Fanpires

Published by New Academia Publishing

Cinema/Film Studies

FORMAL MATTERS: Studies in Film Adaptation and (Re)valuation,
by Bert Cardullo

TERROR ON THE SCREEN: Witnesses and the Re-animation of 9/11 as Image-event, Popular Culture, and Pornography, by Luke Howie

SCIENCE FICTION EXPERIENCES, by Angela Ndalianis

AMERICA REFLECTED: Language, Satire, Film, and the National Mind,
by Peter C. Rollins

MOSCOW BELIEVES IN TEARS: Russians and Their Movies
by Louis Menashe

PIER PAOLO PASOLINI: In Living Memory,
Ben Lawton and Maura Bergonzoni, eds.

HERETICAL EMPIRICISM, by Pier Paolo Pasolini.
Ben Lawton and Louise Barnett, eds., trs.

EVERY STEP A STRUGGLE: Interviews with Seven Who Shaped the
African-American Image in Movies, by Frank Manchel

IMAGING RUSSIA 2000: Film and Facts, by Anna Lawton

BEFORE THE FALL: Soviet Cinema in the Gorbachev Years, by Anna Lawton

Popular Culture/Visual Culture

PASSION AND PERCEPTION: Essays on Russian Culture, by Richard Stites

REMEMBERING UTOPIA: The Culture of Everyday Life in Socialist Yugoslavia,
Breda Luthar and Maruša Pušnik, eds.

WE'RE FROM JAZZ: Festschrift in Honor of Nicholas V. Galichenko,
Megan Swift and Serhy Yekelchyk, eds.

SUPER/HEROES: From Hercules to Superman,
Wendy Haslem, Angela Ndalianis, and Chris Mackie, eds.

SHOPPING FOR JESUS: Faith in Marketing in the USA, Dominic Janes, ed.

VISUAL CULTURE IN SHANGHAI, 1850s-1930s, Jason Kuo, ed.

RUSSIAN FUTURISM: A History, by Vladimir Markov

WORDS IN REVOLUTION: Russian Futurist Manifestoes 1912-1928,
A. Lawton and H. Eagle, eds., trs.

Fanpires

Audience Consumption of the Modern Vampire

Edited by
Gareth Schott and Kirstine Moffat

Washington, DC

Copyright © 2011 by Gareth Schott and Kirstine Moffat

New Academia Publishing, 2011

All rights reserved. No part of this book may be reproduced or transmitted in any form or by any means, electronic or mechanical, including photocopying, recording, or by any information storage and retrieval system.

Printed in the United States of America

Library of Congress Control Number: 2011940925
ISBN 978-0-9845832-1-8 paperback (alk. paper)

New Academia Publishing
P.O. Box 24720, Washington, DC 20038-7420
info@newacademia.com - www.newacademia.com

Contents

Acknowledgments   ix

The Modern Vampire   1

1. Every Age Has the Vampire It Needs: An Introduction
   Kirstine Moffat and Gareth Schott   3

2. Ambivalence about Immortality: Vampires Reveal and Assuage Existential Anxiety
   Jonathan F. Bassett   15

Fans and Anti-Fans   31

3. Pa/trolling the Borders of the Federal Vampire and Zombie Agency Website: Realism, Gender, Authenticity
   Joan Ormrod   33

4. Buffy vs. Bella: The Re-emergence of the Archetypal Feminine in Vampire Stories
   Jennifer Jenson and Anita Sarkeesian   55

5. As Close to Worthless as It Can Get: Twilight Anti-Fans, Teenage Girls and Symbolic Violence
   Catherine Strong   73

6. Vampires, Queers, and Other Monsters: Against the Homonormativity of *True Blood*
   Susana Loza   91

7. True Blood Truebies: *True Blood* Fans and Comic Book Covers
   David Huxley 119

Place and Identity 135

8. Knit One, Bite One: Vampire Fandom, Fan Production and Feminine Handicrafts
   Brigid Cherry 137

9. Gorgeous Monsters and Awful Beauties: The Vampire in the World of Alternative Fashion and Photography
   Rick Hudson 157

10. Mystic Falls Meets the World Wide Web: Where is *The Vampire Diaries* Located?
    Kimberley McMahon-Coleman 169

11. Escape to Ambiguity: The *Twilight* Fan's Playground
    Katie Hoskinson 187

Fan Fiction 203

12. Anyone for a Vampwich? *True Blood*, Online Identity and Copyright
    Melissa de Zwart 205

13. Willing Freshies: Blood, Sex, and Vampires in *Moonlight* Fan Fiction
    Candace Benefiel 223

14. The Recuperated Bite and Issues of the Soul in Vampire Fan Ficiton
    Maria Lindgren Leavenworth and Malin Isaksson 239

Authors and Critics as Fans 255

15. Postmortem Matchmaking: Jane Austen, Vampire Bride
    Amy Elizabeth Smith 257

16. I Demand an Undying Devotion to the Play: *Rosencrantz and Guildenstern are Undead*
    Fiona Martin 275

17. The Critic as Vampire: Parasitic Relations in
    Media Studies and Popular Culture
    Roy Parkhurst   291

Contributors   313
Bibliography   321
Index   351

Acknowledgments

Particular thanks to Dr Fiona Martin, who has served as our proof editor, for her incredible eye for detail, dedication, and professionalism. It has been an absolute pleasure working with you Fiona.

Grateful thanks to Alan Deare at Area Design for his wonderful cover design.

Many thanks to Anna Lawton at New Academia Press for her advice and support through the process.

Adrian Athique, Ted Nannicelli, Anna Kingsbury, Bevin Yeatman, Carey-Ann Morrison, Tanya Krzywinksa, Joe Grixti, Carolyn Michelle, Ann Hardy, Lia Kindiger, Cherie Todd, Sarah Shieff all provided constructive comments and feedback.

Finally, a debt of gratitude to our friends and colleagues for their interest and support. Rachael and Matthew Peploe deserve a special mention; hopefully this collection will go some way to settling the debate about why vampires are so popular.

The Modern Vampire

1

Every Age Has the Vampire It Needs:[1] An Introduction

Kirstine Moffat and Gareth Schott

The vampire of folklore is a mysterious and menacing figure who lives in the shadows, a legend evoking dread because it is hidden, separate, and unknowable. Think of John William Polidori's elusive Lord Ruthven who "gazed upon the mirth around him, as if he could not participate therein," or Sheridan L. Fanu's Carmilla, a "strange and beautiful companion" whose "ardour" is "hateful and yet overpowering," or Bram Stoker's Count Dracula "with a red light of triumph in his eyes, and with a smile that Judas in hell might be proud of."[2] The reverse is true of many contemporary vampires, who seem to be omnipresent and — in part because of their visibility and in part because of their domestication — familiar, known, almost friendly. Writing of the vampires of our age, J. M. Tyree observes that "Edward, Bill, and Eli embody a new combination of undead chum and unnaturally attentive lover, a sort of guardian angel with fangs."[3] If, as Milly Williamson has argued, "we conjure the vampires that we want or need for the cultural and historical times that we find ourselves in,"[4] the contemporary vampire has, in many ways, been "de-fanged" and "re-souled," continuing to beguile because of its supernatural power and immortality, but as hero rather than as monster.

There are, of course, contemporary examples of predatory vampires, such as the sadistic Vlad Tepes of Elizabeth Kostova's *The Historian*, who is described by his creator as "a metaphor for the evil that is so hard to undo in history."[5] Films such as *I am Leg-*

end and *Against the Dark* symbolically link vampirism with disease, while the Federal Vampire and Zombie Agency website (the subject of Joan Ormrod's discussion in Chapter 3) casts vampires as the threatening "other" in a post-9/11 world. Likewise, series such as *Buffy the Vampire Slayer* and *Demons* focus on the heroic exploits of those who protect humanity from supernatural monsters. However, the fictional vampires who currently people the pages of books and the screens of cinemas, televisions, and computers tend to be much less menacing. Think of the many texts which centre on vampire families attempting to live a "normal" life, such as Matt Haig's dysfunctional Radley family, or the conflicted family of *Young Dracula*, or Mitchell in *Being Human*. Many modern vampires are designed to amuse rather than horrify, such as Gail Carriger's witty Lord Akeldama, resplendent in "yellow checked gaiters, gold satin breeches, an orange and lemon striped waistcoat, and an evening jacket of sunny pink brocade,"[6] or the rock-and-roll musicians of *Suck*, or the parodic Edward Sullen of *Vampires Suck*. Alternate or parallel worlds entice readers and viewers with their varied and intricate vampire mythologies: Richelle Mead's *Vampire Academy*, Elizabeth Knox's haunting *Daylight*, Sergei Lukanenko's Nightwatch series, New Zealand film *Perfect Creatures*, the Underworld trilogy. Even the classics can now be read "spiced" with some vampire action, such as Sarah Gray's *Wuthering Bites*, Charlotte Brontë and Sherri Browning Erwin's *Jayne Slayer*, or Louisa May Alcott and Lynn Messina's *Little Vampire Women*. Above all, on page and screen the romantic, moody, charismatic, vampire hero transfixes fans with his hypnotic gaze: Angel, Edward Cullen, Stefan Salvatore, Eric Northman.

The all-pervasive nature of the vampire in contemporary Western culture was brought home to us during a fact-finding trip to one of New Zealand's largest chain stores, the Warehouse. We were literally encircled by vampires. On a stand in front of us vampire texts jostled for attention: Stephenie Meyer's Twilight quartet, Charlaine Harris's Southern Vampire Mysteries, Rochelle Mead's Vampire Academy, Colleen Gleeson's *The Vampire Voss*, Christine Feehan's *Dark Peril*. To the left a display of DVDs enticed us with their vibrant colours: the first series of *The Vampire Diaries*; the third season of *True Blood*; the sci-fi *Daybreakers*, the poignant *Let the Right*

One In. To the right sat a selection of posters and games. Should a shabby or plain interior need beautifying, then a brooding Edward, or the eroticized "Vampire Girl," fangs bared and cleavage on display, was there to offer the perfect solution. Should the detached adoration of the representational qualities of the vampire fall short, fans could turn to the orientational function of an interactive digital game (such as *Vampire Rain* for Playstation) and "become" a vampire. To the left, a display of T-shirts highlighted the insight of Lisa Lewis's proclamation that: "We all know who fans are. They're the ones who wear the colors of their favorite team ... Fans are, in fact, the most visible and identifiable of audiences."[7] By donning T-shirts with slogans such as "I Kissed a Vampire and I Liked It," "Screw Being a Princess I Wanna Be a Vampire!" and "Only Vampires Can Be Your BFFs," the self and identity construction of the vampire fan could be easily cemented and articulated. These aspects of constructing and maintaining fan identity are highlighted by Brigid Cherry, who examines communities of fans who knit in Chapter 8, and by Rick Hudson, who investigates the world of alternative fashion and photography in Chapter 9.

Vampire products, and their positioning within the compositional designs of shop displays, are, of course, evidence of a superb marketing ploy. The "product" which is the contemporary vampire is a highly successful commodity, as David Huxley explores in Chapter 7 in relation to comic books. We argue that this plethora of books, T-shirts, DVDs, and posters is also indicative of fan demands, a heightened audience appetite for all things vampiric. In this collection we seek to understand these fan demands more fully by investigating the context within which vampire texts are produced, circulated and consumed.[8]

Fans are divided on the subject of the contemporary vampire. Some celebrate the romanticizing and domestication of the vampire, while others call for the return of the Gothic vampire who not only titillates but chills and horrifies (such as the authors of the fan fiction discussed by Candace Benefiel in Chapter 13, and Maria Lindgren Leavenworth and Malin Isaksson in Chapter 14). Unsurprisingly, the idea of extending this debate within an edited collection materialized from a conversation between two fans (who also happen to be colleagues). As editors and academics we hail from

English and Media Studies respectively and we share a penchant for texts that engage with vampire mythology. For us, and for the other contributors to this volume, the vampire as an object of study firstly excites our passion as fans, before being related to wider disciplinary interests and located within intellectual frameworks. In focusing our analyses on the vampire as it is expressed in contemporary literature, film, television, graphic novels, and fan activities, this collection serves to acknowledge the power of popular culture to tap into emotions and provoke strong associations, as well as the ability of this medium to release audiences from everyday thoughts and concerns. Cultural hierarchies may continue to separate the activities of fandom from more "valued" cultural artefacts, such as "high" art or literature, but scholars such as Jolie Jenson have been eager to question the boundaries and practices that separate aficionados (such as scholars) from fans, arguing that devotion and loyalties to "high" cultural forms (as opposed to those that are popular, inexpensive and widely available) are not really qualitatively different in terms of levels of knowledge, expertise, research and time investment.[9] Such arguments serve to acknowledge the complexity of the engagement with the popular. Indeed fans typically operate as both avid consumers and passionate yet analytical readers of texts, as Roy Parkhurst highlights in Chapter 17. Herein lies the challenge of this collection: to expand the address of cultural criticism beyond the ivory tower and to account for the place of popular culture in our everyday lives.

While the politics of studying popular culture (which has been well covered elsewhere)[10] is not the central preoccupation of this collection, we share with fans and fan scholars an interest in the everyday and in the modes of cultural expression that form a central role in who we are and how we see the world, be it as part of a regular, scheduled viewing experience on television, or a more pronounced passion for phenomena that others might consider trivial, irrelevant, banal or trite. While the "sympathetic" vampire is a key figure in modern vampire tales, it is not itself a modern phenomenon, having been traced back to the figure of Lord Byron by Milly Williamson.[11] Indeed, the domestication of the vampire can be read as an extension of the desire expressed by the powerful Dracula, who reads in order to free himself from both his physical isolation in a castle surrounded by wasteland and his sense of his redundancy at having no armies to command and no children to rear:[12]

> "... for some years past, ever since I had the idea of going to London, [my books] have given me many, many hours of pleasure. Through them I have come to know your great England, and to know her is to love her. I long to go through the crowded streets of your mighty London, to be in the midst of the whirl and rush of humanity, to share its life, its change, its death, and all that makes it what it is."[13]

More pronounced in contemporary culture is the way in which the sympathetic vampire has been reinscribed with the concerns of fans, focusing on the pragmatics and realism of day-to-day vampire existence and vampire relationships with humans (as discussed by Katie Hoskinson in Chapter 11). By examining the current resurgence of the vampire, we therefore expand the notion of fandom beyond the aca-fan (academic fan) to the "author as fan," with Amy Elizabeth Smith focussing on vampiric recreations of Jane Austen in Chapter 15 and Fiona Martin exploring multiple layers of homage and adaptation in her analysis of *Rosencrantz and Guildenstern Are Undead* in Chapter 16. It can be argued that contemporary treatments of the vampire fulfil a similar performative role to that which has traditionally been associated with media fandom, that is, the creation of texts that "enact, share in, and see scenes that the canonical author never created."[14] The complexities of these fan reworkings and extensions of beloved texts is the subject of Melissa de Zwart's discussion of online identity and copyright in Chapter 12.

Jonathan Gray, Cornel Sandvoss, and C. Lee Harrington have already commented on the "mainstreaming" of fandom, and with it fan scholarship, during the late twentieth and early twenty-first centuries.[15] A predominant theme in contemporary vampire texts is the shift to an open co-existence between vampires and humans, described as "mainstreaming" in *True Blood*. Edward Castronova uses the term "synthetic worlds" (often interchangeably with virtual worlds) to broadly describe spaces in our everyday lives that replicate many of the features of the real world, but also contain a sort of fantastical reality.[16] Taking this idea a little further, the concept of the synthetic age (an advancement of the genetic age) describes the proliferation of the role and presence of synthetic materials, advanced polymers, artificial intelligence, and composite materials in our daily lives. This notion of the synthetic facilitates a blurring of reality and fantasy to such a degree that, in the vampire universe, it has succeeded in lessening the sharp distinctions between good and evil, human and non-human, which Kimberley McMahon-Coleman examines in relation to *The Vampire Diaries* in Chapter 10. *True Blood* (based on Charlaine Harris's Southern Vampire Mysteries) uses a synthetic blood beverage Tru Blood to enable and initiate the domestication of the vampire through its removal of the *need* for cold-blooded murder. The modern vampire has successfully "mainstreamed," literally re-entering public life and popular consciousness.

As is argued in this collection, the plight of the modern vampire also evokes feminism, classism, civil and gay rights, homo-nationalism, and other liberal-progressive politics. These crucial aspects of fan identity are the subject of Susana Loza's analysis of the homonormativity of *True Blood* in Chapter 6, and underpin Jennifer Jenson and Anita Sarkeeesian's discussion of the archetypal feminine in *Buffy the Vampire Slayer* and the Twilight saga in Chapter 4. Simultaneously present in the fictional world of *True Blood* and our navigable virtual worlds (reinforcing the constant presence of alternate realities) is the AVL (American Vampire League) whose members seek to "eradicate the fear and hatred of vampires that is caused by both widespread misinformation and an entire race's punishment for the crimes of a few."[17] The AVL website features a list of "vampire friendly brands," with global corporations (such as Harley Davidson and Gillette) in on the ruse. Mini is credited as one of the first companies to "remove industrial silver from their product line;" in doing so, they have "greatly reduced the contamination risk for thousands of vampires, eliminating silver-oxide from its electrical components and replacing silver-plated bearings with ceramic alternatives". Conversely, the fictional anti-vampire church, Fellowship of the Sun, featured in Season Two of *True Blood*, also holds a web-presence which condemns vampires for undermining "our way of life, sullying our communities with their routine acts of hedonism and cruelty."[18] In doing so, the church presents a defence of humanity and what it means to be human.

In most of the contemporary versions of the vampire discussed in this collection we find a rupturing of the mundane (with the assimilation of the vampire into everyday life), or, put differently, the mergence of worlds. The artistic effect is a breaking down of the frames that previously demarcated vampire texts as belonging to the horror genre, and the rise in popularity of the "dark romance" genre. Prior to the current resurgence of the vampire, Colin Odell and Michelle Le Blanc stated that, as "'supernatural' beings, vampires offer escape from reality."[19] Contemporary vampire texts embrace and generate collision between fantasy and reality, revelling in the juxtaposition created by the transformation of the vampire myth of demonic power into a much more mundane identity faced with the cruel realities of immortality (on which Jonathan F. Bassett reflects in Chapter 2).

C. Lee Harrington and Denise Bielby provide a compelling argument for the need to apply a "life course" perspective to the study of fandom, placing emphasis on the continuing role and influence of media fandom throughout life.[20] Such relationships between individuals and media objects, they argue, also serve as a means of "understanding lives through times."[21] The concept of age and aging also sits well with the thematic focus of our book. The modern vampire text, our object of study, serves to forefront social and historical change via the vampire. On the one hand the vampire remains in physical stasis (reflecting the human age and historical period in which they were made), yet, on the other hand, vampires carry with them the ideals, conventions, beliefs and values of times past into the present. As a media object, the vampire text evolves via contemporary franchises that are also released, read and watched over an extended period of time. In doing so, they constitute something close to a life stage or a "period" themselves, something that Harry Potter fans are confronting with the release of *Harry Potter and the Deathly Hallows: Part 2*, the final instalment of the film franchise. Indeed, the tag line for the promotional poster for the final film reads "It All Ends."

At the time of writing this collection, the Twilight book series has been concluded, yet it remains incomplete as a film franchise. Another popular example, the television series *True Blood* (also a book adaptation), is currently airing its fourth season. Having started with modest viewing figures in the United States, it has now has become cable channel HBO's (Home Box Office) most watched production since the highly successful *The Sopranos*. The life course of many of the texts discussed in this collection thus currently remains ongoing, and is therefore still a significant part of individual lives.

This book focuses on key shifts in the representation and treatment of the vampire in the current age. Within this new era, it appears that different manifestations of the modern vampire hold relevance for specific generations. Clearly the popular Twilight series has been associated with a predominantly female teenage audience, particularly through its encouraged division of loyalties and declaration of preference for either Team Edward (vampire) or Team Jacob (werewolf/shapeshifter) which has, in turn, given it a perceived lower cultural value with some audiences (as discussed by Catherine Strong in Chapter 5). While the Twilight books clearly deal with "normatively appropriate age-based identities and activities," *True Blood* offers a much more adult-themed account of encounters with the ever-expanding supernatural world that converges upon the fictional setting of Bon Temps, Louisiana.[22] In contrast, the Twilight series can easily be read as a text that assists in making sense of significant physical changes, identity formation, and an emerging sense of self during adolescence, although it also identifies graduation from high school as a key transitional life moment, one that holds additional significance for Bella Swan, as her proposed date for transformation and entry into the vampire world.

The pervasive influence and relevance of vampire narratives in the lives of fans was frequently brought home to us while editing this collection, particularly during social gatherings such as birthday parties and weddings. Given the specialist nature of many academic preoccupations, the typical experience of the academic upon meeting a party of strangers and attempting to answer the inevitable, "So, what do you do?" conversation facilitator, is the onset of the "glazed-eye syndrome." Sadly, however appealing academic passions may be to those working in a particular field, non-specialists frequently find these obsessions at best boring and at worst incomprehensible.

This collection has had the effect of actually reversing this eye-glazing process. Through our preoccupation with the dark, compelling figure of the vampire, we have experienced genuine interest in the book project, gaining a kind of glamour by association. Both friends and strangers have clamoured to tell us about either their love or hate relationship with the world of vampires. We have inadvertently initiated arguments and exposed otherwise clandestine devotees of the Twilight saga, who reveal themselves in order to defend the novels against those who cringe at the idea of vampires who sparkle. We have incited those who relish the contemporary fascination with the vampire to share their passion with those who are either baffled by or contemptuous of this interest in the supernatural. In these contexts voices inevitably get raised and arms begin to gesture wildly as fans seek to get their point across and demonstrate what the non-fan fails to appreciate. We present comments surreptitiously jotted down as mention of this collection unexpectedly triggered informal gatherings of fans and anti-fans:

> "Well *Twilight's* just for swooning girls, but every Monday night at 9:30 I tune in to *True Blood*. Sooooo sexy!"
>
> "I kind of get the lure of the supernatural, the defeat of death, the erotic possibilities of the vampire bite. But I just don't see how the vampire can be tamed. He or she is a beast. Surely that's the charm. We want to escape from mortality and powerlessness. Or we just want to shiver in fear, or see evil defeated."
>
> "Why are vampires male? Where are the female vampires?" "Well, there's the whole erotic bite thing going on, and the tortured soul of the immortal. I suppose vampires are the ultimate 'bad boy' hero." "Yeah, but can you name me one vampire heroine? They're usually either irritating victims or slayers like Buffy."
>
> "Well, I'm grateful to the sudden fashionability of vampires! It took the vampire to make pale, skinny guys sexy!"

While most of the debates focused on fictional texts featuring the vampire, we have also been offered more wide-ranging examples of fan practices and preoccupations. A lawyer acquaintance asked whether we had heard about the 2010 case in which two men and a woman were charged with biting and drinking the blood of a man on Mt Victoria in Wellington, New Zealand.[23] Another person mentioned reading an article in a woman's magazine about a middle-aged *Twilight* fan whose weight-loss regime was inspired by tattoo rewards featuring her favourite characters from Meyer's novel. Such engagements with the vampire are the central preoccupation of this book. As the anecdotal examples provided above illustrate, some of the engagements are critical of the influence of vampires on contemporary culture, but most are celebratory of audience consumption of the modern vampire. After all, the contributors in this collection (however critical we may be of some vampire texts, mythologies, or fan practices) are all themselves "fanpires."

Notes

1. Nina Auerbach, *Our Vampires, Ourselves* (Chicago: University of Chicago Press, 1995), 145.
2. John William Polidori, *The Vampyre: A Tale*, Project Gutenberg, accessed 2 August 2011, http://www.gutenberg.org/files/6087/6087-h/6087-h.htm; Sheridan Le Fanu, *Carmilla*, Project Gutenberg, accessed 3 August 2011,http://www.gutenberg.org/files/10007/10007-h/10007-h.htm; Bram Stoker, *Dracula*, ed. Maud Ellmann (Oxford: Oxford University Press, 1996), 50.
3. J. M. Tyree, "Warm-Blooded: True Blood and Let the Right One In," *Film Quarterly* 63, no. 2 (2009), 32.
4. Milly Williamson, *The Lure of the Vampire: Gender, Fiction and Fandom from Bram Stoker to Buffy*, (London: Wallflower Press, 2005), 5.
5. Elizabeth Kostova, quoted by Jane Sullivan, "Dracula and the Human Factor," *The Age*, 7 June, 2006, http://www.theage.com.au/news/books/dracula-and-the-human-factor/2006/06/02/1148956490961.html?page=fullpage.
6. Gail Carriger, *Soulless: An Alexia Tarabotti Novel* (New York and London: Orbit, 2009), 46.
7. Lisa Lewis, ed. *Adoring Audience: Fan Culture and Popular Media* (London: Routledge, 1992), 1.
8. Henry Jenkins, "On Mad Med, Aca-Fandom and the Goals of Cultural Criticism," Confessions of an Aca-Fan: The Official Weblog of Henry Jenkins, accessed January, 25, 2011, http://henryjenkins.org.
9. Jolie Jenson, "Fandom as Pathology: The Consequences of Characterisation," in *Adoring Audience*, 9-30.

10. Henry Jenkins, Tara McPherson and Jane Shattuc, *Hop On Pop: The Politics and Pleasures of Popular Culture* (Durham: Duke University Press Books, 2003).
11. Williamson, *Lure of the Vampire*.
12. Clive Leatherdale, *"Dracula": The Novel and the Legend* (Rayleigh, UK: Desert Island Books, 1993), 232.
13. Bram Stoker, *Dracula* (London: Penguin Books, 2007), 31.
14. Kurt Lancaster, *Interacting with Babylon 5: Fan Performances in a Media Universe*, (Austin, Texas: University of Texas Press, 2001), 131.
15. Jonathan Gray, Cornel Sandvoss, and C. Lee Harrington, eds., *Fandom: Identities and Communities in a Mediated World* (New York: New York University Press, 2007).
16. Edward Castronova, *Synthetic Worlds: The Business and Culture of Online Games* (Chicago: University of Chicago Press, 2005).
17. *The American Vampire League.com*, accessed August 24, 2011, http://americanvampireleague.com/.
18. *Fellowship of the Sun.org*, accessed August 24, 2011, http://www.fellowshipofthesun.org/.
19. Colin Odell and Michelle Le Blanc, *Vampire Films* (Harpendon, UK: Pocket Essentials Series, 2000), 7.
20. C. Lee Harrington and Denise D. Bielby, "A Life Course Perspective on Fandom," *International Journal of Cultural Studies* 13 no 5 (2010): 429-450.
21. Christine L. Fry, "The Life Course as a Cultural Construct," in *Invitation to the Life Course: Toward New Understandings*, ed. Richard A. Settersten, Jr., Towards New Understandings of Later Life Society and Aging Series (Amityville, NY: Baywood, 2003), 271.
22. Harrington and Bielby, 431.
23. "Vampire Attack in Wellington," *Dominion Post*, 6 May 2010, http://www.stuff.co.nz/national/crime/3662417/Vampire-attack-in-Wellington.

2

Ambivalence About Immortality: Vampires Reveal and Assuage Existential Anxiety

Jonathan F. Bassett

In this chapter, my objective is to examine the ambivalence of audience reactions to vampires in terms of whether the psychological effects of consuming vampire fiction are palliative or challenging. Portrayals of vampires could ameliorate existential anxiety by offering hope of death transcendence, or could stimulate deeper contemplation of existential concerns by revealing how infinity might exacerbate the inherent problems of existence. Kirk Schneider argues that there are two disturbing themes in the horror genre: hyper-constriction, involving the shrinking of self into nothingness; and hyper-expansion, involving the expansion of self into an unmanageable dimension.[1] Interpreting vampires through this framework creates a revealing contrast, in that vampires would seem to allay hyper-constrictive concerns about the loss of self through death, while simultaneously raising hyper-expansive concerns by extending the ego into eternity. Therefore, it seems that both the loss of self and the eternal experience of self are challenging to our current psychological equilibrium.

From a psychodynamic perspective, the horror genre is frightening, yet fascinating, because it gives expression to deep-seated and taboo psychological concerns that are typically repressed and denied cultural expression in other mediums.[2] Some scholars have suggested that the corpse has become an increasingly prevalent image in popular media because, in the twenty first century, death has replaced sex as the repressed taboo topic in western culture that needs some outlet for expression.[3] If horror is about giving expression to culturally repressed death anxiety, then do contemporary vampires even belong to the horror genre? Modern vampires are sometimes perceived as so sympathetic as to be no longer horrifying. However, vampire fiction certainly does contain an element of horror in that it makes the threat of death salient. Even the sympathetic vampires are always presented in contrast to the more evil ones. On the HBO television series *True Blood*, the bartender at the vampire bar Fangtasia informs Sookie that all humans who come to the bar want to die because vampires are death.[4] Although vampires do force a confrontation with mortality, they allow audiences to avoid confronting the possibility of total personal extinction.

Vampires would seem simultaneously to both raise the problem of death and allay fears of finitude by questioning the immutability of the natural laws that impose the starkest of existential realities. By exploring immortality in its vampire form, audiences may find it easier to hold out hope that some type of afterlife is feasible.

Vampires Assuage Existential Anxiety

Portrayals of vampires allow one the opportunity to contemplate the question, "would I like an immortal life?" The desire for an immortal life certainly seems to be the motive for the humans who are allowed to choose to be turned into vampires. In *True Blood*, we learn how the 1000-year-old vampire Eric was made. In a flashback sequence, we see the Viking dying of battle wounds. The 2000-year-old vampire Godric is so impressed by Eric's skill in battle that he offers him the chance to become a vampire. When Eric asks what is in it for him, Godric answers, "What you love most — life."[5]

Theorists working from a currently popular perspective in social psychology known as Terror Management Theory assert that abating death anxiety is the paramount human motive.[6] Proponents of this perspective posit that historically, all cultures contain at least some perceived paranormal components in which the laws of the natural world are violated. They further argue that cultural depictions of supernatural events may be so prevalent and appealing because they allow people to sustain hope in personal

The Modern Vampire   17

immortality in the face of empirical observations that seem to imply that personal mortality is inevitable. If the laws of the natural world can at times be overcome, then perhaps the reality of personal death imposed by those laws can also be overcome.[7] If these theorists are correct, then perhaps depictions of vampires are appealing for the same reason that traditional religious notions of immortality are appealing — namely because they quell the dread of death by offering consumers hope of transcending death.

This perspective on the appeal of the supernatural is given voice by vampire characters themselves in the show *True Blood*. The vampire Bill Compton has gone to New Orleans to seek the advice of Sophie-Anne Leclerq, the queen of the Louisiana vampires, regarding the strange happenings in Bon Temps surrounding the influence of Maryann Forrester. Bill believes that Maryann is an ancient creature called a Maenad and that she is exerting her evil influence by turning the inhabitants of Bon Temps into mindless zombies for some nefarious purpose.[8] He has traveled to New Orleans in the hope that Sophie-Anne will have insights into the Maenad's potential motives and how it might be stopped or killed. When Sophie-Anne describes the ancient Dionysian religious beliefs that Maryann ascribes to — involving sexual orgy, sacrifice, and cannibalism — as the ways to come closer to the divine, Bill suggests that they are delusional. She replies, "Never underestimate the power of blind faith. It can manifest in ways that bend the laws of physics or break them entirely." She further explains that Maryann is a pathetic character because her ancient world has changed and she is still waiting for her god to come. When Bill inquires if he ever does come, Sophie-Anne rebukes him, saying, "Of course not. Gods never actually show up. They only exist in human minds, like money and morality."[9]

The majority of human cultures have speculated about some type of life after death. However, most of these religious notions of immortality seem to violate the rules of the physical world people encounter in their day-to-day experience. Consequently, without constant consensual validation, visions of immortality may lose their anxiety-abating power, as nagging doubts persist that these visions may be merely cultural fabrications. Thinking about supernatural creatures such as vampires, even if one does not literally believe in their existence, makes it easier to entertain the idea that there may be a transcendent dimension to reality beyond our ordinary understanding of the material world.

Vampires as an Expression of Anxieties about Immortality

A further analysis reveals that vampires are not solely a means of allaying concerns about death. In addition, they seem to allow audiences the opportunity to question and challenge the viability of an immortal existence. Vampires allow people to explore their ambivalence about eternity by providing imagery that is richer and more detailed than the references to immortality typically provided in traditional religious texts. Two themes of human concerns about immortality that are addressed in scripture relate one, to what an immortal body would be like and two, how human cultural traditions and institutions could hold up to eternity. St. Paul seems to be speaking directly to the former in his letter to the church at Corinth, when he writes

> But some may ask how are the dead raised? With what kind of body will they come? How foolish! What you sow does not come to life unless it dies. When you sow, you do not plant the body that will be, but just the seed, perhaps of wheat or of something else ... So it will be with the resurrection of the dead. The body that is sown is perishable, it is raised imperishable; it is sown in dishonor, it is raised in glory; it is sown in weakness, it is raised in power.[10]

This passage is meant to allay concerns about the possibility of living eternally in a resurrected but injured, corrupted, or otherwise flawed body. These concerns were given more recent literary voice in W. W. Jacobs's story "The Monkey's Paw", in which a man, at the pleading of his wife, uses the magic amulet that gives the story its title to wish for the return of their son who was mangled in a factory accident. Later, the horrified father realizes the folly of his wish that will bring the boy back in an agonizingly disfigured state, and he uses the third and last wish to dismiss the abomination knocking outside the door.[11] Immortality can seem grotesque and torturous under certain circumstances. The horrors of living eternally with a bodily defect are illustrated in the character of Jessica Hamby in the series *True Blood*. The teenage girl, recently converted into a vampire, develops a romantic relationship with the socially awkward human male Hoyt. After their first sexual fumbling is interrupted, Hoyt drives Jessica back to Bon Temps where they attempt to pick up where they left off. Jessica is horrified to discover that intercourse will always be painful, as her hymen grows back each time.[12] Christopher Moore's novel *You Suck: A Love Story* provides a more comical look at the potentially dystopian aspects of the immortal vampire body. When neophyte vampire Jody turns her new lover Tommy into a vampire against his will, the 19-year-old is disgusted by the fact that his foreskin has grown back and is perturbed by the realization that he will never get to follow through on his intentions to work out and become muscular, but instead must live forever skinny and bird-chested. Jody also suffers dysmorphic disappointment, as she herself was "turned" before losing that last unwanted five pounds that she can now never shed.[13]

In addition to worries about the corporeal aspects of immortality, human doubts about the ability of social institutions to endure eternity find expression in biblical scripture. For example, in the Gospel of Matthew we encounter some doubters who ask Jesus a rather fantastical question in an attempt to illustrate just how unfeasible a bodily resurrection would be from a practical standpoint:

> That same day the Sadducees, who say there is no resurrection, came to him with a question. Teacher, they said, Moses told us that if a man dies without having children, his brother must marry the widow and have children for him. Now there were seven brothers among us. The first one married and died, and since he had no children, he left his wife to his brother. The same thing happened to the second and third brother, right on down to the seventh. Finally, the woman died. Now then, at the resurrection, whose wife will she be of the seven, since all of them were married to her?[14]

Participants in psychological research expressed similar doubts at the end of the twentieth century.[15] When college students were asked about the possible negative consequences of a world with no death, one of the most frequently mentioned was the breakdown of social institutions such as marriage. The apparent perception was that the "until death us do part" aspect of the marriage vow would become unbearable if there was no death to ever do the parting. We find the same sentiment in vampire fiction. In Charlaine Harris's novel *All Together Dead*, we witness a vampire wedding between two male vampires — Russell the King of Mississippi and Bart the King of Indiana. There are some notable differences from the traditional human wedding ceremony. In the wedding vows they agree that they will not marry anyone else for 100 years, that they will pay each other a conjugal visit at least once a year, and that they will get their spouse's permission before entering any alliances with other creatures.[16]

Vampires Challenge Typical Defenses against Existential Anxiety

It is unclear whether being a vampire would allow for an existence completely free of existential worries. After all, vampires are free from the ravages of old age, immune to natural death, and able to heal quickly from most types of injuries, but they can still meet with a violent and — perhaps from their perspective — untimely end. In Annette Curtis Klause's novel *The Silver Kiss*, we meet a sympathetic, existentially brooding vampire. Simon is a 400-year-old vampire who feeds on birds when necessary and on humans, gently, without killing them. Simon has developed a relationship with a human teenager named Zoe. Zoe learns that Simon's maker is a child vampire who capitalizes on his female victims' maternal instincts by pretending to be helpless and lost, then luring them to their brutal demise. When she learns that the predator is not only Simon's maker but also his brother, that he is hunting in their city, and that Simon is reluctant to try to stand up to him, Zoe makes a rather astounding accusation, asking, "You're afraid of death?" In his defense, Simon replies, "It doesn't matter how long you live, the idea of nonexistence is still frightening. No matter how tired you are of life it is better than facing the unknown."[17] So it would seem that, at least for some vampires, long life might not ameliorate the dread of personal extinction. In contrast, however, we get a very different perspective from a Hollywood vampire in Adrienne Barbeau's novel *Love Bites*. Ovsanna is an ancient vampire from the old world, who has spent two human lifetimes as a Hollywood actress and now runs her own movie studio. She becomes romantically involved with a police detective of Italian and Catholic upbringing. When Peter inquires about her belief in God and heaven and hell, Ovsanna responds:

> You know, it's not a concept I spend much time considering, Peter. When you are fairly immortal, you don't worry about an afterlife. You don't need to create an idea of what it might be like after you're dead. And you certainly don't need anyone to pray to for forgiveness or anything else ... Plus, I think most of us are so bored after living eight or nine hundred years that the thought of dying doesn't carry with it any fear. Maybe just relief.[18]

Previous scholars have advanced the idea that vampires serve as a vehicle for exploring existential issues. For example, Betty Roberts asserts that "the condition of vampirism represents for the contemporary reader feelings of helplessness in the midst of an awareness of atrocity and a sense of insignificance and alienation in an overwhelming atmosphere of decline."[19] In addition, Paul Priester suggests that vampires are "a rich source of metaphorical allegory" that allow people to struggle with existential issues related to the meaning of life and the conflict over competing urges and desires.[20] I build on this tradition, arguing that vampires reveal the existential struggles facing mortals by showing how the extension of life indefinitely intensifies these struggles.

There is a large body of work in existential and psychodynamic psychology that suggests that people are driven by a fear of death that precludes them from living fully. Perhaps this position is best articulated by cultural anthropologist Ernest Becker, who writes, "The irony of man's condition is that the deepest need is to be free of the anxiety of death and annihilation; but it is life itself which awakens it, and so we must shrink back from being fully alive."[21] Similarly, Robert Firestone posits that people avoid living fully and pursuing the fullness of life and love, in order to protect themselves from the painful awareness of mortality. He puts it this way:

> One of the things that invariably impresses me as a clinician is the extent to which people appear to want debilitating, conventional forms of safety, security and togetherness, yet reject genuine closeness with their loved ones. They tend to relive early, painful experiences from childhood in their present relationships and, at the same time, maintain a fantasy that they somehow can escape death by merging with another person.[22]

We prefer the comfortable tedium of safe but illusory relationships and our preoccupations with pseudo-problems and drama in their culturally trite forms, over more genuine and authentic approaches to living in which we might dare to strive for our ultimate desires in self-actualizing ways. In this sense, we have been conditioned to live in dull and boring ways (although they are also safe and culturally prescribed), because of our fears of mortality.

Becoming a vampire would seem to offer the freedom to live life more fully and courageously, because immortality would negate the need to shrink from life in order to avoid fear of death. Vampires do seem to have a greater richness of experience than do humans. In addition to their greater physical strength, and flash-like movements, they have extremely heightened senses. Even humans who drink vampire blood gain some of these sensory abilities temporarily. In *True Blood*, after Bill lets Sookie drink his blood to help her heal from wounds inflicted by the vampire drainers who have beaten her nearly to death, her sensory acuity is greatly enhanced. While eating sausage at the breakfast table, she tells her grandmother that she can smell the sunshine, see the farm, and taste the texture and complexity of the soil where the pig was raised.[23] These heightened sensory experiences could be read allegorically as a greater appreciation of the fullness of existence that is possible when worries about its finitude are removed. The appeal of vampirism, offering existence without fear, is seen in the character of Jody in Moore's novel *You Suck: A Love Story*. Jody enjoys her new vampire powers and walks through the streets without fear of sexual or physical predators because she is now the physically dominant one. She is the stalker and the hunter, not the prey. Even though their vampire existence is threatening the viability of Jody and Tommy's love, Jody does not want to go back to being human because she cannot face the idea of living in constant fear again: "Until she had been changed and stalked the city as a vampire, she never realized that virtually every moment she had been there as a woman, she had been a little bit afraid … of attack, the shadow around the corner, the footsteps behind." In the absence of such fear, Jody's discovery is that "the city was a great sensual carnival. There was no danger in anything she experienced, no anxiety."[24]

Whereas vampirism has freed Jody from one kind of existential fear, it has exacerbated a different kind of anxiety in Tommy. In describing the nature of the existential angst inherent in the human condition, Becker writes that:

> [W]hat man really fears most is not so much extinction, but extinction *with insignificance*. Man wants to know that his life has somehow counted, if not for himself, then at least in a larger scheme of things, that it has left a trace, a trace that has meaning. And in order for anything once alive to have meaning, its effects must remain alive in eternity in some way."[25]

If the human condition gives rise to a need for a sense of some kind of transcendent significance, then being a vampire would seem to rob one of the opportunity to feel such a sense of contribution to the world. Tommy wants to go back to being human so that he can write and achieve some kind of symbolic immortality, in the sense that his life contributed something meaningful to the history of human affairs. He tells Jody that he wants to be special in a human way because of something he did.

The work of psycho-historian Robert Jay Lifton is useful here in revealing that the main challenge to maintaining a meaningful existence is the ability to connect symbolically with the past and future in a rapidly changing world. Lifton notes that, in the postmodern age, the pace of historical and technological change makes it difficult to symbolize any sense of connection between past and present, leaving people prone to a state of psychic numbing, in which they feel life has no meaning because they can neither envision how the lives of previous generations relate to their own, nor how contributions and accomplishments made in their life will matter in the future.[26] The theme of symbolic immortality seems pervasive among the human characters in *True Blood*. In Episode Two, Season One, Terra tells Jason that everybody is trying to be someone that everyone wants to be seen and to feel that they matter. In Episode Four, Season Two, Sookie's brother, Jason Stackhouse, is attending a leadership-training program, hosted by the anti-vampire organization known as The Fellowship of the Sun. It is the desire for symbolic, rather than literal, immortality that motivates Jason's newfound religious zealotry, as he wants to feel that God has a purpose for his life, that he is special, and that he can contribute something meaningful and enduring that will afford him cosmic significance. We see this same motive for symbolic immortality in Jason's desire for heroism, as he and Andy try to save Bon Temps from the evil influence of Maryann Forrester. Maryann tells Sam that he is lucky she is sacrificing him, because his life will actually mean something and that this is so rare for humans.[27] Although clearly present as a motive for the human characters in vampire fiction, would the literal immortality of vampires free them from the need to pursue symbolic immortality through accomplishments and relationships?

In Klause's novel *The Silver Kiss*, Simon is clearly struggling with the desire for symbolic immortality: "He wanted to be noticed. He wanted people to see him. It was dangerous this want. It was mad. But sometimes he was afraid that he didn't exist."[28] This need to be noticed, to feel as if his life matters, is later evidenced when Simon encounters a gang of ruffians who attack him. Simon tries to exit the encounter without hurting his assailant, until they call him a nobody and provoke his anger. After immobilizing one of his attackers, Simon bites the man's wrist and writes in bloody script on the top of a car the words "I am."[29]

An alternative to pursuing symbolic immortality via creative accomplishment is to abate death anxiety through a romantic solution, in which one attempts to give significance and meaning to existence by merging completely with a lover. Becker argues that this approach to dealing with death anxiety had been growing in popularity with the rise of secularization in western culture. He suggests that the modern human being has

> fixed his urge to cosmic heroism onto *another person* in the form of a love object. The self-glorification that he needed in his innermost nature he now looked for in a love partner. The love partner becomes the divine ideal within which to fulfill one's life. All spiritual and moral needs now become focussed in one individual. Spirituality, which once referred to another dimension of things, is now brought down to earth and given form in another individual human being.[30]

Firestone argues that love is motivated by a genuine concern, respect, and admiration for the other person, whereas emotional hunger is motivated by a desperate need for the other because of the anxieties and distress they quell.[31] If human relationships are frequently a defensive response to death anxiety, then immortality would seem to offer the possibility for vampires to have less needy and dependent relationships. Certainly, vampires have needs, many of which humans must fulfill. They need protection during the day, they need sexual partners, and, of course, they need blood. However, their immortality should free them of the need to have to define themselves through their romantic relationships. They should not need love out of a psychological motive to avoid the fear of being alone by merging their identity with another. In fact, vampires should be free of any anxiety generated by lack of romantic involvement, because the sense of isolation and meaningless evoked by being alone is distressing to humans precisely because it leaves them prone to increased death anxiety. In contrast, while vampires have a physical thirst for blood, analogous to the human drive systems that motivate feeding, they should be free of the emotional hunger that so often taints human romantic relationships. Consequently, it is unclear whether or not vampires could even feel love in the same way that humans experience the emotion.

In the novel *Love Bites*, the vampire Ovsanna argues adamantly that vampires do not experience love in the same way as humans when she declares, "Vampyres don't need caretaking. We don't need anything — except blood. We don't need others to give us a sense of worth; we don't need attention to make us feel valuable."[32] Similarly, the vampire Eric in *True Blood* suggests that vampires do not understand love, but his actions later cast doubt on this statement. When Sookie and Eric are trying to save Godric from the Fellowship of the Sun, Sookie asks if Godric is Eric's maker, to which he replies, "Don't use words you don't understand." Sookie responds by saying that Eric seems to have a lot of love for Godric, to which he replies, "Don't use words I don't understand." Despite his declaration that he does not even understand the concept of love, Eric shows very strong emotion in response to Godric's decision to "greet the sun." Tears of blood stream down his face as Eric begs his maker not to leave him alone.[33]

In the character of Lorena, *True Blood* presents a glaring contradiction to the idea that immortality would free vampires from emotional hunger and the need to feel loved. Lorena is Bill's maker and the pair spent many decades together as lovers and hunters, sadistically torturing and killing numerous human victims. Eventually Bill rediscovered his human conscience, grew weary of his lustful and violent existence with Lorena, and longed for something else. Lorena could not stand the thought of continuing alone without Bill, and only agreed to let him leave when he threatened to kill himself if she forced him to stay with her. Some 70 years later, Lorena still has not overcome her desperate need for Bill. Even when Godric has banished her for attacking Sookie, Lorena still holds out false hope that someday she will see Bill again — telling him that, after all, forever is a long time.[34] Unrequited human love, in which one party needs the other because they feel vulnerable or incomplete, evokes pathos; but the tragedy of eternal unrequited love, in an immortal creature, is almost too much to bear. How could it be that, with so many years to work with, someone could not move on and find a new outlet for their needs or, even better, learn to become comfortable with their own individuality? If vampires can feel love, then in one sense they would seem to be great romantic partners. If humans could be sure that their vampire amours were not just using them as food, then vampire love might be more trustworthy than human love, because people would be confident that their attentions were motivated out of a genuine affection and not out of flight from the terror that they are alone and therefore vulnerable to death.

However, even the appealing depictions of romantic relationships between humans and vampires raise some doubt about whether love can ever be free from selfish motives. In the relationship between Bill and Sookie there is a tension as to whether both parties are motivated by genuine love or trying to compensate for their own deficits. Both are lonely and isolated by their conditions and in need of companionship. Is Bill drawn to Sookie because of her fairy blood, which gives her an irresistible taste and special allure to vampires? Is Sookie drawn to Bill because she cannot read his thoughts, and being around him offers her the sanity-restoring tranquility of mental quiet? Vampire fictions illustrate how romantic love is pursued in order to avoid existential anxieties, but they also cast doubt on whether love can ever have the true transcendent properties that make it so desirable. Here again, vampires seem to be creating ambivalent psychological reactions. In one sense, the vampire lover would seem to offer hope for the romantic solution to existential anxiety by demonstrating that true love can overcome death. In another sense, vampire relationships give expression to doubts about the true transcendent quality of romantic love by exploring the defensive nature of motives in relationships.

Conclusion

In conclusion, there is a complex relation between contemporary portrayals of vampires and the psychological experiences of existential questions raised by these portrayals. At least part of the appeal of vampires seems to be their ability to alleviate death anxiety, by offering the hope of some kind of existence that transcends death. However, vampires also allow audiences to struggle with their uncertainty as to what an embodied immortality would be like, and whether or not a desirable existence could be maintained eternally. The psychological suffering depicted in the lives of vampire characters might serve as a valuable tool for consumers of these fictions to explore the deeper questions of their own mortal existence. In response to depictions of vampires, people can evaluate the role of death in their own psychology, explore how death interacts with other existential motives, and contemplate how to live and love fully in their own finite existence. Vampire fictions are challenging, in that they reveal the potential difficulties involved in satisfying the needs for meaning, novelty, and connectedness in an immortal existence. Further, vampire fictions allow for exploring the viability of the typical defenses employed in minimizing the terror of confronting our existential predicament. By revealing how maintaining love and meaning becomes more difficult in an immortal existence, vampire stories cast doubts on the ability of our symbolic immortality projects to provide any true transcendence. Yet, the confrontation with existential challenges offered to consumers of vampire fictions could be beneficial. Vampires also seem to offer a view of what existence could potentially be like if lived free from existential fears and anxieties. The increased strength, enhanced sensory appreciation, and reduced reliance on conventional morality that characterize vampire life could serve as templates for how humans might live. Vampires could inspire a desire to break free of the human tendency to live safe but provincial and inauthentic lives in order to avoid the painful awareness of mortality.

Notes

1. Kirk J. Schneider, *Horror and the Holy: Wisdom-Teachings of the Monster Tale* (Peru, IL: Open Court, 1993), 13.
2. Robin Wood, *Hollywood from Vietnam to Reagan* (New York: Columbia University Press, 1986), 63. Wood exemplifies this approach by asserting that horror serves the function of giving expression to those aspects of existence that society represses.
3. Jacque Lynn Foltyn, "Dead Famous and Dead Sexy: Popular Culture, Forensics, and the Rise of the Corpse," *Mortality* 13, no. 2 (2008): 153. Foltyn argues that in the twenty first century the proliferation of graphic images of corpses in electronic media has occurred to fill the psychological need created by the fact that most people in industrialized cultures do not come into contact with actual corpses.
4. *True Blood*, "Escape From the Dragon House," Season One, Episode Four, director Michael Lehmann, written by Brian Buckner, New York: Home Box Office, first aired November 28, 2008.
5. *True Blood*, "Never Let Me Go," Season Two, Episode Five, director John Dahl, written by Nancy Oliver, New York: Home Box Office, first aired July 19, 2009.

6   Sheldon Solomon, Jeff Greenberg, and Tom Pyszczynski, "Terror Management Theory of Self-Esteem," in *Handbook of Social and Clinical Psychology: The Health Perspective,* ed. C. R. Snyder and Donelson R. Forsyth, Pergamon General Psychology Series 162 (New York: Pergamon Press, 1991), 21.
7   Sheldon Solomon, Jeff Greenberg, and Tom Pyszczynski, Florette Cohen, and Daniel M. Ogilvie, "Teach These Souls to Fly: Supernatural as Human Adaptation," in *Evolution, Culture, and the Human Mind,* ed. Mark Schaller, Ara Norenzayan, Steven J. Heine, Toshio Yamagishi, and Tatsuya Kameda (New York: Psychology Press/Taylor & Francis, 2010), 99.
8   Maenads were female followers of Dionysus whose name translates as "raving ones." See David Wiles, *Greek Theatre Performance: An Introduction* (Cambridge, UK: Cambridge University Press), 2000.
9   *True Blood,* "Frenzy," Season Two, Episode 11, director Daniel Minaham, written by Alan Ball, New York: Home Box Office, first aired August 30, 2009.
10 1 Corinthians 15: 35–37, 42–43.
11 W. W. Jacobs, *The Lady of the Barge and Others, Entire Collection, The Project Gutenberg,* accessed May 11, 2011, http://www.gutenberg.org/fiels/12133/12133_h/12133h.htm#c2.
12 *True Blood,* "Timebomb," Season Two, Episode Eight, director John Dahl, written by Alexander Woo, New York: Home Box Office, first aired August 8, 2009.
13 Christopher Moore, *You Suck: A Love Story* (New York: Harper, 2007), 8.
14 Matthew 22: 23–28.
15 Robert Kastenbaum, "A World without Death? First and Second Thoughts," *Mortality* 1 (1996): 117. Kastenbaum attempted an empirical test of the appeal of immortality. College students imagined a hypothetical world in which death no longer existed. Although the majority of students found this world initially appealing, after deliberation most people chose the world with death as preferable to a world with no death. Participants' main objection to a world without death was that this form of immortality would deprive them of the heavenly immortality they were anticipating. Even in the absence of this objection, however, they still viewed immortality on earth as undesirable because it would sap motivation, become inevitably monotonous, and cause the breakdown of social order.
16 Charlaine Harris, *All Together Dead* (New York: Penguin, 2007).
17 Annette Curtis Klause, *The Silver Kiss* (New York: Dell, 1990), 136.
18 Adrienne Barbeau, *Love Bites* (New York: Thomas Dunne Books, 2010), 67.

19 Betty B. Roberts, *Anne Rice* (New York: Twayne, 1994), 31.
20 Paul Priester, "The Metaphorical Use of Vampire Films in Counseling," *Journal of Creativity in Mental Health* 3 (2008): 75.
21 Ernest Becker, *The Denial of Death* (New York: The Free Press, 1973), 66.
22 Robert W. Firestone, *Death Anxiety Handbook*, ed. Robert A. Neimeyer (Washington: Taylor & Francis, 1994), 229.
23 *True Blood*, "The First Taste," Season One, Episode Two, director Scott Winant, written by Alan Ball, New York: Home Box Office, first aired September 14, 2008.
24 Moore, 81–82.
25 Ernest Becker, *Escape From Evil* (New York: Free Press, 1975), 4.
26 Robert Jay Lifton, *The Life of the Self: Toward a New Psychology* (New York: Simon & Schuster, 1976), 35.
27 *True Blood*, "Beyond Here Lies Nothing," Season Two, Episode 12, director Michael Cuesta, written by Alexander Woo, New York: Home Box Office, first aired September 13, 2009.
28 Klause, 36.
29 Ibid., 36.
30 Becker, *Denial of Death*, 160.
31 Robert W. Firestone, "Individual Defenses Against Death Anxiety," *Death Studies* 17 (1993): 510.
32 Barbeau, 264.
33 *True Blood*, "I Will Rise Up," Season Two, Episode Nine, director Scott Winant, written by Nancy Oliver, New York: Home Box Office, first aired August 16, 2009.
34 Ibid.

Fans and Anti-Fans

3

Pa/trolling the Borders of the Federal Vampire and Zombie Agency Website: Realism, Gender, Authenticity[1]

Joan Ormrod

> This site is a tribute to the men and women who served in the FVZA [Federal Vampire and Zombie Agency] ... who lost their lives fighting to keep our country safe. In addition to paying tribute to the FVZA, this site hopes to call attention to dangerous research being done at the Santa Rosa Institute: research that runs the risk of bringing back a scourge of vampires worse than any before.[2]

With this opening address, the Federal Vampire and Zombie Agency website presents a story set in an alternate reality. The website consists of a collection of official-looking documents, newspaper and magazine articles that recount the story of the agency. According to this alternative reality, FVZA is a quasi-military organization formed to combat vampire and zombie contagion in America. The vampire and zombie threats arrived in America with the first European settlers in the sixteenth century. The FVZA was set up in the nineteenth century, and thanks to their development of immunization and professional combat techniques and weaponry, the vampire and zombie threats were eradicated. By 1975 the FVZA was disbanded and Dr. Hugo Pecos, the director, pensioned off. However, Pecos believed that the vampire and zombie threats had not died, but merely gone to ground.

The website was produced in 2001 and, given FVZA's interest in combat, it is no great leap of the imagination to connect the threat of vampires and zombies with 9/11. Indeed Richard S. Dargan, the website creator, notes the aims of the website as, "partly an attempt to apply some logic to the undead ... [Partly] ... apocalyptic fears in the age of terrorism."[3] In this statement lie two issues central to the website narrative: first, the link between 9/11, war and the apocalypse; second, in using the word "logic," Dargan opts for a realistic representation of the undead. Indeed, realism is central to the knowledge and the hierarchies developed in the website and maintained principally by Dargan, his various alter egos of Dr. Hugo Pecos, Dangovich, and moderators in the website. The website also has a loyal participant base that defends it from attack by trolls, individuals who post inflammatory messages with the aim of destabilizing or subverting the website. These inflammatory posts are based upon values that challenge the realism of the website, and are discussed in the final section of the chapter.

In FVZA, the vampire is a human infected by a virus that "rewrites the victim's DNA,"[4] dehumanizing them. An understanding of the nature of the so-called viral vampire is crucial to sub-cultural authenticity, as noted in the opening page of Incident Reports in which Pecos asserts that, "learning to separate false reports from the genuine article is an important skill for an FVZA investigator."[5] Facts are continuously invoked to reinforce the stories and documents posted on the website by Dargan and, in this sense, empirical knowledge operates to substantiate ideas. Much rhetoric on the website is predicated on the necessity of generating factual material that concurs with such viral vampire "facts." In Pecos's seeded documents realism is reinforced by the recounting of vampire pathology, quoting from quasi-scientific reports, accounts of famous vampires, and outbreaks of the vampire virus in history, folktales and myths. These stories are reinvented to incorporate vampire elements in what we would half recognize as versions of "real" events. For instance, the website rewrites Valerie Solanas's attempted assassination of Andy Warhol as a vampire attack.[6] There are also lists of famous vampires such as Percy Bysshe Shelley, Rasputin, and Ivan the Terrible. Participants submit incident reports, ask Pecos's opinions, get advice about possible sightings, and discuss the FVZA military and combat weaponry and combat techniques. In the role-playing game (RPG) section, which was partitioned off from the forums in November 2003, weaponry, combat strategies and missions are discussed. Role playing is discouraged in forums; the role-playing section maintains the emphasis on realism and prohibits superpowers or fantastic elements to creep into the missions.[7]

What makes FVZA so interesting in comparison with other vampire fandom is the avowed masculinity, especially in the vampire section, of its rhetoric and participants. This masculinity sets FVZA apart from other contemporary vampire texts that tend to target mainly female audiences. Authenticity and hierarchies in the website cluster around rhetoric based upon perceived traditional masculine discourses: realism and war. FVZA participants express masculine values in their forums and, so far as can be determined, are male[8] in a subgenre that has become feminized.[9] That it was produced in 2001 suggests a close connection with 9/11 and its avowedly masculine rhetoric, a masculinity that has been in crisis since 9/11. Susan Faludi,[10] for instance, proposes that since the arrival of Europeans in the sixteenth century, America has developed a fear of invasion by "other" peoples. 9/11 disrupted the American myth of invulnerability encapsulated in the frontiersman,[11] because it brought forth no masculine lone hero to inspire the collective imagination. Post 9/11, masculinity became defensive and psychologically disempowered, and there was a cultural reaction that reverted to traditional hetero-normative masculinity. Given the rhetoric and the gendered issues that emerge from the FVZA website, Faludi's proposal does seem convincing. For "other" people, read vampires and zombies. It also poses the question: what pleasures do the fans of this masculine-orientated website gain from their participation in fan forums? Superficially, it is the opportunity for the mainly male participants to re-enact 9/11 so that this time we win. But my analysis demonstrates other pleasures gained by all participants within the FVZA forum. The first part of the chapter deals with gender, authenticity and hierarchies in researching fandom. To contextualize the analysis of the rhetoric in the latter part of the chapter, the discourses constructing the two types of vampire that appear on the website are deconstructed. The viral and sympathetic vampires play a key role in the generation of hierarchies. In defining what the FVZA vampire is not, participants define their own identities.[12]

Fandom, Gender and Authenticity

Much debate in academia on fan fiction and fandom concentrates on female identities and hierarchies in subcultures. The first wave of fandom researchers aimed to differentiate the fan from common perceptions of the hysterical mob or the crazed loner. Consequently, writers such as Camille Bacon-Smith[13] and Henry Jenkins[14] showed the creative aspects of fandom and the liberation they afforded the disempowered, such as women. Later research used poststructural and sociological ideas to examine the operation of hierarchies within fandom. John Fiske[15] and Sarah Thornton[16] apply the ideas of Pierre Bourdieu[17] to subcultures to demonstrate the presence of hierarchies and the concept of cultural capital, capital that is not necessarily economic but linked with the accumulation of communal credibility. Bourdieu notes that, "[T]aste classifies and it classifies the classifier."[18] Performance and articulation of communal values, and an understanding of cultural *habitus*,[19] are central to the production of authenticity. Through knowledge and performance within a subculture, participants accumulate "sub-cultural capital."[20] Sub-cultural capital is symbolic rather than literal, as it generates more respect within the community. The values and hierarchical structure therefore become interdependent and the values of a subculture may differ dramatically from those of the broader culture. This leads to an in/out dichotomy within fandom.

The exclusion of dissent in fandom is challenged by Abigail Derecho, who proposes that fan fiction is archontic, an archival activity that is inclusive, and the result of a "hive mind" rather than one producer.[21] Further, the archive is non-hierarchical: "archontic literature is inherently, structurally, a literature of the subordinate against cultures of the dominant."[22] Derecho's argument enables fan fiction to be incorporated into the wider textual unity and this is useful in this analysis of FVZA, which incorporates both the viral and the sympathetic vampire.[23] Nevertheless, although it may be inclusive, participants who construct the archive do so within hierarchical structures. Fan practices often reproduce hierarchies in society and textual boundaries and thus "perform a key strategy that allows fans to construct a self-reflexive reading of the object of fandom. It is a simultaneous process of inclusion and exclusion."[24] What I propose in this chapter is that participatory culture is inclusive, and that participants within fandom can gain pleasures within these hierarchies, whether they operate within or outside of the community.

The Viral Vampire, the Sympathetic Vampire and Gender

The vampire is constructed through gender and realism from its folkloric and literary roots. It is a powerful metaphor of otherness and paradox, representing desire, sexuality, and eternal youth and beauty, juxtaposed with monstrosity and disease within post-Romantic societies from the late eighteenth century. Although paradoxical, these issues are present in "the story itself [which] encodes some central belief or perception that is ... more or less constant from the vampire's very beginnings."[25] Vampirism is linked with hemophilia, blood disorders, rabies, and AIDS in folklore and early vampire novels.[26] Dracula, for instance, arrives on a plague ship from the borders of Europe and Asia, invoking the threat of racial contagion in *fin de siècle* England. He poses as human and insinuates himself into the heart of English society, subverting patriarchal order and sexual propriety, and inspiring desire in English middle-class women. Whereas the vampire was regarded as a sexual and diseased monster in films, plays and novels up to the 1970s, a new breed of angst-ridden, feminized vampires emerged from the 1970s. The sympathetic vampire cycle resulted from the domestication of the vampire and its alignment with melodrama and romance. Key characters in the development of the sympathetic vampire are Louis in *Interview with the Vampire*,[27] Barnabus in *Dark Shadows*,[28] and Angel in *Buffy the Vampire Slayer* (1997–2003),[29] vampires who deplore their blood-lust. Barnabus and Angel also form the basis for the crossover of the vampire from horror to the supernatural romance genre. The supernatural romance subgenre fuses the sympathetic vampire with his original inspirations, Lord Byron and Heathcliff, in texts such as *Twilight*[30] and *True Blood*.[31] These narratives combine horror, romance and teen dramas, and their anti-heroes — Bill Compton and Edward Cullen — tend to appeal to female fans. FVZA, however, is unashamedly masculine in its conception and in its underpinning discourses.

FVZA vampires are unremittingly other, aligned with war narratives in video games and films rather than with literature. FVZA belongs to a subgenre of vampire, demon and zombie horror, in which the emphasis is on the slayers, acting within the context of military institutions in texts such as *Sanctuary*,[32] *Resident Evil*,[33] and *Covert Vampire Organization*.[34] Such narratives stress weapons and combative techniques, and construct vampires and zombies as abject, diseased, and inhuman. FVZA forms a part of war-related texts that since 9/11 have been predicated upon realism and traditional American values. Realism has "permeated nearly every aspect of contemporary life, finding pronounced expression in entertainment media."[35] War texts from 9/11 rely on realism as a tool for the rewriting of history and the validation of the fantasy within the real world.[36] Disease and contagion in this world become metaphors for invasion, not only of the human body but also the nation. The website likewise becomes a battleground to retain a sense of purity in the realistic vision of the vampire as a possible, not a supernatural, threat.

Realism in war narratives reinforces American nation building and expansion in the real world.[37] War games revise history. For instance, *Conflict: Desert Storm II: Back to Baghdad*[38] entices its mainly adolescent male audiences through realism, using documents such as documentaries, newspaper reports and news coverage. These types of war-based narratives are more masculine in their concept and enable their participants to experience war within a risk-free environment.[39] They also give participants a measure of empowerment over future attacks. FVZA continuously reiterates its professionalism and expertise. Documents in the website, for instance, note:

> The tactics of the Federal Vampire and Zombie Agency used to fight the undead from 1868 to 1976 are just the thing the CIA needs to subdue America's new enemies, according to retired Maj. Gen. Mike Blois of Wilmington, North Carolina ... "This would be a different type of soldier ... he would be able to act independently with minimal or no oversight ... such an agent would have prevented the terrorist attacks of September 11."[40]
>
> Top American military brass confirmed yesterday they have

been consulting with Dr. Hugo Pecos ... for help in locating Osama Bin Laden ... Dr. Pecos is confident that Bin Laden will eventually be found. "After all," he noted, "vampires are much more formidable than terrorists, and we eradicated them."[41]

Realism, Hierarchy and Authenticity

Authenticity on the website is constructed through spatial organization and the presentation of knowledge. There is no clear linear narrative of cause and effect in the website, rather, as Marie-Laure Ryan[42] argues, the website narrative is non-linear, akin to a sea anemone where the participants click onto different pages then click back to the center. However, this act in itself implies a hierarchy, in which the homepage privileges the most important material on the site. So, too, do the regulations in the fan forums, which are placed separately at the top of the topic lists. Participants' understanding of viral vampires is crucial in their progression through the hierarchies of the website. A participant's accumulated posts provide them with respect within the community even if they breach the rules, as will be discussed below.

Participant authenticity has been noted in other sub-cultural research. Peter Donnelly and Kevin Young[43] propose four stages of progress within a sports subculture: pre-socialization, selection and recruitment, socialization, and acceptance/ostracism. The first three stages concern the actor's performance of a specific sub-cultural identity. Pre-socialization, for instance, refers to the ways in which new members, or neophytes, become aware of a subculture through family, friends, or the media: "such tenuous knowledge of a specific subculture frequently results in a caricatured and stereotypical image of the group, and certain misconceptions regarding members." Selection and recruitment relate to the participant's introduction and enrolment into the subculture. The fourth stage concerns identity confirmation by the subculture, when the participant is "placed as a social object."[44] Although Donnelly and Young write about sports subcultures, their model for the production of hierarchies and authenticity on the FVZA website is highly appropriate.

The highest authority on the website is its producer, Richard

S. Dargan, and his alter egos, Dr. Hugo Pecos and Dangovich the Unfrozen Caveman. The rules of the RPG forum state that "The highest authority in arguements [sic] ... is Dr. Hugo Pecos (aka Dangovich from the FVZA forum), he will have the final say in any and all arguements [sic]."[45] After Dargan, the FVZA website hierarchies amongst participants are organized around military promotion according to numbers of posts. This arrangement is similar to the video game in the progression from one level to another. Karine Barzilai-Nahon[46] argues that forum gatekeepers can control the information traffic on a forum. Gatekeepers can control the content through deletion, blocking and manipulation. However, the role of gatekeeper is not without its paradoxes in FVZA, as will be discussed below. At the bottom of the hierarchy is the neophyte, who might begin with the position of "zombie chow" before working through rankings such as "scourge of the dead" for over 1000 posts, and choosing their own rank after 1500 posts.[47] These roles are allocated by participants' allegiance to website values and also by their number of condoned posts. Trolls — individuals who sign up to the website to disrupt and cause conflict — can be classed as neophytes as they seldom last more than thirty posts, but they are usually very aware of site values and use them as a tool to cause maximum conflict.

Despite the simplicity of the hierarchies there are paradoxes in website protocol. On the Vampires forum the gatekeeper, Vampyre13, is a self-confessed vampire, thus breaching his own rules and regulations: "NO RolePlayers (RPr's). If you post that your [sic] a 13th century Dracula wanna be or similar, several things will happen. Your post will be mercilessly mocked. You will be flamed.[48] Your post will be moved to the graveyard or deleted."[49] Despite this breaching of his own rules, he claims sub-cultural authenticity through knowledge, as noted by a participant: —he is the resident expert on this subject and Mod. Authenticity seems to be achieved through adherence to "facts" and maturity/age. The latter issue is important because long-term participants have grown up and achieved their authenticity from 2001, so they have a stake in the website content but also have reached maturity within this period: "I'm not a pre-teen, sparkle eyed, youth full of Gen-Y (2000) bullshit in my head that then, spews onto this forum." Indeed, within the site, Vampyre13 is referred to as "the old man." He is also provided with a testimonial: "People believe in vampyre13 not because he shouts from the rooftops 'I am a vampire!' ... Ol vamp works his true character into his posts here ... over time your true colors shine through."

An example of hierarchies at work in the FVZA website can be found in a communication between Stinger 5 (with 309 posts) and Vampyre13. Stinger5 misreads the website values, a common failing of members new to a subculture when, in their enthusiasm for authenticity, they may "deliberately adopt mannerisms and attitudes ... speech, and behavior that [is perceived as] characteristic of established members of the achieved subculture."[50] He remarks that the *30 Days of Night* vampire is a better representation than vampires wearing trench coats and sunglasses: "I have started to become really annoyed with people who claim they are immortal vampires."[51] Although the anti-RPG rhetoric seems to articulate the forum values, and Stinger5 has 309 posts, he is criticized by Vampyre13 who admits he is "a self-proclaimed vampire ... i do somewhat resemble ... Dracula." Stinger5 quickly backs down: "I'm sorry if it offended you ... This is my first "dip" into the vampire part of the forum. I expected to make a mistake somewhere. And yes, I had heard that you had something resembling a vampire lifestyle, and I wasn't meaning to include you in the 'things that annoy me' list." What is significant in this encounter is that authenticity can be acquired by certain individuals in a subculture, but it has to be earned. Given the aggression shown to RPGs in the forum discussions, Stinger5's mistake is understandable. The accidental infringement of rules can be shown in a post, "Vampire Facts," in which Fibonacci, a new participant, attempts to describe the symptoms of the vampire virus, including "Sudden darkening of hair: This virus changes the gene that determines hair color." This is challenged and demolished by three long-term participants for contradicting itself and for its lack of knowledge of "vampire facts." The last notes: "the [myths] you're talking about ALL COME FROM MOVIES! Movies aren't real. They don't even transfer into real life. They make a good story up and then toss it on a screen ... It's no wonder no one believes you. It's very important when you're acting like a know it all jerk that you DON'T contradict yourself.

Cause now you look like an idiot." The continuous assertion that viral vampires are not constructed through media myths is used across the website in forums and the seeded documents.

Rhetoric and Authenticity: Defining Monstrosity

In this section rhetoric is discussed through two types of participant activity, definition and combat. In both sections gender and hierarchies play a major role. Website rhetoric indicates a macho culture in its attitude towards vampires and in their definition. Authenticity clusters around issues of audiences, genre, and, obliquely, gender. Definition is in the comparison of various vampire presentations. Combat is metaphorical and takes place on forum discussions between FVZA agents and trolls. The comparative and combative aspects of rhetoric are definitional. They define participants' values and the authenticities underpinning FVZA. Vampires that bear similarity to the viral vampire or the realistic, masculine values of the FVZA website have more approval than the sympathetic vampires of *Twilight*.

Generically, as noted above, FVZA falls under the war/combat genre linked with films and video games. In contrast, the sympathetic vampire genre is linked with romance and melodrama, both associated with women and therefore tending to be dismissed as culturally credulous. Literary-based texts, such as the Twilight saga, *Interview with the Vampire* and *Vampire Diaries*, are subject to vitriolic attack, with participants particularly scornful of "god-modded" vampires and homoerotic, "girly monsters" in *Interview with the Vampire*. The issues emerging from these quotations define the audiences who are devotees of the sympathetic vampire as immature and female. The crossover of vampires from horror to romance/melodrama is regarded as weakening a previously virile monster. Participants define themselves against female audiences, and the viral vampire encapsulates this difference, as shown in the following quotations:

> I blame Anne Rice and her ilk, they cut the balls off a horror staple and turned him into a brooding angst-ridden loser in a frilly shirt. (Judge Khan)
> … [Twilight saga fans are] young and stupid. (Vampyre13)

> ... IT'S ALL about teenage angst and emo bullshit with some steamy sex scenes ... Vampire books and the genre itself has gone from the Horror section in the book stores to the Young Readers area ... the only Vampire novels worth reading are all STILL in the horror section, though it depends greatly on your bookstore ... (The Dark One)

> ... couldnt get thru the first book [Twilight saga] ... to the part where the girls in school booooooooring ... saw the flick ... way too tenboppish ... Stoker would be rolling over in his grave. (Vampyre 13)

Comments about Stoker "rolling in his grave" indicate the subcultural credibility of *Dracula*, born out in other forum discussions about *Dracula* and *30 Days of Night* above. Both texts are approved of for perceived heteronormative masculine values: violence, predatory sexuality, and objectivity.

Of film vampires FVZA participants approve of Christopher Lee's portrayal of Dracula who:

> ... was especially evil because he brought sexual pleasure to the women. This is one of the things that the Hammer Dracula films got right. In most of them, they show that the female victims took great pleasure in Dracula's embraces, even as it killed them. (Vampyre13)

> Dracula was a brooding sort in a frilly shirt but he brooded about more practical things and wasn't gay and in love with other vampires. (Ricky Strange)

> ... real vamps DO NOT CARE about sex, love, emotions ... there IS NO ROOM for that in their existence. (Vampyre 13)

30 Days of Night has the approval of the FVZA participants because it depicts vampires as unknowable, evil and animalistic. According to Nightstalker, the vampire is "a ruthless, killing machine, hell bent on making itself the only species on the planet." Dr. Bedlam also attests to the authenticity of *30 Days of Night*: "both the movie and the graphic novel brought us back to a vampire I could respect: a creature that may once have been human, but has been turned into a hideous monster."

Pa/trolling the Boundaries: Symbolic Skirmishes in Cyberspace

In the comparisons above, FVZA participants construct their own identities from their concept of the viral vampire against the sympathetic vampire. Although most participants perform in compliance with FVZA values, there are some participants whose intervention in the site challenges FVZA agents. Trolls post contentious messages with the aim of eliciting violent responses. In encounters with these individuals, FVZA participants perform and confirm their sub-cultural identities, reflecting masculinized and idealized identities within the FVZA hierarchy.

Trolls, like other members of online communities, fabricate a range of identities which are used as avatars in different communal contexts.[52] Although the troll may seem a negative phenomenon, like the comparative rhetoric above, they serve to consolidate FVZA boundaries.[53] This is demonstrated in encounters with trolls.

In recent years FVZA interaction has diminished to a small number of hardcore participants patrolling the site and shooting down any trolls claiming to be real vampires. In this sense they are acting out the FVZA narrative metaphorically, as they protect their space from predation by sympathetic vampires.[54] There are three levels of symbolic combat incorporated within the encounters between agents and trolls, and these relate to the viral-versus-sympathetic vampire: the vampire as virus attacking the body; the vampire as virus attacking the website; and the vampire as terrorist/suicide bomber, attacking America. Trolls purposely register and inflame in order to be abused and ultimately killed. But their activity is an important component in the reinvigoration of participation, for they often enact (sympathetic) vampire identities. FVZA agents regard them as young "Twi-hards," and often two or three will take part in an online skirmish to rout the pests.

Trollers relentlessly pursue conflict and confrontation unthinkable in the real world. In the "real world," social etiquette is the province of the middle classes and tends to be conceptually female and constructed through nineteenth-century social discourses.⁵⁵ This courtesy is manifest in social intercourse, in which women defer to men in conversation and floorspace.⁵⁶ In her discussion of female online fandom, Rhiannon Bury defines verbal aggression as masculine and, invoking Herring's study of online politeness, argues that, "women are more concerned with maintaining positive politeness."⁵⁷ As noted above, the website is divided along two separate lines, RPGs and discussion forums. Despite the warning against role-playing, there is regular flame baiting (posts meant to inflame argument) by role-players.⁵⁸ As "[the virtual world] is composed of *information* rather than matter,"⁵⁹ this type of behavior is an attack on fundamental social interaction and communities. Flamebaiting is often posted by trolls using a variety of usernames to escape detection. Trolls attempt to disrupt the flow of information within the virtual world, and because identities on the internet are anonymous and multiple, trollers and virtual combatants⁶⁰ do not face the social stigma of everyday life in their aggressive confrontations.⁶¹ What is significant about FVZA trollers is that some of them are female. The behavior of participants in these online verbal combat encounters seem to overturn accepted norms of male/female behavior in Jenkins's fandom research, and in Derecho's perception of the libratory aspects of archontic texts.

One such encounter between FVZA agents and three troll identities is examined, to show how the realism of the archive discourse is used as a weapon on both sides. "I am a Vampire"⁶² is the first post by role player Iwillnotsuckyourblood, AKA Poppy, February 15, 2010. This is countered by four long-term participants and the forum moderator, Vampyre13. Poppy perhaps uses other identities, for once she disappears two more trolls, DarkLady and Caine, join the fray. The following discussion identifies the strategies in this online skirmish to show how realism and gender are key rhetorical issues.

Iwillnotsuckyourblood's opening address uses FVZA values as a weapon to attack the forum, in an opening phrase similar to Pecos's opening address: "i [*sic*] just want to set you straight with *the difference between myths and facts* ... if you delete this post or block me you are denying many people the *truth*." There is initial skepticism and she is challenged by Vampyre13, who demands facts, including:

How often do you feed on bodily fluids? ... Are you associated with any known (or unknown) groups, covens, associations that would be recognized by the vampire community? 6. Are you aware of any specific vampire community organizations? 7. Are you goth, emo, dark natured, etc ? ... Finally, What evidence or proof do you possess to back your claim to vampiredom?

The post raises discussion of identity through sub-cultural affiliation (Emo and Goth, both regarded as inauthentic), age, and gender. Poppy responds, "www.vampirewebsite.net/forum is the only organization that i [sic] trust via internet ... im [sic] not a emo/goth/darknatured person, but most of my doners are emos." The use of "donors" rather than "victims" proclaims her sympathetic nature. Iwillnotsuckyourblood's profile is also questioned. Vampyre13 describes her as a poser and there is evidence that he knows of her previous activities on other websites: an "initial analysis (estimate really) puts you in the general percentile of a young adult or thereabouts, having been on previous forums and annoying the authorities there ... (hence post deletes). Offhand, I'd give you a 30% chance of sticking around here more than 60 days." Panther, a new recruit, takes up the attack, claiming, "you were banned for being a poser on the http://vampirewebsite.net/forum which ironically is the same website that you claim to get your information from." Panther can claim sub-cultural capital because of his knowledge of and activities on other vampire websites:

> Roughly mid to late 2009, poppy kept coming back with different ip#s [sic] by use of proxy sites for a while after that. On my forum when we IP ban we don't ban their name immediately, that way we know if they are back on a new IP ... Poppy kept coming back with a new proxy site about 15 times before I got sick of it and simply banned by name ...

A day after Poppy's last post a new member, Lady Night, registers, claiming to hail from Sweden and to be over 30,000 years old. Again Vampyre13 demands facts, displaying knowledge of antiquity and history before blocking her content. Whether Poppy, Lady

Night and Caine are the same individual and whether that individual is female cannot be verified.[63] However, the discussion of their encounters with FVZA participants confirms notions of online participation and online fabricated identities as libratory.[64]

Trolls may gain some pleasure from these encounters, but the participants on the website also relish these attacks as they sharpen their discussion skills. More importantly, they keep the website functioning, as Vampyre13 comments: "without them certain sections on here would go inactive." Jenkins notes that participatory culture enables deviant behavior as a form of transgression and resistance. He relates this to the producer/fan, or mass media/fandom relationships. However, FVZA begins as a website — part of the gift economy produced by a fan for fans. The encounters discussed above demonstrate that trolling and online debates construct their own hierarchies. Resistance may not be against the values of the website so much as a form of identity construction or affirmation.

Conclusion

Unlike other forms of contemporary vampire fandom, the FVZA website is constructed through discourses relating to realism and masculinity. Fantasy is discounted, romance is scorned and devalued. The rhetoric of participants, therefore, departs from previous studies of website rhetoric predicated upon narratives relating to fantasy, romance and melodrama in hurt/comfort, Mary Sue and slash fictions. Participants, however, define their alternate reality through the negative "not I" in their comparison of FVZA vampires with sympathetic vampires. The use of realism to underpin FVZA rhetoric raises issues of gender and identity within the community. The construction of the archive — its practices and use of rhetoric — is similar to that of academia. It involves the employment of knowledge, facts, and rational debate to construct hierarchies and authenticity within the community. The close encounters and endless debate about the nature of vampirism suggest that the FVZA archive also includes those oppositional vampire texts through which the community can define itself.

The relationship between producer, participants and texts changes through convergence culture. Research into fan fiction websites has highlighted that fan fiction can be a liberating genre that gives voice to the silenced or disempowered. This chapter has focused on a masculine-based community, so one might conjecture that participants articulate within patriarchal systems from a position of power. Certainly their aggressive rhetoric in flaming, mocking, and reasoning against trolls — and the use of perceived essentialist masculine discourses, such as realism, logic, and war — seems to suggest this. However, the site is based on a call for action and the reassertion of masculine values. FVZA agents do gain satisfaction from their trollish combat. The FVZA archive incorporates these rhetorical encounters within the overall body and, just as male participants gain satisfaction from this combat, so too must the trolls — or else why flamebait? So the combative rhetoric is satisfactory for both parties. Another benefit of trollish behavior is that, in discussing FVZA with trolls, participants identify the boundaries of their alternate world.[65]

What is certain in FVZA rhetoric in a post 9/11 cultural landscape is a picture of national and masculine uncertainty. In this landscape the viral vampire can be regarded as a disease threatening the national body. War games, as Richard C. King and David J. Leonard suggest, use realism to expand American frontiers. However, realism can also act as a tool for combating the irrational. Calls for FVZA professionalism to be applied to the militia and intelligence services act as a critique of the American administration's handling of the War on Terror, but also serve as an affirmation of the possible reinvigoration of American masculinity, with professionalism at the fore. The lack of confidence may change in light of recent events. As this chapter was being prepared, the death of Osama bin Laden, as the culmination of a meticulously planned and executed CIA initiative, was announced. From early reports of rejoicing at Ground Zero, it looks as though the American psyche and honor have been restored. It would be interesting to follow FVZA in these circumstances, to identify any reinvigoration of the site or new directions of narrative; for fan fiction, like the archive, is always a work in progress.[66]

Notes

1. Grateful thanks to Gareth Schott, David Huxley and Hugo Pecos for their generous help and excellent advice in writing this chapter.
2. *The Federal Vampire and Zombie Agency.org*, accessed September 20, 2010, http://www.fvza.org.
3. Richard S. Dargan, "Foreword," *FVZA: Federal Vampire and Zombie Agency*, written by David Hine and illustrated by Roy Allan Martinez, (California: Radical Publishing, 2010), 6.
4. Joan Ormrod, e-mail message to Richard S. Dargan/Hugo Pecos, December 21, 2010.
5. Richard S. Dargan, "FVZA: Incident Reports," *Federal Vampire and Zombie Agency.org*, accessed September 20, 2010, http://www.fvza.org/incidents.html.
6. Richard S. Dargan, "FVZA: Famous Cases: Terror in the Factory," *Federal Vampire and Zombie Agency.org*, accessed September 20, 2010, http://www.fvza.org/warhol.html.
7. The RPG section rules posted by Adminbot3000, December 27, 2005, include: "[No] Magic, Satanic rituals that revive things that've been dead for a long time, Demons, Religious favoratism [sic]. By that I mean that God shall not smite vampires in this RPG, Ghosts, Extraterrestrials, Bigfoot, Bioenhancements that do not currently exist. You can have contact lenses, but no cybernetic arms with rocket launchers, Supersoldier FVZA agents, Superheros [sic]. Although I do like Spider-Man, I don't want to read about him killing zombies unless it's in comic book form by Marvel. Unrealistic actions, such as continents spontanously [sic] combusting. Your character has to learn his/her skills from somewhere. You don't just inherit those skills from family members. They can teach you those skills, but their blood/DNA won't give you those skills for nothing." Adminbot3000, "Rules of the FVZA RPG," *Invision Free.org*, accessed December 24, 2010, http://z14.invisionfree.com/FVZA_RPG/index.php?showtopic=2.
8. Personal correspondence with Richard S. Dargan (April 15, 2011) confirms that vampire participants on the website tend to be male, and that there is a bigger female contingent in the zombie section.
9. Karen Backstein, "(Un)safe Sex: Romancing the Vampire," *Cineaste* 35, no. 1 (2009): 38–41.
10. Susan Faludi, *The Terror Dream: Fear and Fantasy in Post 9/11 America* (London: Atlantic, 2008), 13–15.
11. Richard Slotkin, *The Fatal Environment: The Myth of the Frontier in the Age of Industrialization, 1800–1890* (Middletown, CT: Wesleyan University Press, 1986), 33–48.

12. Kenneth Burke, *Language as Symbolic Action* (Berkeley and Los Angeles: University of California Press, 1966), 9–13.
13. Camille Bacon-Smith, *Enterprising Women: Television Fandom and the Creation of Popular Myth* (Pennsylvania: University of Pennsylvania Press, 1992).
14. Henry Jenkins, *Textual Poachers: Television Fans and Participatory Culture* (London and New York: Routledge, 1992).
15. John Fiske, "The Cultural Economy of Fandom," in *The Adoring Audience: Fan Culture and Popular Media*, ed. Lisa A. Lewis (London and New York: Routledge, 1992), 30–49.
16. Sarah Thornton, *Club Cultures: Music, Media and Sub-cultural Capital* (Hanover: University Press of New England, 1996).
17. Pierre Bourdieu, *Distinction: A Social Critique of the Judgment of Taste*, trans. Richard Nice (Cambridge, MA: Harvard University Press, 1985).
18. Bourdieu, 6.
19. *Habitus* is a term used by Bourdieu to describe the lifestyle and background of an individual which, in turn, defines their taste and knowledge.
20. Thornton, 11.
21. Abigail Derecho, "Archontic Literature: A Definition, a History, and Several Theories of Fan Fiction," in *Fan Fiction and Fan Communities in the Age of the Internet*, ed. Karen Hellekson and Kristina Busse (Jefferson, NC: McFarland, 2006), 64–66.
22. Derecho, 73.
23. The graphic novel adaptation by David Hine for Radical Comics would also be an appropriate part of the archive to analyze, but there is no space to do this in this chapter. However, FVZA poses an interesting problem for the adapter, because apart from Pecos, no hero or heroine is presented on the website.
24. Cornel Sandvoss, *Fans: The Mirror of Consumption* (Cambridge, UK and Malden, MA: Polity Press, 2005), 131.
25. Bruce A. McClelland, *Slayers and Their Vampires: A Cultural History of Killing the Dead* (Michigan: University of Michigan Press, 2006), 17.
26. Nicola Nixon, "When Hollywood Sucks, or, Hungry Girls, Lost Boys, and Vampirism in the Age of Reagan," in *Blood Read: The Vampire as Metaphor in Contemporary Culture*, ed. Joan Gordon and Veronica Hollinger (Philadelphia: University of Pennsylvania Press, 1997), 115–128.
27. Anne Rice, *Interview with the Vampire* (London: Warner, 1994).
28. *Dark Shadows*, created by Dan Curtis, Burbank, CA: ABC, first aired June 27, 1966.
29. *Buffy the Vampire Slayer*, created by Joss Whedon, Los Angeles: 20th Century Fox Home Entertainment, first aired March 10, 1997.

30 Stephenie Meyer, *Twilight* (London: Atom, 2007).
31 *True Blood*, created by Alan Ball, New York: Home Box Office, first aired September 7, 2008.
32 *Sanctuary*, created by Damian Kindler, New York: SyFy Imagine Greater, first aired October 3, 2008.
33 *Resident Evil*, directed by Shinji Makami, Osaka, Japan: Capcom, 1996.
34 Alex Garner, Jeff Mariotte, Mindy Lee, and Gabriel Hernandez, *Covert Vampire Organization* (San Diego, CA: IDW Publishing, 2004).
35 Nina B. Huntemann and Matthew Thomas Payne, "Introduction," in *Joystick Soldiers: The Politics of Play in Military Video Games*, ed. Nina B. Huntemann and Matthew Thomas Payne (New York and London: Routledge, 2010), 10.
36 This replicates the construction of *Dracula* which, according to McClelland, relies upon letters, diaries and newspaper articles for much of the narrative. Stoker does not draw attention through narration to Dracula's evil. Rather, he presents the reader with the information to enable them to make up their minds.
37 Richard C. King and David J. Leonard, "Wargames as a New Frontier: Securing American Empire in Virtual Space," in *Joystick Soldiers: The Politics of Play in MilitaryVideo Games*, ed. Nina B. Huntemann and Matthew Thomas Payne (New York and London: Routledge: 2010), 91–105.
38 *Conflict: Desert Storm II: Back to Baghdad* (Bath; Pivotal Games, 2003). Another example is in the development of the video game *Deadspace* (Redwood City, CA: Electronic Arts, 2008), of which Ian Milham (the art director) noted, "The key I think was to not look at other games and movies too much, but instead look at real life ... and we integrated those real-world influences into the game." Brad Nicholson, "Dead Space's Horror Influence Comes from Life, Not Space Monsters," *Gamezone*, accessed April 4, 2011, http://www.destructoid.com/dead-space-s-horror-influence-comes-from-life-not-space-monsters-103619.phtml.
39 King and Leonard, 92.
40 "Retired Army General Says CIA Should Take a Page From the FVZA," *Federal Vampire and Zombie Agency.org*, accessed February 4, 2011, http://www.fvza.org/prgeneral.html.
41 "Legendary Vampire Hunter Helping in Search for Bin Laden," *Federal Vampire and Zombie Agency.org*, accessed February 4, 2011, http://www.fvza.org/prcaves.html.
42 Marie-Laure Ryan, *Avatars of Story*, Electronic Mediations (Minneapolis: University of Minnesota Press, 2006), 97–125.
43 Peter Donnelly and Kevin Young, "The Construction and Confirmation

of Identity in Sport Subcultures," in *Contemporary Issues in the Sociology of Sport*, ed. Andrew Yiannakis and Merrill J. Melnick (Champaign, IL: Human Kinetics, 2001), 399–412.
44 Ibid., 226.
45 Adminbot3000, "Rules of the FVZA RPG."
46 Karine Barzilai-Nahon, "Gatekeeping: A Critical Review," *Annual Review of Information Science and Technology* 34, no. 1 (2009): 1–79.
47 "I am a Vampire," *Federal Vampire Zombie Agency.org*, accessed August 24, 2011, http://www.*fvza*.org/vampires.html.
48 The virtual demolition of an opponent through mockery, insults and invective.
49 Vampyre 13, "Forum Index: Vampires," *The Federal Vampire and Zombie Agency.org,* October 5, 2008. http://www.fvza.org/phpBB2/viewtopic.php?t=6467.
50 Donnelly and Young, 225.
51 Stinger5, "30 Days of Night ... more like the FVZA vampire?," *The Federal Vampire and Zombie Agency.org,* September 6, 2008, http://www.fvza.org/phpBB2/viewtopic.php?p=179172.
52 See, for example, Sherry Turkle, *Life on the Screen: Identity in the Age of the Internet* (New York: Touchstone, 1995), and Lisa Nakamura, *Cybertypes: Race, Ethnicity, and Identity on the Internet* (New York and London: Routledge, 2002).
53 Michele Tepper, "Usenet Communities and the Cultural Politics of Information," in *Internet Culture*, ed. David Porter (New York and London: Routledge, 1997), 43. See also Judith S. Donath, "Identity and Deception in the Virtual Community," in *Communities in Cyberspace*, ed. Marc A. Smith and Peter Kollock (London: Routledge, 1999).
54 This is noted by a newer member, Ihopdemon: "Currently, it seems like there are about 20–30 of us or so that talk mostly in the guns section ... It seems like nothing but role players and trolls have joined since I got here and are mostly chased away." "What was the forum like in the beginning?" *Federal Vampire Zombie Agency.org*, accessed May 2, 2011, http://www.fvza.org/ phpBB2/viewtopic.php?t=10136.
55 Rhiannon Bury, *Cyberspaces of their Own: Female Fandoms Online*, Digital Formations Vol. 25 (New York: Peter Lang, 2005), 131–35.
56 Robin Tolmach Lakoff, *Language and Woman's Place* (New York: Harper and Row, 1975), and Janet Holmes, *Women, Men and Politeness*, Real Language Series (London and New York: Longman, 1995).
57 Bury, 135.
58 Donath, 28.
59 Ibid.
60 Mark Dery, "Flame Wars," in *Flame Wars: The Discourse of Cyberculture*,

ed. Mark Dery (Durham, NC: Duke University Press, 1994), 1–10; and Howard Rheingold, "A Slice of Life in My Virtual Community," in *Global Networks: Computers and International Communication*, ed. Linda M. Harasim (Cambridge, MA: MIT Press, 1993), 57–80.

61 Erving Goffman, *The Presentation of Self in Everyday Life* (London: Penguin, 1990).

62 Iam a vampire Iwillnotsuckyourblood, "I am a Vampire," *The Federal Vampire and Zombie Agency.org*, accessed April 19, 2011, http://www.fvza.org/phpBB2/viewtopic.php?t=9830.

63 I attempted to contact them through email but received no reply. However, research into troll motivations would be interesting, especially when identifying the pleasures of this type of activity.

64 Nakamura, 13.

65 This can also be likened to academia's endless collection, classification and discussion of research. Indeed the connection to fan and academic participation has been noted by Joli Jenson, "Fandom as Pathology: The Consequences of Characterization," in *The Adoring Audience: Fan Culture and Popular Media*, ed. Lisa A. Lewis (London and New York: Routledge, 1992).

66 Hellekson and Busse, "Introduction: Work in Progress."

4

Buffy vs. Bella: The Re-Emergence of the Archetypal Feminine in Vampire Stories

Jennifer Jenson and Anita Sarkeesian

Introduction

In the battle for brains, beauty, and brawn in the contemporary teen vampire soap-operatic melodrama, female heroes, in particular, are portrayed in varied roles, from love interest, to rebel outsider, to protector of the world. At opposite ends of the spectrum are Buffy Summers, the heroine of the long-running, teenage vampire melodrama, *Buffy the Vampire Slayer*, and Bella Swan, the lead female of the Twilight novels and movies. This chapter will focus on these lead female characters, comparing and contrasting them in reference to situational, popular cultural vampire stories and lore, before concluding with an investigation of how fans write about and interact with the characters. Through each lens we will examine Buffy and Bella "in action," to demonstrate the ways in which certain values and attributes might be associated with each, and to suggest what this might mean for the shifting landscape of femininities, at least as they relate to teenage vampire stories. We also stake out and attempt to summarize the very different communities of fans that are in circulation around those two characters. Whereas Buffy Summers offers her fans an assertive, imaginative landscape for action, Bella Swan offers far less, in that she is marginal to much of the main action in the movies, and is cast centrally as the object of desire for two male protagonists. Our objective is to show how, as many who have written on one or both of these characters have declared, "the wild success of *Twilight* might be cause for despair."[1]

The fictional vampire is a figure that is constantly being reconfigured and recirculated: from the nineteenth-century novels of John William Polidori and Bram Stoker; to films by Boris Karloff (*Black Sabbath*), Tony Scott (*The Hunger*), and Stephen Norrington (*Blade*); to twentieth-century mass paperback fiction by authors such as Stephen King (*Salem's Lot*) and Anne Rice (*Interview with the Vampire, The Vampire Lestat*); to small screen incarnations such as *Forever Night, Buffy the Vampire Slayer* and *True Blood*. As scholars have pointed out, the vampire is a divided figure in most of these narratives; it is inhuman and undead, yet both an outsider and an insider in a world that is predominantly human.[2] Many of these texts focus on vampires who are already "evil," having resigned themselves completely to their soulless existence of feeding on human blood. Other fictions are fascinated with vampires who are struggling to cultivate or maintain a remaining humanity.

The deeply compelling draw of these narratives is, in part, the formation of the Gothic hero who resides outside of social and cultural structures. In some texts, such as Rice's novels, the imaginative landscape centers on characters who have observed the ongoing mistakes of human existence over hundreds of years, yet still yearn to re-enter that fray. In other narratives, such as *Blade* and King's *Salem's Lot*, the attraction is the outright lawlessness and inhumanity that can be explored through the breakdown of human conventions, a result of the overwhelming need simply to feed. These central figures are almost invariably male, and the central object of their desires is principally female. As the focus of a vampire's interest, Bella Swan seems little different from her predecessors Mina Murray and Lucy Westenra in Stoker's *Dracula*. She does share some similarities with Buffy, in that they both experience possessive male behavior — in the form of stalking — and eventually fall in love with a vampire, but the ways in which they manage their situations greatly diverges.

This chapter builds upon and extends the numerous comparisons between Buffy and Bella that have circulated on blogs and in popular media in recent years — especially following the immense popularity of the Twilight franchise, whereby Bella has become the face of the contemporary vampire heroine. Vampire film buffs may disapprove of the turn that vampire lore has taken in this series;

however, what might be even more remarkable (and with long-lasting social impact) is the way in which Bella's character is shaping the future of the female protagonist. She is not a full, complete character who has depth and understanding; rather, she is more like a vessel[3] or a "Mary Sue" (the self-insertion of the author as the main character), who offers the author, readers and viewers the opportunity to live out fantasies about attractive, possessive men. Indeed, in the movie series Bella is rarely portrayed on her own, and usually assumes a secondary role as the heterosexual and feminized counterpart to two different but equally powerful masculinities.

In contrast, the cult classic television show (and spin-off comic series that continues today) *Buffy the Vampire Slayer* gives its audience a female hero who pushes the boundaries of the typical female character. Buffy is not the helpless love interest of the menacing vampire, but a brave young woman with a strength that is equal to or greater than that of her vampire foes and friends. Whereas Bella is rarely in a scene alone, Buffy is central and decisive, and — unlike Bella — is portrayed as someone who has romantic relationships on her own terms, even when she is suffering their consequences. The contrast between Buffy and Bella illuminates the "battle of the story":[4] one character promotes change and a vision of gender, while the other settles into a deeply regressive and patriarchally inscribed gender role.

Buffy vs. Bella

Buffy the Vampire Slayer aired from 1997 to 2003, and remains a widely popular cult classic eight years later, with fan sites still active, the publication of a spin-off comic, and ongoing talks of another full-length movie. The series has been celebrated, criticized, and analyzed by academics and feminists, precisely because it is an unusual show in America's television landscape, with good writing and feminist undertones that has ensured its appeal for seven seasons.[5] *Buffy* tells the story of an average American teenager who has been "chosen" and endowed with superhuman strength to protect the earth from vampires, demons, and the forces of darkness. Throughout the seven seasons, audiences watch her battle vampires and other evil predators; she grows up, loses those who are close to her, is denied her first love (a vampire, Angel), and genuinely struggles with the complexities of adult life. There is also real tension created in the series, between Buffy's being "just a teenage girl" who wants to go to movies with friends and have a boyfriend, and her "other life," which involves slaying vampires after dark. For example, she states in Season One, Episode One, "Welcome to the Hellmouth": "It's my first day! I was afraid that I was gonna be behind in all my classes, that I wouldn't make any friends, that I would have last month's hair. I didn't think there'd be vampires on campus."[6] This trope of the reluctant yet ready heroine continues through the early years of the series; throughout, Buffy's femininity is continually challenged and under siege as she struggles to fulfil her dual roles of female hero and vampire slayer.

The popularity of *Buffy* reaches beyond its fan community, according it the status of a pop culture icon. The show is constantly referenced in the mainstream media, and is often subject to intertextual "nods" in other television shows such as *Xena: Warrior Princess*, *Will & Grace*, and *True Blood*. The point here is that Buffy represents the kind of heroine who breaks with the usual role of the victimized woman in vampire stories. She thus commands the attention of audience members and fans who are compelled by her story to continue viewing, writing, blogging, and exploring.

Not surprisingly, when the Twilight franchise gained instant popularity and the blogosphere was buzzing with talk about the books, the movies and the fans (Twihards), Buffy's name came up often, though usually in contrast to Stephenie Meyer's heroine. The Twilight saga, like *Buffy*, has a central female protagonist, Bella Swan, who is also a young woman in high school. Her story begins and ends with her falling in love and subsequently marrying a vampire, Edward Cullen. Much of the action of the story is centered on this romantic drama, the kindling of Bella and Edward's love, and later on Edward's family saving Bella from the imminent harm of other vampires. The fact that both Buffy and Bella fall in love with a vampire, and that their stories begin when they are nearly the same age, was enough for critics and the pop culture blogosphere to start comparing the two narratives.[7]

That said, the portrayals of Bella and Buffy differ significantly. This is not merely because one is a "slayer" with the strength and power to kill vampires, while the other is an average high school teenager with no special powers; it is also because they are presented with very different problems, and with different methods for solving them. For example, Buffy's story casts her as a young woman who struggles with the trials of teenage life, while also fighting vampires and other demons. In contrast, Bella is faced with minor choices and anxieties (such as concern about her father's safety), but exists more to be battled over by the lead male characters than to face struggles herself. As the fans of the Twilight novels make clear, Bella is tangential; she could be anyone. Or, more specifically, she is the fan, for the stars of the narrative are Edward Cullen and Jacob Black, the romantic rivals. This becomes apparent in the fan-created titles such as, "Team Edward vs. Team Jacob." Where is "Team Bella"? Buffy fans responded by creating "Team Buffy," reclaiming their hero archetype. In one sense, Meyer has created a multi-million dollar global phenomenon, in which the star of the show is more absent than present.

Since Meyer's Twilight books are written as a first person narrative, the reader is immediately invited to identify with Bella, who comes across as a character who lacks depth and complexity. In the books, she is portrayed as "ordinary" in appearance; she is clumsy, awkward, and suffering from low self-esteem, which mirrors the experience of many young women, especially those who have just moved to a new town. However, the film presents a different visual image, casting Kirsten Stewart in the role of Bella, who is anything but an "average-looking" actress. While film makers attempt to use casual, muted clothing and "natural" make up to help Bella appear unremarkable, photographs of the actress consistently defy that categorization. Particularly in the movies, these attempts to brand Bella as just an "average" girl are further contradicted when Bella arrives at her new home in Forks, Washington, and she is instantly popular: all the boys want to date her and all the young women want to be her friend. This inconsistency in Bella's character — socially awkward, accident-prone and clumsy, yet undeniably and instantly popular — has led some critics to call this a "Mary Sue" tale, in which the main character in a story is the idealized version of the author.[8] In addition to her social "imperfections," Bella is not shown to have any interests until she meets vampire Edward Cullen, with whom she quickly becomes infatuated. It is extremely easy for readers to place their desire for popularity and love on to a character who in many ways is an empty vessel. The lack of any real, substantive character development allows Bella to be anyone, and interested in anything, but — most importantly — she is interested simply in being the love of Edward's (undead) life.

While the portrayal of each female lead demonstrates fundamental differences in their characters, it is possibly more important to examine the implicit and explicit intent of the writers and creators of these franchises, especially given their great popularity. A close examination of Buffy and Bella is important, first of all because these characters may be influential in promoting progressive values in terms of relationships and gender roles; or, alternatively, by maintaining the status quo. Secondly, the questionable practice of appealing only to "what consumers want" may well encourage publishers and film makers to continue producing stories with potentially damaging and sexist values.

Initially, it seems almost impossible to compare Buffy and Bella, since they embody such different points of view and such different possibilities for action, but there are a number of similarities in their stories. Both stories are about vampires and teenage women, both women fall in love with and have a relationship with a vampire, and both are offered (though in very different ways) the chance to become a vampire. On the surface, Buffy, like Bella, seems to be just another average high school teenager, interested in boys and shopping, and with blond hair and mini-skirts; but she is, in fact, a warrior with supernatural powers, who is obligated to protect the world from the creatures of the night. While Buffy does not have time to pursue hobbies or interests like other young women her age, she does have close friends and romantic relationships, and socializes at the local music venue, even though she has dedicated her life to her slayer obligations. Throughout the series, Buffy is constantly growing, making mistakes and learning from them. She is often faced with moral dilemmas and emotional struggles. These elements make Buffy's character rich, complex, and appealing.

While both Buffy and Bella fall in love with vampires, their romantic relationships could not be more different. Interestingly, however, both their relationships are initiated through stalking. In the first episode of *Buffy*, the viewer sees a dark figure lurking behind Buffy as she walks down the street.⁹ Instead of running in fear, she turns the tables on her stalker and sets up a trap for him. As he follows her into a dark alley, she knocks him down and demands to know who he is and why he is following her. In the Season Two premiere, "When She Was Bad," Buffy finds the same man following her again, whereupon she pointedly comments, "You know, being stalked isn't really a big turn on for girls."¹⁰ Her stalker, Angel (a vampire), says he is lurking around to protect her because she is in danger, though it has already been made clear that Buffy is strong and capable of protecting herself.

Bella is put into a similar situation, though her reaction is slightly different. When Bella is confronted with aggressive, drunken young men in a dark alley, just as she attempts to defend herself, Edward saves her. Later on, Bella confronts Edward, asking him how he knew where she was; he admits to stalking her, just in case she needed protection, and confesses to entering her bedroom at night and watching her sleep. Instead of responding in consternation, she timidly tells Edward that his behavior is acceptable and that he should not stay away from her. In *Buffy*, overprotective, stalking male behavior is quickly categorized as an offensive act, made clear in Buffy's sarcastic comment. In *Twilight*, this same behavior is turned into a display of affection that initiates a romantic relationship. Thus, one storyline gives agency to its lead female character, while the other denies her the right to protest, under the guise of being "saved."

After their very different experiences of being stalked, both characters are confronted with the knowledge that their stalkers are vampires. When Buffy realizes that Angel is a vampire she screams, even though she has the physical power to be able to fight and possibly kill him if necessary. The tension here is immediately obvious to the audience: first and foremost, Buffy does not usually scream when in danger, and her usual reaction to encountering a vampire is to arm herself for a fight. That Buffy screams at this moment points to the tension between her "real girl life" and her slayer life, and the audience seems to be alerted to the fact that it is Buffy the girl, not the slayer, who has just kissed a vampire. Bella, in contrast, simply responds by pressing her lips together and taking the news stoically, perhaps because — as the audience and readers know — she already knows that Edward is a vampire. In the first *Twilight* film, following his revelation that he is vampire, Edward follows Bella into the woods and dramatically exhibits his strength and power in an attempt to scare her. After this demonstration he asks, "Are you afraid?" and she responds, "No."[11] Again, the writers of *Buffy* and *Twilight* diverge, choosing to frame abusive, threatening, and possibly violent behavior either with seriousness and responsibility, or with flippancy and negligence. There is, however, another way of reading this scene: because Bella does not respond fearfully, it might be possible to interpret her reaction as a challenge to feminine norms, standing up to a masculine display of power by not reacting to it. But this reading appears overly optimistic, particularly when contrasted with the ways in which Buffy confronts patriarchal authority. For example, Buffy's dismissal of the Watcher's Council (the governing body that guides the slayer), and her challenge to the unethical behavior of the American military, characterize her as a person who is unafraid of confrontation. In contrast, Bella's actions are too easily cast as those of a rebellious, naive teenager, who is unwilling to recognize the risks and possible physical harm with which she is threatened.

An under-discussed issue in regard to both shows is the way in which the relationships suffer from the unequal power dynamics resulting from a century-wide age difference. In this, and in the arguably stunted development in both Edward and Angel, the stories diverge in terms of each woman's interaction with her vampire lover and her participation in the relationship. The relationship between Angel and Buffy is a secondary narrative point in the greater story arc, whereas Bella and Edward's relationship *is* the story. Bella's high school crush is quickly turned into a troubling infatuation. Meyer, through Bella's voice, uses the language of worship, variously describing Edward as, "[T]he beautiful one, the godlike one";[12] "godlike creature";[13] "like a Greek god";[14] and "glorious as a young god."[15] An excessive amount of time is spent in emphasizing his appearance, as in, "[A] perfect statue, carved in some unknown stone, smooth like marble, glittering like crystal."[16] Moreover, "[H]is voice was beautiful, like a lullaby,"[17] and "[I]t was hard to believe that someone so beautiful could be real."[18] Edward, or his individual features, are described as "perfect" well over a dozen times in the first book alone.[19]

While Buffy and Angel eventually end their romantic relationship, their affection and respect for one another remains constant. In "Chosen," one of the last episodes, Angel visits Buffy to ask if she needs help in fighting the impending apocalypse. They begin to talk about their relationship and Buffy tells Angel,

> I'm cookie dough. I'm not done baking. I'm not finished becoming who ever the hell it is I'm gonna turn out to be. I make it through this, and the next thing, and the next thing, and maybe one day, I turn around and realize I'm ready. I'm cookies. And then, you know, if I want someone to eat me or enjoy warm, delicious, cookie me, then that's fine. That'll be then. When I'm done.[20]

While she clearly still has feelings for Angel, Buffy tells him that she wants to be alone, that she wants to explore herself and ultimately does not need a vampire, even one with the soul of a man.

While Buffy is a far more intricately created character than this brief comparison suggests, her complexity is one of the reasons that fans continue to celebrate, discuss and create new fan works about her. Much scholarly and fan writing has been devoted to critically analyzing the agency with which Buffy is endowed by the writers of the show. Although Buffy makes mistakes and sometimes does things she knows that she should not, her character continues to evolve and grow, and she has the capacity to learn from those experiences.[21] One example of this is the development of her relationship with the vampire Spike. Fans watched as Buffy spiraled into a dark place during Season Six, projecting her feelings of alienation and depression into violent and aggressive sex with Spike. Rhonda V. Wilcox explains: "It might be said that Buffy brings out the human side of Spike, while Spike brings out the monstrous side of Buffy."[22] Buffy eventually recognizes the self-destructive nature of the emotionally and physically dangerous situation she has entered into, and she ends the affair, but not before Spike attempts to rape her. The depiction of her struggles with her conflicted feelings and actions is a story arc that continues to push and expand the limits of her character.

Conversely, Bella does not have this kind of depth or complexity, and instead remains shallow and somewhat predictable. Indeed, much of what a reader or audience learns about Bella is deflected, other than her desire to be with Edward and to be a vampire. This kind of "secondary" occupation, we want to argue, flattens out her character. As Brendan Shea succinctly puts it, "As Bella understands it, much of her life's purpose is provided by the love she feels for Edward, Jacob Black, and her extended 'family'."[23] Shea, however, does argue that Bella is faced with a very interesting choice between mortality and immortality. This is a place where some depth may be read into Bella's character — not so much in relation to her various "loves," but more in regard to her worries over mortality and growing old. This is evidenced in Bella's refrain in hospital (after being bitten by a vampire and being saved by Edward): "Every minute of the day I get closer [to dying]. And I'm going to get old."[24] These are not the only reasons for Bella's expressed desire to be a vampire; there is also the fact that by not being a vampire she puts her family and friends at risk. Yet it is worth pointing out that Bella wishes to be a vampire partly so that she does not appear older than Edward, a motivation suggestive of her shallowness and vanity.

One way in which Bella asserts herself is through her expressions of sexual desire. As "Pop Psychology" blogger Johannah Cousins writes, Bella is "an openly and unashamedly desirous teenage girl."[25] Throughout the books and films, Bella is clear and consistent in her desire to be sexually intimate with Edward, but he constantly rejects her advances, sometimes even physically pushing her away. Bella's sexual feelings illustrate "the paradox of adolescent girls and sexual desire: they are expected to be desirable but are denied the expression of their own sexual desire. The Twilight series shows the frustration and complication of both desire and restraint."[26] The modicum of agency afforded Bella is, however, undermined by the controlling behavior of Edward, who seems to dictate the terms of their relationship, including when they will have sex.

Another way of exploring the differences between Buffy and Bella is to look at their functional roles within the stories. Buffy's function is that of the vampire slayer, but she exceeds that function at every turn; through the dialogue of the story, through her interactions with other characters, and through the emotional responses she invokes in the audience. Bella's function, in contrast, is wholly derivative: she functions as the damsel in distress or as the young woman in love, but that function is dependent on the roles and functions of others. For example, Edward or Jacob must save her, Edward *must* love her, Edward needs to transform her into a vampire. So it is not simply that Buffy and Bella are very different female characters. Buffy's functional role is exceeded by her character, while Bella rarely exhibits anything beyond that functional role. Buffy becomes a character in whom there is true depth to be explored, so that her role is one in which a strong female protagonist exceeds and surprises her viewers in terms of physical strength and emotional range. In contrast, as Kate Harding comments in her *Salon* article on the topic, "the whole point of Bella's existence is earning the suffocating love of supernatural hotties; even if you think her obsessive devotion to Edward might waver in the face of were-love, you know you're never going to see her throw them both over to stand on her own two feet."[27] Bella's derivative function is evident here for Harding, and this insight is repeated by many others. In her review of *Breaking Dawn*, Jennifer Reese observes, in regard to Bella: "You may wish she had loftier goals and a mind of her own, but these are fairy tales, and as a steadfast lover in the Disney princess mold, Bella has a certain saccharine appeal." She also notes that Bella, during her pregnancy, is "not only hard to identify with but positively horrifying, especially while guzzling human blood to nourish the infant."[28]

In each of these characters, a range of feminities and — in Buffy's case, masculinities — are explored, tried out, and performed. These identities are not necessarily fixed, but move and change and are reconfigured. Judith Butler's well-rehearsed work on gender and performativity is a useful tool for thinking about the inherent tension that is apparent in Buffy's character: both female and aggressive slayer, both vulnerable and "kick ass." Thus Buffy *performs* gender differently, depending on what role she is playing at any given time. Bella, too, performs femininity, although very differently. Bonnie Mann, writing about Bella through the lens of Simone de Beauvoir's classic text, *The Second Sex*,[29] argues that "[I]n Meyer's books, Bella continually discovers boys looking at her in various modes of desire. The masculine gaze confers meaning on her otherwise empty existence by giving her a place in the story as the very location through which masculine action instantiates meaning."[30] The point here is that Bella's performance of femininity, rather than demonstrating the assertiveness of a female protagonist, is regressive, because it is found through the masculine subject.

Fan Engagement

Fan engagement with both Buffy and Bella is evident in blogs, reviews, wikis, fanvids, and fan fiction. It is difficult to specifically characterize the range of fans that mobilize around Bella and Buffy, although it is quite clear from media and other general accounts that Bella attracts many more women than men.[31] Buffy's fans are quite clear: she is a strong female role model who is self-reliant and therefore does not depend upon the male characters in the series. She is also continually described as a kind of "transgressive female warrior."[32] There is near-unanimous agreement, not only among fans, but in scholarly literature as well, that Buffy *is* a strong female role model, one that not only displays true physical strength, but also plays with traditional masculine and feminine roles.[33] As Buffy herself quips after an especially harrowing fight scene, "Tell me the truth: How's my hair?"[34] In asking about her hair, she is breaking open for the audience the tension between her more masculine role as hero/warrior and her re-invoked femininity. Buffy's fans continue to write about her, including continuous postings on fan fiction sites such as The Bronze Beta,[35] Buffy World,[36] and fan sites such as Buffy the Vampire Slayer;[37] new media content is also generated through websites like the Hellmouth Podcast.[38]

Unlike Buffy, Bella's fans are both divided (should she love Edward or Jacob?) and more critical (can she *really* be considered a heroine?). The character of Bella is questionable in the sense that she mostly fulfills functional role in the story — as the damsel in distress, as the person in love with a vampire, and as the person who wants to be turned into a vampire. This means that in the popular press, and indeed fan fiction generally, Bella is mentioned more in relation to other characters than she is on her own. Indeed, despite her transformation into a vampire, she changes very little in the course of the novels and films; she begins and ends as the character who loves Edward, and has little else to offer. As the review of the final novel *Breaking Dawn* in *Publisher's Weekly* so poignantly puts it: "Everygirl Bella achieves her wishes quickly (marriage and sex, in that order, are two, and becoming an immortal is another), and once she becomes a vampire it's almost impossible to identify with her."[39] In a similar commentary on the series, Laura Miller of *Salon.com* writes: "But Bella is not really the point of the Twilight series; she's more of a place holder than a character. She is purposely made as featureless and ordinary as possible in order to render her a vacant, flexible skin into which the reader can insert herself and thereby vicariously enjoy Edward's chilly charms."[40] This is not to say that Bella and the series do not have fans — they most certainly do — from the popular fan site, Twifans[41] to the more specific Twilight Moms,[42] to Twilight Guy.[43] It seems, however, that Bella is still difficult to read as a strong female heroine. Meyer is also ambiguous on the topic, when she states on her blog, "... there are those who think Bella is a wuss. There are those who think my stories are misogynistic — the damsel in distress must be rescued by strong hero ... I emphatically reject the ... accusation. I am all about girl power — look at Alice and Jane if you doubt that. I am not anti-female, I am anti-human."[44] Significantly, even when attempting to argue against accusations of Bella's being a "wuss," Meyer points to other characters (Alice and Jane) and against the charge of misogyny she claims to be anti-human, which is not really an answer.

There are also numerous comparisons of Buffy and Bella in blogs and in the popular online press, with nearly all arriving at the same conclusion: that Bella is no match for Buffy. In one comparison, a blogger succinctly ends their Buffy vs. Bella post with, "In summary, if this were *Celebrity Deathmatch*, *Twilight* would be bleeding and then using all of its self-restraint not to suck its own blood." [45] Beth Woodward, writing for *CC2K: The Nexus of Pop-Culture Fandom*, puts it this way: "Unlike *Twilight*, *Buffy the Vampire Slayer* is not the story of an ordinary girl made extraordinary by supernatural gifts. Instead, it is the story of an ordinary girl — who just happens to have supernatural gifts — struggling through the all-too-human process of growing up."[46] Bella appears to represent the unattainable, while Buffy offers fans a kind of alternative reality that is much more real than the idealized immortality of Bella. As one fan puts it: "I'd rather have stake-wielding Buffy over lip-biting Bella as a role model for my future daughter any day."[47]

Conclusion

Vampire narratives allow readers and viewers to explore dark, Gothic worlds and possibilities for existence (such as living for many centuries) that transcend biological and social norms. In *Buffy*, the darkness of vampires and other forms of evil are literally fought episode after episode by its central character. While there is much that is bleak for Buffy — especially when she transgresses vampire/human boundaries through love and sex — there is never any question that she is, and will remain, human. Bella Swan's character, however, does make the transition between human and vampire, which implies that she has attained some sort of greatness that she did not have before (certainly she has a super power she did not have before). But that does not necessarily mean that her character is any "fuller," or that she somehow becomes a kind of feminist vampire heroine. As a fan, quoted in an MSNBC article, notes, "Bella exists almost solely as an author insert or reader proxy to enjoy the relationships with these two guys, whichever one you like better, in a story that is really geared toward wish fulfillment."[48] Bella Swan is regressive, literally and figuratively pale and weak; she is clearly much less interesting than the two male characters with whom she shares her story (Jacob and Edward), and less engaging than Buffy, who continues to command the interest of audiences and fans.

Of particular note, by way of comparison between these two protagonists, is the imaginative landscape that Buffy offers her fans, in terms of what it might mean to be a fully present female warrior; she battles evil, as do traditional masculine heroes, and also turns a very old, Gothic tale on its head by subverting the narrative of the female victim who needs to be saved. As Buffy herself so aptly puts it: "Do you think I chose to be like this? Do you have any idea how lonely it is? How dangerous? I would love to be upstairs watching TV or gossiping about boys or ... God, even studying! But I have to save the world. Again."[49] And, like so many fans, we feel much better knowing that there is a Buffy out there who slays vampires again and again. In this vampire tale, Buffy is the outstanding heroine, and we are left pondering our own fanfic piece that introduces a very different, Buffy-influenced, Bella Swan.

Notes

1. Bonnie Mann, "Vampire Love: The Second Sex Negotiates the Twenty-first Century," in *Twilight and Philosophy: Vampires, Vegetarians, and the Pursuit of Immortality*, ed. Rebecca Housel and J. Jeremy Wisnewski (Hoboken, NJ: John Wiley & Sons, 2009), 144.
2. See Ken Gelder, *Reading the Vampire*, Popular Fictions Series (London and New York: Routledge, 1994); Janice Doane and Devon Hodges, "Undoing Feminism: From the Preoedipal to Postfeminism in Anne Rice's Vampire Chronicles," *American Literary History* 2, no. 3 (1990); and James B. Twitchell, *The Living Dead: A Study of the Vampire in Romantic Literature* (Durham, NC: Duke University Press, 1981).
3. See Stefanie Scarlett, "Professor Critical of 'Twilight' Gender Roles," *The Journal Gazette*, July 8, 2010, http://www.journalgazette.net/article/20100708/FEAT/307089990/-1/FEAT11. See also PuppetMaster, "Kristen Stewart Interview, TWILIGHT," *MoviesOnline*, accessed January 30, 2011, http://www.moviesonline.ca/movienews_16118.html; and Katharine Trendacosta, "You're Doing it Wrong: *Twilight*," *Glibberal*, accessed March 29, 2011, http://glibberal.com/3100/.
4. For more on the 'battle of the story,' see Patrick Reinsborough and Doyle Canning, *Re:Imagining Change: How to Use Story-Based Strategy to Win Campaigns, Build Movements, and Change the World* (Oakland, CA: PM Press, 2010).
5. See Kevin K. Durand, ed., *Buffy Meets the Academy: Essays on the Episodes and Scripts as Texts* (Jefferson, NC: McFarland, 2009); Frances H. Early, "Staking Her Claim: *Buffy the Vampire Slayer* as Transgressive Woman Warrior," *The Journal of Popular Culture* 35, no. 3 (2001): 11–27; James B. South, ed., *Buffy the Vampire Slayer and Philosophy: Fear and Trembling in Sunnydale*, Popular Culture and Philosophy 4 (Chicago: Open Court, 2003); and Rhonda V. Wilcox and David Lavery, eds., *Fighting the Forces: What's at Stake in* Buffy the Vampire Slayer (Lanham, MD: Rowman and Littlefield, 2002).
6. *Buffy the Vampire Slayer*, "Welcome to the Hellmouth," Season One, Episode One, director Charles Martin Smith, written by Joss Whedon, Burbank, CA: Warner Bros, first aired March 10, 1997.
7. See, for example, Beth Woodward, "Whedon Week: Buffy vs. Bella: The Battle of the Vampire Love Sagas," *CC2K: The Nexus of Pop-Culture Fandom*, August 9, 2009, http://www.cc2konline.com/movies/script-reviews/1378-whedon-week-buffy-vs-bella-the-battle-of-the-vampire-love-sagas.
8. The Mary Sue trope comes out of the fanfic community, see for example: http://anti-twilexicon.livejournal.com/947.html.

9. *Buffy the Vampire Slayer*, "Welcome to the Hellmouth."
10. *Buffy the Vampire Slayer*, "When She Was Bad," Season Two, Episode Thirteen, director Joss Whedon, written by Joss Whedon, Burbank, CA: Warner Bros, first aired September 15, 1997.
11. *Twilight*, DVD, director Catherine Hardwicke (2008; Santa Monica: Summit Entertainment, 2009).
12. Stephenie Meyer, *Twilight* (New York: Little, Brown and Company, 2005), 357.
13. Meyer, 256 and 292.
14. Ibid., 206.
15. bid., 343.
16. Ibid., 260.
17. Ibid., 479.
18. Ibid., 87.
19. Ibid., 79.
20. *Buffy the Vampire Slayer*, "Chosen," Season Seven, Episode 22, director Joss Whedon, written by Josh Wheedon, Burbank, CA: Warner Bros, first aired May 20, 2003.
21. James B. South, ed., *Buffy the Vampire Slayer and Philosophy: Fear and Trembling in Sunnydale*, Popular Culture and Philosophy 4 (Chicago: Open Court, 2003).
22. Rhonda V. Wilcox, "'Set on This Earth Like A Bubble': Word as Flesh in the Dark Seasons," in *Buffy Goes Dark: Essays on the Final Two Season of Buffy the Vampire Slayer on Television*, ed. Lynne Y. Edwards, Elizabeth L. Rambo, and James B. South (Jefferson, NC: McFarland, 2009), 104.
23. Brendan Shea, "To Bite or Not to Bite: *Twilight*, Immortality and the Meaning of Life," in Housel and Wisnewski, 79–80.
24. Meyer, 476.
25. Johannah Cousins, "Sex in *Twilight*: An Argument for Bella," *PsychCentral*, March 15, 2010, http://blogs.psychcentral.com/pop-psychology/2010/03/sex-in-twilight-an-argument-for-bella.
26. Danielle Dick McGeough, "*Twilight* and Transformations of Flesh: Reading the Body in Contemporary Youth Culture," in *Bitten by* Twilight: *Youth Culture, Media, & the Vampire Franchise*, ed. Melissa A. Click, Jennifer Stevens Aubrey, and Elizabeth Behm-Morawitz, Mediated Youth 14 (New York: Peter Lang, 2010), 100.
27. Kate Harding, "Touched by a Vampire." *Salon.com*, July 30, 2008, http://www.salon.com/books/review/2008/07/30/Twilight.
28. Jennifer Reese, "Why Not Team Bella," *Salon.com*, December 2, 2009, http://www.salon.com/life/broadsheet/feature/2009/12/02/new_moon_girls.

29. Simone de Beauvoir, *The Second Sex* (New York, Vintage Books, 1989).
30. Mann, 136.
31. "Twilight Take Me Away!", *New York Magazine.com*, accessed April 25, 2011, http://nymag.com/movies/features/62027/.
32. Frances H. Early, "Staking Her Claim: Buffy the Vampire Slayer as Transgressive Woman Warrior." *The Journal of Popular Culture* 35, no. 3 (2001): 11–26.
33. See Early; see Edwards, Rambo and South; see also Elana Levine and Lisa Parks, eds., *Undead TV: Essays on* Buffy the Vampire Slayer (Durham, NC and London: Duke University Press, 2007).
34. *Buffy the Vampire Slayer*, "I Robot, You Jane," Season One, Episode Eight, director Stephen L. Posey, written by Joss Whedon, Burbank, CA: Warner Bros, first aired April 28, 1997.
35. *The Bronze Beta*, accessed August 24, 2011, http://www.bronzebeta.com.
36. *Buffy World.com*, accessed August 24, 2011, http://www.buffyworld.com.
37. *Buffy the Vampire Slayer.org*, accessed August 24, 2011, http://www.buffy-vampireslayer.org.
38. *Hellmouth Podcast.com*, accessed August 24, 2011, http://hellmouthpodcast.com/podcast-eps.
39. "Breaking Dawn." *Publishers Weekly*, August 4, 2008, http://www.publishersweekly.com/978-0-316-06792-8.
40. Laura Miller, "Touched by a Vampire." *Salon.com*, July 30, 2008, http://www.salon.com/books/review/2008/07/30/Twilight.
41. *Twifans.com*, accessed August 24, 2011, http://www.twifans.com.
42. *Twilight Moms.com*, accessed August 24, 2011, http://www.twilightmoms.com.
43. *Twilight Guy.com*, accessed August 24, 2011, http://www.twilightguy.com.
44. Stephenie Meyer, "The Story Behind the Writing of *New Moon*," *Stephenie Meyer.com*, accessed April 10, 2011http:/www.stepheniemeyer.com/nm_thestory.html.
45. Laura and Lauren, "Buffy Vs. Bella: The Ultimate Showdown," *iwillnotcallyouback.blogspot.com*, February 18, 2009, http://iwillnotcallyouback.blogspot.com/2009/02/buffy-vs-bella-ultimate-showdown.html.
46. Beth Woodward, "Whedon Week: Buffy vs. Bella: The Battle of the Vampire Love Sagas," *CC2K: The Nexus of Pop-Culture Fandom*, August 9, 2009, http://www.cc2konline.com/movies/script-reviews/1378-whedon-week-buffy-vs-bella-the-battle-of-the-vampire-love-sagas.
47. Ms. Manifest, "Buffy vs. Bella", *msmanifest.typepad.com*, May 2, 2010, http://msmanifest.typepad.com/blog/2010/05/buffy-vs-bella.html.
48. Stephanie V. W. Lucianovic, "Why doesn't *Twilight* have a Team Bella?" *MSNBC.com*, June 27, 2010, http://today.msnbc.msn.com/id/37545960/ns/today-entertainment.

49 *Buffy the Vampire Slayer*, "Becoming (Part Two)," Season Two, Episode 22, director Joss Whedon, written by Joss Whedon, Burbank, CA: Warner Bros, first aired May 19, 1998.

5

As Close to Worthless as It Can Get: Twilight Anti-Fans, Teenage Girls and Symbolic Violence

Catherine Strong

In Western societies, cultural products associated with girls or women —whether they are the creators or the main audience — have often been positioned at or near the bottom of the cultural hierarchy.[1] Examples of this include romance novels, soap operas, and "pop" music. This chapter will examine the views of commentators in on-line discussions whose expressed opinions position them as "anti-fans" to the hugely successful Twilight series (both the books and the movies), with a view to demonstrating how the feminine nature of the series is central to the criticisms made of it and its fans. The associated characterization and naturalization of the teenage girl as an uncritical, overly-emotional consumer of bad or even harmful culture will be analyzed as a form of symbolic violence that helps to reproduce power relations between men and women. It will be demonstrated that the themes that arise in the discussion of the Twilight saga coincide in many ways with debates within academia and wider society about the value and effects of popular culture, and ultimately contribute to the maintenance of a hierarchy of tastes that continues to denigrate the feminine.

The gendered nature of the critical reception of the Twilight saga, and the way in which the audience of the books and films has been constructed as problematic, has been noted by a number of writers. For example, Melissa Click, Jennifer Aubrey and Elizabeth Behm-Morawitz[2] have examined the way the Twilight series is marketed towards and mainly consumed by teenage girls, and have noted how Twilight and its fans have been singled out for much fiercer criticism than is directed at culture designed for a male audience, such as action films.[3] Cultural items associated with women are often at the bottom of the cultural "pecking order," in line with the "persistent cultural assumption that male-targeted texts are authentic and interesting, whereas female-targeted texts are schlocky and mindless."[4] Romance novels, soap operas and pop music are labels that are often used as shorthand for "bad" culture, yet they also have a tendency to have women as their main audience.[5] The dismissal of these types of culture, and of the Twilight series, often stems from the way that women have been constructed as irrational and overly emotional, and therefore at risk of becoming too involved in the culture they love.[6] The culture associated with men, on the other hand, is constructed as being thoughtful, intelligent, and, on the whole, more worthy of engagement and discussion.[7] Value is still more likely to be accorded to culture associated with men and boys, despite the efforts of scholars working in fields such as fandom studies, who have struggled to break down the highly gendered as well as highly classed divisions between "high" and "low" culture, and who have demonstrated the possibilities for multiple readings of, and creative and resistant uses for, popular culture.[8] As Lisa Bode notes, "even in the past two decades, with the rise of cult media and their fan cultures, the process of defining a text as 'cult' (and transgressive, resistant and masculine) routinely relies on its opposition to a feminine conception of 'the mainstream' as passive, compliant and over-enthralled."[9]

Despite this, studies of fandom show women using cultural items to explore, create and change aspects of their identities. In the 1980s, groundbreaking work by theorists such as Tania Modleski[10] and Janice Radway[11] began to explore the ways in which feminine culture such as romance novels could be read as potentially resisting hegemonic gender relations, and since then many other aspects of women's and girls' engagement with culture have been explored.[12] Along these lines, studies of fans of the Twilight saga demonstrate that it can facilitate greater communication between mothers and daughters,[13] and can help girls think about and discuss the meaning of feminism.[14] On the other hand, the concerns of scholars about the poor messages that the Twilight series contains, particularly in regard to gender roles[15] and ideas about "true love,"[16] demonstrate an ongoing worry that women and girls will be negatively affected by the culture they consume. Although this chapter will concentrate on the ways in which the discourses around popular culture can be used to shore up existing power structures, it should be remembered that such structures are always contested, and that the imposition of power is never complete.

The subject under consideration here, the Twilight series by Stephenie Meyer, is very strongly associated with the feminine, as it has a female author, a female protagonist, a predominantly female audience, and even (unusually) a female director (for the first film), as well as belonging to the romance genre and offering a generally conventional take on gender roles. The series consists of four books that follow Bella Swan, the protagonist who narrates the majority of the series, and her developing romance with Edward Cullen. The books have sold over 53 million copies worldwide, rarely leaving bestseller lists since their release.[17] The three movies in the franchise that have been released to date have collectively taken over US$1,700 million at the box office around the world.[18] Although in many ways a traditional romance, the Twilight series is unusual in that it takes place in a world in which mythical creatures exist. Edward is a vampire, and Bella's best friend — and Edward's rival for her affections, Jacob Black — is a werewolf.[19] Hence, the romance between Bella and Edward pivots around an unusual focal point. Bella wants to become a vampire as well, to share eternal life with Edward, while he, uneasy about the moral implications of being a vampire, does not want her to become one.

Insofar as it is about vampires and werewolves/shapeshifters, the Twilight saga includes some elements of the horror genre. However, Edward describes himself as a "vegetarian" vampire, meaning that he does not kill or feed from humans, but hunts animals instead. He is part of a vampire "family" of seven that, unusually for vampires, has a very traditional nuclear set up. There is a "father," Carlisle Cullen, who has created most of the other vampires in the family in a way that fits in with most vampire lore (he bites them and they become vampires); a "mother," Esme; three "children," Rosalie and Emmett (who are a couple) and Edward; and two "foster children" who have joined the family from outside,

Alice and Jasper (also a couple). These vampires are cultured, sophisticated, very well off, and polite and the "children" all attend high school. Little traditional vampire lore applies to them, and —most notably — they are not harmed by sunlight as vampires usually are. Instead, when exposed to direct sunlight, Edward is described as follows: "his skin ... literally sparkled, like thousands of tiny diamonds were embedded in the surface."[20] This means that in order to take part in day-to-day human life without drawing attention to themselves, the family lives in Forks, a remote part of Washington State, where the weather is frequently overcast. The series is also difficult to position as part of the horror genre because Bella is a willing participant in the world of monsters, rather than a helpless victim. Lydia Kokkola argues that the series instead has much in common with adult and teen romance fiction (while still not entirely adhering to the conventions of either).[21]

Most of the research that has been done, to date, on audiences of the Twilight saga has focused on people who are easily identifiable as fans or anti-fans, either because they have identified themselves as such, or because of where they have been found by researchers. For example, researchers have gone to websites that are Twilight-specific (either pro or against) to analyze the discourses that fans and anti-fans are creating around the series.[22] While such studies are important to understanding how fans relate to the series, they can be limited in demonstrating how the Twilight series is being understood more generally among consumers of popular culture. The members of websites devoted to talking about the Twilight saga (whether in positive or negative ways) may be engaging in a "closed conversation" with other members of their communities. This chapter will contribute to the growing body of literature on the Twilight series by examining the way it is discussed by people who are not, for the most part, highly invested in it. Therefore, I have chosen to analyze comments about the Twilight books and films that appear on an internet forum devoted to a wide-ranging discussion of all aspects of popular culture, as well as current events and more general "chat." Although this still does not provide a full picture of how society at large views the series (participants in this thread still needed to be motivated enough to go into the thread and write a response), it broadens our understanding beyond Twilight-specific sites and groups.

The discussion of the Twilight series analyzed here is from a "thread" on the discussion boards of comedy website Cracked (www.cracked.com/forums). This is a forum of which I am a member, and occasionally contribute to. It is a forum that is open to be viewed or joined by anyone, and it has a very large membership (at the time of writing this chapter over 273,000). Discussion is not heavily moderated, but there are definite norms of behavior that have been established on the forums, and there is a small group of official moderators who will usually quickly contain any poster who is stepping too far outside these norms. These moderators are therefore treated with a certain amount of respect. Participants on Cracked post using pseudonyms, meaning that the ethical issues associated with using this material for analysis are minimal.[23] The anonymity provided by the forums may in fact allow for a more honest expression of opinions. The discussion that is the current subject of analysis comes from the section of the forum that is dedicated to movies.[24] Despite being located here, the thread deals with the books as much as the movies, with the two often being conflated, which is unsurprising given how faithful the movies are to the books. The thread clearly exists as part of a broader, ongoing discussion of Twilight on the internet, and participants often draw on outside sources to support their arguments. The themes identified in the thread can all be seen in broader discussions of Twilight. As of February 15, 2010 this thread had 600 posts in it, from 202 unique posters. Over half of the participants in the thread did not actively engage in discussion, but posted an opinion about an aspect of Twilight and did not return. The highest number of posts by any one participant was 27, so there was not a lot of "debate," as such, in this thread. However, this is not surprising, given the high level of agreement that *Twilight* was neither a good book nor a good movie.

Three main criticisms of the Twilight series appear during the discussion. Firstly, the Twilight saga is chastised for sending a "bad" message to teenage girls, who uncritically accept this message. Secondly, the Twilight series is criticized as a text written for teenage girls and thus represents "bad" culture, because teenage girls only like bad culture. Thirdly, the Twilight books and films are attacked for feminizing vampires, thereby devaluing them. Each of these will be discussed below.

The "Bad" Message of Twilight

Given the very negative response to Twilight in the thread, it became evident that the best way to understand the contributors was to think of them as "anti-fans" of the series; that is, as people who actively dislike this cultural item. Jonathan Gray discusses how "all texts have moral, rational-realist, and aesthetic dimensions," but the way audiences and anti-fans, in particular, frame a text can have repercussions in terms of their ability to engage with all these possible dimensions, and can also have an impact on how others view the text.[25] In particular, Gray describes how anti-fans can focus their criticisms of a text on specific moral aspects of it that can then come to define the text, reducing the importance of the other dimensions or, in extreme cases, almost erasing them. In the discussion of Twilight on the Cracked boards, much of the focus is on the moral implications of the books' storylines and the way they supposedly send a bad message to young girls about how to relate to men and live their lives. The comments echo the analysis of the gender messages of Twilight made in academic analyses of Meyer's books.[26] The character of Bella is criticized for being overly passive, and for apparently being motivated by nothing other than her desire for Edward. She is perceived as presenting a deeply conservative version of femininity, and is therefore not seen as a positive role model for young girls. The strength of this moral reading of the books is such that possibilities for alternative readings of Bella's character (which certainly exist) are rendered unthinkable (or at least unsayable).

One aspect of the story that is a particular focus is when Edward reveals to Bella that in the months leading up to their becoming involved with each other, he has been coming into her bedroom every night and watching her sleep.[27] During the course of the books Edward also restricts Bella's movements at certain points, always with the excuse that he is trying to protect her in some way (it is, however, noteworthy that Bella never passively accepts these restrictions but always finds a way around them, in the end getting what she wants). These plot points are seen as very sinister by posters:

Anyways all of my cousins read them and I made the mistake of saying in front of their parents that I would never let my teenage daughter read the books. You would have thought I said I ate babies. I explained that I don't think it's healthy for girls who haven't experienced real relationships to read about a boy who cuts a girl's car wires when he doesn't want her to go somewhere, and then to be told that's love. (Tallie)

The message of the movie is that Bella as a character is a blank with no ambition or interests of her own, who wraps her entire existence around a co-dependent, emotionally abusive stalker. Yeah. I call that a bad message. (DBB)

While aspects of Bella and Edward's relationship are not ideal, these posters are presenting an understanding of the effects of culture that can be best equated to the "hypodermic" model, which describes an unproblematic cause-and-effect relationship, whereby teenage girls who like the Twilight books and films will uncritically take on board "the message" of the books and will go on to live their lives according to this message.[28] This is contrasted with the posters' own "knowing" positions, whereby they are able to see through and critique the message of the books in a way that teenage girls are presumed to be unable to do. Posters are concerned that young women will be disempowered by Bella's supposed passivity and reliance on Edward. For many posters, then, this moral dimension of the Twilight saga has become central to their understanding of it, and there is a very high level of agreement among posters as to what these dimensions are and how harmful they may be. In terms of symbolic violence, as will be discussed below, this shows a subtle attack on girls being advanced through explicit statements supporting the position of women. This is done by focusing the criticisms on the *feminine* rather than on females as such, but also through the acceptance, throughout the discussion, of the idea that girls unthinkingly absorb and act on messages they receive in the mass media.

Teenage Girls' Culture is "Bad"

On the other hand, there are posters whose engagement with the

Twilight texts is concentrated on the aesthetic, rather than moral, dimensions of the books and movies. The books are derided as being poorly written, and the movies as badly acted. These criticisms, though, are almost always linked in some way to the perceived gender of the audience. In a somewhat circular way, the posters in the thread argue that since teenage girls like the Twilight series, it must be bad culture, because teenage girls like bad culture:

> Pretty much the only people who *can* enjoy Twilight exist solely within its target audience [teenage girls], which pushes it basically as close to worthless as it can go.
> (St Even 7)
>
> Adolescents, especially adolescent girls, love stupid things, everyone knows that. But rarely do they love something so delightfully stupid, so hilariously inept as Twilight.
> (Billy McGlory 11)

However, central to the connection being made between teenage girls and "bad" culture is the characterization of teenage girls throughout the thread, which is almost universally disparaging. They are described as "squealing" (or, similarly, "squeeing"), "screaming," out of control, and undiscerning. This type of characterization is hardly confined to this thread, and these comments in many ways reflect stereotypical ideas of how teenage girls behave. However, the loop that is created between teenage girls liking "bad" culture and *being* "bad" (or at least behaving badly) works to deprive this group of any authority, in that it renders their opinions worthless.

Twilight Feminizes Vampires

While I do not have the space to elaborate on all possible aspects of how the Twilight series is considered to have misrepresented vampires, what is relevant to this discussion is that the problem most posters have with how vampires have been portrayed by Meyer is that they have been over-feminized. In the words of poster Something Clever, "[Meyer] has managed to turn vampires from unholy abominations into non-threatening, idealized fantasy lovers. Seriously, they're not even vampires anymore ... they're more like blood-sucking My Little Ponies. They *sparkle* for christsakes." Bode has demonstrated how Twilight's reliance on certain aspects of the horror genre allows for more strident criticism of it and its audience, insofar as horror is a more "masculine" genre that relies on audiences being able to endure scariness and gore.[29] Adherents to this way of viewing horror see the introduction of romance and a greater focus on emotion as a "perceived contamination" by the feminine, and are therefore even more critical of Twilight and its audience than critics who approach the Twilight saga as a romance. The comments in this thread reveal similar concerns.

The idea that the Twilight series is corrupting the idea of the vampire further ties into gender issues, as the vampire is often seen as threatening the established gender order and heteronormativity.[30] Vampires perform male and female roles, in that they dominate and penetrate, yet also "give birth" to children and nurture them through suckling, albeit with blood instead of milk. Vampire "families" have almost always challenged the traditional nuclear family set-up, and vampire tales are replete with homoerotic imagery.[31] The Twilight books and films, on the other hand, presents an overwhelmingly heteronormal picture.[32] The Cullen "family" has a conventional nuclear structure; all vampire relationships discussed are male-female and are "for life"; and Edward insists that he and Bella must be properly married before they have sex, despite Bella's protestations.

This much more conventional approach to relationships than is usually portrayed in vampire fiction reinforces what the posters have to say about the "bad role model" Bella provides for young women. But it could be argued that by rejecting the "normalizing" of the vampire in the Twilight saga, these anti-fans may be seen as rejecting conventional gender roles altogether, and, in a way, arguing for open, fluid sexualities. That might be the case, if there was not a definite tendency towards homophobia that lies alongside the condemnation of the "bad" role models:

> If this movie has taught me one thing, it's that contrary to popular belief, sunlight actually makes vampires *even gayer*. (Edward: "This is what the sunlight does to us. Look at me! I'm ... FABULOUS!") (Thor)

There are many examples in the thread of males' interactions with *Twilight* being carefully framed in a way that reasserts their heterosexuality (for example, by explaining that they only went to see one of the Twilight movies because they thought it might result in them "scoring" with the woman they went with), and (jokingly) calling into question the sexuality of males who profess to like the series. So, in addition to explicitly condemning teenage girls and their culture, posters also perform a type of boundary maintenance, between what is considered masculine and feminine, that recreates the binaries and hierarchy between the genders through the use of male homosexuality as a bridge between the two. This then serves as a form of symbolic violence directed not just at girls, but also at gay men, although this cannot be discussed at length here.

Symbolic violence

Examining the Twilight books and films through the lens of the anti-fan is helpful in understanding the criticisms that are levelled at it, and how they can be connected to "naturalized" differences between males and females, and therefore to symbolic violence.[33] One useful application of the study of anti-fans is in examining the role they play in enforcing the dominance of certain tastes and cultures. Cultural hierarchies are not just created through certain forms of culture being praised, but also by the denigration of other forms. The anti-fan, it would seem, plays an important role in this process.[34]

In this way, examining a cultural phenomenon like the Twilight saga is not merely a matter of academic interest. The work of Pierre Bourdieu has demonstrated that taste is not just a matter of personal preference, but is closely tied to power relations in society. The tastes of the powerful come to be seen as "naturally" occupying positions at the top of the taste hierarchy, whereas cultural forms associated with the less powerful (particularly the lower class) are seen as being less worthwhile.[35] Bourdieu sees this as being maintained through the use of symbolic violence, which he defines as "every power which manages to impose meanings and to impose them as legitimate by concealing the power relations which are the basis of its force."[36] Symbolic violence is invisible in that it exists only in the effects that it has on those who are its victims — both in the way they perceive themselves and their place in the world, and in their acceptance of the categorizations that accompany it. Most importantly, those who are the victims of symbolic violence often participate in it, to the extent that certain ways of viewing the world are difficult to challenge. Certain groups (usually determined according to markers such as class, race, age, gender, or a combination of these) are subject to "peremptory verdicts, which, in the name of taste, condemn to ridicule, indignity, shame, silence" them, and it is generally accepted that they *just do not do things the right way*.[37] These groups internalize (and through the habitus, externalize) such judgements, and this makes challenges to the social order harder to imagine or sustain.[38] The discussion above shows that the on-line discussion by anti-fans of the Twilight books and films can be interpreted as a form of symbolic violence, in that the underlying point of the discussion is not about Twilight at all, but about constructing teenage girls as a group not worth taking seriously. This is done through a reliance on a negative construction of the teenage girl that is treated as though it is self-evident, even by teenage girls themselves.

This may be further seen in the way that actual teenage girls who participate in the thread almost always accept the negative image put forward (readers should note that this is in the context of an online forum, where there is always the possibility that posters are lying about, or concealing, their identity). A number of female posters describe how, while they themselves do not read the books, they have friends who are fans of the series. They participate in mocking the behavior of their friends, using the same pejorative terms and unflattering descriptions as other posters in the thread. Jessica Sheffield and Elyse Merlo, in their study of anti-fans on Twilight-specific sites, note how some posters who identify themselves as fans of the series negotiate a position that allows them to (try to) separate themselves from the poor behavior of other fans, usually by distancing themselves from behaviors identified as "feminine."[39] A similar tactic is employed by teenage girls posting in the Cracked thread; however, the effect of this is to put them in a position whereby they are agreeing with the overall negative assessment made of teenage girls as a group. In participating in the mocking of other teenage girls, they are indirectly mocking themselves and accepting their lower social status, even as they are trying to claim greater cultural capital.

There is only one occasion when a serious challenge is made to this portrayal of teenage girls. A poster calling herself "HallelujahRIP" makes the following post:

> I'm a teenage girl. I wouldn't read these books if my eyelids were glued open and the book was forced in front of me ... But ... I take even more offense at the fact that they have so often caused exactly the stereotypes named in this thread to be pushed upon my gender and age group. No, teenage girls, as a giant block, do not all adore Twilight. There are some very smart girls and women that I do know that DO, in fact, like the books, and that alone does NOT make them vapid idiots. However, there are also many, like me, that have no interest in the books and who are also NOT vapid idiots. On the other hand, there are many teenage girls who do not like the books and who are also vapid idiots.

Aside from her willingness to still classify "many" teenage girls as "vapid idiots" (itself a rather gendered term that is utilized on a number of occasions in the thread), HallelujahRIP is explicitly resisting the violence being perpetrated upon the group she belongs to. However, the response she receives quickly contains this challenge. Mortal Wombat, one of the moderators of the site, replies by saying:

> I am sure you are a great kid, but by the time you are 25 or so, you are going to look back and think that you were a vapid idiot, and laugh about it. It's nothing personal, it happens to everyone.

In this way, HallelujahRIP's protest that she is not a "vapid idiot" is negated because vapid idiots are apparently incapable of recognising themselves as such, and teenage girls automatically fall into that category. This response silences HallelujahRIP, and when she posts again in the thread some months later it is to make fun of friends of hers who are excited about the next movie, in a similar vein to the other teenage girls who have identified themselves in the thread.

Of course, there are other aspects of identity that need to be considered along with gender when people are making claims for cultural capital. Age is clearly an important element in the discussion, as is shown in Mortal Wombat's assertion that HallelujahRIP will improve as she gets older. What is being said about the audience for the Twilight series is specifically about *teenagers* (with the occasional reference to "middle aged housewives" also being thrown in). There is not enough space in this chapter to fully examine the way that age can be an overlooked aspect of inequality, and how symbolic violence perpetrated on young people can marginalize them and their concerns.[40] However, Bode notes that films associated with teenage boys are not criticized in the same way as the Twilight series, but are celebrated for the specific pleasures they bring. She argues that "perhaps, then, more so than age, it is *gender* that functions here as a key factor in the relative status of taste formations."[41] Given the centrality of gender to the discussion of the Twilight books and films in general, and the very specific focus on teenage *girls* in the thread, I believe this statement also holds true in this instance. At times this is even made explicit in the thread. For example, when it is suggested that it is unreasonable to think that all movies made for young people are bad, Nimby replies: "[the other poster] didn't say it sucks because it was made for young people, but because it sucked because it was written for *teenage girls*. That is an important difference."

Furthermore, a strong focus on gender is warranted, given the underlying anxieties that emerge from the forum discussion about womanhood and the future of the girls involved. References to the middle-aged women who also participate in Twilight fandom raise the idea that this sort of behavior is something that might *not* be grown out of in time. The way Stephenie Meyer is discussed is a case in point. Meyer is herself a grown woman, but is characterized by posters as still indulging in the same overly-emotional behavior as her younger counterparts. She is presented not only as an example of how "wrong" a girl can go on her journey to adulthood, but is portrayed as actively seeking to lead the readers of her novels down the same path. With the right sort of guidance, and without the poor influence that comes from something like the Twilight saga, there appears to be the possibility that these girls could grow up to become what posters in the thread seem to consider to be the "right" sort of woman; but the lurking danger is that exposure to the Twilight universe could prevent women from ever taking on the more masculine attributes of rationality, reason, and self-control.

In conclusion, the discussion of the Twilight books and movies in the forums of Cracked.com can be read as a form of symbolic violence perpetrated on the purported main audience of the Twilight series; that is, teenage girls. Such discussions naturalize the position of feminine culture at the bottom of the cultural hierarchy and reinforce the idea of the powerlessness of this particular group. Teenage girls are portrayed as unable to separate fact from fiction, as being uncritical receivers of media messages, and as being somehow inherently attracted to "bad" culture. All of these discourses help to maintain hierarchies of both culture and cultural competency, with teenage girls becoming the "other" that is inferior and in need of protection (mostly from themselves). However, it must always be remembered that these girls are not as powerless or as stupid as they are portrayed, and as popular culture is a site of contestation there are places where these ideas and images are challenged, often by the girls in question. Works such as the edited volume *Bitten By Twilight* have begun to explore how this happens, but much more work is required to fully understand the interactions of fans and anti-fans in the context of wider gender relations. [42]

Notes

1   Andreas Huyssen, *After the Great Divide: Modernism, Mass Culture, Postmodernism*, Theories of Representation and Difference (Bloomington and Indianapolis: Indiana University Press, 1986), 710–11; Tania Modleski, "Femininity as Mas(s)querade: A Feminist Approach to Mass Culture," in *High Theory/Low Culture: Analysing Popular Television and Film*, ed. Colin MacCabe (Manchester: Manchester University Press, 1986), 48.
2   Melissa A.Click, Jennifer Stevens Aubrey, and Elizabeth Behm-Morawitz, "Introduction," in *Bitten by Twilight:Youth Culture, Media and the Vampire Franchise*, ed. Melissa A. Click, Jennifer Stevens Au-

brey, and Elizabeth Behm-Morawitz, Mediated Youth 14 (New York: Peter Lang, 2010).
3   See also Lisa Bode, "Transitional Tastes: Teen Girls and Genre in the Critical Reception of *Twilight*," *Continuum: Journal of Media and Cultural Studies* 24, no. 5 (2010).
4   Click, Aubrey, and Behm-Morawitz, "Introduction," 8.
5   Alison Light, "'Returning to Manderley': Romance Fiction, Female Sexuality, and Class," in *Feminism and Cultural Studies*, ed. Morag Shiach, Oxford Readings in Feminism (Oxford: Oxford University Press, 1999), 372; Tania Modleski, *Loving with a Vengeance: Mass-Produced Fantasies for Women* (New York and London: Methuen, 1982), 10.
6   Joanne Hollows, *Feminism, Femininity and Popular Culture* (Manchester and New York: Manchester University Press, 2000).
7   Terry Lovell, *Consuming Fiction*, Questions for Feminism (London: Verso, 1987).
8   Matt Hills, *Fan Cultures*, Sussex Studies in Culture and Communication (London and New York: Routledge, 2002); Henry Jenkins, *Fans, Bloggers, and Gamers: Exploring Participatory Culture* (New York and London: New York University Press, 2006); Henry Jenkins, *Textual Poachers: Television Fans and Participatory Culture*, Studies in Culture and Communication (New York and London: Routledge, 1992).
9   Bode, 707.
10 Modleski, *Loving with a Vengeance*.
11 Janice Radway, *Reading the Romance: Women, Patriarchy and Popular Literature* (Chapel Hill: University of North Carolina Press, 1984).
12 See, for example, Mary Ellen Brown, ed., *Television and Women's Culture: The Politics of the Popular*, Communication and Human Values 7 (Sydney: Currency Press,1990); Kristina Busse, "Introduction," in "In Focus: Fandom and Feminism: Gender and the Politics of Fan Production," *Cinema Journal* 48, no. 4 (2009); Christine Scodari, "Yoko in Cyberspace with Beatles Fans: Gender and the Re-Creation of Popular Mythology," in *Fandom: Identities and Communities in a Mediated World*, ed. Jonathan Gray, Cornel Sandvoss, and C. Lee Harrington (New York and London: New York University Press, 2007); and the essays on gender in Lisa A. Lewis, ed., *The Adoring Audience: Fan Culture and Popular Media* (London and New York: Routledge,1992).
13 Cathy Leogrande, "My Mother, Myself: Mother-Daughter Bonding via the Twilight Saga," in Click, Aubrey, and Behm-Morawitz, eds.
14 Sarah Summers, "'*Twilight* Is So Anti-Feminist That I Want to Cry': *Twilight* Fans Finding and Defining Feminism on the World Wide Web," *Computers and Composition* 27, no. 4 (2010): 315–23.
15 Carrie Anne Platt, "Cullen Family Values: Gender and Sexual Politics

in the Twilight Series," in Click, Aubrey, and Behm-Morawitz, eds., 71–86.
16 Tricia Clasen, "Taking a Bite Out of Love: The Myth of Romantic Love in the Twilight Series," in Click, Aubrey, and Behm-Morawitz, eds., 119–34.
17 Lauren A. E. Schuker, "Harry Potter and the Rival Teen Franchise," *Wall Street Journal Online*, July 9, 2009, http://online.wsj.com/article/SB 10001424052970204261704574276261288253316.html.
18 *Box Office Mojo.com*, accessed August 24, 2011, www.boxofficemojo.com.
19 Although strictly speaking Jacob is a shapeshifter, this is not revealed until the final pages of the last book in the series, so the term "werewolf" will be used here for the sake of simplicity.
20 Stephenie Meyer, *Twilight*, 3rd ed. (London: Atom, 2005), 228.
21 Lydia Kokkola, "Virtuous Vampires and Voluptuous Vamps: Romance Conventions Reconsidered in Stephenie Meyer's "Twilight" Series," *Children's Literature in Education* 42, no. 2 (2011).
22 Jessica Sheffield and Elyse Merlo, "Biting Back: Twilight Anti-Fandom and the Rhetoric of Superiority," in Click, Aubrey, and Behm-Morawitz, eds,. 207–22 ; see also Summers.
23 Gunther Eysenbach and James E. Till, "Ethical Issues in Qualitative Research on Internet Communities," *British Medical Journal* 323, no. 7321 (2001): 1103–105.
24 *Cracked.com*, accessed August 24, 2011, http://www.cracked.com/forums/topic/40234/twilight.
25 Jonathan Gray, "Antifandom and the Moral Text: Television Without Pity and Textual Dislike," *American Behavioral Scientist* 48, no. 7 (2005): 844.
26 Clasen; see also Platt.
27 Meyer, *Twilight*, 256.
28 See Dominic Strinati, *An Introduction to Theories of Popular Culture*, 2nd ed. (London and New York: Routledge, 2004), 10–15.
29 Bode, 710–1.
30 Shannon Winnubst, "Vampires, Anxieties, and Dreams: Race and Sex in the Contemporary United States," *Hypatia* 18, no. 3 (2003).
31 Candace R. Benefiel, "Blood Relations: The Gothic Perversion of the Nuclear Family in Anne Rice's *Interview with the Vampire*," *Journal of Popular Culture* 38, no. 2 (2004); Ken Gelder, *Reading the Vampire*, Popular Fictions Series (London and New York: Routledge, 1994).
32 Kathryn Kane, "A Very Queer Refusal: The Chilling Effect of the Cullens' Heteronormative Embrace," in Click, Aubrey, and Behm-Morawitz, eds., 103–18.

33 Jonathan Gray, "New Audiences, New Textualities: Anti-Fans and Non-Fans," *International Journal of Cultural Studies* 6, no. 1 (2003): 64–81.
34 See also Sheffield and Merlo.
35 Bethany Bryson, "'Anything but Heavy Metal': Symbolic Exclusion and Musical Dislikes," *American Sociological Review* 61, no. 5 (1996): 884–99; see also Lovell..
36 Pierre Bourdieu and Jean-Claude Passeron, *Reproduction in Education, Society and Culture*, trans. Richard Nice, Sage Studies in Social and Educational Change 5 (London: Sage, 1977), 4.
37 Pierre Bourdieu, *Distinction: A Social Critique of the Judgement of Taste*, trans. Richard Nice (Cambridge, MA: Harvard University Press, 1984), 158.
38 See also Angela McRobbie, "Notes on 'What Not to Wear' and Post-Feminist Symbolic Violence," in *Feminism after Bourdieu*, ed. Lisa Adkins and Beverly Skeggs (Oxford: Blackwell, 2004).
39 Sheffield and Merlo.
40 Ron Eyerman and Bryan S. Turner, "Outline of a Theory of Generations," *European Journal of Social Theory* 1, no. 1 (1998): 91–106.
41 Bode, 716.
42 Click, Aubrey, and Behm-Morawitz, eds.

6

Vampires, Queers, and Other Monsters: Against the Homonormativity of *True Blood*

Susana Loza

Whether it is the sparkly vegetarian vamps of the Twilight series, the troubled teen bloodsuckers of *The Vampire Diaries,* or the sexy undead denizens of *True Blood,* one thing is clear: vampires are in vogue. But have they ever truly been out of fashion? The appeal of the vampire sometimes seems as deathless as the monster itself. As journalist Jennie Yabroff reminds us: "The figure of the vampire — a human transformed by a bite into something that looks human but is not, who feeds off the blood of others to survive and has the power to both kill and bestow eternal life — is one of our most powerful and durable myths."[1] The malleability of the metaphor has allowed the monster that lacks a reflection to act as our mirror, crystallizing fantasies and fears, illuminating cultural anxieties and societal structures. Just over a century ago, Bram Stoker's *Dracula* (1897) skulked into Victorian England and stalked into our imaginations. Since then, the vampire has incarnated our deepest desires, embodied our most secret terrors. Its immortal flesh, caught between life and death, has become an ambivalent allegory for immigration,[2] reverse colonization,[3] consumption and capitalism,[4] sexual imperialism and deracination,[5] miscegenation and racial hybridity,[6] the horrors of anti-Semitism,[7] the cannibalistic nature of whiteness,[8] the abject depths of evil,[9] the allure of domesticated otherness,[10] the dangers of female sexuality,[11] the perils and pleasures of homosexuality,[12] the political promise of queerness,[13] the destructive alchemy of AIDS and other blood-borne diseases,[14] and the troublesome instability of sex and gender.[15] As this admittedly abbreviated list indicates, the vampire is a highly mutable being that adapts to fit the demands of particular cultural/political moments.[16] The revenant is not timeless or universal; its blend of race, class, gender, and sexuality, what Judith Halberstam dubbed its "composite of otherness," is historically specific.[17] Because "every age has the vampire it needs,"[18] these representations "expose the unconscious workings of racism, chauvinism, sexism, homophobia, ethnocentrism, religious (Christian) fundamentalism, and other forms of oppression based on social difference."[19] But vampiric texts do not simply frame social reality, they "provoke a perspective, provide a context, produce a way of seeing."[20] In other words, these texts "give image to historically determinate anxieties, wishes, and needs, they simultaneously function by stimulating, endorsing, broadcasting the very anxieties, wishes, and needs to which they give image."[21] This is why it is essential that we deconstruct contemporary representations of vampires. And this is what drew me to *True Blood* as a fan and a critic.

Created by Alan Ball and based on Charlaine Harris's Southern Vampire Mysteries series, *True Blood* made its début on HBO in 2008 and is beginning its fourth season at the time of writing.[22] The supernatural drama chronicles the volatile interspecies romance between Sookie Stackhouse (Anna Paquin), a telepathic waitress who we later learn is a human-fairy hybrid,[23] and Bill Compton (Stephen Moyer), a 173-year-old vampire and former Confederate soldier. The show is set in the fictional rural town of Bon Temps, Louisiana, and takes place two years after the Great Revelation, the day that vampires "came out of the coffin." Thanks to the invention of synthetic blood, vampires no longer need to feed on humans for sustenance. The series tracks their attempts to mainstream into mortal society, including their fight to pass a Vampire Rights Amendment (the amendment would give vampires equal rights to humans in the United States and is championed by the American Vampire League). As many critics and fans have noted, the show is laden with heavy-handed comparisons of the vampire experience with that of modern day queers. It should thus come as no surprise to learn that the Gay & Lesbian Alliance Against Defamation (GLAAD) recently lauded *True Blood* as "the most inclusive program currently on television ... thanks to its large cast (and often sexually ambiguous vampires)."[24] But does *True Blood*'s inclusion of erotically undefined characters signal inclusivity or is it just a risqué version of "gay window advertising," a way for HBO to simultaneously appeal to queer audiences and titillate straight viewers without actually challenging heteronormativity?[25] Do its ham-fisted allusions to gay rights actually serve the Lesbian/Gay/Bisexual/Transgender/ Intersexual/Questioning (LGBTIQ) community as a whole, or do they merely advance the interests of white queers who are, to paraphrase Homi Bhabha, almost the same as white heterosexuals, but not quite straight?[26] Does this make *True Blood* a homonationalist text? Or does the supernatural series reclaim the radical potential of queerness, by conflating monstrosity with homosexuality and thus refusing the neoliberal logic of normalization? These are just some of the questions raised by the fans of *True Blood*, or truebies, as they are more commonly known.

While truebies articulate and circulate their opinions about the show through a variety of means (fan fiction, fan videos, personal blogs, youtube comments), I will focus on the critical discourses generated by the show's self-proclaimed feminist, anti-racist, and queer fans in response to the recently completed third season. Through an analysis of blog-based roundtable discussions, critical recaps, debates on fan boards and forums, and comments on mainstream/new media, I hope to reveal how fans dedicated to dismantling gender, sexual and/or racial oppression appraise the inclusivity of the show. But before we can assess whether *True Blood* promotes queer heterogeneity or bolsters homonormative privilege, we must first sketch out the state of gay politics in America. After this brief theoretical detour, I will return to the truebies and their insights.

Gay is the New Black? Vampires in the Age of Neoliberal (Homo) Normativity

Since the 1990s, the political goals and strategies of LGBTIQ activism have shifted from liberation to assimilation, from principled resistance to acceptance at all costs, from embracing difference to desiring sameness. A growing body of queer scholarship documents the ascendance of this paradigm, its (neo)liberal dimensions and normative aspects, and the subsequent "alignment of gay and lesbian sexual politics with politically and economically conservative and nationalist discourses and projects."[27] This relatively new species of sexual politics has inspired many memorable monikers: queer liberalism (David Eng), homonormativity (Lisa Duggan), homonationalism (Jasbir Puar), gay imperialism (Jin Haritaworn), and the neoliberal politics of normalization (Diane Richardson). These names testify to the increasing influence of center-libertarian-conservative classical liberalism in the LGBTIQ movement.[28] As these scholars conclusively establish, the inoffensive language of equal rights has eclipsed the more radical rhetoric of women's, lesbian, and gay liberation. LGBTIQ political organizations now seek "sameness" with heterosexuals and emphasize the "rights of individuals rather than 'gay rights' and in seeking 'equality' with, rather than tolerance from, the mainstream."[29] Equality is narrowly defined as equal entitlement to rights and to resources, centered upon demands for civil recognition of domestic partnerships, including the right to marry and adopt, and the right to serve openly in the military.[30] In this neoliberal model of citizenship, the "risk" that queers pose to society is neutralized through the construction of the self-regulating homosexual subject, a "normal," "ordinary" citizen who proves their fidelity to the heteronormative state through civil registration and self-surveillance.[31] In the United States, "equal rights" approaches have become the dominant political discourse of the LGBTIQ movement and are the favored strategy of lesbian and gay advocacy groups such as GLAAD, the Human Rights Campaign (HRC), and the National Gay and Lesbian Task Force (NGLTF). But the neoliberal obsession with normativity and citizenship is not without its drawbacks; the passage of Proposition 8 and the subsequent racial backlash testify to the limits of homonationalism.

The California Marriage Protection Act, better known as Proposition 8, was passed in November 2008, on the same day that Californians helped to elect America's first black president. "Gay is the new black" quickly became the rallying cry for disenchanted white liberal queers across the country. The slogan — meant to evoke parallels between the civil rights movement and the gay rights movement — popped up on T-shirts, protest signs, political buttons, and even the cover of *The Advocate*.[32] While "Gay is the new black" is an undeniably catchy phrase, it is a deeply flawed analogy for several reasons. First, it assumes that racism has been vanquished and that homophobia remains to be conquered. The analogy thus propagates the post-racial delusion that the United States has finally, magically, transcended race (a delusion that was only furthered by Obama's election). Unfortunately, as countless scholars attest, racism is not dead;[33] it has simply mutated into what sociologist Eduardo Bonilla-Silva calls the "new racism," a "post-civil rights system of subtle, institutionalized, and apparently non-racial practices that maintain white supremacy — and its accompanying dominant racial ideology of color-blind racism."[34] Secondly, the analogy fractions homosexuality from race, thus implicitly privileging those subjects for whom queerness is their primary or only marked identity: namely, gay white males.[35] Finally, by simplistically equating the experiences of queers with African Americans, by conflating sexual and racial prejudice, the analogy reinforces "antigay bigotry, racism, and sexism; create[s] rifts between LGBT communities and black communities; and further marginalize[s] LGBT people of color."[36] "Gay is the new black" tellingly reveals how the same-sex marriage debate has been "hijacked by a white upper class queer universality that not only renders marginalized queer communities invisible, but — as it is presently framed — also renders them speechless."[37] And yet, despite these pernicious and divisive defects, the homonationalist notion that "gay is the new black," that queers are "the most socially acceptable targets for the kind of casual hatred that American society once approved for habitual use against black people,"[38] persists in politics and also in the realm of popular culture. In fact, as any truebie will tell you, the notion that the struggle for gay equality IS the new civil rights movement is integral to *True Blood*'s vampire mythology.

The post-racial and homonationalist assumption that the vampire state is equivalent to the historical experience of racial minorities and the contemporary realities of (white) gays is telegraphed in the title sequence of *True Blood*. The opening credits locate racial prejudice in the past and homophobic bigotry in the present by juxtaposing grainy 1960s-era images of the Ku Klux Klan, a burning cross, and African Americans at civil rights protests, with a bright neon sign that reads "God Hates Fangs" (an obvious play on "God Hates Fags," the slogan of the Reverend Fred Phelps and his notoriously anti-gay Westboro Baptist Church).[39] By depicting racial struggle as "part of an antique and literally crumbling or melting past,"[40] *True Blood's* title sequence implies that "race has had its day as a concern"[41] and that we have new battles, gay battles, to fight now. The viral materials crafted for the show, which include a rather elaborate website for the American Vampire League (AVL), further cements this association. The AVL site, clearly modeled on the web presences of GLAAD and the National Association for the Advancement of Colored People (NAACP), prominently features a letter from its spokeswoman Nan Flanagan (played by the icy blonde Jessica Tuck), in which she thanks vampire rights supporters and reminds them that: "The arc of the universe is long. But it bends toward justice."[42] The inclusion of a quotation from Reverend Martin Luther King, Jr. evokes the memory and spirit of the civil rights movement and surreptitiously yokes the historic African American struggle against racism to the (supposedly) more nascent liberation movements of gay rights and vampire rights.[43] Potent and evocative as they are, *True Blood's* opening credits and viral media campaign only hint at the homonationalist and postracial assumptions that haunt the show. To fully flesh them out, we must turn to the truebies who dedicate themselves to deconstructing the progressive and reactionary elements of the show on a weekly basis.

Unpacking the Vampire-as-Oppressed-Minority Metaphor: Truebies vs. Alan Ball

While creator Alan Ball admits that "vampires totally work as a metaphor for gays, for people of color, for anybody who is misunderstood and feared and hated for being different,"[44] he believes it is a mistake to equate *True Blood's* vampires with oppressed minority groups. "It's so easy to see them as that. It's just too easy,"[45] Ball moodily cautions in countless interviews.[46] Although truebies duly report Ball's protestations that "*True Blood's* supernatural characters are NOT stand-ins for real-life marginalized groups,"[47] most find his disclaimers difficult to stomach, especially those commenting on anti-racist, queer, and feminist blogs. They see *True Blood* as "an allegorical tale about prejudice, with a strong emphasis on gay rights."[48] And they "relate to the vamps as a marginalized group facing intolerance and inequity."[49] Tami Winfrey Harris,[50] who blogs about *True Blood* at various sites (What Tami Said, Womanist Musings, and Racialicious), concedes that this intense identification with the vampire might have to do with her own minority status ("Maybe it's cause I'm a black woman who spends a lot of time writing online about race, gender and sexual marginalization. Who's to say.").[51] Nevertheless, she urges fans who doubt the vampire-as-minority metaphor to watch the AVL's Public Service Announcement (PSA) promoting tolerance. The PSA features a multicultural cast of humans reciting the following text:

> Don't let anyone tell you that discrimination no longer exists in this country because it does. Our darkest moments as a country have been when good people turn a blind eye to oppression, intolerance, and injustice. Our greatest triumphs have stemmed from unwillingness to accept these conditions. When our citizens have stood up and said no, not in my country, not in my name. Stand up, let yourself be heard.[52]

The screen then goes black and the announcer says, "Vampires were people, too. Support the Vampire Rights Amendment." The ad not only suggests that vampires are stand-ins for marginalized groups, it implies that bloodsuckers suffer the same discrimination that racial minorities once did, and that sexual minorities currently do.

S. E. Smith,[53] a queer, disabled, white feminist who blogs at This Ain't Livin', sees *True Blood*'s "embedded commentary" as more directly "related to LGBQTAI issues."[54] As proof, Smith cites "the clear comparisons drawn between hatred of vampires and homophobia,"[55] and Bill asking Sookie to marry him in Vermont (a state famous for legalizing same-sex marriage and apparently vampire-human unions, too). At After Elton, a gay liberal popular culture website, a reader named Kevin suggests that the "whole Vampire Rights movement/vamps coming out is meant to represent Prop 8/gay rights movement."[56] Homophilic, a commenter at the postfeminist site Jezebel, eagerly concurs: "Vampires = gays has been the allegory from the start ... The Vampire Rights Amendment discourse was [clearly meant to be a] parallel to real-life gay rights in politics (a la DADT, DOMA, Prop 8, etc.)."[57]

Tobi-Hill Meyer, a contributor at Bilerico Project ("The World's largest LGBTQ group blog"), finds these arguments compelling, but suggests that the vampire-as-minority metaphor works even better for the trans community. Hill-Meyer, who describes herself as "your average multiracial, pansexual, transracially inseminated queerspawn, genderqueer, transdyke, colonized mestiza, pornographer, activist, writer,"[58] contends that societal oppression in *True Blood* is based on one person being hated for being "unnatural" and another person being hated for loving them.[59] "There's even a population of humans called 'fangbangers' that exoticize and seek out vampires as the ultimate lovers,"[60] blogs Hill-Meyer. "That's a lot more like transcis relationships."[61]

But just because truebies recognize the vampire as a conspicuous allegory for otherness — racial and sexual — on *True Blood*, this does not mean that they uncritically support how the show depicts difference. In fact, I would argue that truebies personally attuned to the vicious vagaries of oppression are extremely critical of the show's central metaphor and the way in which this allegory can — if not wielded responsibly — simply re-monsterize queers and people of color. These criticisms have only grown sharper with each passing season. But before we delve into the ideological dangers of the vampire-as-minority metaphor, let us pause and consider how queerness, that to which the vampire is symbolically aligned, is treated in *True Blood*.

Beyond the Metaphor: Truebies Take On *True Blood*'s Homonormativity

The monster, as metaphoric construct for the homosexual, has been a staple of American film since *Nosferatu* (1922) stumbled silently from his crypt. As Harry Benshoff observes in *Monsters in the Closet: Homosexuality and the Horror Film*, the generic space of horror has historically been "one of the few cultural spaces in which queerness can be fairly openly addressed, yet, because of the requisite form of the genre, queerness is almost always figured as destructive and monstrous."⁶² However, After Elton's Brian Juergens opines that we have entered a post-gay era in which the vampire is not a stand-in for the homosexual other, but rather the minority upon which they model themselves: "The world of *True Blood* is not a repressed heteronorm where the vampire or 'other' metaphor is required to discuss gay sexuality, as it has been in the past: It is a world where gay sexuality is actually such a given that it is used to define the 'other.'"⁶³ It is a world where vampires appropriate the terms of gay visibility to out themselves (i.e. vamps come out of the coffin), "meaning that gay struggles aren't just acknowledged in this universe, they're a part of the vocabulary."⁶⁴ It is a world in which the undead, like liberal gays, strive for assimilation, to be part of the human-hetero mainstream, to be just like everyone else. It is a world in which "gays and straights mix with ease," where "homosexuality comes off almost banal, offhanded, of minor consequence."⁶⁵ In other words, *True Blood* is a world in which gayness has been homonationalized; it is a world in which queerness has been deracialized, normalized, and sanitized. At least, that is the consensus of truebies who approach the show from an anti-racist, feminist, and queer of color perspective.

Although GLAAD praises *True Blood* for being sexually inclusive, it is important to note that this inclusivity does not extend to race. In fact, the majority of recurring queer characters on *True Blood* are white. There is Yvetta (Natasha Alam), the bisexual Russian stripper at vampire nightclub Fangtasia, and her pansexual bloodsucking boss Pam de Beaufort (Kristin Bauer). There is Sophie-Anne LeClerq (Evan Rachel Wood), the Vampire Queen of Louisiana, and her fairy-human paramour, Hadley Hale (Lindsey Haun). AVL spokeswoman Nan Flanagan also prefers the taste of women. Last but not least, there is Russell Edgington (Dennis O'Hare), the Vampire King of Mississippi, and his royal consort Talbot (Theo Alexander). While most of *True Blood*'s queer characters are white and conventionally attractive (and thus embody the homonormative ideal), the show does feature two working class gay men of color: African-American Lafayette Reynolds (Nelsan Ellis) and Latino Jesus Velasquez (Kevin Alejandro). Unfortunately, since Jesus was not introduced until the third season, Lafayette has been burdened with representing raced queerness on *True Blood* for most of its run. As the sole queer of color in Bon Temps, Lafayette has, understandably, garnered intense scrutiny from queer/raced/feminist truebies.

Black and flamboyantly gay, Lafayette Reynolds is the hardest-working man in Bon Temps. He is a construction worker, short order cook, drug dealer, male prostitute, and online sex provider. Lafayette is magnetic, sardonic, and a constant purveyor of sassy quips.[66] This has made him a fan favorite and one of *True Blood*'s most quoted characters. However, as Truebie JC laments, Lafayette is "one finger snap away from a Wayans Brothers *In Living Color* parody."[67] Feminist Frequency v-logger Anita Sarkeesian reluctantly concurs: "Lafayette, oh, you know we all love him. He's ... dynamic and ... interesting and funny and he definitely has some choice lines BUT he is every stereotype about Black Queer men all rolled into one little pretty package and it constantly infuriates me."[68] Lafayette's role as a prostitute and a drug dealer, argues Renee Martin of Womanist Musings, reifies the "image of Black gay men as predators."[69] Tami Winfrey Harris, who "love[s] Lafayette as much as the next TB fan," nevertheless criticizes Ball for his dysfunctional, one-dimensional, and stereotypical representations of black people on *True Blood*. "When I look at Lafayette together with all the other black folks in fictional Bon Temps," Winfrey Harris bemoans, "I get a little queasy at how 'typical' and uninspired the show's portrayal of my people is."[70] Besides being nauseated by the blatant racial and sexual stereotyping of Lafayette, POC/feminist/queer fans are also sickened by how *True Blood* reinforces the homonationalist assumption that black people are anti-gay, by making Lafayette's mother, Ruby Jean Reynolds (Alfre Woodard), "a hateful, homophobic racist who says God killed her son because 'he's a faggot.'"[71]

In contrast, Brian Juergens pleads with his fellow truebies to not be so quick in their judgment of Lafayette. "A sexually aggressive, cross-dressing gay character who drinks during the day and sass-talks might not seem a huge break from stereotype,"[72] concedes Juergens. "But let's not dismiss Lafayette out-of-hand. He's also physically strong, and utterly unintimidated by anyone or anything."[73] In other words, before we brush aside Lafayette as a big black gay stereotype, we should consider how his character queers gender and resists homonormativity. In many ways, Lafayette resembles Lindy (played by Antonio Fargas), the "flamboyant, stunningly self-assured, gender-bending"[74] character from the blaxploitation classic *Car Wash* (1976). Like Lindy, Lafayette is "defiant, witty, compassionate, well adjusted, and a truly queer blurring of the genders."[75] And like him, Lafayette "exposes the 'queerness' of black masculinity itself, namely, its uncertainty, its fluidity, its vulnerability, its 'boundarylessness.'"[76] But, as the truebies quoted above would no doubt point out, just because Lafayette troubles the boundaries of gender/sexuality does not mean he destabilizes the borders of race. It is possible to simultaneously dismantle one form of oppression while buttressing another, just as it is possible to have a show littered with sexually ambiguous characters that sanitizes, heterosexualizes, and pathologizes queers.

For queer, feminist, and/or Women of Color (WOC) truebies, one of the most problematic aspects of *True Blood* is how gay sex is "sanitized relative to how heterosexual sex is portrayed."[77] Sex scenes featuring gay and lesbian characters are "heavily edited and perfunctory."[78] Each time a queer couple gets intimate, "it shifts to a different scene,"[79] or, worse, in the case of Lafayette and his nurse-turned-witch lover Jesus, occurs "almost entirely off-screen."[80] While having the courtship of Jesus and Lafayette "shrouded in shadow ... makes for very tender and sensual scenes,"[81] it "sets their interactions apart from those of heterosexual characters who generally get it on quickly, aggressively and with all the lights on."[82] Even in depicting the fantasy lives of characters, the show seems "squeamish about gay sex."[83] In one of the third season's steamiest homoerotic moments, shapeshifting barman Sam Merlotte (Sam Trammell) daydreams about taking a long hot shower with Vampire Bill. Sadly for queer truebies, "the scene did not go beyond heavy breathing and shirt removal."[84] Renee Martin suggests the fact that they "never even kissed"[85] sends the message that sex between men is wrong or somehow unseemly.

True Blood's sanitization of queer desire, its tactical homoeroticism, confirms the continued existence and changing dimensions of what Gayle S. Rubin famously christened the "charmed circle" of sex:

According to this system, sexuality that is "good," "normal," and "natural" should ideally be heterosexual, marital, monogamous, reproductive, and non-commercial. It should be coupled, relational, within the same generation, and occur at home. It should not involve pornography, fetish objects, sex toys of any sort, or roles other than male or female. Any sex that violates these rules is "bad," "abnormal," or "unnatural."[86]

Of course, the neoliberal normalization of queerness has allowed some forms of homosexuality to creep towards respectability;[87] namely, those that are "vanilla, coupled, and monogamous."[88] By whitewashing, desexualizing, and normalizing queerness, *True Blood* reveals its complicity with the homonationalist agenda of the gay civil rights movement, its clandestine yearning to join the charmed circle of heterosexual domesticity.

As the fans above make abundantly clear, straight sex and queer sex are depicted quite differently on *True Blood*. But there are also key differences between how gay sex and lesbian sex are portrayed. Sex between men is sanitized or pathologized (more on this shortly), and sex between women is heterosexualized. Although *True Blood* features several characters who have sex with women (Sophie-Anne, Nan, Pam, Yvetta, and Hadley), the characters are coded as bisexual or pansexual on the show and/or via the press. Evan Rachel Wood, the bisexual actress who plays Sophie Anne, insists that her character is "not necessarily a lesbian. Her human partner is a girl, but I'm pretty sure she goes both ways."[89] Yvetta does swing both ways, and is shown having sex with Eric Northmann (Alexander Skarsgård) and Pam. Kristin Bauer claims that she is not surprised that her character Pam goes "for women [but] I think she's pansexual."[90] Having characters who engage in lesbian sexual practices but do not identify as homosexual suggests that *True Blood*, like most mainstream television shows, is "uncomfortable incorporating authentic lesbianism on screen," but is "willing to depict a type of 'watered-down' lesbianism in order to capitalize on the femme-chic trend."[91] *True Blood*'s strategic incorporation of lesbianism can be viewed as a form of gay window advertising. According to Danae Clark, gay window advertising is a dual marketing approach that "consciously disavows any explicit connection to lesbianism for fear of offending or losing potential customers,"[92] while simultaneously appropriating lesbian styles.

The creation of the female characters as bisexual or pansexual and femme allows *True Blood* to court lesbian viewers without alienating heterosexual ones. Limiting the landscape of lesbianism to luscious femmes is unfortunate, because the image of the butch lesbian is arguably "better equipped to challenge conventional notions and perhaps even prejudices involving female homosexuality."[93] By solely presenting feminized and heterosexualized lesbians, *True Blood* reveals that it is less concerned with sexual diversity than with rendering lesbianism more palatable for mainstream audiences.[94] That is, it is more concerned with normalizing lesbianism than challenging the homophobia and heterosexism of its straight audience. It also bears mentioning that in thirty-six episodes there has been only three extremely brief lesbian sex scenes on *True Blood* and they all occurred in the third season (Sophie Anne/Hadley, Pam/Yvetta, and Nan/Unnamed Stripper). Until then, queer truebies had to settle for Pam lasciviously leering at Sookie. But as Malinda Lo of the lesbian popular culture blog, After Ellen, wryly reminds us: "Suggestive gazing has its place (in fact, most of *Twilight* is about this), but it does not make a lesbian vampire."[95] Perhaps even more tragic than the limited number of lesbian sex scenes is how *True Blood* ruthlessly heterosexualizes these encounters to maximize straight male enjoyment. Two of the three scenes involve strippers. The third one involves a buxom blonde (Hadley) who could be a stripper. As Thomas, a Feministe commenter, justly complains: "The woman-on-woman sex and biting seems cheap ... It seems like there isn't a [sexy] powerful woman vampire on the show who doesn't log airtime with her fangs in a skinny, conventionally attractive naked woman."[96]

While *True Blood*'s tactical homoeroticism and strategic lesbianism are disappointing, it is the show's linkage of gay sex with savage demise that truebies find most distressing. Homosexual desire culminates in brutal homicide, not once but twice in the third season. In the first case, Viking vampire Eric seduces Talbot. At the height of their passion, instead of penetrating Talbot, Eric stakes him from behind with a suitably phallic wooden scepter. Talbot dies in a propulsive explosion. But as Harry Benshoff rightfully insists, exploitative scenes like this do "little more than firmly link once again the idea of homosexuality with violence and murder. It titillates the audience with its homosexual foreplay, but instead of reaching a sexual orgasm, the screen is showered with a bloody ejaculate."[97] In the second case, a grieving Russell hires a male prostitute, Tony (Michael Steger), who resembles the recently departed Talbot. After their tryst, Russell repeatedly stabs the prostitute until he is dead. While tears of blood stream down his face, Russell tells the corpse: "I am more sorry than I can ever say. I'm so glad we had a chance to say our goodbye."[98]

Although fans were appalled by Russell's ritualistic murder of Tony, the gay prostitute, they were even more horrified by the Eric/Talbot sex scene. Feministe commenter Queen Emily protests: "It takes to the third season of this show on HBO of all channels for there to be a gay male sex scene and one of them (the bottom!) ends up dead almost straight away? That's just the old homophobic gay sex = death meme to me. You don't have to be Leo Bersani to see that the rectum is a grave in this one."[99] Nor do you have to be Bersani to recognize that the "whole gay-sex = back-stabbing thing" is just a "hoary old cliché right out of *Cruising*."[100] Other truebies, like Andrea Plaid of Racialicious, saw the scene as a stark reminder of "how many men who have sex with men die at the hands of self-identified straight men out of 'gay panic.'"[101] Her fellow roundtable participant, Thea Lim, finds it "difficult to write off as coincidence that the first really open gay love scene in this show … ends with the death of one of the partners."[102] And Renee Martin ruefully observes that Talbot's death "almost make[s] it seem like there is a price for two men having sex."[103] Indeed, it does.

While *True Blood* is exalted for being sexually risqué and queer-inclusive, these fan critiques suggest otherwise. Their readings suggest that the show is sexually conservative and homonormative. On *True Blood*, homosexuality is predominantly the province of whites. On *True Blood*, clear lines are drawn between good queers and bad queers. Good gays are coupled, chaste, and thoughtfully save their sexual antics for off-screen. Good lesbians are luscious bisexuals who appeal to gay women and straight men. Bad gays are promiscuous and kinky; they seduce straights and pursue prostitutes. Bad queers are not interested in joining the charmed circle of normative sex and thus they pose a grave threat to heterosexuals and homonationalists. Now that we have, with the assistance of truebies, laid bare the homonormativity at the heart of *True Blood*, let us close by considering what happens when metaphor and reality collide, when bloodsuckers are not just gay analogues but are actually queer. What are the ideological consequences of conflating homosexuality with vampirism, of comparing minorities to monsters?

Perilous Allegories, Or The Dangers of Conflating Minorities with Monsters

As we have seen, *True Blood* draws explicit parallels between vampirism and homosexuality. In its first two seasons, this metaphor is primarily employed to elicit sympathy for vampires and to elucidate the evils of homophobia. But Russell Edgington, the privileged white gay villain at the heart of the third season, reveals the analogy's limits (and thus, by implication, the political viability of queer liberalism) by demonstrating that even exemplary homonormative subjects cannot be absorbed by the hetero-human mainstream, for even these seemingly benign sexual others remain threatening symbols of alterity.

In many ways, Edgington embodies the ultimate homonationalist subject: "He is [white], able-bodied, monied, confident, well-traveled, suitably partnered and betrays no trace of abjection or shame."[104] Yet, as truebies quickly learn, Russell is only pretending to mainstream. He is, in fact, violently opposed to assimilation and normativity. Unlike Bill, the self-hating bloodsucker who "sneers at vampire culture and customs,"[105] advocates the "complete abdication of [vampire] cultural practices,"[106] and prefers to "hook up with humans,"[107] Russell is a supernatural supremacist[108] who sees integration as fundamentally "contrary to vampire identity"[109] and "tantamount to genocide."[110] In one of the show's most infamous scenes, Russell hijacks a cable news show and rips out the human anchor's spine live on camera. Still clutching the dead man's bloody, quivering spine in hand, Russell addresses the human race and reveals a side of the vampire that the AVL had very much hoped to keep hidden. Because this speech compelled many truebies to re-evaluate the sociopolitical consequences of the vampire metaphor,

I will quote from it at length:

> [T]he American Vampire League wishes to perpetrate the notion that we are just like you. ... But ... we are nothing like you. We are immortal. Because we drink the true blood, blood that is living, organic and human. And that is the truth the AVL wishes to conceal from you. Because let's face it, eating people is a tough sell these days. So they put on their friendly faces to pass their beloved VRA but make no mistake, mine is the true face of vampires! Why would we seek equal rights? You are not our equals. We will eat you. After we eat your children. We need to take this world back from the humans, not placate them with billboards and PR campaigns while they destroy it![111]

Some fans interpret Russell's rampage as Alan Ball's reaction to the "domestication of gay life,"[112] his furious denunciation of the neoliberal logic of sameness. These fans identify with Russell because he symbolizes a "disenfranchised minority figure exact[ing] a violent and gratifying revenge upon a dominant heterocentrist hegemony."[113] This scene prompted After Elton to name Russell their #1 Gay Badass of the year, because he "will definitely cut a bitch. And when we say 'cut' we mean dismember and disembowel — and that's just for lunch."[114] Over at io9, the popular science fiction blog, reader Arryma marvels: "Russell is suddenly the best villain ever ... He took the entire premise of the show — the idea that vamps and humans could live together — and smashed it with a wrecking ball."[115] But it is a fine line between queer avenger and monster terrorist fag.[116] While one can easily understand why gay truebies might "rally around the queer psycho-killer ... avenging [himself] upon straight society,"[117] Benshoff reminds us that the "resultant connotative and cumulative effect of such images on non-queer spectators remains retrogressive."[118]

Fans and critics of *True Blood* echo the concerns of Benshoff. In "Vampire Conservatives," Michelle Goldberg muses that comparing vampires to queers, while "cheeky and clever ... has troubling implications, because the vampires, political rhetoric aside, aren't really interested in joining human society ... [M]ost of the vampires we meet [in *True Blood*] are arrogant, perverse, and cruel — everything the far right believes gays to be."[119] io9 editor Annalee Newitz concurs: "If these murderous, evil creatures are figures for gay people, then they are figures for the religious right's worst nightmare of what gay people are."[120] At *Television Without Pity*'s True Blood forum, leefonthewind broods: "Russell's 'We will eat you, after we eat your children' becomes a disturbing statement, given a large portion of the country's 'think of the children!' approach to justifying discrimination in areas like gay adoption or allowing gay teachers in schools."[121] Anita Sarkeesian frets that equating racial and sexual others with "evil, manipulative, bloodsucking, monstrous, undead beings ... is not a far cry from the actual accusations against Black folks and Queer folks, both historically and currently."[122] Perhaps the most profound and profane denunciation of the gay = vampire allegory comes from Gabe, Videogum's *True Blood* recapper, who finds it "super fucked up ... to have a metaphor for the homosexual community in which the metaphorical homosexuals are ... hyper-sexualized violent mass murderers with whom sex = death."[123] Amazingly, Alan Ball agrees: "Ultimately, if you latch onto that metaphor and become really serious about it, it would make the show extremely homophobic. Because vampires are dangerous, they kill, they're amoral, a lot of them."[124] And Ball is right; it is just too bad that, unlike his fans, he underestimates the ideological power of the gay = vampire analogy. Instead, Ball dismisses the metaphor as a "nice little detail in what is hopefully a big popcorn thrill ride."[125]

Despite its plethora of pansexual vampires, its neoliberal celebration of homonormativity, *True Blood* nonetheless partakes of the same demonizing tropes as do horror texts of the past: queers are terrorists and traitors, queers are liars and schemers, queers are psycho-predators who will deflower and/or devour your children. Instead of dispelling gay stereotypes, the series re-inscribes and validates them. While the presence of white queer characters on *True Blood* indicates a grudging movement towards greater acceptance of certain homosexuals, its commodification of gay racial stereotypes, its tactical homoeroticism and strategic lesbianism, demonstrate the "hegemonic nature of mass culture and the justification of exploitation through tolerance."[126] In the end, *True Blood* is deeply ambivalent about homosexuality. The show definitely does not embrace the diversity of queerness and thus does not merit the plaudits of GLAAD or any other organization claiming to represent the entirety of the LGBTIQ community. Fortunately, queer/anti-racist/feminist truebies bravely unmask the post-racial homonationalism of the series. These fans reveal the sociopolitical limits of white liberal gay rights discourse and thus provide the impetus for a broader queer liberation movement. A movement in which the queer is not synonymous with the "polite categories of gay and lesbian," but represents the "taboo-breaker, the monstrous, the uncanny."[127] A movement that "attacks the dominant notion of the natural" and "revels in the discourse of the loathsome, the outcast, the idiomatically-proscribed position of same-sex desire."[128] A movement that realizes that the queer monster "always represents the disruption of categories, the destruction of boundaries, and the presence of impurities," and that "we need monsters to recognize and celebrate our own monstrosities."[129] What we do not need are homonationalist vampires who deplore difference, reinforce sexual and racial boundaries, and revel in neoliberal sameness.

Notes

1. Jennie Yabroff, "A Bit Long in the Tooth," *Newsweek*, 6 December, 2008.
2. On the xenophobic uses of the vampire, see Dale Hudson, "Vampires of Color and the Performance of Multicultural Whiteness," in *The Persistence of Whiteness: Race and Contemporary Hollywood Cinema*, ed. Daniel Bernardi (London and New York: Routledge, 2008), and Gina Marchetti, "From Fu Manchu to *M. Butterfly* and *Irma Vep*: Cinematic Incarnations of Chinese Villainy," in *Bad: Infamy, Darkness, Evil, and Slime on Screen*, ed. Murray Pomerance, Cultural Studies in Cinema/Video (Albany: SUNY Press, 2004).
3. For an exploration of how vampirism symbolizes white colonial guilt and fear of reverse imperialism, see Stephen D. Arata, "The Occidental Tourist: *Dracula* and the Anxiety of Reverse Colonization," *Victorian Studies* 33, no. 4 (1990): 621–45.
4. On the uncanny similarities between blood-sucking, consumption, and capitalism, see Rob Latham, *Consuming Youth: Vampires, Cyborgs, and the Culture of Consumption* (Chicago: University of Chicago Press, 2002), and Franco Moretti, "The Dialectic of Fear," *New Left Review* 136 (November–December 1982).

5   For a discussion of the de-racializing aspects of vampirism, see John Allen Stevenson, "A Vampire in the Mirror: The Sexuality of *Dracula*," *Publications of the Modern Language Association of America* 103, no. 2 (1988): 139–49.
6   On vampirism as a metaphor for miscegenation, see Eric Lott, "Whiteness: A Glossary," *Village Voice* 38, no. 20 (1993); Steven Jay Schneider, "Mixed Blood Couples: Monsters and Miscegenation in U.S. Horror Cinema," in *The Gothic Other: Racial and Social Constructions in the Literary Imagination*, ed. Ruth Bienstock Anolik and Douglas L. Howard (Jefferson, NC: McFarland, 2004); and Shannon Winnubst, "Vampires, Anxieties, and Dreams: Race and Sex in the Contemporary United States," *Hypatia* 18, no. 3 (2003): 1–20.
7   For more on the historical linkage of vampirism with anti-Semitism, see Bram Dijkstra, *Idols of Perversity: Fantasies of Feminine Evil in Fin-de-Siècle Culture* (New York and Oxford: Oxford University Press, 1986), and Judith Halberstam, "Technologies of Monstrosity: Bram Stoker's *Dracula*," *Victorian Studies* 36, no. 3 (1993): 333–52.
8   On the parallels between blood-sucking and eating the racial other, see Richard Dyer, *White* (London and New York: Routledge, 1997).
9   On the traditional relationship between vampirism and depravity, see Milly Williamson, "Vampire Transformations: From Gothic Demon to Domestication?" in *Vampires: Myths and Metaphors of Enduring Evil*, ed. Carla T. Kungl (Oxford: Learning Solutions On-line Publication, 2004), and Jules Zanger, "Metaphor into Metonymy: The Vampire Next Door," in *Blood Read: The Vampire as Metaphor in Contemporary Culture*, ed. Joan Gordon and Veronica Hollinger (Philadelphia: University of Pennsylvania Press, 1997).
10 To learn more about how the modern vampire got defanged, see Michelle Callander, "Bram Stoker's *Buffy*: Traditional Gothic and Contemporary Culture," *Slayage: The Journal of The Whedon Studies Association* 1, no. 3 (June 2001), Margaret L. Carter, "The Vampire as Alien in Contemporary Fiction," in *Blood Read: The Vampire as Metaphor in Contemporary Culture*, ed. Joan Gordon and Veronica Hollinger (Philadelphia: University of Pennsylvania Press, 1997), Bruce McClelland, "Un-*True Blood*: The Politics of Artificiality," in *True Blood and Philosophy: We Wanna Think Bad Things with You*, ed. George A. Dunn and Rebecca Housel (Hoboken, NJ: John Wiley & Sons, 2010), and Suzanne Scott, "All Bark and No Bite: Siring the Neutered Vampire on Buffy the Vampire Slayer," in *Vampires: Myths and Metaphors of Enduring Evil*, ed. Carla T. Kungl (Oxford: Learning Solutions On-line Publication, 2004).
11 On the enduring association of evil with feminine sexuality, see Barbara Creed, *The Monstrous-Feminine: Film, Feminism, Psychoanalysis*, Popular

Fictions Series (London: Routledge, 1993), Bram Dijkstra, *Evil Sisters: The Threat of Female Sexuality and the Cult of Manhood* (New York: Alfred A. Knopf, 1996), and Carol A. Senf, "'Dracula': Stoker's Response to the New Woman," *Victorian Studies* 26, no. 1 (1982): 33–49.

12 To unravel the many similarities between vampirism and homosexuality, see Richard Dyer, "Children of the Night: Vampirism as Homosexuality, Homosexuality as Vampirism," in *Sweet Dreams: Sexuality Gender and Popular Fiction*, ed. Susannah Radstone (London: Lawrence and Wishart, 1988), David William Foster, "José González Castillo's *Los invertidos* and the Vampire Theory of Homosexuality," *Latin American Theatre Review* 22, no. 2 (1989): 19–29, George E. Haggerty, "Anne Rice and the Queering of Culture," *NOVEL: A Forum on Fiction* 32, no. 1 (1998): 5–18, Barry McCrea, "Heterosexual Horror: Dracula, the Closet, and the Marriage-Plot," *NOVEL: A Forum on Fiction* 43, no. 2 (2010): 251–70, and Andrew Schopp, "Cruising the Alternatives: Homoeroticism and the Contemporary Vampire," *Journal of Popular Culture* 30, no. 4 (1997): 231–43.

13 On the queer potential of vampires, see Harry M. Benshoff, *Monsters in the Closet: Homosexuality and the Horror Film*, Inside Popular Film (Manchester: Manchester University Press, 1997), Sue-Ellen Case, "Tracking the Vampire," *Differences: A Journal of Feminist Cultural Studies* 3, no. 2 (1991): 1–20, and Judith Halberstam, *Skin Shows: Gothic Horror and the Technology of Monsters* (Durham, NC: Duke University Press, 1995).

14 For discussions of vampirism as a metaphor for sexually-transmitted disease, see Vera Dika, "From Dracula – With Love," in *The Dread of Difference: Gender and the Horror Film*, ed. Barry Keith Grant, Texas Film Studies Series (Austin: University of Texas, 1996), and Peter Redman, "Invasion of the Monstrous Others: Heterosexual Masculinities, the 'AIDS Carrier' and the Horror Genre," in *Border Patrols: Policing the Boundaries of Heterosexuality*, ed. Deborah Lynn Steinberg, Debbie Epstein, and Richard Johnson, Sexual Politics Series (London: Cassell, 1997).

15 On the seductively unfixed gender of vampires, see Christopher Craft, "'Kiss Me with Those Red Lips': Gender and Inversion in Bram Stoker's *Dracula*," in *Dracula: The Vampire and The Critics*, ed. Margaret L. Carter, Studies in Speculative Fiction 19 (Ann Arbor: UMI Research Press, 1988), and Cyndy Hendershot, "Vampire and Replicant: The One-Sex Body in a Two-Sex World," *Science Fiction Studies* 22, no. 3 (1995).

16 Joan Gordon and Veronica Hollinger, "Introduction: The Shape of Vampires," in *Blood Read: The Vampire as Metaphor in Contemporary Culture*, ed. Joan Gordon and Veronica Hollinger (Philadelphia: University of Pennsylvania Press, 1997), 5.

17 Halberstam, "Technologies of Monstrosity," 335.

18 Nina Auerbach, *Our Vampires, Ourselves* (Chicago: University of Chicago Press, 1995), 145.

19 Hudson, "Vampires of Color," 128–9.
20 Joshua David Bellin, *Framing Monsters: Fantasy Film and Social Alienation* (Carbondale: Southern Illinois University Press, 2005), 9.
21 Ibid.
22 The fourth season is currently in production and will air in Summer 2011. See Robert Seidman, "'*True Blood*' Renewed by HBO for a Fourth Season," *Zap2It*, accessed August 24, 2011, http://tvbythenumbers.zap2it.com/2010/06/21/true-blood-renewed-by-hbo-for-a-fourth-season/5480.
23 Although the series hints that Sookie Stackhouse is something other than human from the beginning, it is not confirmed until late in the third season. See *True Blood*, "I Smell A Rat," Season Three, Episode Ten, director Michael Lehmann, written by Kate Barnow and Elizabeth R. Finch, New York: Home Box Office, first aired August 22, 2010.
24 "Where We Are on TV: 2010–2011 Season," *GLAAD.org*, accessed August 22, 2011, http://www.glaad.org/publications/tvreport10/overview.
25 For more on gay window advertising, see Danae Clark, "Commodity Lesbianism," *Camera Obscura* 25/26 (January/May 1991): 181–201.
26 Homi K. Bhabha, *The Location of Culture* (London and New York: Routledge 1994).
27 Margaret Denike, "Homonormative Collusions and the Subject of Rights: Reading *Terrorist Assemblages*," *Feminist Legal Studies* 18, no. 1 (2010): 86.
28 Lisa Duggan, *The Twilight of Equality: Neoliberalism, Cultural Politics, and the Attack on Democracy* (Boston: Beacon, 2003), 177.
29 Diane Richardson, "Desiring Sameness? The Rise of a Neoliberal Politics of Normalisation," *Antipode* 37, no. 3 (2005), 516.
30 Ibid., 519.
31 Ibid., 522.
32 See Michael Joseph Gross, "Gay Is the New Black?" *The Advocate*, accessed August 24, 2011, http://www.advocate.com/News/Daily_News/2008/11/16/Gay_is_the_New_Black_/.
33 On the enduring power of race and racism in America, see Eduardo Bonilla-Silva, *Racism without Racists: Color-Blind Racism and the Persistence of Racial Inequality in the United States*, 3rd ed. (Lanham, MD: Rowman & Littlefield, 2010), Joe R. Feagin, *Racist America: Roots, Current Realities, and Future Reparations* (New York: Routledge, 2000), David Theo Goldberg, *The Threat of Race: Reflections on Racial Neoliberalism*, Blackwell Manifestos Series 2344 (Malden, MA: Wiley-Blackwell, 2009), H. Roy Kaplan, *The Myth of Post-Racial America: Searching for Equality in the Age of Materialism* (Lanham, MD: Rowman & Littlefield, 2010), George Lipsitz, *The Possessive Investment in Whiteness: How White People Profit from Identity Politics*, rev. and expanded ed. (Philadelphia: Temple University Press,

2006), Charles W. Mills, *The Racial Contract* (Ithaca: Cornell University Press, 1997), and Tim Wise, *Colorblind: The Rise of Post-Racial Politics and the Retreat from Racial Equity*, City Lights Open Media (San Francisco: City Lights Books, 2010).

34 Eduardo Bonilla-Silva and Victor Ray, "When Whites Love a Black Leader: Race Matters in *Obamerica*," *Journal of African American Studies* 13, no. 2 (2009): 177.

35 Lisa Duggan, "Queering the State," *Social Text* 39 (1994): 4.

36 Catherine Smith, "Queer as Black Folk?" *Wisconsin Law Review* (2007): 383.

37 Irene Monroe, "Gay Is Not the New Black," *The Huffington Post*, accessed August 24, 2011, http://www.huffingtonpost.com/irene-monroe/gay-is-emnotem-the-new-bl_b_151573.html.

38 Gross, "Gay Is the New Black?"

39 Steve Anderson, "*True Blood* Title Sequence," *Critical Commons*, accessed August 24, 2011, http://criticalcommons.org/Members/ironman28/clips/trueBloodTitleSequence.mov/view?searchterm=true%20blood.

40 Michael Peterson, Laurie Beth Clark, and Lisa Nakamura, "Vampire Politics," *FlowTV*, accessed August 24, 2011, http://flowtv.org/2009/12/vampire-politicslisa-nakamura-laurie-beth-clark-michael-peterson/.

41 Ibid.

42 Nan Flanagan, "About: The American Vampire League," *American Vampire League*, accessed August 24, 2011, http://americanvampireleague.com/about/index.html.

43 Ariadne Blayde and George A. Dunn, "Pets, Cattle, and Higher Life Forms on *True Blood*," in *True Blood and Philosophy: We Wanna Think Bad Things with You*, ed. George A. Dunn and Rebecca Housel, Blackwell Philosophy and Pop Culture Series (Hoboken, NJ: John Wiley and Sons, 2010), 34.

44 Alan Ball as quoted in "Vampires Come to Life in *True Blood*," *Canwest News Service*, accessed August 24, 2011, http://www.canada.com/topics/entertainment/story.html?id=47530f3e-7aa4-49d7-9152-2b5b2f697d30.

45 Scott Tobias, "Alan Ball on *True Blood* and Its Relationship to the Source Material," *The A.V. Club*, accessed August 24, 2011, http://www.avclub.com/content/interview/alan_ball.

46 See Denise Martin, "TCA: Alan Ball: *True Blood* Is Not a Metaphor for Gay People," *Los Angeles Times*, accessed August 24, 2011, http://latimesblogs.latimes.com/showtracker/2008/07/tca-alan-ball-t.html; Lauren Gitlin, "Sexy Vampire Alert: Alan Ball Dishes on *True Blood*," *Television Without Pity*, accessed August 24, 2011, http://www.televisionwithoutpity.com/telefile/2008/09/suck-on-this-alan-ball-dishes.php; Christina Radish, "Alan Ball on Making *True Blood*," *Media Blvd.*, accessed Au-

gust 24, 2011, http://www.mediablvd.com/magazine/the_news/celebrity/alan_ball_on_making_true_blood_200811021391.html; Joy Press, "Vampires That Don't Suck," *Salon.com*, accessed August 24, 2011, http://www.salon.com/entertainment/tv/int/2008/09/03/ball/index.html; Joe Rhodes, "After All the Funerals, a Prime-Time Auteur Digs up the Undead," *The New York Times*, accessed August 24, 2011, http://www.nytimes.com/2008/08/03/arts/television/03rhod.html; Jace, "From Dusk Til Dawn: Talking with Alan Ball About *True Blood* Season Two," *Televisionary*, accessed August 24, 2011, http://www.televisionaryblog.com/2009/06/from-dusk-til-dawn-talking-with-alan.html; Emma, "Interview: Alan Ball from *True Blood*," *FanBolt*, accessed August 24, 2011, http://www.fanbolt.com/headline/7203/Interview:_Alan_Ball_from_True_Blood.

47 Tami Winfrey Harris as quoted in Thea Lim, Tami Winfrey Harris, Andrea Plaid, and Latoya Peterson, "Racialicious Presents the *True Blood* Roundtable," *Racialicious*, accessed August 24, 2011, http://www.racialicious.com/2010/06/22/racialicious-presents-the-true-blood-roundtable/.

48 Melissa McEwan, "On *True Blood*," *Shakesville*, accessed August 24, 2011, http://shakespearessister.blogspot.com/2010/06/on-true-blood.html.

49 Tami Winfrey Harris, "*True Blood* Epiphany: If Bill Compton Were a Black Man, He'd Be Clarence Thomas," *What Tami Said*, accessed August 24, 2011, http://whattamisaid.blogspot.com/2009/09/true-blood-epiphany-if-bill-compton.html.

50 In the About Me section of her blog, *What Tami Said*, Tami Winfrey Harris describes herself as "a writer, black woman, bibliophile, music lover, nappy head, geek, eccentric, Midwesterner, wife, stepmother, sister, aunt and daughter. I am a liberal progressive. I believe in equality ... of gender ... of race ... of sexuality ... and I believe in working PROACTIVELY toward same. I am anti-oppression. I believe in justice for ALL." http://whattamisaid.blogspot.com/.

51 Winfrey Harris, "*True Blood* Epiphany."

52 American Vampire League, "Pro-Vampire Rights Amendment Commercial," *BloodCopy.com*, accessed August 24, 2011, http://www.youtube.com/watch?v=ZEhG5DKmkHQ.

53 S. E. Smith's profile for *Bitch Magazine* saucily reads: "I am a writer and mischief-maker living in the small town I grew up next to. Queer, disabled, transgender, and highly likely to trounce you at backgammon." http://bitchmagazine.org/profile/se-smith.

54 S. E. Smith, "Finally, I Have Watched *True Blood* Season Two," *This Ain't Livin'*, accessed August 24, 2011, http://meloukhia.net/2010/06/finally_i_have_watched_true_blood_season_two.html.

55 Ibid.

56. Kevin from the comments of Snicks, "'*True Blood*' Episode 3.10 Recap: 'I Smell a Rat!'" *After Elton*, accessed August 24, 2011, http://www.afterelton.com/tv/recaps/trueblood/310.
57. Homophilic from the comments of Dodai Stewart, "The *True Blood* Finale Is All Questions & No Answers," *Jezebel*, accessed August 24, 2011, http://jezebel.com/#!5636669/the-true-blood-finale-is-all-questions--no-answers.
58. Tobi Hill-Meyer, "About This Contributor: Tobi Hill-Meyer," *Bilerico Project*, accessed August 24, 2011, http://www.bilerico.com/contributors/tobi_hill-meyer/.
59. Meyer, "*True Blood* a Metaphor for Trans Folks?," *Bilerico Project*, accessed August 24, 2011, http://www.bilerico.com/2010/09/true_blood_a_metaphor_for_trans_folks.php.
60. Ibid.
61. Ibid.
62. Benshoff, *Monsters in the Closet*, 284.
63. Brian Juergens, "'*True Blood*' Review and Interview with Creator Alan Ball," *After Elton*, accessed August 24, 2011, http://www.afterelton.com/TV/2008/9/alanball_trueblood?page=0%2C0.
64. Ibid.
65. Jason Zinoman, "A Shirt Shortage Strikes Bon Temps: *True Blood*'s Very Sexy, Very Gay Season 3 Debut," *Slate*, accessed August 24, 2011, http://www.slate.com/id/2256939/.
66. See "Quotes for Lafayette Reynolds (Character) from '*True Blood*'," *IMDb*, accessed August 24, 2011, http://www.imdb.com/character/ch0060862/quotes, "Lafayette Reynolds Quotes," *TV Fanatic*, 2010, http://www.tvfanatic.com/quotes/characters/lafayette-reynolds/, Vanessa Wesley, "Top 10 Lafayette Reynolds Quotes from *True Blood*," *Wet Paint*, accessed August 24, 2011, http://www.wetpaint.com/true-blood/articles/top-10-lafayette-reynolds-quotes-from-true-blood.
67. JC from the comments of Tami Winfrey Harris, "*True Blood*, Tired Stereotypes," *Racialicious*, accessed August 24, 2011, http://www.racialicious.com/2008/09/24/true-blood-tired-stereotypes/.
68. Anita Sarkeesian, "Beyond *True Blood*'s Sensationalism [Transcript of Youtube Video]," *Feminist Frequency*, accessed August 24, 2011, http://www.feministfrequency.com/2009/11/beyond-true-blood-sensationalism.
69. Renee Martin, "When Is Gay Love Not Problematic on Television?" *Womanist Musings*, accessed August 24, 2011, http://www.womanistmusings.com/2010/03/when-is-gay-love-not-problematic-on.html.
70. Lim et al., "Racialicious Presents."
71. Trish Bendix, "'*True Blood*' Mini-Cap 3.2 'Beautifully Broken'," *After El-*

len, accessed August 24, 2011, http://www.afterellen.com/blog/trishbendix/true-blood-mini-cap-3-2-beautifully-broken.
72 Juergens, "'*True Blood*' Review and Interview with Creator Alan Ball."
73 Ibid.
74 Joe Wlodarz, "Beyond the Black Macho: Queer Blaxploitation," *The Velvet Light Trap* 53 (2004): 16.
75 Ibid.
76 Ibid., 17.
77 Renee Martin, "*True Blood*: Bad Blood," *Womanist Musings*, accessed August 24, 2011, http://www.womanist-musings.com/2010/06/true-blood-bad-blood.html.
78 Michelle Dean, "'The Bridge of You and Me Ain't Never Gonna Happen': Against *True Blood*," *Bitch*, accessed August 24, 2011, http://bitchmagazine.org/post/tube-tied-the-bridge-of-you-and-me-aint-never-gonna-happen-against-true-blood.
79 Renee Martin, "*True Blood*: Everything Is Broken " *Womanist Musings*, accessed August 24, 2011, http://www.womanist-musings.com/2010/08/true-blood-everything-is-broken.html.
80 Dean, "'The Bridge of You and Me Ain't Never Gonna Happen'."
81 Tami Winfrey Harris quoted in Thea Lim et al., "The Snot Factor, Death and Sex, & Improper Firearm Use: *True Blood* S03 E08," *Racialicious*, accessed August 24, 2011, http://www.racialicious.com/2010/08/11/the-snot-factor-death-and-sex-improper-firearm-use-true-blood-s03e08/.
82 Ibid.
83 Dean, "'The Bridge of You and Me Ain't Never Gonna Happen'."
84 Ibid.
85 Martin, "*True Blood*: Bad Blood."
86 Gayle S. Rubin, "Thinking Sex: Notes for a Radical Theory of the Politics of Sexuality," in *The Lesbian and Gay Studies Reader*, ed. Henry Abelove, Michèle Aina Barale, and David M. Halperin (New York: Routledge, 1993), 13–14.
87 Ibid., 15.
88 Katherine Sender, "Sex Sells: Sex, Taste, and Class in Commercial Gay and Lesbian Media," *GLQ: A Journal of Lesbian and Gay Studies* 9, no. 3 (2003): 333.
89 Evan Rachel Wood, interview by Katy Hall, "Evan Rachel Wood Talks Nudity, Lesbian Vampire Sex," *The Huffington Post*, August 27, 2009, http://www.huffingtonpost.com/2009/08/27/evan-rachel-wood-talks-nu_n_270421.html.
90 Trish Bendix, "Kristin Bauer Could Play the Next Lesbian Vampire on '*True Blood*'," *After Ellen*, November 3, 2009, http://www.afterellen.com/blog/trishbendix/kristin-bauer-could-be-the-next-lesbian-vampire-on-true-blood.

91 Tricia Jenkins, "'Potential Lesbians at Two O'Clock': The Heterosexualization of Lesbianism in the Recent Teen Film," *The Journal of Popular Culture* 38, no. 3 (2005): 492.
92 Clark, "Commodity Lesbianism," 193.
93 Jenkins, "Potential Lesbians at Two O'Clock," 494.
94 Ibid.
95 Malinda Lo, "Notes & Queeries: The Allure of the Lesbian Vampire," *After Ellen*, accessed August 24, 2011, http://www.afterellen.com/column/2009/6/notes-queeries.
96 Thomas from the comments of Lauren, "Tuesday *True Blood* Roundtable, 'Everything Is Broken'," *Feministe*, accessed August 24, 2011, http://www.feministe.us/blog/archives/2010/08/17/tuesday-true-blood-roundtable-everything-is-broken/.
97 Benshoff, *Monsters in the Closet*, 248.
98 *True Blood*, "I Smell a Rat," Season Three, Episode Ten.
99 Queen Emily from the comments of Frau Sally Benz, "Tuesday *True Blood* Roundtable: Night on the Sun," *Feministe*, accessed August 24, 2011, http://www.feministe.us/blog/archives/2010/08/10/tuesday-true-blood-roundtable-night-on-the-sun/.
100 Steven Frank, "'*True Blood*' Episode 3.08 Recap: 'Yes, Daddy!'" *After Elton*, accessed August 24, 2011, http://www.afterelton.com/tv/recaps/trueblood/308.
101 ndrea Plaid as quoted in Lim et al., "The Snot Factor."
102 Thea Lim as quoted in Ibid.
103 Martin, "*True Blood*: Everything Is Broken."
104 Jasbir Puar, "In the Wake of It Gets Better," *The Guardian*, accessed August 24, 2011, http://www.guardian.co.uk/commentisfree/cifamerica/2010/nov/16/wake-it-gets-better-campaign.
105 Winfrey Harris, "*True Blood* Epiphany."
106 Gabe, "Can the *True Blood* Metaphor Get Any More Fucked Up?" *Videogum*, accessed August 24, 2011, http://videogum.com/23001/how_much_worse_can_the_true_bl/everyones-a-critic/.
107 Buymywings from the comments of "*True Blood* General Gabbery >>3-3: "It Hurts Me Too [Forum]," *Television Without Pity*, accessed August 24, 2011, http://forums.televisionwithoutpity.com/ lofiversion/index.php/t3196618-250.html.
108 Russell's supernatural supremacy is famously revealed in an exchange with Eric, in which he tells him: "Preening little fool that he was, Adolph was right about one thing: there is a master race. It's just not the human race" [*True Blood*, "I Got a Right to Sing the Blues," Season, Three, Episode Seven, director Michael Lehman and written by Alan Ball, New York: Home Box Office, first aired July 25, 2010.

109 William M. Curtis, "'Honey, If We Can't Kill People, What's the Point of Being a Vampire?': Can Vampires Be Good Citizens?" in Dunn and Housel, eds., 74.
110 McClelland, "Un-*True Blood*: The Politics of Artificiality," 83.
111 *True Blood*, "Everything is Broken," Season Three, Episode Nine, director Scott Winant and written by Alexander Woo, New York: Home Box Office, first aired August 15, 2010.
112 Laura Sundstrom, "*True Blood* Is Right Wing's Worst Nightmare," *Young Feminist Adventures*, accessed August 24, 2011, http://youngfeministadventures.blogspot.com/2009/07/true-blood-is-right-wings-worst.html.
113 Benshoff, *Monsters in the Closet*, 220.
114 Snicks, "13 Gay Badasses We Love," *After Elton*, accessed August 24, 2011, http://www.afterelton.com/people/2010/07/thirteen-gay-badasses.
115 Arryma from the comments of Meredith Woerner, "Best *True Blood* Ending Ever. Ever. Ever. Ever.," *io9*, August 16, 2010, http://io9.com/5613435/best-true-blood-ending-ever-ever-ever-ever.
116 I borrow this term from Jasbir K. Puar and Amit S. Rai, "Monster, Terrorist, Fag: The War on Terrorism and the Production of Docile Patriots," *Social Text* 20, no. 3 (2002).
117 Benshoff, 223.
118 Ibid., 232.
119 Michelle Goldberg, "Vampire Conservatives," *The Daily Beast*, accessed August 24, 2011, http://www.thedailybeast.com/blogs-and-stories/2009-07-18/vampire-conservatives/.
120 Annalee Newitz, "Let's Face It: *True Blood* Hates Gay People," *io9*, accessed August 24, 2011, http://io9.com/#!5071755/lets-face-it-true-blood-hates-gay-people.
121 Leefonthewind from the comments of "*True Blood* General Gabbery >> 3–9: "Everything Is Broken [Forum]," *Television Without Pity*, accessed August 24, 2011, http://forums.televisionwithoutpity.com/index.php?showtopic=3197707&st=195.
122 Sarkeesian, "Beyond *True Blood*'s Sensationalism."
123 Gabe, "Can the *True Blood* Metaphor Get Any More Fucked Up?"
124 Ball, "From Dusk Til Dawn."
125 Ibid.
126 Michael J. Yaksich, "Consuming Queer: The Commodification of Culture and its Effects on Social Acceptance," *Elements* (Spring 2005): 25.
127 Case, "Tracking the Vampire," 3.
128 Ibid.
129 Halberstam, *Skin Shows*, 27.

7

True Blood Truebies: *True Blood* Fans and Comic Book Covers

David Huxley

Fans of the HBO television *True Blood* series, which first aired in September 2008, call themselves "truebies." This appellation seems to be a badge of honor and there is not (as yet) the kind of division that developed between "trekkies" and "trekkers," which sought to divide the younger, simpler *Star Trek* fans from those who saw themselves as more sophisticated and analytical. The choice of term, with its aural and linguistic associations with "true," is enticingly ambiguous given that the series is an adaptation of Charlaine Harris's Southern Vampire Mysteries novels. The series is thus neither "true" in the sense of being "real" or "genuine" — it is a spin-off, a copy, a version of the original — or "true" in the sense of being "faithful," for the series makes substantive changes to Harris's original, in keeping with its desire to appeal to an adult audience of both genders (in contrast to Harris's paranormal romances which have a predominantly female market and fan base). In the world of fandom such subtle distinctions are perhaps irrelevant, with fans pledging allegiance to the vampire world which has captured their interest and loyalty. Nevertheless, given that "truebies" are vocal in terms of the pros and cons of fresh adaptations arising from the television series, these issues of the relationship between source and spin-off are pertinent. One such adaptation or spin-off of the *True Blood* HBO series is the comic book arising from it, which both draws on the source material of the series and embellishes and departs from it in a variety of ways. This chapter will consider the conception and design of this comic book adaptation by its creators, and its ensuing reception by "truebies." A specific focus on selected comic book covers provides a useful means of considering the complex issues of adaptation and fandom in a clear and detailed way.

Adaptation and Authenticity

In any transition from one medium to another there is inevitably a debate about the issue of authenticity in relation to the original source. While the televised *True Blood* had already been adapted from The Southern Vampire Mysteries novels of Charlaine Harris, in the context of this discussion of the comic book adaptation the "original" will be taken to be the television series, created by successful writer Alan Ball (*Six Feet Under*). Given the popularity of the series it was perhaps inevitable that it should be adapted into other media, both to satisfy "trubies" and to attract new fans through a merchandizing drive that also included bottles of "Tru Blood" (a soft drink rather than the human blood substitute of the program). The comic book adaptation of the series was launched at the San Diego comic convention in July 2010.

The central characters from the series are also prominent in the comic book, covering its possible demographic with two strong female characters, one of whom is black, four male characters of varying ages and supernatural abilities, and a gay black male. Sookie, Tara, Bill, Eric, Jason, Sam, and Lafayette all feature on the comic book covers, as does another, more minor character, eighteen-year-old new vampire Jessica Hamby. Significantly, some of the characters who feature fairly prominently in the television series do not feature in the comic or its covers. These include Sam's main barmaid, Arlene, and law enforcement officer Andy Bellefleur. While these characters are as integral to the show as Jessica Hamby, their exclusion from the comic book seems to be based largely on the fact that they are not as young or attractive as either Jessica or the other central characters. This suggests that the appeal of the comic may be a marketing ploy directed at the younger proportion of the show's demographic — or, at least, at the potential comic book reader who is as interested in the sexual attractiveness of *True Blood*'s characters as the supernatural and mythological elements of the show, perhaps signaling a divide in "truebie" tastes and loyalties.

The narrative of the comic uses the device of putting the major characters of the series into one of the key locations — Sam's bar, Merlottes. There, an energy-sucking entity forces them to reveal secrets from their past so that he can feed off their pain. This device allows these stories to be removed from the main narrative flow of the television program, although the back-stories are certainly plausible to those familiar with the television series. For example, Sookie reveals her parents' fear of her powers before their early death; Eric tells of the death of a human he loved at the time of the Inquisition; and Lafayette laments that the discovery of his homosexuality by his unbalanced, deeply religious mother leads to her final mental breakdown. In the final episode Bill confesses that during the Civil War he bit and killed the sister of one of his comrades and the entity uses the power he has gained from the misery of others to send a huge bolt of energy at Eric. The vampire survives and the story ends on a teaser for the next series, with Eric telling Sookie that he is being hunted by an insane vampire, and that they are all in danger again.

Few successful fantasy television series in recent years have not been adapted into the comic book form, and several, such as *Star Trek*, *Xena: Warrior Princess* and *Buffy the Vampire Slayer*, have been highly successful. The question remains whether these comics appeal to the original fans of the television series, or whether they extend the appeal of the program to a new audience. It was certainly the case that there was some resistance from "trubies" who regarded the comic book as perhaps a "lesser" medium than television. Fan sites and blogs provide an insight into "truebie" reaction. For some fans, the comic books hold little appeal; for example, Tiffany, who took the time to post that she was "not into comic books and doubt i would buy."[1] Other fans display the kind of blind devotion previously associated with media fandom as indiscriminate consumers prior to the birth of the "prosumer" (proactive consumer). For example, MsStabby, commenting on the previews of the comic covers, declared that she was "a spazzy TB [*True Blood*] fan girl with squee to spare, but hmmmmmmmm. I'm undecided on these. Perhaps they look different in life?"[2]

Acceptance of the comic book appears to center around whether "truebies" can agree on the "authenticity" of the comic book, which, for fans of the television series, appears dependant on the involvement of the show's originators. Liz, responding to an accusation that Alan Ball was copying Joss Whedon, the creator of *Buffy the Vampire Slayer*, replies:

> Alan Ball has enough talent NOT to NEED to copy anyone! In fact, he really made *True Blood* his own thing, much better than the books. I could buy the comic, if he's the one who wrote it...[3]

The above quotation demonstrates a deeper loyalty to Alan Ball's vision in translating *True Blood* to television, again reinforcing the notion of the television series as authorial original. However, for another fan, Isolde, the comic book represents a step too far:

> So this is a comic book based on a television show based (somewhat) on a book series. Hm. Sounds about half-step up from fan fiction to me, but whatever floats your boat. BTW – my vote goes to whichever cover shows more delicious Eric![4]

Isolde's comments speak of the complex attitudes and engagements of fans. A contempt for fan fiction as a lesser genre, and a perception of the cycle of adaptation as a process which steadily dilutes the original works, is set against the willingness to participate in any activity which will feed the professed obsession with Eric as hero and sex symbol.

In spite of the "truebie" unease evident within fan sites and blogs, the comic nevertheless achieved financial success. As True Blood Net asserted in 2010:

> The first series broke sales records when it debuted this year, which makes perfect sense considering the graphic novels were created as a means to keep Truebies up-to-date on their favorite characters' secret lives once the cameras stopped rolling each season.[5]

One of the key debates engaged in by fans of the series and the comic book revolves around depictions of sexuality. The television series of *True Blood* distinguished itself from two of its major precursors, *Buffy the Vampire Slayer* and *Twilight*, in that its major characters are not teenagers. Combined with its transmission on the HBO cable channel, famed for productions such as *The Sopranos*, *Six Feet Under* and *Generation Kill*, the adult characters featured in *True Blood* have allowed the show to deal with the sexual aspects of the vampire myth much more explicitly than some of its recent predecessors. Heightened and frequently unconventional, sexual appetites and desires are, of course, part of vampire mythology and are a constant in the vast majority of vampire literature, to one extent or another. Although Bram Stoker might not recognize the description, the most famous vampire novel of all, *Dracula*, has been summarized by Maurice Richardson as being: "a kind of incestuous, necrophilious, oral-anal-sadistic all in wrestling match."[6]

Indeed it can be difficult to totally de-sexualize the vampire. When writing *Salem's Lot*, Stephen King declared that he "decided to largely jettison the sexual angle," yet the intrinsic sexuality of the myth still pervades both his novel and the television film based on it.[7] Publicity for, and reviews of, *True Blood* rarely fail to note its more adult or sexual approach to the portrayal of vampires. In 2009 *SFX* magazine announced that *"True Blood* isn't just sexy, it's positively raunchy."[8] The official press release for the comics emphasized that the comic series was intended to appeal to fans who appreciated the television show's sexual content, stating that they would be a "sexy, visually striking comic series," and that the "first six-issue *True Blood* comic series offers the same erotically-charged romance, wry humor and intriguing mystery and suspense the show has become known for."[9]

However, there has been some disagreement among fans about the extent to which the comic replicates the sexual atmosphere of the show. In May 2010, fan Meredith Woerner claimed that:

> First six pages of the *True Blood* comic are just as dirty as the show. Check out the four different covers, and the first six pages, of IDW Publishing's *True Blood* comic. We're happy to find that it's just as wonderfully pervy as our favorite vam-

pire show, including almost see-through sketches of Sookie's work-wear in the rain.[10]

However, another fan, Shini: R.O.A.C.H., replies: "They didn't strike me as dirty at all. My meter for such things may be calibrated high, though. Seems like a pretty good read, but not that dirty yet."[11]

It is not just the sexual content that some fans see as being reduced in the comic book. On the fan site *The Vault (The True Blood Fansite that Satisfies your Bloodlust since 2008)* a review explains that in the comic:

> They stay true to their characters, even if their foul language is downplayed significantly. For the fans of the show, it's a lot of fun to see these guys on the paneled page. That said, the lack of profanity in *True Blood* comic #1 is definitely noticeable. The HBO series is well known for its risqué subject matter – heck, that's what draws viewers on a weekly basis ...[12]

Despite missing the bad language and some of the sexual content of the show, the overall response to the comic is positive, producing recommendations that fans of the show should buy it. The comments of fans provide a fascinating insight into the sense of ownership many "trubies" feel in relation to the television series. Criticisms of the comics revolve around a perceived lack of authenticity and fidelity to the television series, with fans posting their comments in order to defend and protect the series. Likewise, fans praise the comics when the adaptation is seen to reflect the aims of the series and to offer an enhanced understanding of the characters, as in the amplification of the television characters' back stories.

The Collector, The Investor, and the Variant Cover

Comic books have been, since the 1960s, an increasingly active area for the collector and investor. Russell Belk argues that the collector is different to the "bricoleur," who "accumulates potentially useful things, whereas the collector acquires things without use."[13] Belk continues to differentiate between the collector and the connoisseur, claiming that "the amateur collector is a passionate subjective consumer, while the connoisseur is a rational objective expert."[14] Fans of *True Blood*, it can be argued, might fall into the category of amateur collectors, in their extended engagement with the show via bottles of the "Tru Blood" drink and action figures of the stars. Comics add a further collectible to this list, and although the issue of whether all these items are "without use" is open to question, it is certainly the case that they have the potential to increase in value, and thus may be bought by the collector as an investment. A further way of attracting investors to the comics is the variant cover, which became very popular in the comic book industry in America during the 1990s. Variant covers can obviously be viewed as a cynical marketing ploy — as a way of maximizing revenue by appealing to "completists," and persuading collectors to buy multiple copies in the hope that one particular cover may prove to be a particularly good investment. The rise in value of rare or desirable editions of comic books has made it a medium that has attracted increasing levels of interest amongst investors. This has arguably led to the process of "slabbing," whereby a comic's condition is definitively graded and then it is sealed in plastic to preserve and maintain its continuing value. While modern comics are unlikely to see the dramatic rise in value of *Action Comics* number one (DC comics, 1938) — from ten cents to over a million dollars in seventy years — Bradford Wright notes that "[B]y the 1990s, comic books had become the nation's third largest collectible market, just after coins and stamps."[15] Thus, to a large degree the purchasers of the comics may not be considered fans, either of comics or any given subject matter.

True Blood Covers

The variant covers of the *True Blood* comic series can broadly be divided into three types: caricatured (often in a slightly manga style); photographic; and "photo-based," in which although the image is drawn it relies very heavily on photographic sources (and indeed may be partially photographic in origin). Photographic comic covers are by no means a new phenomenon. They make the most obvious claim to authenticity and were widely used by Dell comics in the 1950s and 1960s for its tie-in titles, particularly television westerns such as *Maverick* and *Have Gun, Will Travel*, and indeed for Gold Key's 1970s vampire tie-in series, *Dark Shadows*. Of course there is a potential mismatch between these covers and the interior artwork, although Dell tended to use experienced artists who could catch a likeness, such as Dan Speigle and Alberto Giolitti.

True Blood covers produced by David Messina, in particular, not only have a broadly photographic feel but are also in much the same style as the more recognizable interior artwork of a comic book. The advent of computer coloring and image manipulation has allowed the line between the photographic and the drawn to be blurred. Messina's artwork will sometimes feature photographic backgrounds, and the line artwork with its flat colors is reminiscent of the effect in the film *Through a Scanner Darkly*, where live action footage was manipulated to give the appearance of animation. In contrast, J. Scott Campbell's covers demonstrate a much more angular, manga-influenced style. By the third printing of Issue One there were 13 different covers available, but if minor design and color variations are ignored there are six different images: Cover A (Messina); Cover B (Campbell); Cover C (Currie); Cover D (Corroney); a photographic cover; and a wraparound cover by Messina based on a *True Blood* poster. Some of these, such as the latter cover, were only available at particular conventions or shops.

The cover of a comic book, like a movie poster, is there to sell a product and to entice readers. In comic books adapted from television series the main character or characters tend to be displayed for the viewer's delectation, often appearing to look back, or return, the viewer's gaze. Here there are two key gazes: the potentially scopophilic view of the reader and the gaze of the characters back at the reader. There is at least one other gaze, which is that between the comic characters portrayed on the cover, but in the main that is an element I will not focus on in this analysis.

The "gaze-back," or "extra-diagetic gaze" — from the character in a photograph, drawn image or painting — can be crucial. Yet, as art critic John Frederick Anderson has pointed out, "[T]here remains to be done a major study on the dynamic between the viewer and the object in photography."[16] For the purpose of this analysis, the photographic and drawn or painted image, assuming that the latter depicts clearly recognizable characters, will be treated as broadly the same. In practice, of course, it might well be argued that the mimetic quality of the photographic portrait — giving a fan the sense that this actor was there and, "posed for my benefit" — could be seen as having a greater cachet for fans. Nevertheless, I would argue that both kinds of images carry a broadly similar appeal. Various authors have considered some of the implications of images, in which the "viewed" appear to "look back" at the viewer in both photographic and painted forms. Feminist scholar Maria Buszek comments on the different meanings in two photographs of the nineteenth-century poet, actress and activist Adah Menken. In one she is shown at a desk, writing, looking down, her head in her hand as she contemplates her work. In the other her image is totally different:

> Menken smiles shyly up at the viewer, eyes peering through her eyelashes from her slightly downcast face. Appearing as if caught momentarily exposing her face ... the notorious Menken successfully represents herself in the role of a shy and submissive object of desire – the thinking-man's crumpet, perhaps ...[17]

Art critic John Berger argues that the expression of the observed figure, whether it is a painted nude or a modern pin-up, has a specific meaning:

> Compare the expressions of these two women: one the model for a famous painting by Ingres and the other a model for a photograph in a girlie magazine. Is not the expression remarkably similar in each case? It is the expression of a woman responding with calculated charm to the man whom she imagines looking at her — although she doesn't know him. She is offering up her femininity as the surveyed.[18]

The situation with the *True Blood* covers is even more complex; we have to take into account the gaze of not just female but also male protagonists, the clothes they are wearing (on covers at least they are not naked), and possibly the fact that the gender and sexual orientation of the viewer may vary.

The issue four Joe Corroney cover B portrays Sookie in the foreground with a tray of the "Tru Blood" drink, with a large image of Bill in the background. Both gaze back at the reader, Sookie with wide-open eyes; but Bill, with half-closed eyes, glowers much more threateningly. The sexual appeal of the vampire can of course be masochistic and on this cover Bill's threatening gaze might be as appealing to his fans (female or male) as a more conventional "come-hither" look, whilst on the other hand, it also positions the reader as a rival vampire, given the presence of the "Tru Blood" beverage and Sookie's reaction and role as waitress. From the very first issue of the comic, fans have discussed the covers in some detail, happy with the wider choice, but not all in agreement as to which constitute the most desirable covers. Indeed, fan Mandi Bierly comments: "Were I to purchase one, it would be the Disney-fied Cover B … Cover C just features Tara, Jason and Sam (How pissed would you be if that was the only one left to purchase?)." However, Darcy replies: "I like the Sam, Tara, Jason cover." Fan Orville adds: "I like the one with Sam — he's one of my favorite characters. Gotta love a guy who can sub as an adorable pet."[19] The covers therefore serve to draw out fan preference and individual tastes in relation to the large cast of characters.

Of course, when examining online reaction, response and discussion, it is not possible to be absolutely certain whether fans are male or female. It is possible to guess at their gender from the usernames they adopt, but in the virtual world of pseudonyms and avatars there is a level of uncertainty. Yet, in a sense gender identification is not vital. The fans' responses indicate the appeal of various characters and specific images; whether that fan is female, male, bisexual, or gay is not central to this investigation. This is not to say that these issues are not interesting, or that program makers or comic book producers are not aware of the potential appeal to gay audiences, for example, of certain characters or storylines. Season Three of *True Blood* introduced a gay vampire king, Russell Edgington and his partner. This season also includes a gay love scene featuring one of the show's most brutal vampires, Eric, although his motives are revealed to be motivated by revenge rather than sexual desire. Several covers in the comic series contain all seven central characters — Bill and Sookie, Eric, Sam, Lafayette,

Tara and Jason — but the three most commonly fore-grounded characters remain Bill, Sookie and Eric.

Cover A (Messina) of issue three of the series combines both the gaze-back and the masochistic sexual element of the vampire legend. Sookie stares at the reader, wide-eyed again, as Bill, standing behind her, this time bites her neck. He looks up too, glowering again, and blood is clearly visible on the wounds on her neck. Her open, frank gaze at the reader makes her compliant in the act of vampirism, and it also draws the reader into feeling complicit in the act. She holds his arm protectively, and the image begins to hint at the anti-vampire prejudice elements of the television show, with Sookie appearing as an unashamed "fang banger," as the show describes humans who have sex with vampires.

Drawing Style and Meaning

The visualization of the *True Blood* characters in the comic raises a whole series of issues. Some of these echo problems in casting the show, and meeting expectations of the fan base of the original Southern Vampire Mysteries novels. Fans of any given novel are likely to have formed a mental picture of the main characters. Alan Ball explained that "in casting, there was more of a focus on who would portray the character in a compelling way rather than who would physically resemble the characters from the book."[20] Thus the makers of the show were very aware of this phenomenon, to the extent that they talk of "physical resemblance" to characters who at that stage just existed on the written page. In producing the comic the artists had perhaps an even more pressing problem: how close should their images be to the physical appearance of the stars of the show? Some fans seem to have been particularly taken with the likeness of key characters. Thus Sarah comments: "I'm loving comic book Eric!! Hott!! I'm going to catch all kinds of crap from my husband when I buy these but I don't care!!"[21] Here the "comic book Eric" seems to have taken on a separate life that the fan seems to find even more engaging than the "original" television version.

However, if comics are drawn in a broad "cartooning" style, or in the increasingly popular Japanese "manga" style, then the characters will inevitably be only vaguely reminiscent of any photographic original. Although it may be too broad a generalization to say that manga-style artwork appeals to a younger generation of comic fans, it is certainly the case that the *Twilight* graphic novel by Young Kim, which appeared in the same year as the first *True Blood* comic, is in a manga style. This means that it looks very different to the *True Blood* comic. The stylization of eyes and noses, in particular, means that in Kim's rendering the central characters bear only a vague resemblance to their real life incarnations, Robert Pattinson as Edward Cullen and Kirsten Stewart as Bella Swan. Whilst this is potentially a problem for fans of the live action series, in more general terms, and for some kinds of fans, it may not be such a problem. Scott McCloud, in one of the first serious attempts to analyze the structure and nature of the comic book form, argues that: "by de-emphasizing the appearance of the physical world in favor of the idea of form, the cartoon places itself in the world of concepts." He writes that, "When drawing the face ... nearly all comic artists apply at least some small measure of cartooning," and concludes that this simplification "allows readers to mask themselves in a character and safely enter a sensually stimulating world."[22]

Thus, perhaps the readers of the *Twilight* graphic novel may experience a different kind of pleasure to viewers of the film. While the audience of the *True Blood* series (and perhaps readers of the *True Blood* comic) recognize, admire and gaze on simulacra of their favorite characters, with the *Twilight* graphic novel fans arguably project their emotions onto more physically ambiguous figures who act as ciphers.

Fan Mandi Bierly also sees this kind of "masking" or identification in Scott Campbell's *True Blood* cover B, for issue number one. She comments:

> Judging how Sookie looks nothing like Anna Paquin while the other characters are at least close to their actors. I suspect the artist was purposely trying to distance her so women who want to pretend *they* are Sookie could.[23]

Here a fan has instinctively come to the same conclusion as proposed by McCloud after a great deal of consideration and research. If they are both correct, it would seem that the less a character in a comic looks like the actual actor on which it is based, the better it is for fans who want to put themselves in the shoes of that character.

Yet many fans of the *True Blood* comic are certainly concerned about the physical accuracy of the representations of their favorite characters. For example, orville comments on the first issue cover (Campbell): "Is the woman in the one on the top left really meant to be Sookie? Looks more like Pam to me for some reason" (Pam is Eric Northman's assistant).[24] Indeed, the whole issue of likenesses divides fans, with Lee Rodriguez articulating similar views to McCloud in relation to the first issue:

> The art is okay, albeit inconsistent. There's nothing wrong with the panel layouts or the actual storytelling. Unfortunately, Messina falls into the trap many artists do when adapting a television or film property in that there's clearly a strong focus on nailing the actors' likenesses over creating a definitive visual take on the established characters. The result in this issue are panels that look like Anna Paquin and Alexander Skarsgard talking to each other followed by a panel of Stephen Moyer talking to a version of Anna Paquin who's been left in the microwave a little too long.[25]

Consistent likenesses are extremely difficult in any lengthy comic, and this seems a little harsh on Messina, whose artwork is, in the main, highly effective. Some of the flashback sequences in the comics are done by other artists (for example, Elena Casagrande in issue two, Serena Ficca in issue three), but these sequences require less accuracy in the way of likenesses, and the difference in style is normally not jarring. When the flashback and the contemporary scenes appear on the same page, however, the effect is more disconcerting. In the last two panels on the first page of the last episode (issue six) Bill, as drawn by Messina, transforms into a much more angular, cartoony version of himself in exactly the same pose as when the flashback begins. In effect, then, we have two "Bills" on the same page, occupying two different universes, thus drawing attention to the "device" and to the artificial nature of the drawing process itself.

Conclusion

Fan responses to the comic book series of *True Blood* have been ambivalent. Narrative styles, drawing styles, the problem of likenesses, and, indeed, the cost of buying multiple copies have all been criticized. However, through the power of their cover imagery and their contribution to the backstories of characters, these comics arguably provide a kind of pleasure for fans which is different from their direct enjoyment of the original television series. At their best, comics are able not just to imitate another media source, but to add to it with the creation of iconic images and scenes of key characters; and, if McCloud is right, at times it may provide a "masking" experience that brings readers closer to their favorite characters. It is possible that the *True Blood* comics might provide an afterlife for the characters in the same way that the *Buffy* comics have done for that series.

Whilst the show continues to be screened, the comics perform a different function. Actor Michael McMillian, who played Steve Newlin in the first series of the show and wrote the second comic book series, "Tainted Love," describes the relationship:

> The comics aren't entirely independent of the show, but obviously the show is the main *True Blood* storyline. We're the supporting act. The comic is a great way to expand the mythology and explore certain corridors of the True Blood world that the show may perhaps leave untouched.[26]

McMillian has also addressed fan criticism — of the first series of the comic — regarding its downplaying of sexual content and bad language. He argues that he and co-writer Marc Andreyko "haven't really censored ourselves as writers ... I'm not opposed to dropping the f-bomb, but too many times and you start to look lazy. Bad words can lead to redundant writing, so I try to keep it fresh on my end."[27] Marc Andreyko adds:

> Sex is a huge part of *True Blood*, both from a narrative standpoint and metaphorically, so eliminating it from the comics would be a conspicuous absence. That being said, we are not doing 'adult comics' here ... less is much more when it comes to moments of graphic sex or violence.[28]

While some fans fear that, without proper editorial control, the comics could move away from, or dilute, the original concept (whether that is taken to be the original novels or the television series), reader response also shows that the comics still have the potential to become an important part of the *True Blood* canon, providing a different, yet significant, form of pleasure for the dedicated "truebie."

Notes

1 Tiffany, May, 16, 2010 (7:50 p.m.), comment on Mandi Bierly, "'True Blood' Comic Book Series Coming in July, Hold On To Your Fangs, Or Fang," *Entertainment Weekly*, May 13, 2010, http://popwatch.ew.com/2010/05/13/true-blood-comic-book-series/.
2 MsStabby, 14 May, 2010 (5:44 p.m.), comment on Meredith Woerner, "First Six Pages of the True Blood Comic are Just as Dirty as the Show," *io9, We Come From the Future*, 13 May, 2010, http://io9.com/5538531/first-six-pages-of-the-true-blood-comic.
3 Liz, May 12, 2010 (5:08 p.m.), comment on Mandi Bierly, "'True Blood' Comic Book Series Coming in July, Hold On To Your Fangs, Or Fang," *Entertainment Weekly*, May 13, 2010, http://popwatch.ew.com/2010/05/13/true-blood-comic-book-series/.
4 Isolde, 13 May, 2010 (5:43 p.m.) comment on Mandi Bierly, "'True Blood' Comic Book Series Coming in July, Hold On To Your Fangs, Or Fang," *Entertainment Weekly*, May 13, 2010, http://popwatch.ew.com/2010/05/13/true-blood-comic-book-series/.
5 Maurice Richardson, quoted in Clive Leatherdale, *Dracula: The Novel and the Legend: A Study of Bram Stoker's Gothic Masterpiece* (Wellingborough, UK: Aquarian Press, 1985), 144.
6 Richardson, in Leatherdale, 144.
7 Tara Bennett, "Yours Truly," *SFX Special Edition: Vampires* (Bath: Future Publishing, 2009), 86.
8 CBR News Team, "IDW, HBO Announce 'True Blood' Comic," *Comic Book Resources*, Friday, April 2, 2010, http://www.comicbookresources.com/?page=article&id=25537.
9 CBR News Team, "IDW, HBO Announce 'True Blood' Comic."
10 Meredith Woerner, "First Six Pages of the True Blood Comic are Just as Dirty as the Show," *io9, We Come From the Future*, May 13, 2010, http://io9.com/5538531/first-six-pages-of-the-true-blood-comic.
11 Shini: R.O.A.C.H, 13 May, 2010 (3:27 p.m.), comment on Meredith

Woerner, "First Six Pages of the *True Blood* Comic are Just as Dirty as the Show," *io9, We Come From the Future*, 13 May, 2010, http://io9.com/5538531/first-six-pages-of-the-true-blood-comic..

12. Lynnpd, "Review: True Blood Comic Book No. 1," *The Vault*, July 16, 2010, http://www.trueblood-online.com/?s=review%3A+true+blood+comic+book+no+1.
13. Russell W. Belk, *Collecting in a Consumer Society, Collecting Cultures* (Oxford and New York: Routledge, 1995), 45.
14. Belk, 45.
15. Bradford W. Wright, *Comic Book Nation: The Transformation of Youth Culture in America* (Baltimore, MD: John Hopkins University, 2003), 279.
16. John Frederick Anderson, "The Gaze in Portraiture," *Reveal*, accessed 23 August, 2011, http://www.dshed.net/digitised/reveal/resources/the_gaze_adv_part1.html.
17. Maria Elena Buszek, *Pin-Up Grrrls: Feminism, Sexuality, Popular Culture* (Durham, NC: Duke University Press, 2006), 49.
18. John Berger, *Ways of Seeing* (Harmondsworth: Penguin Books, 1972), 55.
19. Mandi Bierley, "'True Blood' Comic Book Series Coming in July, Hold on to your Fangs, Or Fang," *Entertainment Weekly*, May 13, 2010, http://popwatch.ew.comic/2010/05/13/true-blood-comic-book-series/.
20. Heather Day, "*True Blood* Comics are a Mega Hit," *True Blood Net*, December 10, 2010, http://truebloodnet.com/true-blood-comic-books-mega-hit/.
21. Sarah, 13 May, 2010 (2:19 p.m.), comment on Lividity, "True Blood Comic Book, 4 Covers + Inside Pages," *True Blood News, The Place To Feed Your Obsession*, May 13, 2010, http://www.trueblood-news.com/true-blood-comic-book-4-covers.
22. Scott McCloud, *Understanding Comics* (Northampton, MA.: Kitchen Sink Press, 1993), 42–3.
23. Mandi Bierley, "True Blood comic book series coming in July."
24. Orville, 14 May, 2010 (6:37 a.m.), comment on Mandi Bierly, "'True Blood' Comic Book Series Coming in July, Hold On To Your Fangs, Or Fang," *Entertainment Weekly*, May 13, 2010, http://popwatch.ew.com/2010/05/13/true-blood-comic-book-series/.
25. Lee Rodriguez, "True Blood #1," *Panels on Pages.com*, July 20, 2010, http://panelsonpages.com/?p=25980.
26. Gianna Sobel, "An Interview with Michael McMillian," *HBO, Inside True Bood Blog*, February 18, 2011, http://www.inside-true-blood-blog.com/.
27. Shaun Manning, "McMillan & Andreyko Spill 'True Blood'," *Comic Book Resources*, March 1, 2011, http://www.comicbookresources.com/?page=article&id=31073.
28. Manning.

Place and Identity

8

Knit One, Bite One: Vampire Fandom, Fan Production and Feminine Handicrafts

Brigid Cherry

The first images of vampires and vampire fandom that come to mind are unlikely to involve knitting needles, yarns and patterns. Nevertheless, in the thriving world of feminine handicrafts, vampires have come, in recent years, to occupy a well-loved source of inspiration for knitting, crochet and other handicraft projects, as well as an extremely commercial niche for entrepreneurial fans who sell vampire-themed home-spun and hand-dyed yarns and their own patterns. Furthermore, the launch at Comic-Con 2010 in San Diego of the book *Vampire Knits*, a collection of vampire, werewolf and gothic themed knitting patterns, draws attention to the way in which feminine handicrafts are gaining a higher profile as a significant fan activity.[1] Taken alongside pre-existing female followings for vampire film and fiction, the publication of a pattern book and its marketing at a major fan event recognizes a significant niche market. *Vampire Knits* is typical of a vast range of fan handicrafting already taking place. The recognition of handicrafts alongside other forms of female fan production, such as fan fiction (fanfic), music video (vidding) and costuming (cosplay), represents an opportunity to explore the ways in which gendered fan production is subject to socialization, politicization, eroticization and commodification.

Knitting a Vampire Fan Culture

In researching fan knitting (this is part of a wider study also focusing on *Harry Potter*, *Doctor Who*, *Alice in Wonderland* and *Lord of the Rings* knitting culture), participant observation and data collection has been carried out within the Ravelry online community for knitters, crocheters, spinners, weavers and designers.[2] This member-only community was formed in 2007 and has quickly grown in size and recognition: by November 2010 over a million members had joined and in the same month it won the .net Magazine Awards 2010 Community Site of the Year (beating Twitter and Facebook). Of paramount importance in selecting Ravelry as the focus of the data collection is that it works as a closed and close-knit social space for anyone with an interest in feminine handicrafts. The site consists of a database providing searchable information on four key areas: a) yarns; yarn companies and stores; books and magazines, and patterns; b) an e-commerce marketplace where members can sell their own patterns (or advertise goods that they sell on other online market sites such as Etsy) and buy Ravelry branded T-shirts, bags, badges, mugs and glasswear; c) a social network with member profiles (these allow for the recording of yarn stash and project progress as well as friending and personal messaging); and d) a forum where members can join groups reflecting their own specific interests and take part in group discussion or chat with like-minded members on those topics.

It is the personal projects and forums that have been the particular focus for data collection in this research. In terms of the empirical research design, discussion can be tracked in threads on specific topics and, since it is archived and searchable, can be traced forwards and backwards in time; postings by individual members can also be tracked across groups. Whilst the personal projects reflect the member's fan interests, it is in the groups that fan knitting communities emerge. Members can set up groups on any topic and whilst many of these are dedicated to brands of yarn, local knitting groups or stores, indie dyers, sock yarn clubs, specific books or patterns, techniques and groups for learners, and yarn swaps, there are almost 19,000 groups in total dedicated to everything from family and homecare (for example, cooking) to jobs and workplace, to the media and arts, as well as groups for those who identify as Pagan, Catholic or Muslim, gay, lesbian and bisexual, Goth, tattooed, over 50, and so on. Popular culture is reflected in many groups: for example, there are 44 film groups, 53 for television, 40 on comics and graphic novels, 39 on popular novels and novelists, 18 for science fiction and 21 for the horror genre. Specific texts are well represented, from soap operas such as *Neighbours* to pop music performers such as Lady Gaga. There are a total of 61 groups chatting about various aspects of the Harry Potter series alone.

Vampire fandom is well catered for within the Ravelry community; there are 46 groups dedicated to vampires in fiction and popular culture. These groups differ in both size – with memberships ranging from several thousand to less than 10 – and levels of activity – with postings varying anywhere between 145 posts in a 24-hour period (this was around the transmission of the Season Three finale of *True Blood* in a specific episode thread in the True Blood group) to less than ten posts a week in the discussion as a whole in less active groups. The largest of these groups are the ones dedicated to vampire texts in general: Blood and Yarn (with 860 members), Crocheters Darkly Dreaming (959), Horror Knits (1068), Vampires Purrrl (225) and Paranormal Romance Novel Fans (187). In terms of activity levels, groups focused on specific examples of current vampire fiction and media are the most active at any one time; unsurprisingly, current texts generate the most interest. During the period of the research there were 24 Twilight saga groups, six *True Blood* and two *Vampire Diaries* groups, and one group each for *Being Human*, *Sanctuary* and *Supernatural* (all of which feature recurring vampire characters or monsters). Similar groups exist for other recent novels or television series, as well as older cult series and films, including *Buffy the Vampire Slayer* and *Angel*, *Moonlight*, *Blood Ties*, *Interview with the Vampire*, *The Vampire Chronicles*, *Dark Shadows*, *House of Night* and *Black Dagger*. There are also geographical or national groups for contemporary series; for example, the existence of the True Blood UK group reflects the fact that British fans fall out of the spatio-temporal rhythms of the US-based discussion due to the different national broadcast dates and scheduling patterns.[3]

Just as in fan culture generally, distinct communities form around specific tastes, such as favorite characters, desired relationships, and beloved actors. Breaking down the Twilight saga groups further, there is a main group (Twilight Saga Fans with 3603 members); a group of Twilight saga fan fiction readers (Unicorns Unlimited which has 538 members); groups for specific characters or actors (♥Edward Cullen♥ has 282 members – in comparison, groups for the characters Bella, Carlisle and Jacob have under ten members each, making it clear where the interest lies amongst these fans); a group for Teenage Twilighters with 91 members and another for Twilight Kids with 33 members (discussion on the main Twilight boards tends to contain material only suitable for adults); and a group for the not-fans (Sparkles Aren't Our Thing which has 121 members). Other groups are for discussion of specific films or books in the Twilight saga (Breaking Dawn Lovers, for instance, with 61 members); for crossover interest (Bella v Harry, for example, which has 116 members); or for quirky and light-hearted groups (such as The Twilight Chocaholics with 30 members). It is not possible to say for certain without further intensive research exactly how many women who handicraft consider themselves to be fans or participate in "fannish" activities, or indeed how many fans practice handicrafting, but the snapshot presented here suggests that there is a significant community of fan handicrafters with an interest in vampire fiction and media. The account that follows draws on observations of the discussion groups noted above, online interviews with a selected sample of fans, and case studies which illustrate particular aspects of the activities and production being undertaken by the fan handicrafters.

The Politics of Feminine Handicrafting and Fandom

As Cornel Sandvoss outlines, fandom per se is not necessarily gendered, but specific fan interests, activities and communities are often marked out as feminine or masculine. Vampire fandom is a culture that has always attracted a significant female demographic.[4] The vampire has always held great appeal for female viewers (see Williamson for example),[5] and readerships for the Twilight saga and other paranormal romances are largely female.[6] It therefore follows that the associated fan communities will include activities that are accessible and attractive to female fans. For example, in her study of British vampire fans, Maria Mellins identifies the ways in which fashion, dress practices and performative identity are significant aspects of female fan culture.[7] Many female vampire and Gothic fans who express their identity through their dress and appearance, or take part in cosplay, make their own clothing and accessories. With handicrafting still regarded, for the most part, as a feminine activity, it is little wonder that female fandom and knitting have come together. As Genevieve Miller explains in her introduction to *Vampire Knits*:

> I'm a knitter who loves vampires — and I'm not the only one. I started out as your average knitter [but] it didn't take me long to find a group of knitters and designers who were similarly enthralled by modern day vampire stories. We fans of mysterious, brooding and sexy vampires shared ideas and inspirations with one another, creating patterns inspired by beloved immortal characters. And so the idea for this book was born.[8]

Although Miller does not say "We female fans," it is implicit in her book. The patterns are all designed by women, and — as with the membership of the other groups outlined above — the membership of the *Vampire Knits* group on Ravelry is predominantly (over 99%) female.

Gender is a primary factor in discourses of handicrafting. According to Debbie Stoller, knitting is frequently belittled as a traditionally women-centered activity. Handicrafts are seen as domestic activities linked to the home and women's lives.[9] Stoller's work, and the Stitch'n Bitch phenomenon that resulted, was a defining moment in feminine handicrafting and contributed to a resurgence of interest (including amongst men, although they remain a small minority of handicrafters).[10] With knitting traditionally considered to be a feminine pursuit, it follows that online knitting communities are predominantly female. This is important in considering knitting as a fan activity.

Henry Jenkins highlights that Web 2.0 has "made visible a set of cultural practices and logics [...] expanding their cultural influence by broadening and diversifying participation".[11] This, he points out, is "fandom without the stigma." Fan knitting, whilst it may include intensely fannish production (cosplay, for example), also broadens and diversifies participation within fandom. However, as Kristina Busse argues when discussing this mainstreaming of fan culture, the fannish behaviors encouraged when casual viewers engage with trans-media texts in the context of Web 2.0 should not be wholly conflated with fandom per se. She proposes instead the notion of "a continuum that acknowledges the more intense emotional and actual engagements of many TV viewers today without erasing the strong community structures which have developed through media fandom."[12] The fan knitters on Ravelry represent many trajectories (to borrow a term from Busse) of fannish activity. This includes knitters with intense emotional attachments to cultural texts that have no or little experience of fandom, as well as active members of participatory fan communities outside of Ravelry. The shared interest in knitting brings these "casual" fans into the same community as the "intense" fans, the latter bringing their knowledge and experience of the fandom itself (including sets of fan competencies and other "producerly" activities) into play. The fan knitting community thus works to create a sociable space for both fans and others with fannish interests. This creates a support network for knitters new to fandom and can be an intensely pleasurable shared experience for all the fan knitters.

Furthermore, as Beth Ann Pentney argues, the growth of interest in the fiber arts can be understood in the context of third-wave feminist practice.[13] Although Pentney rightly points out that not all knitting can or should be regarded as feminist, the practice of handicrafting as art or for personal pleasure needs to be understood in relation to "the complexities of being both critics and consumers of popular culture, as well as critics and participants in gendered spaces and subjectivities."[14] Although many of the vampire fan knitters would not identify themselves as feminist, they are taking pleasure in engaging with forms of popular culture in a gendered space, and this is significant in its own right. It is pertinent in this respect that the circulation, discussion and sharing of fan knitting is taking place largely within the spaces of the online handicrafting community, rather than within established (and possibly masculine) online fan communities. Whilst it is unrealistic to assume that fan knitting practices are unproblematically feminist, the expression of fandom and fan status within a handicrafting community (as opposed to a fan community) should be recognized as gendered fan practice reflexively organized around women's activities and pleasures. In many respects it is unsurprising that female fans congregate in such gendered spaces. As Busse points out in discussing geek hierarchies:

> [F]ans replicate negative outsider notions of what constitutes fannishness, often using similar feminizing and infantilizing concepts. Accusations of being too attached, too obsessed, too invested get thrown around readily, and all too often such affect is criticized for being too girly or like a teen.[15]

Women's fandom has been frequently "demoted" in the fan hierarchy in this way, especially with respect to young women's interests and their intense emotional responses (the Twilight saga is a case in point, evidenced by negative press reactions to the female audience "squeeing" over Edward).[16] Despite the opening up of fan culture in general to women, women's tastes and activities are still relegated to a subordinate status in many instances.

Knitting itself is similarly subordinated. Despite being reclaimed as feminist art and a trendy pastime, it is still often seen as a somewhat old-fashioned activity undertaken by "little old ladies" or grandmothers. This goes some way to explaining why fan handicrafters have a higher profile in the online knitting community than in online fandom (and clearly this may include a separation from the wider female fan communities). Whilst fan knitting clearly occupies the boundary between traditional hobby and fannish interests, in terms of sociability and community it exists largely within knitting and other handicrafting groups. In this respect, it can be argued that fan knitters are a community in their own right, related to and sharing members with, but also separate from, other areas of fandom or participatory culture. Though this is not an inherently feminist practice, it occupies a gendered position that the fans themselves have negotiated.

Projects of the Self and Eroticized Narratives

These fan knitters both participate in fannish activities and self-identify to varying extents as "fangirls." Some fan knitters may choose a Ravelry name which reflects their fan identity or interest in vampires; these include Blooferlady, Vampirate, Spikeknits, Acullen, Horrorchc and Horrorghoul. A larger number declare their fan interests in their avatars (or Ravatar); these might depict a favorite character, such as Eric or Edward, or contain an iconic image that suggests vampirism (pointed teeth, bite marks or blood droplets). Some even proclaim their team membership in a communal group activity, such as Team Bite Me in Nerd Wars, or Team Twilight in Ravelympics. Hills's notion of projects (or reflexive narratives) of the self, in which he suggests there are links between discourses of fandom and the fans' biographical sense of self, is informative here.[17] The status of being a fan, and not simply a fan *per se* but a female fan is overtly displayed within the Ravelry community. Furthermore, fan status is a defining characteristic in the sociability of these fan knitters, even when they have no experience of actual fan culture or typical fan competencies (which in any case may be deemed masculine fan traits). The expression of fan interest is orientated around the cultural texts themselves, as well as the handicrafting projects they inspire.

With respect to the latter, much fan knitting is inspired by texts. Close readings of novels or viewings of the films or television series offer opportunities to discuss the onscreen knitted items that might be copied or adapted. Fan knitters frequently create patterns (which they share within the community) for items worn or used by characters in their favorite texts. *Twilight*, being set in a cold climate, offers many opportunities for such text-related knitting, and popular patterns include Bella's mittens, baseball scarf and La Push hat, and Alice's arm warmers (several different patterns existing for each). By this means, the fan knitters can construct and express their fan identity in everyday life (the fan herself is aware of the significance and such items will be recognized by other fans), though because they are commonplace items of clothing without logos or branding they may well pass unnoticed as fan productions in daily life. For some, this may be useful in not overtly drawing attention to their status as a fan, and this might be especially significant where the fandom is one subject to ridicule (as the Twilight saga is). However, the evidence suggests that the fans are not particularly sensitive to such concerns, and they also create clearly branded items. These include several kinds of colorwork charts enabling fans to create items depicting book covers and font styles. Such items include the Be Safe iPod cover, Eclipse socks, Stupid Shiny Volvo Owner tote and the Team Cullen Crest hat. Fans creating these items express their love explicitly, and are not concerned about copyright issues — feeling, like the fans in Jenkins's *Textual Poachers*, that they have imaginative ownership by dint of their intense love for the text.[18]

Furthermore, such projects may be either personal or collective – the latter being organized group activities that enhance the sociability of the groups. The True Blood group members, for example, have participated in a knit-a-long (KAL) for the duration of each season's run of the television series (as well as organizing a Lafayette Afghan crochet-a-long), making the My Vampire Boyfriend socks during Season Two and the Tiger Eye Lace Scarf during Season Three. The knitters of the My Vampire Boyfriend sock all choose appropriately blood red yarn to make their socks, and often made reference to their attraction to the vampire characters Bill and Eric (and sometimes others such as Angel or Spike from *Buffy the Vampire Slayer*, suggesting these fan knitters' prior interests). For example, as Nogs comments on her project: "These days I'm feeling like my Vampire Boyfriend would be TB's Godric. Either him, or Puppet Angel :D (and always Spike and Eric as backup. OK, I'm greedy)." For the Season Three KAL, members of the group voted on which pattern to choose, the winner reflecting the popularity of the character Quinn, a weretiger introduced in the fifth *Southern Vampire Mysteries* novel *Dead As a Doornail*, even though the character had yet to appear in the television series. Some members felt this pattern should have been saved until the character "showed up on *True Blood*," but the voting does reflect the character's appeal to female readers (he is described as muscular, well over six feet tall, and olive-skinned, with deep purple eyes "like pansies.") Some members demonstrated their love for the character by naming their projects Quinn or Quinn's Eyes; one even labeled it Seduced by a Tiger (aka: Quinn's dreamy eyes), knitting it in warm oranges and brown or, in the latter case, purple. Others "adapted" it for a stronger vampiric theme, knitting it in shades of blood red, and naming their projects TruBlood, Eric, Jessica's Tears, or Midnight in a Louisiana Bayou.

In these indicative examples, the naming of projects and the comments in the notes section of project pages both work to create fan narratives. Such expressions of attraction to particular characters or favorite aspects of the text, work to flag fan status within Ravelry in general. More detailed discussion takes place within the group, and within specific threads. Like all fans, the fan knitters discuss each episode of the television series or film, and as in other fan communities they discuss their reactions and responses to narrative developments; they nitpick if they do not like the way a character or event is portrayed, and they frequently express the desirability of their favorite characters. As some of the examples from the *True Blood* KALs suggest, discussion often arises around the sexual appeal of the characters, evidenced by threads entitled More Skarsgard [sic] Nakedness in Upcoming True Blood and Shun, Shag or Marry: The Men of True Blood in the True Blood group (similar threads appear in the Twilight saga, *Vampire Diaries* and other groups).

Emphasizing the visual appeal of the characters, the groups also frequently contain threads for the sharing of pictures, for example the Sharing Pics of Twilight Guys in the Twilight Saga Fans group. Discussion of this kind contains typical female fan chat, and certainly eroticizes the text in ways that are not unique to the fan knitting community (see accounts of female fandom from Camille Bacon-Smith onwards).[19] Fan knitters create fan art using needles as others would use pencils or paint: they reproduce the likeness of favorite characters. Projects include crochet portrait panels of Edward and Jacob, a Twilight Illusion Knit portrayal of Edward and Bella (the image only appearing when the fabric is looked at from an angle, appearing plain when seen straight on), and amigurumi (crochet stuffed figures) of Edward. Moreover, fan narratives are often created around the projects. In exhibiting their fan-themed projects in the group threads or on their own project pages, fan knitters often stage or photoshop their knitted items with or alongside their favorite vampires. For example, Satonika — knitting for Team Bite Me in Nerd Wars — posts pictures of Eric Northman in the bath, from a Season One episode of *True Blood*, and then poses her bath set (a knitted washcloth with runes and crochet bath puff in light blue cotton to match both Eric's eyes and a sweater — extremely popular with the Eric fans — that he wore in episodes from Season Three) on the edge of a similar roll-top bath. Fans are already accomplished users of the internet and social networking, and such image making with screengrabs, publicity stills, other art work and their own photographs, echoes the remix culture also observed in vidding.

Spinning and Stitching Words

Jenkins identifies the creation and circulation of fan art such as the examples above as one of the key characteristics of fan cultures, blurring the boundaries between producers and consumers.[20] Fan knitting is clearly embedded in the social and eroticizes the text, as outlined above, but it is also significant that it can be a producerly activity that extends and reworks the narrative. As Jenkins asserts, fans involve themselves in the creative process by re-mediating and re-writing the text, and fan knitting exists at the heart of an intertextual relationship with the originating text. Fan films and fanfic are the predominant forms of fan production that re-mediate the narrative of the cult text. These frequently occupy an overt (if sometimes oblique) relationship to the original text and involve, for the most part, some form of narrative development. Kustritz points out that fan writing often serves to make the relationship with the characters more intimate by turning them into real people.[21] Fan knitting is similarly located in the interfaces between fan identity and character identity and the processes of projected interactivity result in the text becoming manifest for the fans. Though fan knitting cannot really be considered an intensive rewriting of the text, the fans' knitted objects can be directly tied into the text and even tell stories of their own. They certainly represent an intense emotional investment in the narrative. Furthermore, fan knitting is also sometimes linked to existing re-mediations of the narrative in fanfic (either the knitter's own or an example she particularly enjoyed or remembers keenly).

Furthermore, the fact that projected interactivity comes about through stitches rather than (or in addition to) words is significant. According to Constance Classen, pens and needles are often conflated in reference to women's art, in the spinning of words for poetry, for example.[22] Since female fans have so enthusiastically taken up pens to write fanfic, is it any wonder that they have also enthusiastically taken up needles? Indeed, there are direct links between these two forms of fan production, and the knitter/writers interviewed for this research see strong links between them. BizarreYarns (as a writer of vampire fiction and a handicrafter, her chosen Ravelry name could easily refer to either activity), responds typically when asked whether she feels a connection between her writing and her handicrafting:

> I do indeed. Often while spinning, knitting, crocheting, tatting, etc. I will mull over the story in my head and let it wander aimlessly. On many occasions I've had my best ideas while making or working with yarn. When I wrote my novels [...] it all clicked while I was spinning yarn, in fact. One minute I was fingers deep in seacell fiber, and the idea just popped into my head of exactly what my characters were, and why it took a whole lot more than a stake to kill them.

Describing herself as "a bit of a jack of all trades in the creative realm," BizarreYarns brings her interests together in her novel *Lamia* (she writes generic – not fan – fiction). She also describes how: "[O]ne of the main characters, Nemesis, tries to focus his attention onto things other than mass murder and he takes up knitting. In the process, his lady-love Lamia gets a series of hand knit items that are of impressive skill." Thus, knitting and writing inform each other. Similarly, Twilight and its fanfic are inspirations to knitter and dyer Tri'coterie, who sells her hand-dyed vampire-themed yarn. She states that:

> I have been dyeing yarns for some years and recently started combining them with my fascination with vampire lore. Most of my yarns are theme dyed to either *True Blood* or *Twilight* (including *Twilight* fanfiction).

Her interpretations pick up themes or descriptive passages in favourite fanfics which she outlines on the website for her Etsy shop.[23] In her description for a skein of Landscapes, for example, she writes that:

The colours black, green and shades of brown from gold, through bronze to chestnut are inspired from the following phrases in Chapter 2: "His hair was an amazing mix of bronze, gold and red." [and] "Those green eyes were piercing mine through his trendy black rimmed glasses."

"Landscapes", the Twilight saga fanfic on which the colourway is based, was written by Lambcullen, a knitter and member of Ravelry herself.[24] Several of her projects reflect her interest in Twilight and vampires, including the Forks Beany Hat and Quick Knit Cullen Wristbands with Cullen family crest. Interestingly, her fanfic has a colour theme in its own right (though this is not to suggest that all the fanfics used as inspiration by the dyer do), with chapter titles such as Crimson, Emerald, Indigo, and Flame. The colors chosen for titles are intense shades signifying passion and vibrancy (themselves factors in the appeal of vampires for these fans). Maura Kelly maintains that even at a basic level (as when following a pattern) knitting is a creative and highly technical process involving combinations of different stitches and shaping elements which the crafter needs to have mastered.[25] Color is one of the choices (others are fiber, texture, and drape) of a creative process that reflects the knitter's tastes and desires, and is thus a creative outlet according to the model devised by Stella Minahan and Julie Wolfram Cox.[26] These creative links across both knitting and writing are relatively frequent, and certainly they suggest that color can be an important aspect of creativity for fan knitters (as also evidenced by the choices made by the knitters taking part in the *True Blood* KALs discussed above).

The Micro-economy of Fan Knitting

Such re-mediations of the text are important for dyers who are part of a micro-economy of fan handicrafting. Ravelry facilitates the commodification of fan knitting by allowing members to sell their own patterns via the site marketplace and offering opportunities for micro-businesses to advertise to niche markets. In respect to the former, many pattern writers on Ravelry sell their patterns for small payments. In its pattern database Ravelry offers over 90 generic vampire and over 150 Twilight-inspired patterns, almost all of which are designed by fans and, where not available to download for free, are available to buy for between $3 (for the Jardin Sauvage Vampire Mitts for example) and $12 (for Dracula's Bride, a complex lace shawl). When it comes to obtaining yarn with which to knit these or other patterns, vampire fan knitting is highly commodified. The array of vampire-themed yarns provides a thriving micro-economy of fan production. Frequently, ads for vampire-themed yarns and sock clubs will appear in the relevant fan groups in the forum. In other cases the dyer's yarns develop a cult status in their own right and become highly sought after within certain groups. For example, fan knitters can buy skeins of Fresh From the Cauldron's 'Stupid Shiny Volvo Owner' or Alice Cullen yarn with silver thread to replicate the Twilight vampire's sparkle; the dyer also produces colors inspired by *True Blood*, Bram Stoker's *Dracula*, *Interview with the Vampire* and *Underworld* for those fans who do not find the Twilight saga to their taste. Fans can also buy a membership to Bloodlines, a vamp and hunter sock club featuring yarns and patterns for Bill and Eric, Edward and Jacob, and Sam and Dean — "One drop is all it takes" reads the ad. On Etsy, they can purchase yarn inspired by lines of dialogue from *True Blood* (Cosmic Fibers) or *Buffy the Vampire Slayer* (716Knit).

Such commodification, however, is not necessarily straightforward, and is certainly not unproblematical. For the yarn dyers themselves, this can result in a thriving micro-business, many of the dyers being mothers (with young children) who are not working outside the home, or other women wishing to supplement their income whilst using their skills in an enjoyable way. For dyers like Dharmafey of Cosmic Fibers, her home-dying micro-business is a way of combining her artistic talents with her fannish interests in horror and vampire media and fiction. Her comments on her dyeing demonstrate that such activities are deeply embedded in her fan interests and the sociability of the fan knitting community on Ravelry:

> I first started dyeing because though another indie dyer was producing the yarn I wanted, they were never available. That was a fan-based yarn: Harry Potter self-striping House Yarns, so even my first inspirations were from fandoms.

From those first four yarns, I started to get inspired by *other* pop culture references. I've always been into the more macabre end of things and an artist. Yarn and fiber have been the mediums I've really fallen in love with and dyeing is another way of expressing that passion and enthusiasm. Now, when I see something I enjoy, I envision how I could make a yarn from it. It gives me a place to focus. And as a business, I get to geek out with my customers/friends about these secret things we both enjoy, as well as having a niche market — anyone can dye a Hydrangea yarn, but not everyone can research and apply blunt force trauma blood splatter. I've thought of another correlation in that both yarn and vampires are rather occult knowledge, considering "occult" just means "hidden," and so we get to connect on a level that few others understand.

Dharmafey dyes yarns inspired by each new episode of *True Blood* (these are pre-ordered in the week before transmission) and some of her customers will guess which line she will select as they are watching the episode. Such shared love of the text between the dyer and her customers is indicative of Sal M. Humphreys's hybrid market environment in which there is no clear distinction between social and commercial economies, they co-exist in the same space.[27] As she suggests of the social network market, the social matters here as much as the commercial and financial. Furthermore, the social network influences both production and consumption within the fan knitting community. This is an idealized fan marketplace, one that exists outside of the culture industries that see fans as an exploitable market. The dyers and pattern designers are fans themselves and interact within the fan community as fellow fans as well as customers. As Hills also points out, fan culture is both distanced from commodification and yet bound up within it. This "suspensionist" position can accommodate a both/and position in which fans can be "simultaneously inside and outside processes of commodification," but more important here are issues of copyright.[28] According to Humphreys, as the dominant mode of practice of feminine handicrafting has shifted from domesticity to commerce, the issue of intellectual property for pattern writers can become a challenge. Humphreys's argument is focused on wider issues of publishing and copyright law, but it is clear that fan knitting (as with other "poaching" of the cultural text in fan production) can be in breach of the culture industries that hold copyright for the text. However, such concerns are often sidelined (as they are in fanfic) by declarations that the fans are just playing with the text and the characters they love. Fashion in general has long been inspired by media texts and the reproduction of items of clothing in similar designs or yarn colourways as seen in the Twilight saga or *True Blood* is seen as falling into the same category. In the case of Miller's *Vampire Knits*, the patterns do not make explicit references to the Twilight saga, though items such as the Bellissima mittens are very similar to those worn by Bella when Edward saves her from being crushed by the out-of-control van in the first film.

Knitting as Gendered Fan Practice

In considering fan knitting as an "alternative" fan practice, it is important to question whether it is deflected in a similar manner to that which Courtney Bailey suggests is the case with feminist art.[29] In respect to the tensions that are raised by the association of particular fan practices with gender, the fan spaces provided within the Ravelry community could be seen as a refuge from the competitiveness of male fan communities and the recognition given to male fan production (notably fan films) by the culture industry (just as female fanfic writers have created their own communities). As the internet has facilitated the opening up of fan culture and made it accessible to all viewers, the line between casual and intense fans has blurred. Francesca Coppa suggests that as fandom opens up there is a risk that it is re-marginalizing the very female groups that once represented fan culture.[30] Groups of female fans, such as those discussed by Bacon-Smith in *Enterprising Women*, now represent a very small segment of the fan audiences, and Coppa is concerned that they are increasingly seen as a minority voice in a "mixed gender fannish culture".[31] This may be, as Coppa argues, a form of re-marginalization, but it could also be seen as representing a new politicization (where fan handicrafting has strong links to the gendered politics of new knitting).

In this respect, it is significant that fan knitting is not necessarily organized around specific fan events and fan cultural practices. It might be expected that feminine handicrafts be employed by fans in the practices of costuming: in the creation of costumes to be worn at fan conventions or cosplay events, as an activity integral to fan film production or in live action role play. The making and wearing of costumes in this way is usually linked to specific characters and "performed" in the specialist environments of fan culture (such as a fan convention or meet-up). Fan knitting, however, is predominantly embedded in the everyday. Knitting in this respect is not necessarily a straightforward fan activity, it shares its space with a common-or-garden pastime, taking place inside and outside the home, both as a hobby undertaken simply for pleasure and as a means to an end — the production of wearable clothing or useful domestic items, for example. As such it brings casual followers of vampire fiction and popular culture into close contact with intense fans, and allows them to easily communicate through their shared knowledge, vocabulary, and interest in knitting (whilst simultaneously, and rather ironically, continuing to exclude these mostly female vampire fans from male-dominated fan culture in general). The fan groups in the Ravelry forum provide multiple entry points and potential initiations into fan culture. The various trajectories of fan participation in these groups work to blur the boundaries of established fan culture in increasingly fluid and complex ways, and contribute to the mainstreaming of fannish activities. Regardless of the fact that this merging of mainstream and fannish activities is taking place in a largely gendered community, it is significant that it represents opportunities for fan knitters to share their intense passions and renegotiate the politicized status of feminine handicrafts.

Notes

1 Genevieve Miller, *Vampire Knits: Projects to Keep You Knitting From Twilight to Dawn* (New York: Potter Craft, 2010).
2 Ravelry (http://www.ravelry.com/) is a member-only community. All the patterns, members' project pages and forum groups mentioned in this chapter can be easily found via Ravelry's search facility, but because overall access is restricted no further direct links are provided.
3 Matt Hills, *Fan Cultures* (London: Routledge, 2004), 139.

4   Cornel Sandvoss, *Fans: The Mirror of Consumption* (Cambridge: Polity, 2005) 16–18.
5   Milly Williamson, *The Lure of the Vampire: Gender, Fiction and Fandom from Bram Stoker to Buffy* (Brighton: Wallflower, 2005).
6   Amy M. Clarke, "Introduction: Approaching Twilight," in *The Twilight Mystique: Critical Essays on the Novels and Films*, eds. Amy M. Clarke and Marijane Osborn (Jefferson, NC: McFarland, 2010), 3.
7   Maria Mellins, "Dressing up as Vampires: Virtual Vamps — Negotiating Female Identity in Cyberspace" *Networking Knowledge: Journal of the MeCCSA Postgraduate Network* 1, no. 2 (2007): 5–6.
8   Miller, *Vampire*, 8–9.
9   Debbie Stoller, *Stitch'n Bitch: The Knitter's Handbook* (New York: Workman Publishing, 2003), 9.
10 Male fan knitters are in a very small minority. Just over 2% of members in the HorrorKnits group are men (26 out of 1059), 0.33% of the Twilight Saga Fans (12 out of 3603) and just over 1% in True Blood (19 out of 1713). The gender split of Ravelry members as a whole is unavailable, but there are 2102 members of the online community *Men Who Knit* (http://www.menwhoknit.com/community/), and if there are comparable numbers in Ravelry, this would give a figure of around 0.2%.
11 Henry Jenkins, "Fandom, Participatory Culture and Web 2.0," *Confessions of an Aca/Fan*, January 9, 2010, http://henryjenkins.org/2010/01/fandom_participatory_culture_a.html.
12 Kristina Busse, "Fandom-is-a-Way-of-Life versus Watercooler Discussion; or, The Geek Hierarchy as Fannish Identity Politics," *Flow TV* 5 no. 13 (2006): http://flowtv.org/2006/11/taste-and-fandom/.
13 Beth Ann Pentney, "Feminism, Activism, and Knitting: Are the Fibre Arts a Viable Mode for Feminist Political Action?" *Thirdspace, A Journal of Feminist Theory and Culture* 8, no. 1 (2008): http://www.thirdspace.ca/journal/article/viewArticle/pentney/210.
14 Beth Ann Pentney, "Feminism, Activism, and Knitting: Are the Fibre Arts a Viable Mode for Feminist Political Action?"
15 Kristina Busse, "Geek Hierarchies, Boundary Policing, and the Good Fan/Bad Fan Dichotomy," *Antenna: Responses to Media and Culture*, August 13, 2010, http://blog.commarts.wisc.edu/2010/08/13/geek-hierarchies-boundary-policing-and-the-good-fanbad-fan-dichotomy/.
16 The term refers to the excited, squealing sounds fans, usually female, make when taking pleasure in the text or the star.
17 Hills, *Fan Cultures*, 52.
18 Henry Jenkins, *Textual Poachers: Television Fans and Participatory Culture* (London: Routledge, 1992), 162–177.

19 Camille Bacon-Smith, *Enterprising Women: Television Fandom and the Creation of Popular Myth* (Philadelphia: University of Pennsylvania Press, 1992).
20 Jenkins, *Textual Poachers*, 47.
21 Anne Kustritz, "Slashing the Romance Narrative," *Journal of American Culture* 26 (2003): 375.
22 Constance Classen, *The Colour of Angels: Cosmology, Gender and the Aesthetic Imagination* (London: Routledge, 1998), 99.
23 Tricoterie, "Twilight Fanfic – Landscapes Edward – Merino and Tencil Sock Yarn" *Etsy*, accessed August 22, 2011, http://www.etsy.com/transaction/17884418.
24 Lambcullen, "Landscapes," *Fan Fiction Net*, accessed August 22, 2011, www.fanfiction.net/s/4980544/1/bLandscapes_.
25 Maura Kelly, "Knitting as a Feminist Project? Untangling the Contradictions of the 'New Knitting' Movement," *Proceedings of the American Sociological Association Annual Meeting*, July 31, 2008, 15. http://www.allacademic.com/meta/p241231_index.html.
26 Stella Minahan and Julie Wolfram Cox, "Stitch 'n Bitch: Cyberfeminism, a Third Place and the New Materiality," *Journal of Material Culture* 12, no. 1 (2007): 8.
27 Sal M. Humphreys, "The Challenges of Intellectual Property for Users of Social Networking Sites: A Case Study of Ravelry," *Proceedings Mind Trek* (2008): http://eprints.qut.edu.au/14858/.
28 Hills, *Fan Fictions*, 44.
29 Courtney Bailey, "Feminist Art and (Post)Modern Anxieties," *Genders* 32 (2000): http://www.genders.org/g32/g32_bailey.html.
30 Francesca Coppa, "Women, *Star Trek*, and the Early Development of Fannish Vidding," *Transformative Works and Cultures* 1 (2008): http://journal.transformativeworks.org/index.php/twc/article/view/44.
31 Coppa.

9

Gorgeous Monsters and Awful Beauties: The Vampire in the World of Alternative Fashion and Photography

Rick Hudson

The vampire has become synonymous with both sex and sexuality in the late twentieth and early twenty-first centuries. For adolescents and young adults the vampire has proved to be an object of sexual fascination and a mechanism through which they can articulate both their sexual desire and sexual identity. In the fiction of Anne Rice, Poppy Z. Brite, and Laurell K. Hamilton, the Vampire Romance genre of novels, films such as *Underworld* and *Daybreakers*, and in such television programmes such as *Buffy the Vampire Slayer* and *True Blood*, the vampire has increasingly become a narrative figure that enables young people to explore and express desires and concerns regarding sex and sexuality. Popular music has also provided an arena in which the vampiric image has been exploited for its sexual possibilities, in terms of dress, make-up, philosophy (such as that of the death metal band Draconian), and in terms of lyrical content (see, for example, My Chemical Romance's "Vampires Will Never Hurt You" and Nox Arcana's album *Transylvania*).

In the popular imagination the current image of the vampire has been created from a fusion of the Romantic hero/heroine; popular fiction; punk and rock music; and fashion, to become a sexual image through which teenagers and young adults are able to express a sexual identity that simultaneously conforms with and challenges ideologically dominant notions of sexuality and sexual attraction. This is particularly evident in the field of "alternative" or "alt" modelling, wherein male and female models working in the fashion and erotic photography business have created identities which are highly eroticized syntheses of punk, heavy metal and gothic styles, fetish fashion, and vampire imagery.

The phenomena of the alt model emerged in the wake of the work of Vivienne Westwood and the paradoxical eroticization of the Riot Grrrl movement. It produced a loose faction of male and female models, working in the fashion and erotic photography industries, that ran in uneasy alliance and productive opposition to the "conventional" fashion and "adult" entertainment industries. Initially, it gained widespread recognition through the publication of *SuicideGirls* in 2004, and *Burning Angel* in 2008.

This paper, informed by Mikhail Bakhtin's conception of the carnivalesque as articulated in *Rabelais and His World*,[1] explores the use of vampire imagery by young adults in relation to their sexuality and sexual identity, specifically focusing on the alt model phenomenon. It questions the degree to which such articulations of sex and sexuality can be considered to be complicit with or challenging to ideologically dominant conceptions of sexuality. What is more, it raises the question of whether the assimilation of the marginal into the mainstream should be considered a success or a failure. This argument is supported by interviews with a number of alt models.

From the emergence of Black Sabbath and Alice Cooper in the late 1960s — if not earlier — rock music has allied itself with the horror genre and utilized horror imagery as a means of articulating feelings of alienation, discontent and frustration. Heavy metal and punk bands have been particularly disposed to draw heavily on horror movies, novels, comics and other media/cultural forms, not only in their lyrical content, but also in their respective fashions and album cover designs. Indeed, as punk music morphed into gothic punk (as it was then called) in the 1980s, this association strengthened to the degree that the "gothic" transcended a repertoire of stylistic devices to become an all-embracing lifestyle.[2] Exactly which bands qualified as being "truly" gothic remains open to debate; however, horror imagery may be seen to manifest itself quite clearly in the playful darkness of the Damned in albums such as *Damned, Damned, Damned* (1977), *Machine Gun Etiquette* (1979) and *Grave Disorder* (2001). The Cramps drenched themselves in horror B-movie and bubble-gum card symbolism in *Songs the Lord Taught*

Us (1980), *Smell of Female* (1983), *Stay Sick* (1986) and *Big Bad from Badsville* (1997); Bauhaus solemnly intoned "Bella Lugosi's Dead" for a full nine minutes on their 1979 single of the same name. However, of all the punk bands to adopt the gothic style, the first and perhaps most significant was Siouxsie & the Banshees, whose first album, *The Scream* (1978), distinguished the band from such contemporaries as the Sex Pistols and The Clash, through their use of spooky, jangling guitars and dark, fantastical imagery which employed sinister dreamscapes, broken dolls and perversions of *Alice in Wonderland*. For the purposes of this paper, the importance of the Banshees lies more in the dress and style of lead vocalist Siouxsie Sioux than with the musical output of the band.

Siouxsie Sioux created her on- and off-stage image by incorporating the dress and make-up styles of the 1920s flapper; the prostitute; the dominatrix; the Nazi officer; Louise Brookes; the femme fatale; and the vampire, to present herself as a figure who simultaneously mocked and rejected conventional notions of female sexual attractiveness whilst being highly sexually alluring. As such, she heralded a new kind of female icon that both problematized and embodied notions of desire: "punk/vampire chic." By the mid-1980s the links between horror and punk had become so established that not only did the punk movement draw upon horror movies, but horror movies began to incorporate punk into its catalogue of motifs; particularly that of "punk chic," as epitomized by the character of Trash (played by Linnea Quigly) in Dan O'Bannon's film *Return of the Living Dead*. Since the degree to which this figure has become an object of male fantasy or an empowering role model for women has been the subject of much debate, this paper does not concern itself with how this figure is used or understood by its audience, but rather how and why it is employed by women who choose to utilize such an image themselves within a professional environment. In order to do this it is useful to interrogate women's uses of horror figures — particularly the vampire — in horror texts as a whole, before moving on to assess their own emulation of such figures.

The vampire's position as a sexual figure in the eyes of readers has become a *de facto* reality: the vampire (male or female) is unquestionably a dark, seductive figure for consumers of vampire texts and represents the threat of the predatory sexual outsider while also indulging the fantasy of being such an outsider. Indeed, critical explorations which seek to identify an either/or answer to the question of whether the seductive vampire is an empowering figure for women, or a repressive one embedded in phallocentric discourse, may be fruitless. Importantly, we must note that since the 1980s there has been a boom in vampire fiction by women, which places the vampire in the role of protagonist. This was undoubtedly initiated by Anne Rice and expanded by the work of Poppy Z. Brite, Caitlín R. Kiernan, Christa Faust, Laurell K. Hamilton and their imitators. The popularity of such fiction can be attributed to the representations of female sexuality and sexual identity that is enjoyed by many female readers. Much received wisdom regarding female characters in fantasy, science fiction and horror fiction assumes that these characters function chiefly as sexual fantasy figures for adolescent males; however, Kirsten Clemens's recent study, "Graphic Novels and the Girl Market," makes a strong case for these same figures, providing young women with a figure through which they can understand and articulate their own identity, sexual or otherwise.[3] Gina Wisker interrogates the appeal of the sexual female vampire and attributes the popularity of this figure to women readers:

> In conventional fictions, women vampires connote unlicensed sexuality and excess, and as such, in conventional times, their invocation of both desire and terror leads to a stake in the heart — death as exorcism of all they represent. Contemporary women writers, however, have found in the figure of the vampire marvellous potential for radical reappropriation. The status of vampires as cultural indices and metaphor has been revalued by contemporary women vampire-fiction writers, aligning them with a new feminist carnivalesque.[4]

Indeed, Nancy Kilpatrick, herself a writer of vampire fiction, defines the contemporary vampire as "a predatory being that preys on human beings in a sexually arousing or satisfying and/or sexually repulsive way," and elaborates upon this point to stress that such sexual material is liberating and challenging, rather than a perpetuation of masculine ideological norms.⁵ Such perspectives position the contemporary female vampire as a powerful agent of female sexuality, not to be considered solely as a representative of the threatening "other" to be exorcized, but rather as a joyful figure through which our fantasies and desires are exercised. In writing on monsters in general, Jeffrey Jerome Cohen states:

> Fear of the monster is really a kind of desire. The monster is continually linked to forbidden practices, in order to normalize and to enforce. The monster also attracts. The same creatures who terrify and interdict can evoke potent escapist fantasies; the linking of monstrosity with the forbidden makes the monster all the more appealing as a temporary egress from constraint. This simultaneous repulsion and attraction at the core of the monster's composition accounts greatly for its continued cultural popularity, for the fact that the monster can seldom be contained in a simple, binary dialectic (thesis, antithesis... no synthesis). We distrust and loathe the monster at the same time we envy its freedom, and perhaps even its sublime despair.⁶

Cohen continues to develop this notion of the monster as a fantasy figure, and maintains that the monster facilitates sexual fantasies:

> The habitations of monsters (Africa, Scandinavia, America, Venus, the Delta Quadrant —— whatever land is sufficiently distant to be exoticized) are more than dark regions of uncertain danger: they are also realms of happy fantasy, horizons of liberation. Their monsters serve as secondary bodies through which the possibilities of other genders, other sexual practices, and other social customs can be explored. Hermaphrodites, Amazons, and lascivious cannibals beckon from the edges of the world, the most distant planets of the galaxy.⁷

Both Wisker and Cohen allude to "the carnival," and suggest that the contemporary vampire's or monster's liberating function is played out in the form of a sexual, carnivalesque fantasy figure. As such, our understanding of monstrous attraction can perhaps be explored more successfully by drawing upon Bakhtin's writings on the carnivalesque. I have written in depth elsewhere on Bakhtinian theory in relation to fantasy narratives;[8] however, it may be useful to consider some of Robert Stam's thoughts on Bakhtin and the carnivalesque in relation to sex and sexuality.[9] Such an approach is helpful, as Bakhtinian theory is comfortable with ambiguity and contradiction — indeed it celebrates it — in contrast to attempting to arrive at an "A or B" answer, as some Marxist-informed critical perspectives have a tendency to do. Indeed, Bakhtin himself was a scathing (if codified) critic of Marxism. Stam summarizes the way in which Bakhtinian theory sees bodily and sensual cultural products as subversive and liberating, and highlights the flaws of Marxist interpretations:

> The view of the body developed by Bakhtin in *Rabelais and His World*, it goes without saying, was not designed to please the Soviet authorities. Originally presented as a dissertation, the text divided the Moscow scholarly community, and the State Accreditation Bureau ultimately denied Bakhtin his doctorate. Bakhtin's thesis, as Clark and Holquist point out, can be seen as a subtle Aesopian attack on the puritanical rigidities of Stalinism, its conservative aesthetic tastes, its fondness for 'order and hierarchy' ... In a superegoish climate where nonmainstream sexual practices were denounced as deviant manifestations of 'bourgeois decadence', Bakhtin applauded human sexuality and the right to difference.[10]

For Stam, the bodily, the sensual, and the erotic can constitute a subversive assault on authoritarian ideologies (whether of left or right wing origins) which depend upon an austere, dour, humorless conservatism; such self-righteous mindsets are threatened by the ill-disciplined and chaotic human body and human desire.

The appropriation of monstrous figures by the punk movement is not at all surprising: punks sought to alienate themselves not only from the conservatism of the bourgeoisie and of institutional authority, but also from the preceding counter-cultural generation of hippies and "flower power." The monstrous image was not only antagonistic towards "the establishment," but was also a visual gesture that signified hostility towards the hippie movement, by drawing upon the bloody vampire and the zombie rather than flowers and rainbows. Indeed, the punk fusion of the monstrous with the erotic, in its dress and imagery, can be interpreted as an affront to the hippie generation — a mockery of the principal of "free love" and a rejection of the liberal and left-wing philosophical backbone of the hippies (although, under its more aggressive surface, punk shared the same anarcho-socialist/libertarian principles), particularly in relation to gender and sexuality.

Nevertheless, we are confronted with a situation wherein, in the 1990s and 2000s, the sexualized "vampire punk/chic" appears to have lost its desire to affront, and has become a marketable commodity and sexualized image that is used for titillation rather than subversion. The alt model has become a recognizable staple of the fashion world, and "alt porn" — as in the pages of *SuicideGirls* and *Burning* — can be argued to be no different from regular porn. In regard to these publications and websites, we have to ask ourselves whether the alt model (whether fashion or erotic) is challenging anything at all, or merely offering her (or him) self for exploitation in masturbatory material. However, I think it is of interest to consider the views of alt models themselves; to consider first of all their thoughts on their adoption of the punk/vampire image, and, secondly, their opinions as to whether or not they are being sexually exploited.

At this point it is perhaps useful for me to produce the card I have hitherto kept up my sleeve: yes, I am an academic (specializing in the study of horror and fantastic narratives); yes, I am a writer (specializing in horror and fantastic fiction); but I am also a photographer — and yes, you have guessed it, here too I specialize in the production of horror and fantastic material. Consequently, I am in a privileged position which grants me access to the views and opinions of alt models. The following section of this chapter includes highlights of interviews conducted with a number of alt models, which will be used in more depth in a later study. The models in question work under the following pseudonyms: Bastard Tuesday (male); Veronica Waste (female); Debbie Debris (female); and Lucy Vandal (female).

> **Interviewer:** So, you're all obviously very involved in the punk scene, and your images are all very much based on vampires and zombies. Do you think there's a link between punk and vampires? What's the attraction?
> **Vandal:** I've always been in love with punk and metal — the look and style and the music's just so exciting and energetic. I get bored listening to anything else. I get bored *looking* like anything else. I love fashion and make-up, but regular fashion's just so boring.
> **Tuesday:** Yeah, it's the only scene where a bloke can be extravagant and experiment without being seen as weird [laughs]. Or rather *is* seen as weird but praised for it. I love dressing up, and vampires *and* punks and metal-heads dress up. They're all dandies, and that's cool.
> **Interviewer:** And being cool's important?
> **Tuesday:** Yeah, as long as there's a person behind the image. Depth, you know. People are going to judge you whatever you do ... so you may as well control how they judge you.
> **Waste:** And vampires are smart too. Educated. Artistic. They're not like thick chavs[11] or anything. Can you imagine a chav vampire?
> **Debris:** Yeah, vampires are like an elite gang of smart kids. Too smart to be fooled by the bollocks most people fall for. They're like the intelligent outsiders.
> **Interviewer:** Does that make them like punks?
> **Debris:** Oh yes. But it's cool *and* sexy too. But not in a normal boring way.
> **Tuesday:** That's true, but I don't think it's as superficial as it sounds. People say I'm an attractive guy [laughs awkwardly], and I'm quite a sporty, muscular bloke. I'm a straight bloke, but I don't buy into the usual look — I don't see why the way I dress and stuff has to be dictated. And although I'm straight I don't see why I have to dress in a way that kind of makes me have to be say-

ing all the time, "hey, just in case you were wondering — I'm straight," by the way I look.

Interviewer: So, are both the punk and vampire looks androgynous then?

Tuesday: Yeah, it's a look that says "this is how I am, this is how I want to be irrespective of whether I'm a man or a woman, whether I'm gay or straight or whatever." It's kind of sexless and sexy at the same time.

Interviewer: Do you think that there's a problem with the alt model scene in that it could be seen as exploitative?

Vandal: In a sexual way?

Interviewer: Yes. Not exclusively, but yes.

Vandal: Well, it could be I suppose. But what's so wrong with doing sexual stuff? If you're saying "oooh alt models are doing stuff that people might wank over" then you're kind of saying that there's something wrong with doing art that people wank over? I don't see it as a problem.

Tuesday: Hmmm. If you're asking me about exploitation, then my answer would be this; I have a choice, I can get a job in a call centre for £6.50 an hour and be told that I can't behave or dress or look the way I want, or I can do modelling for £50-£100 an hour, do and look how the fuck I like and have loads of free time to do my own stuff. If you want to talk to people about exploitation, phone a call centre, or speak to Tesco's or somewhere like that.

These comments are a fraction of a large body of material I shall return to at a later date.

Although the comments of some of the models are a little naïve and require further interrogation, they nonetheless reveal some interesting insights into these young men and women's appropriations of the vampire (over 100 years after the publication of Bram Stoker's *Dracula*) and punk imagery and fashion (nearly 30 years after the release of the album *Never Mind the Bollocks, Here's the Sex Pistols*). For these young men and women, the monster — particularly but not exclusively the vampire — becomes the mask that reveals their identities to the outside world: a rebellious non-conformist, an alienated outsider, a figure who rejects conventional notions of sexual attractiveness, yet believes himself to be, and is seen by others to be, sexually attractive and "cool." They see the vampire as a figure they can emulate; one that is sensitive and intelligent and not bound by gender norms. For the alt models interviewed, the vampire offers them an identity (both sexual and political) that is attractive and yet does not conform to conventional conceptions of either the "masculine" or the "feminine." Furthermore, as a romantic outsider, the vampire's appeal also provides them with a role model with whom they can identify.

Although it would be easy to suggest that a young person's attraction to the vampire is grounded in the vampire being the mopey bedroom-bound teenager *par excellence*, this paper indicates that this identification is also grounded in the vampire being an outsider who is critical of societal norms. As such, the vampire has been adopted as a metaphorical figure within punk and heavy metal music, as both the voice of romantic and sexual desire, and the emblem of political dissatisfaction. These individuals place themselves socially within the borderlands of popular culture, and also utilize the vampire as a resource, drawing upon a repertoire of images, motifs and archetypes in the construction and communication of their sexual and political identities. Indeed, it is possible to suggest that the subcultures in which these young people are active allow them to become dynamic authors and performers of their identities within their social milieu. If so, then this perhaps demonstrates a principal tenet of the Bakhtinian carnivalesque:

> [The] carnival does not know footlights, in the sense that it does not acknowledge any distinction between actors and spectators. Footlights would destroy a carnival, as the absence of footlights would destroy a theatrical performance. Carnival is not a spectacle seen by the people: they live in it, and everyone participates because its very idea embraces all the people.[12]

Notes

1. M. M. Bakhtin, *Rabelais and his World*, trans. Hélène Iswolsky (Bloomington, IL: Indiana University Press, 1984).
2. See David Punter and Glennis Byron, *The Gothic: Blackwell Guides to Literature* (Oxford: Blackwell, 2004), 59–64.
3. Kirsten Clemens, "Graphic Novels and the Girl Market," *The CEA Critic* 72, no. 3 (2010).
4. Gina Wisker, "Love Bites: Contemporary Women's Vampire Fictions," in *A Companion to the Gothic*, ed. David Punter, Blackwell Companions to Literature and Culture (Oxford: Blackwell, 2001), 167.
5. Nancy Kilpatrick, "Archetypes and Fearful Allure: Writing Erotic Horror," in *On Writing Horror*, ed. Mort Castle, revised ed. (Cincinnati: Horror Writers Association, 2007), 173–74.
6. Jeffrey Jerome Cohen, "Monster Culture (Seven Thesis)," in *Gothic Horror: A Guide for Students and Readers*, ed. Clive Bloom (Basingstoke: Palgrave Macmillan, 1998), 212.
7. Cohen, 214.
8. Rick Hudson, "The Derelict Fairground: A Bakhtinian Analysis of the Graphic Novel Medium," *The CEA Critic* 72, no. 3 (2010): 35–49.
9. Robert Stam, *Subversive Pleasures: Bakhtin, Cultural Criticism, and Film*, Parallax Re-visions of Culture and Society (Baltimore: Johns Hopkins University Press, 1989).
10. Stam, 158.
11. A "chav," in British slang, is understood to be an uneducated — usually unemployed, usually in social housing — white member of the working class who has no ambition or wish to elevate him- or herself from a position of poverty and violence. The term is usually used to suggest that someone is an aggressive, unintelligent individual with criminal tendencies, and is of course problematic; however, it has great currency in contemporary British culture and society. The term is used with particular vehemence by other members of the British working class. The nearest US equivalent is probably "trailer trash"; however, the two terms do not signify exactly the same thing.
12. Bakhtin, *Rabelais and His World*, 7.

10

Mystic Falls Meets the World Wide Web: Where is *The Vampire Diaries* Located?

Kimberley McMahon-Coleman

In the northern fall of 2009, an adaptation of L. J. Smith's *The Vampire Diaries* débuted on the CW Network to unexpectedly high ratings.[1] From its inception, notions of authorship within this project were necessarily complex, given that Smith did not retain the copyright to the original novel series she produced over a nine month period in 1990,[2] and was not involved in the development of the television series.[3] Consequently, the narrative was uniquely positioned to be open to adaptation by multiple authors, including the creative team at the CW Network and the series' fans. It is difficult to imagine other writers of popular fiction, such as the Twilight Saga's Stephenie Meyer or Harry Potter's creator J. K. Rowling, allowing their creative works to be altered so significantly; indeed, both have achieved some notoriety for their insistence on creative control over their intellectual property. Because of these complex notions of authority and adaptation, questions about the location of the narrative have become paramount: does *The Vampire Diaries* exist in the imagination of L. J. Smith, as represented by Fell's Church; in Mystic Falls, as envisioned by the television program's executive producers; or in cyberspace with its fandom?

In addition to the contested relationship between the television series and the novels on which it is based, there has also been discussion over its position in relation to other contemporary vampire narratives such as *True Blood* and *Twilight*, and its relationship with the earlier vampire narratives from which it self-consciously borrows, such as *The Lost Boys*. Notions of authorship are further complicated by the role of the cyberspace fandom in influencing the love triangle around which the storyline centres. Fans of this show have had unprecedented access to writers, directors, producers, actors, and music director via Twitter and fansites from the outset. Fansites such as www.vampire-diaries.net were established when the series was first in development, and thus predate the existence of the actual show. As actress Candice Accola notes, the internet is a significant resource for the cast as well as the fans: "Nina [Dobrev] lived with me for a while in Los Angeles. So before we knew that the show was getting picked up ... there was this one website, vampirediaries.net, we would check constantly and consistently, 'cos they'd always have new information."[4] It is unclear to what extent the information posted online has influenced the actors' interpretations of the characters, but as Smith's imagined township morphed into television's Mystic Falls, the impact of cyberspace as a third and intermediary location became clear; the internet has facilitated direct conversations between writers, producers, actors and fans. The following discussion examines the impact of the contested and combined authorship between the novelist, executive producers, television writers, actors, and fans in the development of the series' narrative, characters and indeed, location.

With the sequential release of the Twilight movies (2008–2010; the final instalments to be released in 2011 and 2012, respectively, are now in production) and the première of Alan Ball's small screen adaptation of Charlaine Harris's Louisiana vampire novels beginning in 2008, there was always going to be some debate as to whether there was room for yet another filmic representation of vampires. The CW Network already held the rights to Smith's novels when executive Jennifer Breslow met with Kevin Williamson and Julie Plec, however, and it "wasn't opposed to the idea of a third major vampire franchise to fill the void between abstinence and orgies."[5] All three filmic narratives are based around bestselling novel series, and each centers on a love triangle between a mortal girl and her competing supernatural suitors. Moreover, all three feature vampires seek to be valued members of the small communities in which they live, necessitating that they control their blood-lust in order to live harmoniously alongside humans. In each instance, this peaceful coexistence with humans is threatened by the arrival of vampires more closely aligned with traditional horror representations, who make no effort to control their monstrous ways and, in so doing, threaten to expose the already-embedded vampires. In the case of *The Vampire Diaries*, however, this threat is intensely personal; the opposing vampires are also brothers.

Crissy Calhoun argues in the preface to her Companion to the series that while CW may have been interested in the narrative because of the current vampire craze in popular culture, its audience continues to follow the show because of the "heartfelt and human" relationships within that supernatural framework, as exemplified by the Salvatore brothers, their shared love interest, Elena Gilbert, and her friends and family.[6] The development of the relationship between the brothers is almost as important as their respective relationships with Elena, in terms of fans' decisions as to which brother they prefer, and the rivalries between Team Stefan and Team Damon are publically played out in cyberspace.

Arguably, what makes *The Vampire Diaries* an intriguing example of the current filmed vampire drama is the contested nature of its authorship and its impact on the development of storylines. The narrative centers around the Salvatore brothers, Stefan (Paul Wesley) and Damon (Ian Somerhalder), who are configured as foils to each other in both the novels and the television series. They became estranged over their romantic involvement with the same women: first, the vampire Katherine, who "turned" them both, and second, her contemporary lookalike, Elena (both played by Nina Dobrev). There are notable variations between the two iterations of the story, however, including the reconfiguration of characters in terms of age and gender. Notably, Elena's older and responsible Aunt Judith becomes cool graduate student Aunt Jenna in the series, while pre-school-aged sister Margaret becomes the teenage Jeremy. Likewise, Elena's rival at school, Caroline Forbes (Candice Accola), who is a possessed and pregnant shapeshifter in the novels, becomes a vampire in the television series. Perhaps the most significant changes, however, are intrinsically linked to location, such as the change in the brothers' origins from Renaissance Italy to America's South during the Civil War, and altering the family history of

Elena's best friend, Bonnie (Katerina Graham), to include witches from Salem, Massachusetts, rather than druids from Stonehenge. As Claudia Gray argues, this links not only the Salvatore brothers to the town's history, but also links Bonnie, through her ancestry, to Katherine, to the Salvatore brothers in their original lives, and to the establishment of the township of Mystic Falls.[7]

Just as the narrative is simultaneously and uncannily located in Fell's Church, Mystic Falls and cyberspace, the story also spans a number of genres. If Gothic stories rise to prominence during times of cultural upheaval, and serve to "negotiate the anxieties of the age by working through them in a displaced form,"[8] it is interesting that both the novels (1991–1992 and 2009–2011) and the television series (2009 onwards) were created during times when the United States had a significant presence in Middle East conflicts. This kind of reading is further supported by some of the self-reflexive dialogue which typifies the postmodern tone within the series, such as when Elena's younger brother Jeremy (Steven R. Gilbert) earnestly explains to his girlfriend Anna — who, unbeknownst to him, is herself a vampire — that the vampires in his ancestor's short stories were

> a metaphor for the demons of the day... The Union soldiers. I read the stories myself. They talk about the demons that attack at night ... Allegorical vampires, which is what it is: creative expression during a very volatile time. A country at war doesn't want realism, they want fantasy, thus: vampire fiction.[9]

The decision to change the name of the township, from Fell's Church in the novels to Mystic Falls in the television series, perhaps inadvertently encapsulates the contested location of *The Vampire Diaries*. In addition to the linguistic signal that the restrained vampire Stefan could easily "fall" from grace and behave more like his hedonistic brother, the Falls features in a number of key scenes in the first season. For example, Mystic Falls is the backdrop for a party where the budding romance between Elena and Stefan is marred by the vampire attack which signals Damon's return.[10] The town is also the location for the shallow grave of failed teen vampire Vicki Donovan.[11] The use of the word "Mystic" links the Gothic and supernatural to the landscape in which the events take place, while the decision to excise "Church" from the town's name arguably reflects the more secular nature of contemporary society. The Fell family, after whom the town was named in the novel series, is largely sidelined in the television program.

Although these changes appear to focus viewers' attention squarely on the supernatural elements of the series, it is worth noting that the program straddles several generic borders, drawing on what film historian Angela Aleiss argues is a long history of vampires crossing genres. She argues that vampires "have appeared in Science Fiction, they've been superheroes, anime, Western."[12] The program irrefutably has a horror/fantasy base, but features romantic storylines which are soap operatic, and is also identifiably a teen drama. As Glyn Davis and Kay Dickinson argue in *Teen TV: Genre, Consumption and Identity*, recurrent focuses in teen dramas "even within the most fantastical of shows — are sex and sexuality, drug and alcohol use, family tensions and negotiating one's place among one's peers, all issues encountered by the average teenager."[13] Williamson himself agrees, noting, "[w]e have the teen element, the teen drama aspect, which you can compare to *Dawson's Creek* ... It's more of a small-town show ... [but] the vampire story is our way in."[14] The youth demographic is a contributing factor to the show's prominence in cyberspace, a presence on which the CW network has capitalized, creating, for example, a Facebook page for the show.

Williamson is widely regarded as the *auteur* of the television series, even though executive production is shared with Julie Plec, and storyline development with a writing team which includes Plec. This is perhaps because the "small-town show" model and clever dialogue are reminiscent of Williamson's earlier teen program *Dawson's Creek*, as well as his ongoing work within the horror film genre. Nevertheless, he has gone to great lengths to promote the notion of shared authorship, noting in an interview that he has read Smith's books and that they provide the "skeleton" for the show.[15] Both executive producers are also regular users of Twitter, dropping hints about future storylines and posting photos from the set, as well as engaging in public discussions with the actors and fans.

The love triangle which has so mobilized the cyber fandom shares many characteristics with earlier teen drama. Late twentieth- and early twenty-first century teen dramas such as *Beverly Hills 90210* (1990–2000),[16] *Party of Five* (1994–2000),[17] and, of course, Williamson's *Dawson's Creek* (1998–2003)[18] all featured male co-leads who were constructed in binary opposition to each other. In each of these texts the hero of the narrative, as identified through screen time, storylines and narrative perspective, was the more responsible teen rather than the bad-boy anti-hero.[19] Yet, as Miranda Banks argues, even though "the text privileged the pouty-lipped, doe-eyed beautiful boy ... fans would often state their preferences for the rebellious one."[20] *The Vampire Diaries* is no exception, with rivalry between fans over their preferred brother leading them to form allegiances around which they base their online identities.

In both the novels and the series, the privileged male lead is Stefan Salvatore, a 162-year-old undead adolescent who still looks 17, and is constructed as a "good" vampire; a romantic hero who seeks to retain his humanity, refuses to kill humans in order to sustain himself, and tries to make moral choices. His decision to return to his family's hometown of Mystic Falls is predicated on his romantic interest in the protagonist, mortal teenager Elena Gilbert. His "romance novel stare,"[21] their shared interest in journal-writing, and their "epic" conversation[22] seem to suggest that this is little more than an intense teenage romance, but as the series progresses this is complicated by soap-operatic plot twists and moments of unexpected horror. These include the revelations that that he is a vampire;[23] that he had met and rescued Elena on the night of her parents' fatal car crash;[24] and that he has discovered the family secret that she was adopted.[25] Viewers learn that his decision to drink only animal blood, previously constructed as a moral stance, masks the management of an addiction to "the human stuff."[26] As the series progresses, the reasons for both Damon's apparent hatred of him and Stefan's own self-loathing become apparent,[27] and questions about the reasons for the brothers' attraction to Elena appear more sinister than romantic when we learn that she and Katherine are blood-related doppelgangers.[28]

Stefan's rival and brother Damon is initially configured as the vampire of horror films. When first seen on screen he is a shadowy figure, a threatening and not clearly identifiable person in the background; he is always accompanied by fog and a menacing crow,[29] symbols which immediately resonate with the horror genre because of their use by creative artists such as Bram Stoker, Edgar Allan Poe, and Alfred Hitchcock. The early episodes in Season One are framed by horror moments before the opening credits and immediately prior to the closing credits, drawing on Williamson's writing credentials within the horror genre, including the *Scream* movies,[30] *I Know What You Did Last Summer*,[31] and *Cursed*.[32] Damon is the instigator in each of these vignettes; it is he who murders innocent couples in the openings of Episodes One and Two,[33] he who suddenly becomes a fanged monster and attacks his lover Caroline Forbes in her bed in Episode Two,[34] and he who tears out the throat of Stefan's school football coach, Mr Tanner, in Episode Three.[35] He is typically impetuous, promiscuous and immoral, and he appears to embrace the darkness and its associated powers. By the Season One finale, however, his attitude has changed markedly, much to his own confusion: "I came to this town wanting to destroy it. Tonight I found myself wanting to protect it. How's that happen?"[36] By the middle of Season Two, the writers further surprised audiences with Damon's declaration of love for Elena, a confession which he promptly erases using his vampire powers of compulsion, arguing that while he may not deserve her, perhaps his brother does.[37] Plec described this as "the true hero moment ... It was saying, I don't even want you to know about it because I don't even want you to think about it."[38] These redeeming moments permit fans on Team Damon to enthuse about the male lead, despite his often callous actions. As Calhoun argues, "what makes Damon ... romantically interesting ... is the idea of some counterpart or soulmate who is capable of changing this already attractive person into someone who is nearly perfect, leading him to discover the heart of goodness lurking beneath the surface."[39] This hope for his redemption is also key to the character's online followership; viewers need to feel that the character is worthy of their devotion.

In the adaptation of Smith's novels for television, the writers and producers have consciously highlighted that there is more to Damon's character than merely being a figure of horror. It is Damon who is configured as the romantic hero in the early back-story to present-day events; he claims that he required no compulsion to be "turned," because he wanted to spend eternity with Katherine.[40] He was caring towards an injured and vulnerable Elena when they were in Atlanta together,[41] carrying her from a smoking car wreck and agreeing not to use his powers of compulsion to influence her actions; later, he tells her that they were having fun and he thus preferred that the situation "be real,"[42] rather than influenced by his supernatural powers. In the series of novels, Damon disappoints his aristocratic father by dropping out of his University studies in Renaissance Italy; the writers of the television series, however, significantly change the impetus for Damon's return to the family home, using it as an opportunity to tell viewers that in his mortal life he was a person with morals. Stefan reminds their father that Damon deserted the Confederate army "on principle,"[43] rather than because of a lack of commitment. In Season Two the writers also create the character of Rose (Lauren Cohan), a vampire who becomes both friend and occasional lover to Damon. When Rose sustains a fatal werewolf bite from Jules (Michaela McManus), Damon uses his powers of influence to take her back to her favourite place from her original life; he waits until she says she is not afraid anymore before euthanizing her, and shows genuine grief for this loss.[44] All of these moments humanize Damon and demonstrate that he is capable of emotion and loyalty.

There has already been some debate about the romantic hero roles as represented by the Salvatore brothers, notably Alyxandra Harvey's comparison with romantic heroes from canonic English literature texts.[45] Harvey argues that, because of the complexities of characterization, each brother is both Romantic hero and Gothic hero at different points in the series. Because it is fundamentally predicated on a love triangle, the viewers have to believe that Elena could be interested in either suitor; this necessitates a complication of their personas, and raises complex questions about forgiveness and trust. There has also been a lively debate online about Damon's "worthiness," based on Williamson's comments in October 2010, that after snapping the neck of Elena's younger brother, Jeremy, Damon was not "worthy of [Elena], yet ... that's why we have a show! We can go episode to episode and build toward all sorts of romance and love."[46] In the same article, Julie Plec poses a rhetorical question about the appeal of Damon: "I love Damon. Who doesn't love Damon? But if everybody loves him *no matter what he does*, then how does what he does have impact? How is there anything profound about your anti-hero or your villain?"[47]

The shifting position of Damon is not simply demonstrated in online intervention in the series, however, for his creator, L. J. Smith, has noted in an interview:

> ... the idea was that there were two brothers who were both in love with the same girl: one good brother, one bad brother. And I kind of like the bad brother better. That's Damon, and he's one of my favourite characters to work with. So it didn't come out exactly as it was intended, but it seems that people enjoy the effect.[48]

The producers of the television series have heightened the appeal of Damon and moved him closer to the position of male hero by casting Ian Somerhalder, who has what Carina Adley Mackenzie refers to as "inherent charm."[49] Damon is the most unpredictable of the characters and is allocated the darkest and wittiest lines by the show's writers, such as when he announces that he does "believe in killing the messenger ... [B]ecause it sends a message."[50]

The cast and crew are aware that, just as Damon's selfless moments destabilize his "bad boy" image, so too does Stefan's role as hero need to be undermined on occasion in order to maintain interest in the complex relationship dynamics. The episode "Miss Mystic Falls" sees the brothers in reversed positions; Stefan, with his addiction to human blood out of control, becomes a liar and a thief, while Damon takes on the role of protector, trying to hide his brother's actions.[51] As Calhoun explains: "With human blood in his system, Stefan's personality changes — he's ostentatious, flirty, fun, cavalier and mocks his usual broody self ... Like a drug or alcohol addict, Stefan is now a "closet blood junkie," and his primary concern is his next fix — not Elena or the town's safety."[52] Somerhalder himself articulates his awareness of the impact of these character shifts in the online fandom, noting in an interview: "I think we are going to find out more about Stefan that might make fans switch teams ... He isn't all goodie-two-shoes hero-boy."[53] In the episode which follows, a guilt-racked Stefan vows never to drink blood again, but instead to face the sun and end his eternal life. Elena finds him and persuades him to reconsider, instinctively knowing that, just as he was born and died in Mystic Falls, he will have returned to the quarry where he was made a vampire to complete this next life cycle. Stefan is constantly seeking familiar places, spaces, and relationships, even when they are made uncanny by his undeath.

As with the 1987 film *The Lost Boys*, which introduced the notion of the "half-vampire,"[54] there is an element of choice to vampirehood within the mythology of *The Vampire Diaries* as it is envisaged by the television program's creative team. In this version of the narrative, becoming a vampire is not as simple as dying with vampire blood in one's system, as it is in Smith's books; rather, a conscious decision to drink human blood is required in order to complete the transition. The television series makes it clear that both Damon and Stefan were resolute that they would not complete the process; Damon, because Katherine was dead and there was therefore no longer a reason to seek eternal life, and Stefan because he believed much of his father's rhetoric about the vampire as monster. Upon visiting his father to say goodbye, he learns that his father had been the one to assassinate the boys for consorting — or "sympathizing," as he delicately puts it — with a vampire. In an accident which occurs while he is trying to stake his son, Giuseppe Salvatore is injured. Unable to contain his blood-lust, Stefan feeds on him. The writers lead us to believe that moments after expressing his disgust and horror that a father could murder his own sons, one of those sons kills his father and becomes the very thing which his father found most abhorrent. This lends support to the line which is later written for Damon, who tells Elena that "[f]rom the moment Stefan had his first taste of human blood, he was a different person."[55]

The writers have established the importance of family as a point of differentiation between the two brothers. In his initial hours as a vampire, Stefan compelled a girl into being a donor and led her to Damon, encouraging him to feed so that they could discover their new lives together. Through flashbacks over the course of the series it becomes apparent that Stefan had hoped to remain in Mystic Falls, and indeed, often returned to his "home," the Salvatore boarding house. Damon, on the other hand, has no such attachment to place, and only returns to Mystic Falls when he believes that Katherine has survived and is entombed there. Damon's desire to rescue the love of his life is as strong as Stefan's desire to protect Elena, making each character a flawed but devoted romantic hero; or, as Calhoun phrases it, "two sides of the same coin — each brother's primary concern is the woman he loves."[56] This perhaps goes some way to explaining the divisions between Stelena and Delena shippers.

The audience of *The Vampire Diaries* includes a vocal online fan community, whose members regularly engage in online conversations with each other, the writers, and the producers about the characters and events depicted within the series. Fans are typically divided into two camps, in line with the program's central love triangle. "Stelena" shippers are those fans who champion the coupling of Stefan and Elena, whereas "Delena" fans wish to see the heroine choose older brother Damon. Members of fansites such as www.vampires-diaries.net and www.vampirediariesonline.com often identify themselves by their "team," either under their name and avatar, or in their online identity itself. Some of these names are based on the characters (for example, StelenaAlways, TeamSTELENA, Damon Girl, PeaceLoveDamon), whereas others are based on the actors' names (PaulWesleyFans, I_love_IanS). Rivalry between the two teams sometimes spills over into "ship wars" on Twitter, even though both "teams" refer to themselves as "the TVD Family," a metaphor that sometimes extends to asking the show's creators — and therefore, presumably, the "parents" of the family — to adjudicate these spats.[57]

The show's fans have utilized the Internet and social media as a means of feeling immediate connections with those involved in the production of the show. Matt Hills has noted that with increased access to the Internet has come the evolution of "just-in-time-fandom."[58] In 2002 he argued that this manifested in fans discussing episodes online immediately after their broadcast, "or even during ad-breaks — perhaps in order to demonstrate the 'timeliness' and responsiveness of their devotion."[59] The variety of time zones in which the program airs, however, poses problems for fans who wish to Tweet live during the broadcast, leading to a prolific use of "spoiler" and "live Tweet" warnings on Twitter. At the time of writing, the use of Twitter to discuss *The Vampire Diaries* has become such a phenomenon that particular topics often "trend," and on more than one occasion a particular hash-tag has become a "top tweet" — that is, the most commonly discussed topic on Twitter at a given point in time. Notable examples include Ian Somerhalder's birthday in December 2010, when fans were encouraged to donate to the Ian Somerhalder (Environmental) Foundation, and, more recently, when the "CatchPetrovaFire" hash-tag (referring to Katherine Pierce's alias, Katerina Petrova) became a top tweet immediately prior to the mid-season hiatus (February 24, 2011). Fans of *The Vampire Diaries* again generated a trend on Twitter on February 26, 2011: upon the release of ratings figures which showed that the program had come second to *American Idol* in that week's ratings, they circulated the message "Longlive TVD."

This kind of fandom, according to Ruthie Heard from www.vampirediariesonline, is "like no other. We have all become very close via Twitter. Also, having the connection with the cast and crew has added to our experience in ways you can't imagine. They make us feel a part of the show."[60] The writers and fans of the show include what they term "shout-outs" to fans of the books, as when they borrowed the name of Mrs Flowers (a significant character in the novels, for the keeper of a boarding house where Katherine was staying in Mystic Falls),[61] or in the use of one of L. J. Smith's book titles, "The Return," for the first episode of Season Two.[62] These "moments" are also circulated within both the book and television branches of the fandom via Twitter. In an ironic variation on the shout-out, the characters also use modern means of technology within the show's storylines, as when Elena uses text messaging to convey information by a means that is beyond the enhanced hearing of vampires, or when Caroline asks whether Bonnie's description of Damon as "Older Sexy Danger Guy" is an "official Witch Twitter tweet."[63] The actresses who portray these characters, Candice Accola and Katerina Graham, are both active Twitter users who regularly engage in online conversations with the show's fandom, thus providing an in-joke targeted squarely at that audience.

By providing the opportunity to debate the show within the fan community and to directly contact the actors, writers and executive producers, Twitter allows fans a forum to address the future form and direction of the series. As Kaplan argues, "[m]anifestos on characterization, reactions to individual moments in the source text, community in-jokes rooted in the source text and the community's reaction to it, and creative fan works such as fan fiction, artwork, and vids all contribute to a shared understanding of the source text."[64] Indeed, on occasion this kind of feedback has been solicited, as when writer Mike Daniels posted on Twitter: "Coffee. Check. Breakfast. Check. Now to write some Stefan/Elena. Anything you want to hear or see?"[65] Arguably, then, authorship is shared with these fans, who write about their preferred future directions of the storylines and characters.

The immediate and interactive nature of this kind of feedback to the show's producers and writers raises pertinent questions about the ongoing storylines of the show, and how fan opinions and marketing decisions are worked into the already complex interaction with the storylines of the original novels by L. J. Smith. Fans are also implicitly encouraged to engage with the show's characters and storylines in creative ways. Vids, or fan-produced montages of CW network footage set to music, are apparently sanctioned by the show's executive producers, given that Julie Plec has retweeted links to a number of them to facilitate their movement to a wider audience of fans.

Notions about authority and authorship were recently raised when HarperTeen produced and marketed a new *Vampire Diaries* sequence, *Stefan's Diaries*, in which an uncredited author rewrites the vampires' backstories in order to align them with the narrative arc within the alternative universe depicted in the TV series. L. J. Smith, Julie Plec and Kevin Williamson are cited as "consultants" on the cover, but copyright is allocated to "Alloy Entertainment and L. J. Smith."[66] The growing disconnect between stakeholders CW, Outerbanks Entertainment, HarperTeen, Alloy Entertainment, the fans, and Smith herself about the direction of the narrative ultimately led to Smith being dropped by HarperTeen in February 2011. Controversially, future *Vampire Diaries* novels will be written by another author, although Smith believes that some of her recent writing involving the characters will appear in the next instalment, *Phantom*, which she had intended to be Book One of the forthcoming *Vampire Diaries* trilogy, The Hunters. In late 2010, prior to the announcement about the estrangement with HarperTeen,

L. J. Smith used her blog to encourage disgruntled fans to write fanfiction, rather than lobbying her for their preferred "endgame" point of a happy ending for Stefan and Elena, or Damon and Elena, or even the smaller number of "Bamon" shippers, who hope to see Damon ultimately paired with Elena's witch best friend, Bonnie,[67] an outcome which is hinted at in Smith's latest novels.[68]

The erosion of the boundaries between authors and fans has cemented the modern-day vampire as arguably the ultimate uncanny being in popular culture. The vampires, as represented in the different incarnations of *The Vampire Diaries*, are simultaneously and antithetically outsiders and members of a town which itself shifts uncannily between the parallel universes of the novels and the television series. They are at once the predatory, nomadic loners of folklore, and respected founding members of their close-knit Southern township; characters whose relationships and interactions within that township are themselves mediated by an active community of online fans. It is perhaps fitting, then, that *The Vampire Diaries* is itself so uncannily located, simultaneously existing with the world of the novels and the world of the television series; within a number of genres, including Gothic horror, teen drama and romance; in Fell's Church, Mystic Falls, and on the worldwide web.

Notes

1   David Tanklefsky, "Vampire Diaries Sets Debut Record for CW," *Broadcasting and Cable.com*, September 11, 2009, http:www.broadcastingcable.com/article/346165_Primetime_Ratings_Vampire_Diaries_Sets_Debut_Record_For_CW.php; Ruthie Heard, "Interview with the Vampire Fandom," in *Love You to Death: The Unofficial Companion to The Vampire Diaries*, by Crissy Calhoun (Toronto: ECW Press, 2010), 189–196; Michael Ausiello, "Vampire Diaries Ratings: They Don't Suck!" Inside TV, September 11, 2009, http:/www.insidetv.ew.com/2009/09/11/vampire-diaries-ratings-they-dont-suck.

2   Heather Cordova, "L. J. Smith and Vampire Diaries Rumors — Author Confirms They're True," *Vampire Diaries.net*, accessed August 22, 2011, http://www.vampire-diaries.net/books/l-j-smith-vampire-diaries-rumors-author-confirms-theyre-true.

3   L. J. Smith, "Thank you but don't boycott," *Official Site of L. J. Smith.net*, accessed August 22, 2011, http://www.ljanesmith.net/www/blog/297-thank-you-but-dont-boycott; Cordova.
4   *The Vampire Diaries: The Complete Season One*, DVD, "Featurette: Into Mystic Falls," (2009, Neutral Bay, NSW: Warner Brothers Home Video, 2010).
5   Calhoun, 12.
6   Calhoun, xi.
7   Claudia Gray, "The War Between the States," in *A Visitor's Guide to Mystic Falls: Your Favorite Authors on The Vampire Diaries*, ed. Red and Vee, with Leah Wilson (Dallas: SmartPop Books, 2010), 35–49.
8   David Punter and Glennis Byron, *The Gothic* (Oxford: Blackwell, 2004), 39.
9   *The Vampire Diaries*, "Pilot," Season One, Episode One, director Marcos Siega, written by Kevin Williamson and Julie Plec, Neutral Bay, NSW: Warner Brothers Home Video, first aired September 10, 2009.
10 *The Vampire Diaries*, "Pilot."
11 *The Vampire Diaries*, "Let the Right One In," Season One, Episode 17, director Denis Smith, written by Julie Plec, Neutral Bay, NSW: Warner Brothers Home Video, April 8, 2010.
12 *The Vampire Diaries: The Complete Season One*, DVD, "Featurette: When Vampires Don't Suck," (2009, Neutral Bay, NSW: Warner Brothers Home Video, 2010).
13 Glyn Davis and Kay Dickinson, ed., *Teen TV: Genre, Consumption and Identity* (London: British Film Institute, 2004), 3.
14 Calhoun, 13.
15 *The Vampire Diaries: The Complete Season One*, DVD, "Featurette: When Vampires Don't Suck."
16 *Beverly Hills 90210*, created by Darren Star, Aaron Spelling and E. Duke Vincent. Los Angeles: Fox Entertainment, first aired October 4, 1990.
17 *Party of Five*. Los Angeles: Fox Entertainment, first aired September 12, 1994.
18 *Dawson's Creek*. Burbank, CA: Warner Brothers, first aired January 20, 1998.
19 Miranda J. Banks, "A Boy for All Planets: *Roswell*, *Smallville* and the Teen Male Melodrama," In *Teen TV: Genre, Consumption and Identity*, ed. Glyn Davis and Kay Dickinson (London: British Film Institute, 2004), 17–28.
20 Banks, 21.
21 *The Vampire Diaries*, "Pilot."
22 *The Vampire Diaries*, "The Night of the Comet," Season One, Episode Two, director Marcos Siega, written by Kevin Williamson and Julie

Plec, first aired September 17, 2009.
23. *The Vampire Diaries*, "The Lost Girls," Season One, Episode Six, director Marcos Siega, written by Kevin Williamson and Julie Plec, first aired October 15, 2009.
24. *The Vampire Diaries*, "Bloodlines," Series One, Episode 11, director David Barrett, written by Kevin Williamson and Julie Plec, first aired January 21, 2010.
25. *The Vampire Diaries*, "Bloodlines."
26. *The Vampire Diaries*, "Miss Mystic Falls," Season One, Episode 19, director Marcos Siega, written by Bryan Oh and Caroline Dries, first aired April 22, 2010.
27. *The Vampire Diaries*, "Blood Brothers," Season One, Episode 20, director Liz Friedlander, written by Kevin Williamson and Julie Plec, first aired April 29, 2010.
28. *The Vampire Diaries*, "Katerina," Season Two, Episode Nine, director J. Miller Tobin, written by Andrew Chambliss, first aired November 11, 2010.
29. *The Vampire Diaries*, "Pilot."
30. *Scream*, DVD, director Wes Craven (1996; Darlinghurst, NSW: Icon Home Entertainment, 2009); *Scream 2*, DVD, director Wes Craven (1997; South Yarra, Vic.: Village Roadshow, 2011); *Scream 3*, director Wes Craven (2000; South Yarra, Vic.: Village Roadshow, 2011); *Scream 4*, director Wes Craven (2011; forthcoming).
31. *I Know What You Did Last Summer*, DVD, director Jim Gillespie (1997; Sydney, NSW: Columbia Pictures, 2008).
32. *Cursed*, DVD, director Wes Craven (2005; Anaheim, California: Walt Disney Studios, 2005).
33. *The Vampire Diaries*, "The Pilot" and "The Night of the Comet."
34. *The Vampire Diaries*, "The Night of the Comet."
35. *The Vampire Diaries*, "Friday Night Bites," Season One, Episode Three, director John Dahl, written by Barbie Kligman and Bryan M. Holdman, first aired September 24, 2009.
36. *The Vampire Diaries*, "Founder's Day," Season One, Episode 22, director Marcos Siega, wriiten by Bryan Oh and Andrew Chambliss, first aired May 13, 2010.
37. *The Vampire Diaries*, "Rose," Season Two, Episode Eight, director Liz Friedlander, written by Brian Young, first aired November 4, 2010.
38. Carina Adly Mackenzie, "The Vampire Diaries' Kevin Williamson and Julie Plec: Is Damon Worthy of Elena?" *Zap 2 It.com*, accessed August 24, 2011, http://blog.zap2it.com/frominsidethebox/2010/10/the-vampire-diaries-kevin-williamson-and-julie-plec-is-damon-worthy-of-elena.html.

39 Calhoun, 118.
40 *The Vampire Diaries*, "Friday Night Bites" and "Blood Brothers."
41 *The Vampire Diaries*, "Bloodlines."
42 *The Vampire Diaries*, "Fool Me Once," Season One, Episode 14, director Marcos Siega, written by Brett Conrad, first aired February 11, 2010.
43 *The Vampire Diaries*, "Children of the Damned," Season One, Episode 13, director Marcos Siega, written by Kevin Williamson and Julie Plec, first aired February 4, 2010.
44 *The Vampire Diaries*, "The Descent," Season Two, Episode 12, director Marcos Siega, written by Elizabeth Craft and Sarah Fain, first aired January 27, 2011.
45 Alyxandra Harvey, "In Which Intrepid Heroines Discuss the Merits of the Bad Boy versus the Reformed Bad Boy with the Help of a Couple of Dead Women Who Know About Such Things," in Red and Vee, with Leah Wilson, 67–84.
46 Mackenzie.
47 Ibid.
48 Matthew Peterson, "Interview: L. J. Smith," *The Author Hour.com*, November 19, 2009, http://theauthorhour.com/l-j-smith/.
49 Mackenzie.
50 *The Vampire Diaries*, "Isobel," Season One, Episode 21, director J. Miller Tobin, written by Caroline Dries and Brian Young, first aired May 6, 2010.
51 *The Vampire Diaries*, "Miss Mystic Falls."
52 Calhoun, 161.
53 Kris De Leon, "*The Vampire Diaries*: Updates on Team Damon, Werewolves, and a Shocking Death," *Buddy TV.com*, accessed August 24, 2011, http://www.buddytv.com/articles/the-vampire-diaries/the-vampire-diaries-updates-on-35832.aspx.
54 *The Lost Boys*, DVD, director Joel Schumacher (1987; Neutral Bay, NSW: Warner Brothers Home Video, 1998); Nina Auerbach, *Our Vampires, Ourselves* (Chicago: University of Chicago Press, 1995), 168; Ken Gelder, *Reading the Vampire* (London and New York: Routledge, 1994), 106.
55 *The Vampire Diaries*, "Blood Brothers."
56 Calhoun, 107.
57 For example, on February 22, 2011, one fan made direct appeals to actress Nina Dobrev and executive producer Kevin Williamson to "read all the nasty things that SE fans are saying about DE fans!" (Quintana 2011).
58 Matt Hills, *Fan Cultures*, Sussex Studies in Culture and Communication (London and New York: Routledge, 2002), 178.
59 Hills, 178.

60 Heard, 189–196.
61 *The Vampire Diaries*, "Masquerade," Season Two, Episode Seven, director Charles Beeson, written by Kevin Williamson and Julie Plec, first aired October 28, 2010.
62 *The Vampire Diaries*, "The Return," Season Two, Episode One, director J. Miller Tobin, written by Kevin Williamson and Julie Plec, first aired September 9, 2010.
63 *The Vampire Diaries*, "Family Ties," Season One, Episode Four, director Guy Ferland, written by Andrew Kreisberg and Brian Young, first aired October 1, 2009.
64 Deborah Kaplan, "Construction of Fan Fiction Character Through Narrative," in *Fan Fiction and Fan Communities in the Age of the Internet*, ed. Kristina Busse and Karen Hellekson (Jefferson, NC: McFarland, 2006), 134–152.
65 Mike Daniels, "mikedaniels101," *Twitter.com*, November 8, 2010, http://twitter.com/#!/MikeDaniels101.
66 Alloy Entertainment and L. J. Smith, *The Vampire Diaries: Stefan's Diaries, Vol 2: Bloodlust* (New York: HarperTeen, 2011); *The Vampire Diaries: Stefan's Diaries, Vol. 1: Origins* (New York: HarperTeen, 2010); *The Vampire Diaries: Stefan's Diaries, Vol 3: The Craving* (New York: HarperTeen, 2011).
67 L. J. Smith, "About These Just for Fun Polls," *Official Site of L. J. Smith.net*, accessed August 24, 2011, http://www.ljanesmith.net/www/blog/2010/277-about-these-just-for-fun-polls.
68 Smith, *The Vampire Diaries: The Return, Vol 1: Nightfall* (New York: HarperTeen, 2009); *The Vampire Diaries: The Return, Vol. 2: Shadow Souls* (New York: HarperTeen, 2010); *The Vampire Diaries: The Return, Vol 3: Midnight* (New York: HarperTeen, 2011).

11

Escape to Ambiguity:
The *Twilight* Fan's Playground

Katie Hoskinson

Something is happening in Forks, Washington. Since 2005 the town at the foot of the Olympic mountain range has experienced a 600% increase in tourism. This jump has given the struggling timber town an economic boost.[1] The cause of this boost is evident in the tourists that flock there. On a daily basis, 350 to 400 giggling girls, people asking about vampires and werewolves, and mothers in Team Edward T-shirts, crowd into Forks's Chamber of Commerce.[2] They come because of the Twilight saga. Yet, an influx of "Twi-hards" is not the only change Forks has experienced since the publication of the first book in the four-part series. The town has recreated itself as the fictional Forks, Washington where Stephenie Meyer set her story. This recreation is both a reaction to and a partnership with the hundreds of Twilight saga fans that visit the town each day. The changes that have taken place in Forks offer insight into the way that fandom and the mundane work together to recreate a space.

A debate in fan scholarship has arisen over the subversive nature of fan practices. This debate juxtaposes the nature of fandom with the concept of the mundane. In *Mundane Reason: Reality in Everyday and Sociological Discourse*, Melvin Pollner describes mundane reasoning as a belief system that assumes that "an 'out there', 'public' or 'objective' world is a central feature of a network of beliefs about reality."[3] Pollner argues that those who participate in the mundane believe they are confronting a "real world."[4] I find Pollner's sociological description of the mundane is best put into the context of fandom by Joe Sanders and Rich Brown, in their glossary of fanspeak. Sanders and Brown define the mundane, as it relates to fan studies, as "describing the majority of the human race that is content with familiar types of literature and thinking [and is] frequently used with disdain to describe people who denigrate fandom because it differs from the mainstream."[5] Sanders and Brown's definition of the mundane suggests a clear distinction between the realm of the mundane and the realm of the fan.

This current debate in fan scholarship problematizes the notion of a strident distinction between fandom and the mundane, and enables critics to ask questions such as: are fans able to subvert the mainstream or mundane culture? Do fans replicate the hierarchical practices of the mundane in a different setting? Is there common ground between the mundane and fandom? Jonathan Gray is a fan scholar who participates in the fandom/mundane debate. He, Cornel Sandvoss and C. Lee Harrington take issue with the notion of fandom as wholly distinct from the mundane. In the introduction to *Fandom: Identities and Communities in a Mediated World*, the authors argue that fan practices "are tied to wider social structures" and that fans manage to "extend the conceptual focus beyond questions of hegemony and class to the overarching social, cultural, and economic transformations of our time."[6] They suggest that fan practices share similarities with the mundane, and argue that scholars should further an understanding of the relationship between fans and the mundane beyond these general similarities.

Henri Lefebvre's theory about the production of space, specifically his description of social space, makes it possible to see beyond the general similarities of fans and the mundane into the potential for cooperation between these categories. In *The Production of Space*, he writes that "(social) space is not a thing among other things, nor a product among other products: rather, it subsumes things produced, and encompasses their interrelationships in their coexistence and simultaneity ... At the same time there is nothing imagined unreal or 'ideal' about [(social) space] as compared, for example, with science, representations, ideas or dreams."[7] According to Lefebvre, social space is the ether around everything we encounter, but unlike ether, (social) space is tangible. The concept (social) space is tangible in people's perceptions of concrete objects,

Place and Identity   189

like a building perceived as a school. In the (social) space of Forks, fandom and the mundane cooperate to recreate the town.

In this chapter, I draw on the fandom debate, using the term "mundane" to describe those outside of fandom who believe that reality is an "out there" or "real world," but I will do so to explain how the cooperation between fandom and the mundane in the recreation of (social) space in Forks, Washington challenges the distinction made between the mundane and fandom. Following the suggestion of Gray, Sandvoss and Harrington, I look beyond similarities between the mundane and fandom to argue that contemporary theories about the production of space suggest that fandom and the mundane can work together to create reality. Specifically, I point to the recreation of Forks, Washington as a site where cooperation between fandom and the mundane is evident. Since the publication of the first installment of the Twilight saga, the real life setting of Meyer's fictional novels — Forks, Washington — has undergone significant changes. These changes have transformed the town into a playground of ambiguity, where the typical borders between fiction and reality are intentionally blurred.

Forks: Before and After *Twilight*

Forks's recreation was made possible through the relationship between the citizens of Forks, representatives of the mundane, and the Twilight saga fans. Before *Twilight*, Forks was floundering economically; since the release of the series, fans and citizens have transformed the town into a thriving, fictional reality. The benefit of Forks's transformation is twofold. Firstly, the town has been economically resurrected. The second benefit, which I find more intriguing and will further explore here, is the opportunity for Twilight saga fans to continue to experience the texts at a physical location. In an attempt to thoroughly explore this recreation, I will designate the city as it existed before *Twilight* as Forks, Washington "B.T."[8] My examination of what Forks B.T. used to be like serves as a comparison to what the city became after *Twilight* (referred to as Forks Washington "A.T.").

In "Timber Towns," a 1992 article by D. Fisher and C. Schubert about the economic decline of towns relying on timber, Forks is the model of this downward spiral.[9] The authors report that in Forks, "unemployment among the 3,400 residents is soaring, families are stressed and the people are angry ... the community food and clothing banks are being emptied."[10] During Fisher and Schubert's research, Forks did not have an economically bright future. Although the authors cite timber town enthusiasts who express hope for some towns, they conclude that "towns like Forks will probably never see the booming economy of the 1970s and the late 1980s again."[11] Clearly, Fisher and Schubert did not anticipate *Twilight* fans and their desire to continue experiencing the text and the mundane's willingness to cooperate with such a desire.

The future was bleak, but the relationship that the mundane Forks would build with the fictional Forks of *Twilight* solved the town's economic woes. I have already mentioned Chris Gray's report that Forks has seen a 600% increase in tourism since 2005.[12] Citizens interviewed in Jason Brown's documentary, *Twilight in Forks: The Saga of a Real Town,* corroborate Chris Gray's findings and speak of the changes caused by this influx of tourism. Marcia Bingham, from Forks's Chamber of Commerce, states that Forks is visited by 350 to 450 people a day, most of whom are presumably Twilight saga fans.[13] Bruce Paul, co-owner of Forks Outfitters, explains that his store has begun to stock new merchandise to appeal to the "different demographic" of customers.[14] Bert Paul, the other co-owner, gives the Twilight saga phenomenon credit for transforming Forks, saying, "it's been so good for our economy."[15] A teacher at Forks High School, John Hunter, admits there was a "time when it looked pretty bleak,"[16] but, as Mayor Reed states in Tom Henheffer's article, "*Twilight* Central's Sobbing Pilgrims," "*Twilight* has been an absolute blessing. It's kept the last person from turning out the lights, as a matter of fact, lights are going on in abandoned buildings."[17] The lights in Forks illuminate the ambiguity between reality and fiction developed during the recreation of the town.

In order to reap such economic benefits, Forks citizens actively transform their town into a Twilight saga fan's dream. In Henheffer's article, Mike Gurling, manager of Forks's visitor center, highlights that "we realized these folks would be coming to Forks and we wanted to give them an experience."[18] The experience Forks gives Twilight saga fans, is created by blurring the boundary between text and reality. For example, Annette Roots calls her gift shop "immersive" and says, "I sat down and thought: what would it feel like for me to walk into the book?" The result of her pondering is a gift shop divided into four sections: "a forest with giant fake trees, a beach with sand and driftwood, a broken down castle and a dim back-lit dungeon."[19] Roots's immersive shop mimics the physical descriptions in *Twilight*, bringing the fiction into reality. Bert Paul explains why he pages Bella Swan to the sporting goods section of his store: "we just help them add to the fantasy and make it real when they come here."[20] Paul, Roots, and Gurling are citizens of Forks who understand that in order to benefit from Twilight saga fans, they must transform their mundane town into the fictional experience that fans desire.

Before delving much deeper into a discussion of the changes in Forks, I would like to clarify a definition of ambiguity that I will use to describe the production of (social) space in Forks. In *The Flight from Ambiguity*, Donald N. Levine offers clues to understanding ambiguity, which he suggests encompasses "studied skepticisms toward ... exclusively univocal formulations."[21] Levine also suggests that ambiguity is a practice of "devious imprecision" and the ability "to harbor a multiplicity of meanings."[22] Drawing on Levine's clues, I understand ambiguity to refer to people's capacity to embrace intentional multiplicity in meaning. In Forks, such multiplicity arises between the layers of reality and fiction and is embraced by citizens and Twilight saga fans alike. The town is never totally a mundane reality or completely Meyer's fictional creation.

The ambiguous (social) space of Forks parallels Edward W. Soja's concept of Thirdspace, which he describes as "a creative recombination and extension, one that builds on the Firstspace perspective that is focused on the 'real' material world and a Secondspace perspective that interprets this reality through 'imagined' representations of spatiality."[23] The mundane, or the assumption of a real world, is identified as Firstspace by Soja; the desire of fans to see the fictional text is identified as Secondspace. As both "spaces" interact, Forks becomes a Thirdspace, or a place where the real and imaginary recreate reality. The intentionally imprecise distinction between the reality and the fiction of Forks (the Thirdspace) can be divided into categories: people, places, and mythology. Through a close examination of these three in the following sections, I will demonstrate concrete, contemporary ways in which Thirdspace operates, while expanding the scope of Thirdspace beyond place to both the people and narratives of space.

The People of Forks

The people living, working, and visiting Forks cultivate ambiguity between fictional characters and human individuals. Because filming of the Twilight saga occasionally takes place in the town, actors — who have come to embody the fictional characters — are spotted in Forks, blurring distinctions between mundane Forks and Twilight saga fans' fictional fantasy. Lindsay Mcghee and Tomoko Yuzawa, fans interviewed in Brown's documentary, came to watch the filming of *Twilight*. On the streets of Forks, they ran into Kirsten Stewart, Robert Pattinson, and Taylor Lautner. While both girls occasionally use the actors' names, they describe their experience as if they interacted with characters from the book. For example, Mcghee recounts how she shouted, "Oh my gosh Jacob's here, Jacob's here,"[24] when she saw Taylor Lautner. The presence of the actors who have come to represent Meyer's fictional characters helps Forks to appear as the fictional *Twilight* Forks. It is clear from Mcghee's and Yuzawa's stories that some fans, when confronted by the actors, do not automatically distinguish between what is real and what is fiction.

It is not just actors who enhance the fictional aspects of Forks. Citizens are frequently confused with, or purposely identified as, fictional characters. When she was interviewed for *Forks: The Saga of a Real Town*, Christyna Whatman explained that children are frightened to have their pictures taken with her when she plays Alice Cullen in Leppell's Flowers and Gifts. Staying in character, Whatman tells them she has "already eaten,"[25] suggesting they are safe because she is not hungry for blood. Roy Black Jr., a wrinkled Quiluete tribal elder, once introduced himself as Jacob's Grandpa to a speechless young fan.[26] Less intentionally, Sassy Belford adds to the production of ambiguity as a fair-skinned, brown-eyed, long-haired brunette cashier at Forks Outfitters. She was repeatedly asked to work at the Twilight saga gift store, but did not understand why until someone told her she looked like Bella Swan. Fans visiting Forks frequently ask to take her picture.[27] The ambiguity between fictional characters and real people demonstrates an important claim Lefebvre makes about the production of (social) space.

As they slip between characters, actors, and citizens, these people recreate relationships between objects in the (social) space of Forks, thereby portraying the town as the fictional setting of the *Twilight* series. Lefebvre explains that, in this process, the space produced is "not a thing but rather a set of relations between things."[28] According to Lefebvre, objects are not a part of the production of space; rather it is the relationship between these objects that builds (social) space. In Forks, the relations between civilians and/or actors and/or characters are recreated. The development of these different relations recreates Forks as Thirdspace. Soja explains, "*everything* comes together in Thirdspace: subjectivity and objectivity."[29] As fans of the Twilight saga and citizens of Forks build new relationships between the characters and townspeople together, they produce a (social) space that combines the objectivity of fictional characters with the subjectivity of actual people. Through this shared production, fandom and the mundane cooperate to create a Thirdspace.

Places of Forks

As its people are both real and fictional, so too are Forks's physical places. Real locations are manipulated to parallel Meyer's fiction. Although the hospital, school, and homes of Forks were built before Meyer's fictional portrayal of them, they are recreated by citizens to transform Forks. While these preexisting buildings assume their identity from the text, they propagate the lack of distinction between Meyer's Forks and the mundane. For example, the *Dazzled by Twilight* Tour stops at places in Forks referring to them as if they were from the series. Tour guide Travis Belles identifies Forks High School as "the high school of the Cullens."[30] Like the relation between people, the relation between places in Forks — in this case, its buildings — are recreated to bring together the abstract and the concrete into a Thirdspace.

Many citizens interviewed in the documentary discuss places in their town as if they are from *Twilight*. Hunter, the teacher, says, "actually, the Swans kind of live in my neighborhood," and Kevin

Rupprecht, the principal, identifies the crash site, sectioned off in the school parking lot, as the place where Bella was saved by Edward.[31] In the school, the Cullens and Bella have designated lockers.[32] Kenneth Romney, a doctor at Forks Hospital, describes the location of Dr. Cullen's parking spot.[33] These are examples of how fictional elements of *Twilight* are literally recreated in Forks. These reconstructions bridge the gap between the Forks outside of fandom and the Forks alive in the minds of Twilight saga fans.

As a fan myself, I experienced the blurring of fiction and reality while watching the tour included in Brown's documentary. I have read the series and seen the movies multiple times, and when the tour took the documentary crew to Jacob Black's house, I had difficulty deciding if the house had been stylized or was Jacob's fictional house. Like Forks High School, Belles identifies the little red house as Black's home.[34] A motorcycle is on the porch, a barn is located at the back, and "Black" is on the mailbox. The worn look of the home made it appear as if it had been at this location for some time. This house is not a set, but it is identical to the house of the fictional character. The indistinguishable line between my imagined fiction and the "reality" at Jacob's house transformed Forks. For me, the town no longer seems the mundane setting of a series about teenage love and mythical creatures, but a real space where those elusive beings exist.

To explain my experience of Jacob's house as a Thirdspace, I turn to Matt Hills's *Fan Cultures*. Hills suggests that D. W. Winnicott's idea of a transitional object, or an object with which a child plays in a "near-withdrawal state" and "enacts delusions of omnipotence,"[35] is useful in understanding fan relationships to reality. He explains that "the transitional object must always have some kind of physical and intersubjective existence; it cannot be some kind of imagined entity or hallucination."[36] The object with which a child or fan plays must be abstract and concrete. It must occupy a Thirdspace. Applying Hills' theory to my experience with Jacob's house, the house becomes my transitional object, or the object through which I experience both the inner-subjectivity of fandom and the outer-objective reality. Playing with a transitional object, according to Hills, is a creative process. He writes that this play "produces an enduring affective 'structure' which corresponds to the subject's personalized third space."[37] My play with Jacob's house helps me create Forks as a Thirdspace.

Mythology of Forks

The ambiguous reality of people and places is mirrored in stories told about Forks. Together, fans and citizens create the town's mythology. Unlike the people and places of Forks, mythology does not have concrete objects around which new relationships can be developed. However, these narratives do build upon the knowable and unimaginable, and this development is one aspect of Soja's Thirdspace.[38] Examples of such narratives are discussed in Brown's documentary. Charlene Leppell, the owner of Leppell's Flowers and Gifts, has discovered that people with the last name Cullen lived on a ranch near La Push. She also comments on parts of the woods where she and her friends mysteriously knew not to play.[39] Leppell's eerie descriptions of life in Forks B.T. add credence to the town's current, fantastic recreation. Since historically Forks is connected to people named Cullen and forbidden woods, the Forks presented to Twilight saga fans is not mimicry but reality. Marcia Bingham blatantly claims, "we've got vampires and werewolves."[40] The same doctor who spoke of Dr. Cullen's parking spot alludes to a very handsome doctor who spends a large amount of his time in Seattle, and wonders whether the doctor is going there to work or hunt.[41] Stories such as these, told by both citizens and Twilight saga fans, continue to blend fiction into reality. By intertwining mundane Forks with the narrative of *Twilight*, these stories tie the knowable reality of the town to the unimaginable fiction of the text, recreating the relationship between fiction and reality and effectively building a Thirdspace narrative about Forks.

Larry Carroll, a senior writer for MTV, describes the ambiguousness of Forks, saying: "Stephenie's world isn't as imaginary as some people would have you believe."[42] The people, places, and stories of Forks help transform the mundane, faltering timber town to an imaginative world where lines between fiction and reality are not defined. The ambiguity between fiction and reality produces a space where the opposing forces of fantasy and reality coexist. A tribal elder is also the grandfather of a fictional hero. A normal high school educates vampires. A quiet town has forbidden woods.

These examples of ambiguity have drawn Twilight saga fans to Forks for a special experience of their favorite series.

Ambiguity at Play

The 350 to 450 fans who come to Forks every day come to continue their experience with the text. Robyn Duong, a fan who made the journey, says that she came to get in touch with the *Twilight* story. In her words, she came "to keep going on the journey."[43] Fan actions speak as loudly as their words. Gurling reveals that the Chamber of Commerce receives numerous letters addressed to *Twilight* characters. Bella receives the most — usually love letters and book club invitations — but Alice and Jasper also get their share.[44] The beliefs and actions of Duong and those who have written letters demonstrate the extent to which Forks has been transformed from the mundane to the fictional. For these fans, Forks exists in between the lines of reality and fiction where the story of *Twilight* lives.

The ambiguity between fiction and reality helps fans escape into the fiction of *Twilight*. Levine describes several functions of ambiguity in modern culture. Most relevant to understanding the circumstances affecting Forks and Twilight saga fans is Levine's description of ambiguous communication and expressiveness. He argues that precise presentations of facts strip communication of its "expressive overtones and suggestive allusions."[45] Levine continues: "[A]mbiguous communication, by contrast, can provide a superb means for conveying affect."[46] In other words, through imprecise distinctions one can allude to shared experiences and sentiments that evoke a "wealth of affective responses."[47] Ambiguity can better communicate an experience than precise, stripped-down communication. Levine's description of ambiguous communication applies to the people, places, and stories of Forks.

The dimensions of reality and fiction expressed in Forks evoke an experience of the text that would be impossible through a precise depiction of facts. For example, if the young fans reluctant to have their pictures taken with Whatman were informed that she is a human dressed up as a fictional character, their experience of *Twilight* would end due to the precision of the communication. Instead, they are told she has "just eaten," and thus they remain a little longer in the fictional realm through Whatman's intentionally ambivalent re-

Place and Identity   197

sponse. Forks facilitates the experience of *Twilight* through ambiguous communication. Citizens could shrug and say, "remember, *Twilight* is just a story." Instead, they have accumulated fictional characters, cultivated fictional locations in reality, and developed the story of *Twilight* to better express the fictional Forks. The citizens of Forks have transformed their struggling timber town, that existed outside fan practice, into a fictional reality that appeals to *Twilight* fans' desire to continue to experience the text.

"The Act of Reading" *Twilight*

While the ambiguity at work in Forks is mainly propagated by citizens of Forks, it would not exist without the desire of Twilight saga fans. Without demanding fans, Forks would never have been recreated. The desire of fans to continue the journey begun in the text is an important aspect of Forks's changes, and parallels Janice Radway's description of female reading habits in *Reading the Romance: Women, Patriarchy, and Popular Literature*. The readers Radway interviewed for her book have a relationship with romance novels that is similar to the relationship Twilight saga fans have with the series and — by extension — Forks.

While interviewing women about their romance novel reading habits, Radway's surprise at their explanations prompted her to develop "the act of reading."[48] Radway explains that "although I learned later that certain aspects of the romance's story do help to make this event especially meaningful, the early interviews were interesting because they focused so resolutely on the significance of the *act of romance reading* rather than the meaning of the romance."[49] According to Radway, simply reading offers a special experience to readers, something that other forms of entertainment cannot. Picking up any novel is the first step in an important process of escape, that women experience while reading. Radway argues that the act of reading is a "special gift" to one's self.[50] In other words, reading is an inner exchange or a way to achieve pleasure without outside help. Through Radway's theory, the power of the text in relation to the *Twilight* phenomenon becomes clear. According to Radway, while Twilight saga fans read the series, they feel the pleasure of self-gratification. This pleasure is a break from the mundane for the reader. Radway relates that the main goal of the interviewees was to do something different from their usual daily routine.[51] Radway's theory suggests that the act of reading *Twilight* empowers readers to escape from the routine or ordinary.

Evidence of this escape is found in the fans interviewed in Brown's documentary. Duong says that the story gives readers hope, and Whatman claims that *Twilight* is the story "[readers] always wanted to live out."[52] Yuzawa explains that "people want to know there could, maybe, be something like that out there."[53] The statements of these fans echo Radway's theory of reading as an escape from the mundane and extend her theory beyond the act of reading to the content of the text. While Radway argues that the mere act of reading breaks the routine of the everyday, it is clear from their testimony that Twilight saga fans find escape through the series' content as well. For fans, the Twilight saga offers a narrative different from their lives and is thus an experience outside the ordinary. The recreation of Forks is a continuation of this experience. As Duong explained, Forks is an extension of the journey begun in the text. The union of fans' escapist fantasies with concrete aspects of Forks is yet one more way in which the town demonstrates the relations possible in Lefebvre's (social) space, and which facilitates the fluidity of Soja's Thirdspace.

Conclusion

Forks's recreation parallels the conclusion of Brian Longhurst, Gaynor Bagnall, and Mike Savage in "Place, Elective Belonging, and the Diffused Audience." After surveying reactions to the media present in their communities, they conclude that "performance, imagination, and spectacle are embroiled in practices of attachment and identity in everyday life of media drenched societies."[54] Their conclusion is demonstrated in Forks's new relations to *Twilight*. The ambiguity evident in Forks suggests that the mundane can exist alongside the imaginative spectacle of fandom. Longhurst, Bagnall, and Savage suggest that "[f]andom is not significant in its generality, but as indicating aspects of everyday performance and imagination that are informing mundane practices."[55] Fandom and the mundane are most significant in their interactions with each other. The recreation of Forks as Thirdspace is evidence that fandom and the mundane can cooperate.

Place and Identity   199

This cooperative transformation demonstrates how (social) space can develop a Thirdspace. As Lefebvre explains, (social) space is evident in the relations between objects. After *Twilight*, the relations between objects in Forks are not the same. In the (social) space of Forks, fans and citizens have developed new relations between reality and fiction. This meeting has recreated Forks as a form of Soja's Thirdspace. This somewhat incredible work testifies to the transformative capabilities of pairing fandom and the mundane. These previously opposing perspectives unite to recreate a town limited only by the stretch of imaginations.

"*Everything* comes together in Thirdspace." Soja's previously quoted statement includes a comprehensive list thus far missing from my argument, but, in conclusion, the expanse of Thirdspace illuminates the breadth of possibilities for Forks. Soja lists: "subjectivity and objectivity, the abstract and the concrete, the real and the imagined, the knowable and the unimaginable, the repetitive and the differential, structure and agency, mind and body, consciousness and the unconsciousness, the disciplined and the transdisiplinary, everyday life and unending history."[56] These dichotomies speak of the infinite fluidity of Thirdspace. In the (social) space of Forks, the fluidity of relations exists not just in place, but among people and mythology. Forks's citizens, actors, and fictional characters join subjectivity with objectivity. The places of Forks relate concrete reality to what is abstractly imagined. Finally, the mythology of the town brings together knowable stories about the reality of Forks with the unimaginable fiction of werewolves and vampires in the Olympic forest. Through the cooperation of fandom and the mundane, the recreation of Forks, Washington demonstrates how the fluidity of Thirdspace is possible in the places, people, and mythologies of our contemporary reality.

Notes

1   Chris Gray, "It is *Twilight* Time in the Pacific North West," *USA Today*, sec. Life, November 6, 2009, http://web.ebscohost.com.
2   *Twilight in Forks: The Saga of a Real*, DVD, directed by Jason Brown (Universal City, CA: Summit Entertainment, 2010).

3   Melvin Pollner, *Mundane Reason: Reality in Everyday and Sociological Discourse* (Cambridge, UK: Cambridge University Press, 1987), x.
4   Pollner, 127.
5   Joe Sanders and Rich Brown, "Glossary of Fanspeak," in *Science Fiction Fandom*, ed. Joe Sanders, Contributions to the Study of Science Fiction and Fantasy 62 (London: Greenwood Press, 1994), 268.
6   Jonathan Gray, Cornel Sandvoss, and C. Lee Harrington, "Introduction: Why Study Fans?" in *Fandom: Identities and Communities in a Mediated World*, ed. Jonathan Gray, Cornel Sandvoss, and C. Lee Harrington (New York and London: New York University Press, 2007), 8.
7   Henri Lefebvre, *The Production of Space*, trans. Donald Nicholson-Smith (Oxford: Blackwell Publishing, 1991), 73.
8   Tom Henheffer, " *Twilight* Central's Sobbing Pilgrims," *Maclean's* 122, no. 45 (2009): 74, http://web.ebscohost.com.
9   D. Fisher and C. Schubert, "Timber Towns in Trouble," *Progressive* 56, no. 4 (1992): 28, http://web.ebscohost.com.
10 Fisher and Schubert, 28.
11 Ibid., 28.
12 Chris Gray, "It is *Twilight* Time."
13 *Twilight in Forks*.
14 Ibid.
15 Ibid.
16 Ibid.
17 Henheffer, 74.
18 Ibid.
19 Ibid.
20 *Twilight in Forks*.
21 Donald N. Levine, *The Flight from Ambiguity: Essays in Social and Cultural Theory* (Chicago: University of Chicago Press, 1985), ix-x.
22 Levine, ix-x.
23 Edward W. Soja, *Thirdspace: Journeys to Los Angeles and Other Real-and-Imagined Places* (Malden, MA and Oxford: Blackwell, 1996), 6.
24 *Twilight in Forks*.
25 Ibid.
26 Ibid.
27 Ibid.
28 Lefebvre, 83.
29 Soja, 56.
30 *Twilight in Forks*.
31 Ibid.
32 Ibid.
33 Ibid.

34 Ibid.
35 Matt Hills, *Fan Cultures* (London and New York: Routledge, 2002), 104.
36 Hills, 104.
37 Hills, 111.
38 Soja, 56–57.
39 *Twilight in Forks*.
40 Ibid.
41 Ibid.
42 Ibid.
43 Ibid.
44 Ibid.
45 Levine, 32.
46 Ibid.
47 Ibid.
48 Janice A. Radway, *Reading the Romance: Women, Patriarchy, and Popular Literature* (Chapel Hill: University of North Carolina Press, 1991), 87.
49 Radway, 86.
50 Ibid., 91.
51 Ibid., 88.
52 *Twilight in Forks*.
53 Ibid.
54 Brian Longhurst, Gaynor Bagnall, and Mike Savage, "Place, Elective Belonging, and the Diffused Audience," in *Fandom: Identities and Communities in a Mediated World*, ed. Jonathan Gray, Cornel Sandvoss, and C. Lee Harrington (New York and London: New York University Press, 2007), 137.
55 Longhurst, Bagnall, and Savage, 137.
56 Soja, 56–57.

Fan Fiction

12

Anyone For a Vampwich? *True Blood*, Online Identity and Copyright

Melissa de Zwart

> Well, if you're their poster boy, the mainstreaming movement is in trouble: "TruBlood: It'll keep you alive, but it will bore you to death."
> (Eric Northman to Bill Compton, *True Blood*, Season One, Episode Nine)[1]

When Bill Compton walks into Merlotte's Bar and Grill and into the life of waitress Sookie Stackhouse, vampires have been "out of the coffin" for four years, although none have previously ventured into Bon Temps.[2] Sookie observes:

> We had all the other minorities in our little town — why not the newest, the legally recognized undead? But rural northern Louisiana wasn't too tempting to vampires, apparently; on the other hand, New Orleans was a real center for them — the whole Anne Rice thing, right?[3]

In her opening observations Sookie neatly draws us into her universe: vampires are living amongst us, as a minority with a special "problem." She assumes that her audience, like her, has some understanding of vampires, drawing upon the wealth of vampire literature and films; in particular, Anne Rice's *Interview with the Vampire* and the later Vampire Chronicles.[4,5] However, the development of synthetic blood by the mysterious Japanese Yakonomo

Corporation provides an intriguing outcome for the vampires in Charlaine Harris's Southern Vampire Mysteries and their even sexier television adaption *True Blood*, produced by Alan Ball for HBO. It provides a unique scenario for the vampires of the *True Blood* universe, meaning that they are no longer dependent upon human blood and can, if they so choose, liberate themselves and become "mainstream," as law-abiding members of society (their legal status is somewhat uncertain; they pay taxes, but cannot, for example, get married in the Louisiana of the television series).[6] Thus these Southern Vampires are yet another evolution of the sympathetic vampires with which modern culture has become fascinated; they are tragic, beautiful, and misunderstood. This view portrays the vampire as the eternal outsider, romantic and complex, rather than as an evil monster who seeks only his or her own fulfilment.[7]

Does the ability of vampires to "mainstream" also provide fans with a similar capacity to explore the other side of vampire existence, and to engage with the text (used in this context to mean both the books and the HBO series) — to explore their own creativity in the Sookie universe? This chapter will argue that the nature of the HBO content promotes and invites audience interaction. Fans are provided with a wealth of conflicted and complex characters through whom they can explore and interact with a range of issues; these include both Harris's characters, and the enhancements and additions introduced by HBO. They reflect the fractured and contested nature of post-modern society. There is no binary distinction between good and evil, and, as Sookie discovers when she questions Bill on the subject, even the vampires are not clear on the subject:

> "Do you really believe you've lost your soul?" That was what the Catholic Church was preaching about vampires.
> "I have no way of knowing," Bill said, almost casually. It was apparent that he'd brooded over it so often it was quite a commonplace thought to him. "Personally, I think not. There is something in me that isn't cruel, not murderous, even after all these years. Though I can be both."[8]

This chapter will consider the copyright issues that arise with respect to the recreation and reuse of the vampire story, both by Harris and HBO, and by the fans on the TrueBlood Wiki. It will use this forum in order to explore the scope within modern copyright law for the creation of fan fiction and will consider, in particular, the invitation given by HBO to engage with Sookie's universe in a range of commercial and non-commercial spaces, wherein fans can explore vampire identity. It will also consider what is novel in the True Blood series (looking at both the Southern Vampire Mysteries and the HBO version), and what aspects of that novelty may be appropriated by fans in retelling their "own" stories. It will examine why this is important from a cultural and social perspective, and will include a consideration of Gilles Deleuze and Félix Guattari's theories of "becoming," as particularly relevant to the nature of vampires, shifters, and "weres".

The Southern Vampire Mysteries

As of May 2011, Charlaine Harris has written eleven books in the Southern Vampire Mysteries series. Harris has stated that she is "not finished with the series," although she is not sure how many more books she will write about Sookie.[9] The first of these, *Dead Until Dark*, was published in 2001 and explores the relationship that develops between Sookie Stackhouse and Bill Compton, a vampire "turned" during the Civil War. Bill has now returned to Bon Temps and taken up residence in his family home. Bill tells Sookie's grandmother that, following the death of Jessie Compton, "The land reverted to me, and since things have changed in our culture toward people of my particular persuasion, I decided to claim it."[10] Bill's ability to return to "normal" society is made possible by the invention of "Tru Blood", synthetic blood which provides the full nutrition required by vampires but does not satisfy their "hunger" for human blood.[11] Sookie is intrigued by Bill for two reasons. First of all, although she possesses the ability to read minds, she cannot read Bill's thoughts because he is a vampire and is therefore technically dead. Secondly, Sookie is — like Bill — also, implicitly, an outsider. Sexually abused as a child, Sookie has never had an adult romantic or sexual relationship, but with Bill she quickly develops an intense love affair (with plenty of hot vampire sex). However, the course of true love never runs smooth, and throughout the series of books she enters into a relationship with the Sheriff of Area 5, 1000-year-old vampire Eric Northman.

Eric, the tall, blond Viking warrior, is the opposite of Bill, who is shorter, dark-haired, and with "curiously old fashioned" side burns.[12] Eric is attracted to Sookie for her usefulness as a mind reader, and is initially intrigued by the intense attraction she arouses in Bill. However, we also come to learn that despite Sookie's general attractiveness to vampires, due to her fairy blood, Eric's pursuit of Sookie is motivated by his feelings, and he eventually declares his love for her.[13]

As well as acting as a love rival to Bill, Eric provides a foil for Bill's attempts at "mainstreaming". He is openly scornful of Bill's adherence to Tru Blood and appears comfortable with his vampire habits, at one point telling Sookie:

> "Sookie, you have to understand that for hundreds, thousands, of years we have considered ourselves better than humans, separate from humans." He thought for a second. "Very much in the same relationship to humans as humans have to, say, cows. Edible like cows, but cute, too."[14]

Of course, Sookie is offended and nauseated by his comment, but in the end she comes to see that his approach is, at least, honest. Thus Eric and Bill reflect very different aspects of vampiredom: blond-versus-brown hair; modern-versus-old fashioned; honest-versus-secretive; and blood drinking-versus-synthetic feeding.

The juxtaposition of Eric and Bill naturally results in a love triangle that is a key focus of the HBO series, and provides a rich seam of material for the creation of fan fiction.[15] You can be Team Eric or Team Bill or, if you cannot choose between them, you can write your own story featuring yourself (or Sookie) as the center of a "vampwich."[16]

HBO: Television's Third Wave

HBO is a US subscription channel, owned by Time Warner, known for the production of high quality, cinema-like programs such as *Deadwood*, *The Sopranos* and *Six Feet Under*. As a subscription channel it is outside the regulatory framework of the United States Federal Communications Commission, enabling it to include material with a higher level of graphic content (essentially, offensive language and sex) than free to air television.[17] Such freedom may suggest that the HBO would aim for wide audience appeal through gratuitous adult content, but it has instead consistently aimed for the high end of the production output, in line with its claim: "It's not TV, it's HBO."[18] This is due to changing viewer habits, and to recognition of the value of a niche audience with a larger disposable income. The average HBO subscriber, as Nelson explains, wants to be challenged as well as entertained, and requires programs which present excellent production values and also reward repeated viewings.[19] In addition, the backing of Time Warner means that the show has a large promotional budget. This means that the resulting product invites and facilitates audience interaction.

Alan Ball had previously developed and produced *Six Feet Under* for HBO, a series that followed the fortunes of the family-run Fisher & Sons Funeral Home. *Six Feet Under* ran for five seasons to great critical acclaim; it was lauded for its production quality and its portrayal of taboo subjects, such as death and homosexual romance.[20] Looking for new material, Ball encountered *Dead Until Dark* whilst waiting for a dental appointment, and sought the adaptation option.[21] Production commenced in 2007, with the first episodes going to air in the United States in September 2008.[22] The promotion of the upcoming series included a "viral" marketing campaign which focused upon the drink Tru Blood, and upon vampires being liberated from dependence upon human blood, so that they are able to "come out of the closet" and "mainstream" with human society.

In addition to advertizing for Tru Blood, URLs for websites and blogs advocating vampire rights were distributed strategically.[23] Marketing did not end with the beginning of Season One. Season Three was heralded with a series of posters advertising Tru Blood, such as one featuring a coffee pot full of blood, with the caption "Nothing Like A Good Cup of Joe."[24] Thus the ongoing marketing campaign, directed at the spectrum of viewers from hardcore fans to more casual observers, set the scene for users to explore and respond to a range of material associated with the *True Blood* universe.[25] *True Blood* therefore represents a branded universe, which enables those who choose to join it — for example, by becoming a member of the Official True Blood Wiki and posting to the site, using a picture of a character from the show as an avatar — to signal, through association with *True Blood*, a range of liberated, fun, sexy ideas.[26]

The True Blood Wiki

True Blood has inevitably attracted a large number of unauthorized fan sites. There is also an official *True Blood* site at http://www.hbo.com/true-blood/index.html, which provides information about the television show and links to authorized content. In addition to unofficial fan sites, and fan fiction posted to general fanfic sites, there is an "official" True Blood Wiki sponsored by HBO. It actively invites fans to engage with the show, and hosts a range of content areas, including a discussion forum, a fan fiction archive, photographs, and artwork. In sponsoring such a platform, HBO is reaching out to fans and inviting their participation in a broader fan community. HBO also produces http://babyvamp-jessica.com/, a blog maintained by the character Jessica.[27] Fans respond to Jessica's blog posts both in and out of character, and this provides yet another platform for extending the *True Blood* universe.

This is an excellent example of Sara Gwenllian-Jones's identification of the fan experience as "world building for profit."[28] Fans are actively invited to engage with the text (here, referring both to the series and the books) in a way that brings them within the commercial cultural production process. Fans are fully complicit with, and integrated as, developers of content within the bounds prescribed by the commercial providers.

In her study of the commercialization of television fan culture, Gwenllian-Jones argues that fans are part of a symbiotic relationship with the content producers. Television shows are deliberately produced to elicit this kind of fan response, and intellectual property owners are thus not inclined to bring infringement proceedings against fan creators, as they recognise this form of creation as evidence of success. She notes: "fan culture is already co-opted from the moment it comes into being. By definition, fandom is an effect of the culture industry; it is commercial culture's adoring and irreverent offspring, not its nemesis."[29] According to this view, the production of content within the bounds of the True Blood Wiki thus reflects another mode of consumption, rather than a true act of creation. Derek Johnson, however, argues that fan engagement involves both risks and benefits for the television producer.[30] By inviting the audience to participate in the creation of content, the producer encourages consumers to believe that they have an investment in the resulting creation. In line with this sense of investment, they are encouraged to consume aspects of that creation (such as spending significant amounts of money on related items and content, including games, T–shirts and figurines), and to encourage others to make a similar investment — in other words, to participate in the promotion of the product. He concludes that the fan in this context is like a housekeeper: "Though the housekeeper might come to feel a sense of personal investment and even territoriality in that home, he or she has little matching authority within it."[31] This ambiguous relationship both rewards and exploits the participating fan base.

The True Blood Wiki has a Code of Conduct, as well as more comprehensive Terms of Service. In relation to copyright material, the Code of Conduct simply provides, under the heading "Act in Good Faith," the following directive: "Don't pilfer material — Don't publish content to which you have no rights. Period. Full stop."[32] The Terms of Service section includes the slightly more detailed requirement that users accept sole responsibility for any postings to the site, and that such posts do not violate any third party rights. By making use of the service, users agree to terms that require them to warrant that they will not upload any infringing material. Further, they grant Wetpaint (the commercial site providers) an "irrevocable, perpetual, non-exclusive, fully paid, royalty-free, worldwide licence to use, copy, perform, modify, adapt, publish, display, translate, and distribute" those submissions, and to prepare derivative works and sub-licence the use of the submissions. Users also agree that Wetpaint has exclusive rights to the Collective Content (content appearing on the site). Finally, Wetpaint grants third parties a Creative Commons Non-Commercial Share-Alike licence with respect to the Collective Content and the submissions, with attribution to Wetpaint rather than the individual authors.

Thus a constructed commercial environment exists, in addition to the creation of non-commercial fan fiction. Users are probably unaware of the extremely broad license that they grant, both to Wetpaint and the world at large, to reuse their contributions without compensation. Whether this commercial approach will survive in the context of fan fiction is open to debate, although conflicts between owners and fans so far appear to have arisen, not with respect to content ownership and use, but rather in relation to censorship.

The True Blood Wiki site is actively moderated. However, in response to member feedback, the following post was made by the moderators on June 9, 2009:

> Hello everyone
>
> We have been reading your thread regarding over-moderation with interest and we want to do something about it. Although we are not fan moderators, we do empathize with your wishes to be able to say what you feel.
>
> Moderation is absolutely not about disrupting communities or quashing creativity and the last thing we want to do is upset people. We do, however, need to ensure that the site Code of Conduct is adhered to. Here is a reminder of the site Code of Conduct regarding profanity.
>
> "Do not use offensive language — inappropriate, crude, or abusive language is not only unacceptable, it's a lousy way to convince anyone of your point."
>
> So here's what we're going to do:
>
> — We will not delete profanities that appears [sic] in your fanfic. Please do be careful with your other posts though, as we will need to remove them.
>
> — We will remove illicit/illegal/extreme pornographic material from any type of post without prior warning.
>
> — We followed your lead and totally accept that this is an adult community. We hope we can work together to keep content at an acceptable level.
>
> — We hope this will be acceptable to you and look forward

to reading some more of you [sic] amazing fanfic!

The Moderation team.[33]

Note here that the True Blood Wiki moderators clearly specify that they are "not fan moderators." They appear to be struggling with some of the difficulties previously encountered by other commercial enterprises who have sought to monetize fan fiction.[34] So what scope is there for fan fiction authors to write their own "vampwich" fiction?

Charlaine Harris and Fan Fiction

Charlaine Harris has an official website which provides information about Harris's books, tours, interviews, and frequently asked questions. In addition, there is a discussion list for fans. The General Site Information states that the appropriate place for discussion of the *True Blood* HBO series is the HBO site, and directions are given to the True Blood Wiki. However, there is a clear prohibition against fan fiction:

> Fanfic that uses any author's characters, especially my own, is absolutely forbidden on this site for legal reasons. Speculation on further plot developments is fine, should be confined to one or two thoughts and should contain no dialogue.
> Example: "I wonder if Sookie will even meet the maenad again?" is acceptable.
> "If Sookie met the maenad again, and she walked up to the maenad and asked if she'd murdered all those people, and then the maenad said, "I'm going to come to the bar and kill everyone ..." is fanfiction and unacceptable.[35]

Further on the FAQs page, in response to the question, "Can I post my cool story about Sookie on this site?" Harris responds as follows:

> A. No, and I'll tell you why. No fanfic can appear on this website. Not only does it make me feel strange to have other

people use my characters, but there are legal issues to consider.

Here's an example:

Enthusiastic Reader: Wouldn't it be great if Sookie adopted Hunter?

Would be okay.

TooEnthusiaticReader: Wouldn't it be great if Hunter came to Sookie's house and said, "Aunt Sookie, can I play in your attic?" And then Sookie let him in, and Hunter came down and said, "Did you know there's a ghost in your attic?"

This is NOT okay.[36]

Typically, this displays a lack of understanding regarding what is and what is not permitted under copyright law with respect to the creation of derivative works. Harris does not identify what is wrong with the second example in either case, and, with respect to Harris, there is nothing in these examples that transgresses the law. It certainly may make Harris "uncomfortable," in the sense that it promotes a reading and direction of the text that she does not wish to follow, but it is not an infringement of her work. Of course, Harris is not alone in this. Anne Rice notoriously posted an open letter on her web site, stating:

> I do not allow fan fiction. The characters are copyrighted. It upsets me terribly to even think about fan fiction with my characters. I advise my readers to write your own original stories with your own characters. It is absolutely essential that you respect my wishes.[37]

However, apart from upsetting the authors, is there anything actually illegal or infringing about reusing characters in fan fiction? In the United States, copyright protection does extend to a derivative work, defined in Section 101 of the Copyright Act as:

> ... a work based upon one or more pre-existing works, such as a translation, musical arrangement, dramatization, fic-

tionalization, motion picture version, sound recording, art reproduction, abridgment, condensation, or any other form in which a work may be recast, transformed or adapted. A work consisting of editorial revisions, annotations, elaborations, or other modifications, which, as a whole, represent an original work of authorship, is a "derivative work."[38]

This means that under United States law, protection granted to a character may extend beyond copying of the actual text or footage. United States Courts have not consistently recognized imitative works as infringing. While there have been cases such as Walt Disney Productions v. Air Pirates, where the Ninth Circuit held that the depiction of Disney characters in pornographic and lewd contexts was an infringement, the outcomes of such cases have not been consistent.[39] However, it is likely that the appropriation of a well-developed character and storyline, for the purposes of fan fiction, would constitute copyright infringement in the United States.[40]

Under Australian law, in order to infringe the original work, the fan fiction creator would need to take a substantial part of the original work or infringe the author's right to make an adaptation of their work.[41] The question of what constitutes a "substantial part" of the original work is a difficult matter, given that many fan fiction creators appropriate the characters and place them in a novel context. They are not using the words of Charlaine Harris or Alan Ball (or other scriptwriters), but they are using the characters and, possibly, certain incidents of plot. The key Australian case in this area is Universal City Studios v. Zeccola, which concerned the issue of whether the Italian film *Lo Squalo* infringed *Jaws*.[42] In that case the Court was prepared to find that the characters and plotlines in the Italian film sufficiently resembled those in *Jaws* to warrant a finding of infringement. However, there was a great degree of similarity between the two films, a degree that would not usually be found in fanfic, which consciously and deliberately explores other angles of the text. Thus it is open to argument whether fan fiction is in fact infringing the subject text.

When the creator extends an explicit or implicit invitation to engage with the text, is there a more persuasive argument that creative re-writings should be permitted? It has been argued that Joss

Whedon, creator of the Buffyverse, deliberately developed that environment in a manner which acknowledged the subtext sought by fans as a point of engagement: "BtVS is deliberately constructed to be consumed by fan groups in a fannish or "cult" manner — in other words, fans are invited to immerse themselves in the text and produce subtextual readings from the many textual clues."[43] Further, Whedon even made direct reference to that subtext in the program, such as when Giles remarks, "I think the text is quickly becoming the subtext."[44] By providing the forum for posting fan fiction on the True Blood Wiki, it is even clearer that some level of fan fiction is accepted and endorsed by HBO, and through her link to the site, by Charlaine Harris.

Given the success of Alan Ball's interpretation of Harris's imagined community of Bon Temps, it is reasonable to ask what latitude was given to him regarding its creation, on the basis of Harris's original storyline.[45] In an interview in 2008, Ball discussed his thoughts on turning the books into a television series.[46] Displaying acute awareness of the context of creating within an established universe, he noted the benefits of having a "built in fan base" (surely a challenge as much as a benefit). He observed:

> As was the case with Charlaine's books, they work. The world is complete ... in a lot of ways she [has] done a lot of the heavy lifting and I'm really, really indebted to her for that. I think the challenges are to remain true enough to the material so you don't lose what it was that attracted you to it in the first place, but at the same time, to open it up and make changes when you feel like they would improve it.

Ball also noted that Harris had been supportive of his adaptation of the novels, noting that, "Charlaine has been a complete sweetheart about this and she really understands that the medium of television is completely different than the medium of the printed page and she's been really on board."[48]

Fan fiction authors are usually acutely conscious of the intellectual property issues relating to their work. In fact, the desire to remain non-commercial is often cited as the reason that fan fiction remains a gift economy.[49] It appears that by creating a venue for the publication of fan fiction, HBO are actively inviting fans in, to participate in the creation of the meta-text of the *True Blood* universe; as Gwenllian-Jones has noted, in so doing, fans become a part of the commercial process. This invitation would likely prevent any finding of copyright infringement, except in a clear case of copying the text or the dialogue itself. Finally, then, we may ask, "Why is the creation of vampire fan fiction so popular at this time?"

Deleuze, Guattari and the Becoming Vampire

Vampires are a natural fit for fan fiction because they can be killed and resurrected as many times as required. In addition, their immortality means that the author can place them in virtually any time period they desire, allowing for the discussion of multiple time periods, each different context facilitating the exploration of different aspects of the vampire's personality.[50] Does the reworking and rewriting of the vampire story uncover new meanings and understandings? Why are we so fascinated with the vampire story, and how should this inform society's response to controlling and regulating the reuse and adaptation of content? In *A Thousand Plateaus*, Deleuze and Guattari develop their theory of "becoming":

> We believe in the existence of very special becomings-animal traversing human beings and sweeping them away, affecting the animal no less than the human. From 1730 to 1735, all we hear about are vampires.[51]

They explain that structuralism "does not account for these becomings, since it is designed precisely to deny or at least denigrate their existence." Rather, "it sees them only as phenomena of degradation representing a deviation from the true order and pertaining to the adventures of diachrony."[52]

However, in exploring these "becomings," Deleuze and Guattari are not concerned with the transformed beings themselves but the event of the becoming: "becoming is not an evolution, at least not an evolution by descent and filiation." Rather, it involves alliance and symbiosis, and thus their preferred term is "involution."[53] Involution is not regressive and is always creative.[54] They assert that every becoming-animal involves a pack or a band. These bands proliferate by "contagion, epidemics, battlefields, and catastrophes."[55] However, society rejects this mode of propagation; hence the vampire is shunned, because it "does not filiate, it infects."[56] Deleuze and Guattari consider the liminal role of the sorcerer who haunts the fringes of society, living at the borderline of the village:

> In sorcery, blood is of the order of contagion and alliance. It can be said that becoming-animal is an affair of sorcery because (1) it implies an initial relation of alliance with a demon; (2) the demon functions as the borderline of an animal pack, into which the human being passes or in which his or her becoming takes place, by contagion; (3) this becoming itself implies a second alliance with another human group; (4) this new borderline between the two groups guides the contagion of animal and human being within the pack.[57]

The politics of becomings-animal, as well as the politics of sorcery, express the interests of the oppressed and the prohibited, as well as those of minority groups (anomic).[58] These are the very groups dealt with in *True Blood* and the Southern Vampire Mysteries. Vampires are excellent exemplars of becomings.[59]

Conclusions: Vampires for Everybody

At the beginning of *Dead Until Dark*, Sookie tells us that she had been waiting for her "own" vampire.[60] Milly Williamson asserts that "we conjure the vampires that we want or need for the cultural and historical times that we find ourselves in."[61] Sookie is attracted to Bill because he is "different," as she is, but she is also attracted to Eric, who more characteristically represents the powerful defender and lover. Bill and Eric both have the ability to rescue Sookie when she is in danger, saving her from shifters, humans, and other vampires. As J. M. Tyree observes, this role seems to reflect the vampire of our age: "Edward, Bill, and Eli embody a new combination of undead chum and unnaturally attentive lover, a sort of guardian angel with fangs."[62] *True Blood* solves and avoids the question of needing to feed on human blood and the messy question of who to feed on, through the creation of synthetic blood.[63] Feeding and biting thus become connected with sexual intercourse rather than basic need.

Deleuze and Guattari conclude, "Of course there are werewolves and vampires, we say this with all our heart; but do not look for a resemblance or analogy to the animal, for this is becoming-animal in action."[64] Vampires and werewolves "are becomings of man," and synthetic-blood-drinking, charming vampires — who sympathize with the human condition — are the becomings of those who devote their time to creating fiction for the True Blood Wiki.

Notes

1 *True Blood*, "Plaisir D'Amour," Season One, Episode Nine, director Anthony M. Hemingway, written by Brian Bruckner, New York: Home Box Office, first aired November 2, 2008.
2 Bon Temps is the fictional small town in Louisiana where the majority of the action in the Southern Vampire Mysteries is set.
3 Charlaine Harris, *Dead Until Dark* (London: Orion, 2001), 1.
4 Anne Rice, *Interview with the Vampire* (London: Futura Books, 1976).
5 *Interview with the Vampire*, DVD, directed by Neil Jordan (1994; Burbank, California: Warner Home Video, 2000).
6 Nan Flanagan, spokesperson for the American Vampire League, states: "We're citizens. We pay taxes. We deserve basic civil rights just like everyone else," in *True Blood*, "Strange Love," Season One, Episode One, director Alan Ball, written by Alan Ball, New York: Home Box Office, first aired September 7, 2008. See also Joseph J. Foy, "Signed in Blood: Rights and the Vampire-Human Social Contract," in *True Blood and Philosophy*, ed. George A. Dunn and Rebecca Housel, Blackwell Philosophy and Pop Culture Series (Hoboken, NJ: John Wiley & Sons, 2010), 51–64. In Harris's books, vampires and humans cannot marry; however, they can in *True Blood*, but only in certain states. See Patricia Brace and Robert Arp, "Coming Out of the Coffin and Coming Out of the Closet," in *True Blood and Philosophy: We Wanna Think Bad Things with You*, eds. William Irwin, George A. Dunn and Rebbeca Housel (London: Wiley, 2010) 93–108.
7 For a discussion of the Gothic melodrama of the sympathetic vampire, see Milly Williamson, *The Lure of the Vampire: Gender, Fiction and Fandom from Bram Stoker to Buffy* (London: Wallflower Press, 2005), 40–50.
8 Harris, *Dead Until Dark*, 60.
9 Charlaine Harris, "Frequently Asked Questions", *Charlaine Harris.com*, accessed August 22, 2011, http://www.charlaineharris.com/faqs.html.
10 Harris, *Dead Until Dark*, 53.

11 Ibid., 5.
12 Ibid., 2.
13 Charlaine Harris, *Dead in the Family* (London: Gollancz, 2010), 16.
14 Charlaine Harris, *Dead As A Doornail* (London: Gollancz, 2005), 214.
15 Comparisons may inevitably be drawn to the love triangle between Edward, Jacob and Bella in *Twilight*, and the Damon, Stefan and Elena triangle in *The Vampire Diaries*.
16 "Vampwich Stories," *True Blood Wiki*, accessed August 22, 2011, http://truebloodwiki.hbo.com/page/Vampwich+Stories#fbid=skeuuMynP78.
17 Robin Nelson, "HBO Premium: Channelling Distinction through TVIII," *New Review of Film and Television Studies* 5, no. 1 (2007): 25–40.
18 "Home Box Office," that is, it is like a cinema in your own home. See Nelson, 25.
19 Reflecting the "gaze" associated with the cinema viewing experience, as distinct from the "glance" viewing of television. See Nelson, 27.
20 Nelson, 29–31.
21 "True Blood," *Wikipedia*, accessed August 22, 2011, http://en.wikipedia.org/wiki/ True-Blood.
22 "True Blood," *Wikipedia*.
23 Jenna Wortham, "HBO Brews a Viral Campaign With Tru Blood," *Wired*, July 9, 2008, http://www.wired.com/underwire/2008/07/hbo-brews-a-vir/. See the vast range of videos at BloodCopy.com, http://www.archive.bloodcopy.com.
24 "*True Blood*, Season Three Collectable Posters: A Good Cup of Joe," *HBO*, accessed August 22, 2011, http://www.hbo.com/true-blood/inside/posters/download/poster-cup-of-joe.html#.
25 Jonathan Hardy, "Mapping Commercial Intertextuality: HBO's *True Blood*," *Convergence* 17, no.1 (2011): 7–17.
26 Naomi Klein, *No Logo: Taking Aim at the Brand Bullies* (Toronto: Knopf Canada, 2000), 30. See also Judith Donath, "Signals in Social Supernets," *Journal of Computer-Mediated Communication* 13, no.1 (2007): 231–251, and David Lindsay, Melissa de Zwart and Francesca Collins, "My Self, My Avatar, My Rights: Rights of Avatar Identity and Integrity in Virtual Worlds," in *Humanity in Cybernetic Environments*, ed. Daniel Riha (Oxford: Inter-Disciplinary Press, 2010), 150.
27 Jessica does not appear in the Southern Vampire Mysteries; Bill was forced to transform her after killing another vampire in defence of Sookie. See *True Blood*, "Plaisir D'Amour," Series One, Episode Nine.
28 Sara Gwenllian-Jones, "Web Wars: Resistance, Online Fandom and Studio Censorship," in *Quality Popular Television: Cult TV, the Industry and Fans*, ed. Mark Jancovich and James Lyons, BFI Modern Classics (London: British Film Institute, 2003), 163–177.

29 Jones, 173. See also Simone Murray, "'Celebrating the Story the Way it is': Cultural Studies, Corporate Media, and the Contested Utility of Fandom," *Continuum: The Journal of Media and Cultural Studies* 18, no. 1 (2004): 7–25.
30 Derek Johnson, "Inviting Audiences In: The Spatial Reorganization of Production and Consumption in 'TVIII,'" *New Review of Film and Television Studies* 5, no. 1 (2007): 61–80.
31 Johnson, 78.
32 "The True Blood Code of Conduct," *True Blood Wiki*, accessed August 22, 2011, http://truebloodwiki.hbo.com/conduct.
33 "Read Before Posting: Discussion Forum Rules — True Blood," *True Blood Wiki*, accessed August 22, 2011, http://truebloodwiki.hbo.com/page/Read+Before+Posting%3A+Discussion+Forum+Rules.
34 Karen Hellekson, "A Fannish Field of Value: Online Fan Gift Culture," *Cinema Journal* 48, no. 4 (2009): 113–118. See also Suzanne Scott, "Repackaging Fan Culture: The Regifting Economy of Ancillary Content Models," *Transformative Works and Cultures* 3 (2009): http://dx.doi.org/10.3983/twc2009.0150.
35 "General Site Information," *Charlaine Harris.com*, accessed August 22, 2011, http://www.charlaineharris.com/rules.html.
36 "Frequently Asked Questions," *Charlaine Harris.com*.
37 "Anne Rice Readers Interaction: Anne's Messages to Fans," *Anne Rice.com*, accessed August 22, 2011, http://www.annerice.com/ReaderInteraction-MessagesToFans.html.
38 § 101 Copyright Act 1976 (US).
39 "Walt Disney Productions vs. Air Pirates," 581 F 2d 751 (9th Cir, 1978). For a more recent discussion of character and storyline copyright, see the "Harry Potter Lexicon" case, "Warner Bros Entertainment vs. RDR Books," 575 F Supp 2d 513 (SDNY, 2008).
40 Rebecca Tushnet, "User-Generated Discontent: Transformation in Practice," *Columbia Journal of Law and the Arts* 31, no. 4 (2008): 101–120.
41 See section 36(1) and 14(1) Copyright Act 1968 (Cth). See further, Melissa de Zwart, "Angel(us) is my Avatar! An Exploration of Avatar Identity in the Guise of the Vampire," *Media & Arts Law Review* 15, no. 3 (2010): 330–336.
42 "Universal City Studios Inc vs. Zeccola" AIPC 90-019 (Vic. SC, 1982) and "Zeccola vs. Universal City Studios Inc" 46 ALR 189 (FFC, 1982).
43 Milly Williamson, "Spike, Sex and Subtext: Intertextual Portrayals of the Sympathetic Vampire on Cult Television," *European Journal of Cultural Studies* 8, no. 3 (2005): 296.
44 See Williamson, *Lure of the Vampire*, 91.
45 Jim Halterman, "Interview: 'True Blood' Creator Alan Ball," *The Fu-*

ton Critic, September 5, 2008, http://www.thefutoncritic.com/interview/2008/09/05/interview-true-blood-creator-alan-ball.
46 Halterman, "Interview."
47 Ibid.
48 Ibid.
49 See Hellekson; see also Scott.
50 Rebecca Tushnet, "Economies of Desire: Fair Use and Marketplace Assumptions," *William and Mary Law Review* 51, no. 2 (2009): 529–530.
51 Gilles Deleuze and Félix Guattari, *A Thousand Plateaus: Capitalism and Schizophrenia*, trans. Brian Massumi, Athlone Contemporary European Thinkers (London: Athlone Press, 1988), 237.
52 Deleuze and Guttari, 237.
53 Ibid., 238.
54 Joshua Delpech-Ramey, "Deleuze, Guattari, and the 'Politics of Sorcery,'" *Substance* 39, no. 1 (2010): 11.
55 Deleuze and Guttari, 241.
56 Ibid., 242.
57 Ibid., 247.
58 See also the use of the vampire analogy in the context of an exploration of identity in Donna J. Haraway, *Modest_Witness@Second_Millennium. FemaleMan©_Meets_OncoMouse™:Feminism and Technoscience* (New York: Routledge, 1997), which echoes Deleuze and Guattari's exploration of evolution and relationship through infection rather than kinship; and Shannon Winnubst, "Vampires, Anxieties, and Dreams: Race and Sex in the Contemporary United States," *Hypatia* 18, no. 3 (2003): 1–20.
59 Trevor Holmes, "Becoming-Other: (Dis)Embodiments of Race in Anne Rice's *Tale of the Body Thief*,'" *Romanticism on the Net* 44 (2006): http://www.erudit.org/revue/ron/2006/v/n44/ 014004ar.html. See also Anna Powell, "Duration and the Vampire: A Deleuzian Gothic," *Gothic Studies* 11, no. 1 (2009): 86–98.
60 Harris, *Dead Until Dark*, 1.
61 Williamson, *Lure of the Vampire*, 5.
62 J. M. Tyree, "Warm-Blooded: *True Blood* and *Let the Right One In*," *Film Quarterly* 63, no. 2 (2009): 32.
63 Synthetic blood is more consumer-friendly than the non-human alternatives used by Angel (pig's blood, *Buffy* and *Angel*), and Louis (rat's blood, *Interview with the Vampire*).
64 Deleuze and Guttari, 275.

13

Willing Freshies: Blood, Sex, and Vampires in *Moonlight* Fan Fiction

Candace Benefiel

Victims and Blood Donors in Vampire Literature

A significant amount of ink, and more recently, bandwidth, has been spilled in discussing the figure of the vampire, but somewhat less on the food source of the creature. Vampires range from those who thrive on a diet of animal blood, like the "vegetarian" Cullens of Stephenie Meyer's Twilight Saga,[1] to those who can subsist on animal blood, such as P. N. Elrod's Jack Fleming,[2] or Chelsea Quinn Yarbro's Comte Saint Germain,[3] to those for whom human blood is the only sustenance. Within this last category, the trope ranges from vampires who require small amounts of blood on an irregular basis (Yarbro's Comte, for example, takes barely enough to fill a wineglass, and goes for months between feedings) to those who cannot feed without killing, and must take a life every night to support their continued existence. The first major vampire in British literature, John William Polidori's Lord Ruthven, inevitably causes the moral destruction of his victims, and often their physical demise as well.[4]

Arguably the seminal vampire of both literature and film, Bram Stoker's Count Dracula tends to select a human target and, over the course of several feedings, causes that victim to decline and die. Lucy Westenra, despite heroic measures (including a horrifyingly primitive blood transfusion), grows ever more pale and languishing, and eventually expires, only to rise again as a vampire.[5] In nineteenth-century vampire literature, this was frequently the result of a vampire's attentions. Vampirism was regarded as a blood-borne disease, and caused by a risky exchange of bodily fluids. Likewise, one of the most influential modern vampire novelists, Anne Rice, tends to show her vampires killing their prey, with few exceptions.[6] Louis and Lestat, as memorably depicted in the Neil Jordan film, can drink animal blood — the unforgettable and somewhat nauseating scene of Louis dispatching a pair of French poodles springs to mind — but they much prefer human blood, and usually kill when they feed, unless the goal is to create a new vampire.[7]

While the idea of the bite of the vampire, with its obvious sexual overtones of perverse penetration and unnatural procreation, has been a fixture of vampire literature almost since the inception of the genre, until recently the human part of the equation was either an unwitting (and usually unwilling) victim, or one who sought the power and immortality of vampirism for themselves. However, as vampires have become more sympathetic characters, the necessity for them to indulge in rampant homicide has decreased significantly. With this shift, the figure of the willing blood donor has emerged.

In classic vampire literature, vampires have human servants, but these function as considerably more than dinner. A closer analogue to the concept of a sustainable food source is found in Laurell K. Hamilton's Anita Blake novels. Here readers are introduced to the *pomme de sang*, usually a shapeshifter, who is better able to stand up to the demands of feeding a vampire on a regular basis than an ordinary human would be.[8] In the plethora of vampire romance novels published in the past decade, human women (and less frequently, men) often serve as regular food sources for vampires, but there is almost inevitably a concept of "life-mate" included, which enables the vampire hero to remain functionally monogamous. The woman frequently gains a demi-vampire status which confers a greatly enhanced life-span, and allows her to live happily almost-ever-after with her noble hero vampire, without the necessity of blood-drinking on her part, except perhaps from her vampire mate.

One novelist who has come up with a twist on this formula is J. R. Ward, in her Black Dagger Brotherhood novels, in which vampires feed only on other vampires.[9] Similarly, in MaryJanice Davidson's Undead series, Betsy Taylor, who suddenly finds herself not only undead, but queen of the vampires, tries to limit her blood consumption to exchanges with her lover/consort, Eric Sinclair, an old and powerful vampire.[10]

More recently, in Charlaine Harris's Southern Vampire Mysteries, which are the basis for the HBO series *True Blood*, the author discusses what she calls fangbangers, or vampire groupies, who are mostly habitués of vampire clubs, and are there more for sex than for the bite.[11] One interesting aspect of this is that since in the world of the novels, as in Hamilton's, vampires have come "out of the coffin" to gain tenuous legal status, the vampire clubs and "fangbangers" are known not only to the vampires and a select group of humans, but also to the general public, who regard the vampire-addicted humans as scum. This may be emphasized more heavily in the television adaptation, but in either version, Sookie Stackhouse comes in for considerable disapprobation through her association with vampire Bill Compton. Concerning the fangbangers generally, when Sookie is searching for information about one in particular, the vampire bartender Long Shadow observes, "She wanted to die ... Everyone who comes here does, to one extent or another."[12] In this constructed world, the vampires are often all too happy to oblige.

Then, there is the instance of the short-lived television series, *Moonlight*, which aired in the truncated season of 2007–2008.[13] Although only lasting for 16 episodes, the series gained a devoted fanbase, which has produced a significant body of fan fiction. In some ways, the very brevity of the series spurred fans to extrapolate more extensively. The fact that the canon was not only limited, but closed, created a prime opportunity for fan imaginations to range widely. As Sheenagh Pugh comments in *The Democratic Genre* (her study on fan fiction from a literary standpoint), "Whenever a canon closes, someone somewhere will mourn it enough to reopen it."[14]

Summary of Freshies in Canonical *Moonlight*

As the series is not as well-known as some other recent vampire texts, before discussing fan utilization of the blood donor concept from *Moonlight* in fan fiction, it will be useful to summarize the more important representations of the "willing freshie" in the series. The depictions of freshies are limited, but striking. At the beginning of the series, early in Episode One, the protagonist, vampire P. I. Mick St. John, is paying a visit to his best friend, Josef Kostan, described in a voiceover as "one of the oldest vamps in Los Angeles." Kostan is presented as a ruthless, driven businessman, surrounded by the trappings of wealth. At his futuristic, palatial house, one can see naked women lounging by the pool outside the glass-walled living area. During the course of their conversation, the older vampire asks if Mick would "care for any liquid refreshment?" and shouts a command, "Hungry!" — whereupon an attractive, scantily-clad young woman appears, to serve them. Josef handles the woman carelessly, and speaks of her as "delicious." Mick declines the offer, and as he leaves, Josef lifts the young woman's gracefully offered wrist; he allows his vampiric side to emerge, and sinks his fangs into her, to her evident and erotically-charged delight. Later Josef is seen in Mick's loft and, after complaining about the poor quality of the bottled blood Mick has on hand, inquires if Mick has any freshies around, adding, "No, of course you don't." These two exchanges are critical in establishing both Mick's estrangement from human contact and the essential nature of his vampiric needs.[15]

Another key instance occurs in Episode Ten, "Sleeping Beauty."[16] Left alone in hiding at Mick's home after an assassination attempt, Josef "orders in." When Mick returns, he can hear sounds of a party, and Josef's voice saying, "All right, we're going to play a little game ... the rules are, you kiss her ..." Mick walks in to see one girl perched on Josef's lap, the other two dancing in front of him. Upset, he orders the women to leave, which they do, once Josef has seconded the order. Upon leaving, each of them kisses Josef on the cheek, and murmurs affectionately to him, the last of the three saying, "Love you, Josef." The freshies are presented as party girls, and Josef as a hedonistic pleasure-seeker, a perception that will be altered by later revelations of Josef's tragic past.

There are no further discussions of freshies, or depictions of them, until the final episode of the series, "Sonata," in which the relationship between Josef and one of his willing blood donors is foregrounded.[17] In this episode, viewers are introduced to Simone, a lawyer who donates on "Tuesdays and Fridays." Simone and Josef are presented as a playful couple, although Josef treats her rather cavalierly during the opening party sequence, announcing to Mick and Beth that "it's time for a drink," and abruptly taking Simone out of the social setting to feed from her wrist. Subsequently, Mick, clearly uncomfortable, explains the concept to Beth. She quizzes him about how many freshies he has been with, much in the manner of a woman asking about old girlfriends, and reinforcing the notion that vampire feeding is sexual in nature. Later, Beth comments (rather cattily) that she suspects that "blood isn't the only bodily fluid [Josef and Simone] are sharing." When Beth has an opportunity to speak with Simone privately, the freshie insists that, for vampires, feeding is not as intimate as it seems for humans, because they cannot afford to become emotionally attached to short-lived mortals. In another scene, when Mick and Beth are speculating about the exact nature of the relationship between Josef and Simone, Mick comments that Josef is unlikely to have a freshie for a lover, adding, "he has rules." Presumably, the self-imposed rules protect his own emotions, as there is no indication it has much to do with safeguarding the humans involved.

While the co-creators of the series, Trevor Munson and Ron Koslow, were not associated with it past the first 12 episodes, and were therefore not involved with the elaboration of the vampire/freshie dynamic in "Sonata," they were the writers of two of the episodes in which the concept was established, "No Such Thing as Vampires" and "Sleeping Beauty." Trevor Munson comments:

> One of the things Ron and I had discussed early on for a character was a vampire who kept a sort of "blood gimp" around for his or her personal feeding. We realized that there would have to be alternate ways for vampires to get blood other than hunting if the secret was going to be maintained. We further realized that in the larger world of vampires there would necessarily be certain humans (or "renfields" as they are called in other vamp fiction) who are drawn to the vampires and will do anything to be involved in the secret vampire world ... however, it seemed that even if someone was a freshie and knew that vampires existed, even if they went around yelling it from the rooftops everyone would assume they were wackos ...[18]

Munson, Koslow, and the other writers of *Moonlight* have not commented in print on their conception of the willing freshie, and this has led to a range of fan reactions and extrapolations, both to both the series itself, and to the opinions and arguments of other fans.

Fan Interpretations of the Willing Freshie

As Henry Jenkins comments on fan culture generally, "fans often display a desire to take [a] program apart and see how it works."[19] This is certainly true of the *Moonlight* canon, with fan writers analyzing the ramifications of the existence of freshies and commenting on their possible lifestyle and relationships to the vampires of *Moonlight*. From canon, we move into fanon. There are five related issues, extrapolated from the canon, which have become accepted fixtures in the corpus of *Moonlight* fan fiction. Firstly, Josef Kostan is believed to keep a "harem" of freshies at his house, on call day and night, most of whom are devoted to him. Secondly, Mick St. John is regarded as having sworn off freshies around the time he rescued the child Beth Turner from his ex-wife, Coraline, in 1985. Thirdly, freshies are seen as young and beautiful; generally kept as pets for a few years, they are then dismissed. Fourthly, fans posit the idea that there are a number of ways in which vampires and freshies can be connected, or "hooked up": in clubs; through agencies, much like escort services, where vampires can call and arrange for freshies who are paid for their work; and through the employment of a freelance freshie (the fanon term is 100% freshie), who may be exclusively contracted to a particular vampire. Finally, it is generally accepted that while some vampires are not averse to having intimate relations with their freshies, most do not.

I am going to discuss how some of these concepts play out in fan fiction, focusing on a few of the many available works on the subject. It is one of the paradoxes of modern fan culture that, while fan fiction is published more widely, and more readily, than ever before — because of the internet — writers also have unparalleled control over the availability of their work. A fanzine might only have been printed in a small run, but it would be difficult for a writer to regain all copies of it, once distributed. A story can be deleted from the web, with some assurance it is gone, although this may be trusting to the good offices of enthusiastic readers (who may have copied it for personal use) to honor the wishes of the writer and not distribute it without permission. One of the problems intrinsic to the study of fan fiction is its inherent ephemerality. Stories may be available on one website, or several, and many fan fiction archive sites are accessible to registered members only. In *Moonlight* fan fiction, one of the most fully realized explorations of the freshie lifestyle — which was originally available on multiple websites — has subsequently been pulled from all of those venues, as the author is seeking legitimate publication of her fiction. And, as an example of the mutability of the world of fan fiction, that work is, at present, once again available. But for how long? Not even the author knows.

That being said, fan fiction has been an important part of fan participation, and significant archives of fan fiction are currently available at over half a dozen websites all, or in part, dedicated to *Moonlight*. In addition, there are more general venues where fan fiction can be posted, such as Fanfiction.net and LiveJournal. As Susanna Coleman has commented,

> Online participation in fan fiction enables female fan fiction authors to have a voice in the elements of popular culture with which we fill our free time. Our participation goes beyond merely consuming cultural products such as television shows, movies, and videogames. Instead, we invest considerable time and effort online both researching the original text that is the basis for our fan fiction and interrupting this text as we write, reshaping it into what we deem a more satisfactory narrative and exposing this new text to other fans.[20]

From the beginning of *Moonlight* fan fiction, the interaction between the main vampire characters and freshies has been an important trope, even spawning a recognized genre of "freshie fic." These range from thoughtful explorations of the probable dynamic of the vampires with humans who willingly feed them, to out-and-out "Mary Sue" wish fulfillment. I will briefly examine a few examples from the more literate and thoughtful end of the spectrum.

One of the earliest examples of *Moonlight* fan fiction to feature freshie characters is "Damaged Goods," by wynmc.[21] Posted in November, 2007, when the series was not yet two months old, the story presents Mick St. John aiding an abused freshie to escape from her contract. While Josef, the holder of the girl's contract as a freshie, is not the vampire who abused her, he is portrayed as someone who not only utilizes "willing" freshies, but also those who are coerced into making blood payments to fulfil debts. In this case, a young woman is forced to be a blood donor to redeem the gambling debts of her brother. Mick is able to put the girl in touch with a modern Underground Railway, and she is quietly relocated out of reach of the vampires. In this case, the resemblance of the freshies to involuntary servants, or slaves, is inescapable, and Mick's noble and altruistic assistance in rescuing the girl highlights his hero status. It is interesting to note that this story was written and posted before the episode "Sleeping Beauty" first aired. There seems to be little concern about handling Josef's character and motivations carefully, as many fans, judging from fanboard comments, thought of him at that time as simply a snarky, slightly sinister sidekick.

A much more ambitious work, "Losing Beth," by PNWgal, has two themes which extrapolate from the freshie lifestyle.[22] In one thread, a flashback to the tragic life and death of a young woman, Rosie, is explored. Canonically, Mick was shown drinking from a red-headed freshie in "Out of the Past," the second episode of the series. In a subsequent episode, he comments to his love interest, Beth Turner, that in the past he has done terrible things as a vampire, and that he carries a "tremendous load of guilt" for his actions. From these two things, "Losing Beth" postulates that the redhead fell in love with an uncaring and abusive Mick, back in the early 1980s. She is depicted as sexually submissive, addicted to the pleasures and pain the vampire inflicts on her, and his mistreatment of her eventually leads to her death. Lest this make him into an unsympathetic character, however, he is in the present finding redemption through his selfless love for Beth Turner, and even experiences a visionary dream of Rosie in which she grants him forgiveness for his earlier actions.

In another thread of this work, which is not yet completed, PNWgal delves into the dynamics of Josef's household, and introduces a group of women, the Kaslov family. The daughters of the family have, over several generations, served Josef in their youth as freshies, and later, as managers of his household, before marrying a mortal man of Josef's choosing. That such personnel would be necessary, in order to deal with the complexities of resident freshies, seems reasonable. This is an example of the careful thought about the ramifications of such arrangements that has been a hallmark of fan involvement in the series. As PNWgal writes in Chapter 20 of "Losing Beth":

> As Natalia drove home, she reflected on the life of being the oldest daughter of the oldest daughter in the Kaslov line. An accident of birth, she mused, that tied her to one of the most powerful vampires in North America. Some would call it indentured servitude; Natalia called it a small price to pay for the continued safety and existence of the Kaslov line. Kaslov women had served Josef since he'd saved the first of them, a tiny 16-year-old girl named Maria, from a gang rape in 1872. Maria had been quietly accepting of Josef being a vampire and quickly became an efficient and trusted member of his staff. When Maria reached an age where she could no longer carry out her duties, her oldest daughter took over. It became understood the oldest Kaslov daughter would always take over her mother's duties, thus ensuring the protection of the line.[23]

Josef has thus acted as a protector and savior to the women of the family, although his mercenary, predatory side is served as well, giving him a devoted cadre of household managers. Compared to the traditional "renfield," a human servant who guards and obeys the vampire either from fear or from the hope of attaining vampiric immortality for him- or herself, the Kaslov women serve Josef out of love and respect for his special relationship with the family. His initial rescue of Maria from the sexual predations of humans, and his later relations with the succeeding Kaslovs, presents him in a peculiar light. He has a semi-sexual relationship with generation after generation of these women, yet serves as their protector from unwelcome sexual advances. As a predator, he is more interested in their blood, and how they can serve him domestically, than he is in their sexual charms. While Josef will never be (in fan fiction, as in the series canon), the selfless protector of human beings represented by Mick St. John, neither is he the vicious predator who uses humans only as a disposable source of "food."

One of the side plots of "Losing Beth" presents the next heir to the Kaslov legacy, who has known of Josef Kostan's vampirism, and his relationship to her family, since she was a young child. Anastasia, aged about 17 and coming into her service as a freshie, has fallen in love with her "Uncle Josef," and expects a more intimate relationship with him. Chapter 25 of "Losing Beth" details her initiation into her freshie duties, and includes not only his first feeding from her wrist, but also his bite on her throat as he manually brings her to orgasm. Anastasia reacts with explosive anger when Josef does not complete her sexual initiation, despite his temptation to do so. The complications of the vampire/freshie dynamic are highlighted, in a perspective that moves beyond the vampire view of the freshie as an object of sex/food and enters the realm of emotional relationships. The series episode "Sonata" began to delve into this issue, but the door was barely opened before it shut again with the cancellation of *Moonlight*. In the canon, Josef was presented as a sympathetic character, albeit a ruthless one; in fan fiction he moves ever further into the role of romantic hero. In "Losing Beth," for example, despite his inclination to pursue a romantic relationship with Anastasia, he holds back from doing so, out of a sense of responsibility to her family.

How this story line will play out is not yet known, but it explores the issue of vampire and human relationships in a very original way. Josef is the protector of this line of remarkable women, but they are also fierce in their protection of him, serving as an effective counterpoint to the tragic plot involving Mick and Rosie. To illustrate this point, while popular culture provides other examples of vampire and human relationships that are invested in the "vampire as protector" model — such as Sookie Stackhouse's relationships with Bill Compton and Eric Northman — these almost inevitably involve a romantic love angle. In contrast, the Kaslov women have a multi-generational relationship with Josef, based more on mutual respect and shared responsibility.

A more recent addition to the fan fascination with freshies is the production, in 2010, of several issues of the magazine *Freshie!* This joint effort involves input and writing, graphics, and ideas from between five and ten people, and the finished product, appearing to be scans of a print publication, appears on Moonlightaholics.com.[24] *Freshie!* creates a popular magazine, much like those aimed at a market of women and teens, with articles on fashion, relationships, and careers, as well as product and personal ads, with the twist that all the articles and ads are geared toward a specific audience of willing blood donors to vampires. References to key tenets of the canonical *Moonlight* "take" on vampirism keep it in the specialized fan area (I should note that there is a sister publication, *Fangtastic*, for the vampire point of view). Of particular note in the first issue is a long article on femoral bites, which describes the practice as a slightly scandalous, highly sexualized one, and urges freshies not to be pressured into anything they dislike. The February issue includes, among other things, a transcript of a supposed radio interview with a freshie, describing the lifestyle and her relationship to her vampire, along with the results of a poll offered in the first issue. Responses to the poll were sought through the fan board, with respondents taking on the role of freshie to offer opinions. The magazine offers an interpretation of the freshie as a typical young woman (or man) who happens to have an unusual lifestyle, but one not that far removed from everyday life. For these freshies, vampires are a consuming interest, much in the way that teenage girls adore the current celebrity heart-throb. While freshies are presented as adoring their vampires, the feelings largely run only one way. In the companion magazine, *Fangtastic*, freshies are presented very much as inferior beings who are unworthy of much discussion.

The *Moonlight* fan base is not large, but it continues to produce fan fiction and other artistic creations three years after the end of the initial run of the series. Sheenagh Pugh speaks of fan fiction writers who explore "what else and what if," as they broaden the canon of their chosen cultural production.[25] Two recent examples of freshie fic, written for a website challenge, illustrate this perfectly. The impulse to expound on "what else" is usually expressed as expanding a canonical scene, or providing a hypothetically missing scene from the canon. "Hunger" gives a voice to that first freshie from Josef's house in "No Such Thing as Vampires," providing a character who has no spoken lines in the series with motivations, passions, a sexuality that craves the penetration of the vampire's bite, and an understanding that she and Josef fulfil each other's needs. The transaction is seen as necessary — not only for the vampire, but for the freshie as well. While Lilly's description of the actual bite does not deviate from what was seen in the episode, it provides a rich sensuality that was never verbalized in the series:

> You turn toward me and, finally, you show me what I've been denied. The air is charged between us and my skin tingles as you draw near. Like a wave of cool silk, your breath teases its way down my arm, and you catch my wrist with two fingers. You could so easily break me, empty me, and that knowledge just brings me closer to the brink. Your touch is light, though, and your movement precise, like the thrust and pull of this blood tango that we do. And, always, you are in control.
> Beautiful creature, breathe me in and let me intoxicate you. Put your fangs in me and take what you want. Take my breath, my blood — release these bonds. Make me feel alive. Do it now. *Please.*[26]

The sensuous prose here highlights the power imbalance between vampires and humans, and makes the encounter reminiscent of consensual sado-masochistic "power play," suggesting that while the physical power resides with the vampire, the mutuality of the transaction gives him not only nourishment, but sexual and emotional intimacy. The submissive freshie is not merely used, but receives fulfilment from the encounter.

A story by Luxe de Luxe, "You Really Wanna Know?" takes a different approach. In this short piece, also narrated in first person, a young woman describes how she became a freshie, but this is no "Princess Mary Sue" who will win the undying love of her chosen vampire. Instead, we are given a street-smart girl with a plan to take her knowledge of the existence of vampires, and manipulate it for all she can get. She has, as she puts it, a "ten year plan" which involves finding a rich vampire. She describes meeting with her first vampire, a male nurse:

It was Jimmy, of course, who told me about all the other vampires, the ones who live amongst us — I hope you could tell the creepy way I said that — and how hard it was for them to make a 'living' as it were. He also told me something very interesting, almost like a vampire fairytale for girls like me. He said girls could make do selling blood to vampires, that if they were smart, they could even get somewhere nice to live, nice clothes, jewelry and a car as well as getting cold, hard cash for the stuff.[27]

This girl has no illusions about romance, obviously, and no expectations of sensual enjoyment from the vampire's bite. She only wants to profit from her experience. This is a harsher world, and one that fits in well with the *noir* sensibility of the series. Even so, she comments that, in her relationship with Josef, "the old guy was going to become a little more and a little less than a friend to me," implying that there will be some mutual benefit in the future.

The figure of the willing freshie, which is a concept that is largely unexplored in mainstream and romance vampire literature, has found a host of amateur theorists and proponents in the fan creations surrounding *Moonlight*. As an intersection between the exotic world of the vampire and the mundane life of humanity, the freshie provides an opportunity for fans to make a closer connection with their media source. This is an opportunity fans embrace, for the fans of *Moonlight* are definitely willing to supply their narratives, art, and thought in order to keep the vampire series alive.

Notes

1 Stephenie Meyer, Twilight (New York: Little, Brown and Company, 2005).
2 P. N. Elrod, *The Vampire Files: Bloodlist*, Vampire Files (New York: Ace Books, 1990).
3 Chelsea Quinn Yarbro, *Hôtel Transylvania: A Novel of Forbidden Love*, Chronicles of Saint Germain (New York: St. Martin's Press, 1978).
4 John William Polidori, *The Vampyre and Ernestus Berchtold; or, The Modern Œdipus*, ed. D. L. Macdonald and Kathleen Scherf (Peterborough, ON: Broadview Press, 2007).

5   Bram Stoker, *The New Annotated Dracula*, ed. Leslie S. Klinger (New York: W. W. Norton, 2008).
6   Anne Rice, *Interview with the Vampire* (New York: Knopf, 1976).
7   *Interview with the Vampire: The Vampire Chronicles*, DVD, director Neil Jordan, screenplay by Ann Rice (1994. Burbank, CA: Warner, 1995).
8   Laurell K. Hamilton, *Guilty Pleasures*, Anita Blake, Vampire Hunter (New York: Berkley Books, 2002).
9   J. R. Ward, *Dark Lover*, The Black Dagger Brotherhood (New York: New American Library, 2005).
10 MaryJanice Davidson, *Undead and Unwed* (New York: Berkley Sensation, 2004).
11 *True Blood: The Complete First Season*, DVD (2008, New York, NY: Home Box Office, 2009).
12 Charlaine Harris, *Dead Until Dark*, Southern Vampire Series (New York: Ace Books, 2001), 114.
13 *Moonlight: The Complete Series*, DVD, created by Ron Koslow and Trevor Munson (2007, Burbank, CA: Distributed by Warner Home Video, 2009).
14 Sheenagh Pugh, *The Democratic Genre: Fan Fiction in a Literary Context* (Bridgend, UK: Seren, 2005), 47.
15 *Moonlight*, "No Such Things as Vampires," Season One, Episode One, director Rod Holcomb, written by Ron Koslow and Trevor Munson, first aired September 28, 2007.
16 *Moonlight*, "Sleeping Beauty," Season One, Episode Ten, director John Kretchmer, written by Ron Koslow and Trevor Munson, first aired December 14, 2007.
17 *Moonlight*, "Sonata," Season One, Episode 16, director Fred Toye, written by Ethan Erwin, first aired May 16, 2008.
18 Trevor Munson, e-mail message to author, July 19, 2009.
19 Henry Jenkins, *Textual Poachers: Television Fans and Participatory Culture*, Studies in Culture and Communication (New York and London: Routledge, 1992), 65.
20 Susanna Coleman, "Making Our Voices Heard: Young Adult Females Writing Participatory Fan Fiction," in *Writing and the Digital Generation: Essays on New Media Rhetoric*, ed. Heather Urbanski (Jefferson, NC: McFarland, 2010), 95–105.
21 Wynmc, "Damaged Goods," *Moonlight Fans.com*, accessed August 17, 2010, http://moonlightfans.com. /index.php?option=com_fireboard&Itemid=38&func=view&id=35111&catid=10 ().
22 PNWgal, "Losing Beth," *Moonlightaholics.com*, accessed November 30, 2010, http://moonlightaholics .com/viewforum.php?f=567.
23 PNWgal, "Losing Beth," *Moonlightaholics.com*, accessed November 30,

2010, http://moonlightaholics .com/viewforum.php?f=567.
24 "Freshie!," *Moonlightaholics.com*, accessed February 3, 2011, http://moonlightaholics. com/viewforum.php?f=704.
25 Pugh, 47–68.
26 Lilly, "Hunger," Moonlightaholics.com, accessed February 20, 2011, http://moonlightaholics.com/ viewtopic.php?f=60&t=7840.
27 Luxe de Luxe, "You Really Wanna Know?" *Moonlightaholics.com*, accessed February 20, 2011, http://moonlightaholics.com/viewtopic.php?f=115&t=7847.

14

The Recuperated Bite and Issues of the Soul in Vampire Fan Fiction

Maria Lindgren Leavenworth and Malin Isaksson

In contemporary narratives such as Stephenie Meyer's Twilight novels and Alan Ball's HBO series *True Blood*, the vampire protagonist is portrayed as a partner who is aligned with humanity, albeit still maintaining qualities and abilities which signal an otherness. In comparison with other vampires featured in the texts, these vampire characters often make active choices based on human morals. Similarly, in Joss Whedon's television series *Buffy the Vampire Slayer*, the central and ensouled vampire characters' individual choices are significant, and differentiate them from the evil, soulless creatures the eponymous heroine is fated to slay. The depiction of the vampire as sympathetic is a tendency that can be traced back to the Byronic variation of the nineteenth century;[1] however, the preponderance in contemporary texts of morally "good" vampires who are "de-fanged," in the sense that they manage to control their blood-lust and that they represent romance rather than fear, points to an increased interest in exploring humanized and relational aspects of the trope.

While some readings have focused on the fear and repulsion produced by the vampire's inherent monstrosity, the modern instantiation is often presented "as an attractive figure precisely *because* he or she is a vampire."[2] As Nina Auerbach has claimed, "every age embraces the vampire it needs,"[3] and the twenty-first century attraction to vampires may be a consequence of the emphasis on youth and eternal togetherness. The vampire further represents different kinds of marginalization, with all that that entails, including boundary breaking and alluring transgression. Veronica Hollinger connects the contemporary popularity of the vampire to postmodernism; in its deconstruction of "innumerable kinds of inside/outside oppositional structures, [the vampire] is the monster that used to be human, it is the undead who used to be alive; it is the monster that *looks like us*."[4] In the worlds of *True Blood*, *Buffy*, and the Twilight novels, similarities as well as tensions between human and vampire are explored, as the vampires remember their human past; reflect on their own monstrosity; and ponder what their new existence might mean in terms of having or losing their souls. That is, the monster that "looks like us" in these texts might be just as well-recognized by the monsters themselves.

The "new wave" vampires in the Twilight novels, *True Blood*, and *Buffy*, thus problematize a definite line between good and evil as they increasingly come to resemble humans, particularly when relationships are foregrounded. Romantic and/or sexual relationships are also often central in fan fictions — amateur-authored, internet-published stories based on an already existing text world (referred to as the canon). That is, the centrality of "pairings" resonates with the more or less complex "ties of intimacy" that characterize the vampire[5] and make vampire canons particularly suited to fanfic treatments. Although inscribing themselves within the logic of the canon, fanfic authors' new pairings — or alternative elaborations of already existing ones — are evidence of the multiple ways in which themes, characterizations and plot lines may be questioned.

The close readings of fan fictions in this chapter are not designed to increase the understanding of fandoms per se, nor of individual authors. Rather, the texts are approached from a purely literary perspective, with the aim of tracing (re)used themes and examining the strategies employed. While the canons, through downplaying the menace of vampires, address issues concerning the increasingly blurred boundaries between humanity and monstrosity, there are tendencies in the selected fan fiction to move in the opposite direction. The fanfic authors' literal or figurative re-fanging of the vampire implies a reclaiming of its predatory status, as well as the amorality connected both to a "non-vegetarian" vampiric diet, and to the transgressive, unbridled sexuality traditionally associated with the trope. The reworked, dangerous vampire is, in some of these texts, still a heroic protector of humans, with clear ties to the new wave vampires of the canons. However, the focus on issues of marginalization, monstrosity, and metaphysics — such as discussions about the soul and (potential) eternal damnation — connects with both vampires of earlier periods and a contemporary postmodernist state characterized by complex depictions of identity and otherness.

In "Hunger", Eternallybills retells events from the first episode of *True Blood*, suggesting more sinister reasons for how the situation between Bill and Sookie develops. An analysis of levitatethis's "Aberration and Dismantled" further suggest that the liminality of *True Blood*'s main vampire illustrates more general issues considering otherness. WayBeyond's "Paresthesia," based on the Twilight canon, focuses on blood-lust and desire, depicting a recently turned Bella struggling with desensitization and strict sexual morals. The vampire's potential loss of soul is elaborated on in two of the selected fanfics, Lizardmm's *Soulless* (building on *Buffy*), and 5by5creations's "Soul Searching" (which crosses elements from the Twilight canon with the *Buffy* spin-off series *Angel*). These fanfics illustrate, respectively, how a soul is simultaneously transcendent and intimately connected to identity, and how an active soul-searching is linked to very human issues concerning individual guilt and responsibility.

Humanity, Monstrosity and Otherness

The boundaries between the human and the monstrous are blurred and problematized in various ways. In *Buffy*, "good" vampires (those with souls) take the side of vampire slayers in the fight against evil; in *True Blood*, they elicit sympathy as members of a new minority group; and in the Twilight canon, they pass for human, despite their supernatural beauty and power. Discussing the vampire as a metaphor in 1980s and 90s narratives, Joan Gordon and Veronica Hollinger claim that "one of the functions of our monster [is] to help us construct our own humanity, to provide guidelines against which we can define ourselves."[6] To some extent, this notion hinges on the difference between humanity and monstrosity — a difference which, in the new wave canons, is toned down in favor of the vampires' humanized morals — and an equation between the vampire's plight and the human condition. Re-fanging the main vampire in fan fiction often implies concrete recuperation of more menacing traits, and with the added dangerousness comes further opportunities to discuss the monstrous sides of both blood-lust and sexual desire. The heightened dangerousness of the vampires, along with switched perspectives, can also be read as a sign of a desire to further illuminate the vampire's otherness, often in ways which coincide with or echo human moral dilemmas and issues of belonging.

In the various vampire canons, the cultural and social "othering" of the vampire enables a focus on issues of marginalization, which is as likely to produce sympathy as fear. In a discussion about Anne Rice's *Vampire Chronicles*, Fred Botting observes:

> Existing on the borders of society, the lone predator becomes a solitary wanderer seeking companionship and security, intensely aware of his difference and fascinated by the frailty and mortality of the humans around him ... His alienation and disquieted solitude, his love of beauty and knowledge, along with his humane concerns endow him [sic] the qualities of a Romantic self, tortured by self-consciousness and a questing spirit.[7]

Rice's brooding Louis, who is the model for Botting's delineation of the Romantic vampire subject, is mocked in *True Blood*, as Bill self-reflexively states, "I AM a vampire, I'm supposed to be tormented." However, it is not the solitary state which produces this torment, nor a futile search for belonging and kinship. Rather, Bill states that, "When I was made one was forced to live outside society. As an outlaw, a hunter. Humans were prey and nothing else."[8] His previous existence has been uncomplicated, with clear boundaries established between killer and victim. In contrast to Louis, torment comes from the blurring of these boundaries, and from the close relationship Bill, and other vampires like him, now have with human beings. The ties to humanity, the love, distrust, and hate which develop because of their co-existence, produce a new, postmodern anxiety. Several *True Blood* fanfics reinstate clear boundaries to approach issues of humanity and monstrosity from other perspectives, often shifting to a first-person narration from the vampire's point of view. Anxieties connected to identity and human/vampire co-existence are not necessarily diminished by these alterations; rather, the fanfics effect an internal view of monstrosity and non-belonging.

Eternallybills' fanfic "Hunger" suggests that the initial moral choices made by Vampire Bill stem from rather more sinister reasons than a will to peacefully co-exist with humans, particularly given the view he holds of himself as a monster. Although the sequence of events is rearranged, the story closely follows the first episode of *True Blood*, "Strange Love." Since Merlotte's Bar, where Bill first makes an appearance, is out of the synthetic blood substitute which (in part) gives the television series its name, it is, as the fanfic's title suggests, a very hungry vampire we meet. Bill is struggling to come to terms with his mainstreaming existence and obsessively returns to the image of himself as a product of the evil of his maker; he is "Lorena's monster."[9] Considering the close ties to the canon — including recycled dialogue — the fanfic's second chapter initially represents quite a break from fidelity to the original, as it features a graphically described sex scene between Bill and Sookie. Towards the end of the chapter it is revealed as a day-dream, a common strategy for fanfic authors who want to respect the canon, yet include new takes on the story. The author stays true to the logic of her own text, however, as the hunger for blood mingles with a heightened sexual appetite. In the process of seduction, Bill reflects on the possibility of the emergence of a new moral self: "I was my own creation now, not Lorena's. I would not take, but give." Giving sexual pleasure is thus represented as tempering a monstrosity defined by selfishness. But Bill's slightly altered view of his monstrosity is temporary and imaginary, since it is voiced from inside a dream. Back in the 'reality' of Merlotte's, there is a renewed focus on Bill's need to protect Sookie and, combined with his increasing blood-lust, Bill is given a logical reason to follow the vampire drainers, the Rattrays, into the parking lot (a choice which is not explained in the canon). EternallyBills writes: "the one [Sookie] most required protection from was me. I needed to get away from her, fast, and these two monsters were my way out." By placing himself in the hands of moral, if not supernatural, monsters, Bill aims to protect Sookie from his own monstrosity. The Rattrays are also driven by a form of hunger, an addiction to vampire blood, which suggests that self-control may be a defining aspect of humanity.

The switched perspective in "Hunger" provides an internal view of the long battle Bill has had with his own nature. As he awaits painful death at the hands of the drainers he sees it as a most "fitting end ... to a brutish and violent journey," and he imagines a cheering crowd made up of "every human [he] ever killed." He ascribes the dangers both he and humanity confront to the Vampire Rights Movement and the new possibilities for co-existence. His thoughts echo the blurring of boundaries in new wave vampire narratives: "The more I looked and acted as a human, the more they had expected me to be one ... This is my dilemma, the dichotomy of my unlife: play 'human,' deny my inner beast, and break some poor soul's heart, or play the brute, deny what little humanity remains in me, and sink deeper into darkness." The image of the vampire presented here is of a liminal figure, an other, regardless of perspective, who is forced into playacting in his twin existences. Bill's view of himself as a monster makes him other to the vampire community, but his physical difference from humans, regardless of how close he comes to imitating them, makes him "other" as well.

Bill as a liminal figure also appears in two short fan fictions by levitatethis: "Dismantled" and "Aberration". In "Dismantled," Bill assesses his metaphysical struggles, and the view of himself as a monster, as "a joke to those who accept their rebirth" and, as in "Hunger," he is depicted "as much an anomaly in the midst of his immortal peers as he is amongst the humans who populate the world he tries to inhabit."[10] In "Aberration," Bill thinks back on his turning, describing it as being "reborn as *other*." That is, from the moment his new existence starts he cannot identify himself as a vampire, but his turning also means that he is excluded from human society. "Existing between two realms, Bill stands alone."[11] These fan representations suggest that Vampire Bill is particularly useful when exploring issues of otherness. The menacing, "fanged" vampires in the canon, who embrace their otherness and resist a mainstreaming existence by refusing the synthetic blood,[12] do not seem to allow the same kinds of questions to be asked about liminality, and about repeated but failed attempts to belong. Although Bill is a dangerous creature in the three fanfics, he expresses ethical concerns which align him with the sympathetic, new wave vampire. The fears expressed are internalized: he fears himself and the destruction he can bring to the humans who become involved in his "unlife."

Diet choices as a sign of ethics also feature initially in WayBeyond's "Paresthesia." In this fanfic the protagonist also goes through various processes of "othering." Rather than figuratively re-fanging a vampire, the fanfic, set after the battle in Meyer's *Eclipse* and working from the premise that Edward has been killed and Bella has been turned, explores how Bella's new identity affects her moral choices.[13] Bella wakes up to a vampire existence, adopted by the Volturi coven. Following the logic of the Twilight canon, the option of "vegetarianism" (feeding upon animals rather than humans) is open to vampires, and Bella is familiar with this diet choice, through having lived with the Cullens. WayBeyond suggests, however, that the diminished threat to humans produced by the vegetarian diet, the particular de-fangedness of the Cullens, requires guidance and support from a larger group. Without this guidance, and faced with the necessity of feeding for the first time, Bella thinks: "I'd never doubted that my golden-eyed family would have kept me on the straight and narrow [but t]here were no golden-eyed vampires here in Italy."[14] In her new existence, group or coven traditions override individual choice, and Bella's initial otherness is supplanted with belonging as she easily gets used to killing humans. The moral quandaries Bella could be expected to wrestle with, both as a human and as a potentially vegetarian vampire, are replaced by an emotional numbness, a lack of remorse after feeding from and killing a human, which conforms to the attitudes of her Volturi peers. "The fact that I'd just fed on a human should have bothered me, but it didn't," she observes; "I'd felt nothing but intense pins and needles in my chest. No remorse and no regret. It was the coldness that stunned me most." This desensitization is thematized throughout the text and presented as a characteristic discovered by the newborn vampire, as she awakes as undead and experiences "the memories of [her] short life" quickly fading away.

The "emotional agony" which has plagued her only "hours before" is replaced by a disquieting "nothing." The emotional numbness and the absence of remorse are presented as more shocking to Bella than her actual choice to leave the ethical diet choice behind.

Feelings of self-disgust and something resembling ethical considerations, absent in the taking of blood, surface in issues pertaining to sexuality. Bella's virginity at the beginning of "Paresthesia" also functions as a mechanism of "othering," as the Volterra vampires shamelessly display sexual desire and practices, suggesting that this is appropriate vampire behavior. The virginal and innocent portrayal of Bella is only in part modeled on the canon, in which Bella remains a virgin until her wedding night. She is not unfamiliar with lust, however, and Meyer portrays her as the one trying to increase the level of intimacy in her relationship with Edward. Her strict sexual morals in the fanfic, contrasted to her lack of remorse when feeding from humans, is evidence of the author's separation of blood-lust and sexual lust, rather than her imitation of the canon's close link between the two.

Although Bella eventually loses her virginity in "Paresthesia," her decision to have sex is not made as swiftly as her acclimatization to the non-vegetarian diet. Hindering Bella's adjustment to the Volterra vampires' uninhibited sexual practices is her conviction that sexual relations should be monogamous and based on love, a conviction which apparently is rooted deeply enough to live on in her undead existence. When the Volturi vampire Demetri seduces her, Bella enjoys the act itself, but loathes herself for transgressing another set of sexual morals: she has "slept with [her] best friend's boyfriend." This strong emphasis on both fidelity and the connection between romantic love and sex, presented in "Paresthesia" as an undying ideal, evokes the literally eternal love between Bella and Edward which constitutes the center of the romantic Twilight canon.

Vampires, Souls and Questions of Evil

The central metaphysical issues in the canons examined here are often linked to the theme of the soulless/ensouled vampire. The choice of a morally responsible life, which some of the contemporary vampires make, is often based on the conviction that transformation into a vampire entails a loss of the human soul and will thereby lead to eternal damnation. This conviction has implications first and foremost for the characters' relationships with their human love interests; the potential lack of a soul may be perceived as corrupting or, at least, may make the vampire unworthy of love and admiration. The turning of the main vampire is, in all three canons, linked to force and betrayal, which furthers the notion of an unwilling loss of soul. Bill falls victim to what could be construed as rape; Edward is only turned because his human life cannot be saved; and Angel is bitten rather than kissed by a female vampire he mistakes for a prostitute. The attitude exhibited towards general or individual processes of turning enables the sympathetic vampire to illustrate "dilemmas of the self: how to have meaning in the world which demands it, how to act in circumstances we did not choose, how to be a good human."[15] When the fanfic authors considered here shift perspectives, or when they present human characters who are turned into vampires, issues related to potential soullessness connect to both involuntary circumstances surrounding the turning itself and to how a morally sound (human) existence may be reached. The fanfics suggest that the soul is associated with identity and essence, but also that the ensouled state can be intimately connected to issues of guilt and individual responsibility.

Lizardmm's "Soulless" revolves around two central issues: identity, and good vs. evil. Soulless vampirism is presented as unequivocally evil, while the capacity to do good is linked to the human soul. Buffy is mortally wounded in this fanfic, and turning her is a way of rescuing her from final death. That is, although represented as a final option, perhaps preferable to death, Buffy cannot express an active will to be turned (which links her to the male vampires in all three canons). Lizardmm builds on the canon's representation of what happens after a human is turned, as it is explained by Buffy in a Season Two episode: "You die, and a demon sets up shop in your old house, and it walks, and it talks, and it remembers your life, but it's not you."[16] In "Soulless," Buffy's body, or "old house," returns from the grave; it looks like her but is inhabited by an evil demon. Vampire Buffy's soulless existence is characterized by cruel, immoral, and violent acts, often linked to sexuality. The Buffy-shaped demon goes hunting in night clubs and is seen feeding from, and having sex with, a number of humans. When Buffy's soul is temporarily restored by the Powers That Be (god-like, good creatures featured in *Angel*), the demon no longer controls her body and she becomes Buffy again, although in the shape of a ("good") vampire. As an ensouled vampire, Buffy cannot recall events from her soulless period, whereas the soulless Buffy has all of Buffy's human memories, along with some of her linguistic tics and occasional flashes of feeling, which are perceived as annoying to the demon who possesses her body. The soul represents her "essence," which is something more profound than memories and personality; it equates to Buffy's being, minus her bodily shell. Willow, who first attempts but fails to restore Buffy's soul, explains that the process is complicated, since she is "looking for *a specific* soul."[17] The quest for Buffy's soul, then, becomes the quest for Buffy's "essence," separated from her undead body, which suggests that parts of human identity are fundamental or even transcendent, while others are socially constructed and imitable.

The discussions about the soul in Lizardmm's fanfic pertain to metaphysical as well as theological questions. Wishing to return Buffy's soul to her undead body, Buffy's friends face a dilemma: "If they returned the slayer's soul, not only would they be ripping the California slayer from Heaven for a *second* time, but Buffy would now be forced to share a body with a demon."[18] Again, the author draws on the canonical knowledge that an undead body is an empty "old house," in order to represent it as a dwelling alternately for the demon and for Buffy's soul. The restoration of Buffy's soul takes place only because the Powers That Be foresee that the ensouled vampire Buffy can serve a greater good by her continued presence on earth. Unlike Angel in the canon, whose soul is restored as the result of a curse, Buffy's soul is brought back to her undead body by a kind of divine intervention. It is worth noting that the amnesia that follows upon her "re-souling," then, appears as somewhat of a blessing, since it saves her the torment caused by memories of the terrible acts she committed as an evil vampire. In contrast, the ensouled Angel constantly experiences torment and guilt, and therein lies the curse of returning his soul. The transfer of Buffy's soul between different realms is motivated by events of greater importance than the fate of individual humans and is controlled by god-like creatures, while the attempts of Buffy's friends to bring her soul back are presented as selfish and morally doubtful. The suggestion that mortals should not interfere with the borders between metaphysical realms evokes beliefs from numerous religions. Through these representations of matters to do with the soul, Lizardmm injects religious elements into a contemporary, secular vampire canon, in ways that differ from the eighteenth- and nineteenth-century focus on religion in relation to the vampire trope. Hollinger notes that, "however threatening Stoker's vampire is, it serves a crucial function in his novel: in its role as evil Other, it necessarily guarantees the *presence* of the Good."[19] In contrast to Stoker's *Dracula*, there is no absolute good in Lizardmm's "Soulless," only a human soul capable of making morally sound choices, and absolute evil is linked not to the vampiric state per se but to the absence of soul. Connecting the soul both to a conscience and to a transcendent part of the self, Lizardmm associates matters of the soul with individual responsibility as well as with metaphysical realms beyond human reach.

Similarly, individual responsibility is central to 5by5creations's "Soul Searching," but it is coupled with a more definitive view of vampirism itself as eternally damning. The fanfic presents a first-person account from Edward's perspective, and crosses the Twilight canon with *Angel*. "Soul Searching" is set in a narrative gap in the Twilight canon; that is, in the four months in *New Moon* when Edward leaves Bella in order to protect her. From the outset, Edward is racked with guilt, not only for placing Bella in harm's way because of her association with vampires, but because he has hurt her by lying about his feelings for her: "If I had a soul, my lies would be consuming every last piece of it like the fires of hell."[20] At this point in the canon, Bella has expressed a desire to be turned, and this is also something which torments Edward: "I *would* not allow her to sacrifice her chance at heaven for me." Edward's thoughts illustrate a deeply-held Christian belief: his conviction is that souls after death have different destinations that are not dependent on the individual's choices in life, but on what the individual *is*: human or vampire.

To create a purpose in his existence, Edward decides to track and kill the vampire Victoria, one of the main threats to Bella's life, and his quest brings him to Los Angeles, where he encounters another vampire in the form of Angel. The differences between the two vampires are pronounced and it takes some time before they can convince each other of their true natures; this is evidence of 5by5creations cleverly playing on the diverse manifestations of the trope, and of the logical gaps which are the result of crossing two vampire canons.[21] External differences aside, however, the main discrepancy between the two stems from their alternate view of whether or not they have souls. Angel's access to two experiences, his ensouled good state and his existence as the evil Angelus, enable him to argue in favor of vampires having souls, whereas Edward remains hesitant, emphasizing that the taking of human life is a sin so grave that it eliminates the possibility of having a soul. In an effort to convince him, Angel mentions "the countless humans with souls that killed for lesser reasons than survival." Edward is forced to admit that his own vegetarian diet and the fact that he has chosen to take the lives only of "murderers and rapists that preyed on the weaker humans," proves hopeful in comparison; yet he remains convinced that the vampire state itself disqualifies him from having a soul.

Lengthy conversations gradually prompt Edward to reevaluate his views, particularly Angel's suggestion that the very presence of guilt is a sign of a soul and that, without it, Edward would rather "embrace every selfish drive." The canonical elements of protection and love are repeatedly invoked in these conversations as proof of Edward's lack of selfishness, his humanity as it were. When encountering and defeating clearly inhuman creatures — vampires among them — a further level of comparison is reached, since Edward has nothing in common with these monsters. It is thus through continuous comparisons with other vampire representations — the good Angel, the stories about Angel's evil alter ego, and the decidedly soulless creatures Edward helps to slay — that the idea of his own soul emerges. The comparisons are also made against the backdrop of memories of talks with Edward's "father," Carlisle, who is convinced that the transformation into vampire does not mean a forfeiting of one's soul. The end result of Edward's soul searching is the tentative idea that: "Maybe the soul was more a product of choice than an inherent quality. You could choose to have a conscience or to ignore it." Edward does not completely abandon the view of himself as a monster in this fanfic, but his conviction of his soullessness and certain damnation is at least partly tempered. He finds meaning is his involuntary existence, since his strength can be used in the continuing protection of Bella, and becomes more convinced that a morally responsible life may open the doors of heaven to a vampire.

Undead Desires: Some Conclusions

As written reworkings of a canon, fan fictions illustrate how readers and viewers have reacted and responded to various kinds of narratives. The new wave vampire has elicited a number of fanfic responses, arguably because it invites explorations of deeply human concerns. It has been said that the trope no longer necessarily provokes fear, but rather "speaks ... to our undead desires" by "return[ing 'otherness'] as a source of empathy and identification."[22] The fanfic authors' deep investment in the canons is certainly, in many cases, grounded in a sense of recognition of, and identification with, different forms of otherness. The "undead desires" may be connected to a plethora of contemporary issues such as eternal youth, undying love, self-control, and physical as well as mental strength. Naturally, there is ample opportunity in fanfic for interrogations of good and evil, humanity and monstrosity; this is evident in writings which stay relatively close to the canon, and which maintain the blurred boundaries between human and vampire, mirroring the complexity of the new wave vampires' location in "a humanized terrain."[23]

When turning to fan fiction of the kinds discussed here, however, the "undead desires" are also connected to aspects of vampire fiction which are downplayed in the new wave canons. By both literally and figuratively re-fanging the vampire protagonists, and by presenting the canons' human characters in vampire shape, the fanfic authors considered here illustrate a wish to reestablish and reinforce the boundaries between good and evil, between human and monster. The vampires in several of the texts discussed here are to be feared: they are fanged and decidedly "other," and since the fanfics are told from their perspective (a narrative stance in the main unexplored in the canons), they allow for questions of a more internal nature and for self-reflexive recognitions of the monster that looks like us.

Issues connected to the absence or presence of vampire souls, and related questions about eternal damnation or potential redemption, are present to varying degrees in the canons but are explored in more detail in the analyzed fan fictions, once again because of an enforced difference between human and vampire, and an altered narrative perspective. Since fan fiction authors (to varying degrees) follow the logic of the canon they inscribe themselves within, they focus on different sets of problems and probe different metaphysical issues. Questions concerning the individual's responsibility and the redeemable soul are thus variously explored and contested, but the selected texts still evidence similar tendencies to highlight deeply human moral dilemmas, in making the choice between good and evil.

NOTES

1 Milly Williamson, *The Lure of the Vampire* (London: Wallflower Press, 2005), 29.
2 Margaret L. Carter, "The Vampire as Alien in Contemporary Fiction," in *Blood Read: The Vampire as Metaphor in Contemporary Culture*, ed. Joan Gordon and Veronica Hollinger (Philadelphia: University of Pennsylvania Press, 1997), 27.
3 Nina Auerbach, *Our Vampires, Ourselves* (Chicago: The University of Chicago Press, 1995), 145.
4 Veronica Hollinger, "Fantasies of Absence: The Postmodern Vampire," in Gordon and Hollinger, eds., 201.
5 Williamson, 31.
6 Joan Gordon and Veronica Hollinger, "Introduction: The Shape of Vampires," in Gordon and Hollinger, eds., 5.
7 Fred Botting, *Gothic Romanced: Consumption, Gender and Technology in Contemporary Fictions* (Abingdon, UK: Routledge, 2008), 77.
8 *True Blood*, "Shake and Fingerpop," Season Two, Episode Four, director Michael Lehmann, written by Alan Ball, New York: Home Box Office, first aired July 12, 2010.
9 Eternallybills, "Hunger," *Fan Fcition.net*, accessed August 24, 2011, http://www.fanfiction.net/s/6031096/1/Hunger.

10 levitatethis, "Dismantled," *Archive Four Own.org,* , accessed August 24, 2011, http://archiveofourown. org/works/56913.
11 levitatethis, "Aberration," *Archive Four Own.org,* , accessed August 24, 2011, http://archiveofourown. org/works/56914.
12 Bill's senior Eric, for example, feeds on human blood with relish. About "Tru Blood" he says: "It'll keep you alive, but it'll bore you to death." *True Blood,* "Plaisir d'amour," Season One, Episode Nine, director Anthony M. Hemingway, written by Brian Buckner, New York: Home Box Office, first aired November 2, 2008.
13 Bella is turned also in the canon, but not until the fourth book in the saga, *Breaking Dawn.*
14 WayBeyond, "Paresthesia,"*Twilighted.net,* accessed August 22, 2011, http://www.twilighted.net/viewstory.php?sid=14083.
15 Williamson, 50.
16 *Buffy the Vampire Slayer,* "Lie to me," Season Two, Episode Seven, director Joss Whedon, written by Joss Whedon, Los Angeles: Twentieth Century Fox, first aired November 3, 1997.
17 Lizardmm, "Soulless," *Slayer Time.net,* accessed August 24, 2011, http://slayerstime.net/english-fanfics/allauthors/lizardmm-qsoullessq-buffyfaith-rating-nc17-part-1.html.
18 Lizardmm. The author makes an intertextual reference to the third episode, "AfterLife," in the sixth season of *Buffy,* in which Willow brings Buffy back to life, unaware that she was leading a perfectly happy afterlife in a heavenly place.
19 Hollinger, "Fantasies of Absence," in Gordon and Hollinger, eds., 202.
20 5by5creations, "Soul Searching," *Twilighted.net,* accessed August 24, 2011, http://www.twilighted.net/viewuser.php?uid=11399.
21 This aspect is further explored in Maria Lindgren Leavenworth, "Variations, Subversions, and Endless Love: Fan Fiction and the *Twilight* Saga," in *Bringing Light to Twilight: Perspectives on a Pop Culture Phenomenon,* ed. Giselle Liza Anatol (Houndmills: Palgrave MacMillan, 2011), 69–81.
22 Williamson, 29.
23 Ibid., 31.

Authors and Critics as Fans

15

Postmortem Matchmaking: Jane Austen, Vampire Bride

Amy Elizabeth Smith

Jane Austen's early death, with only four novels in print and two ready for publication, was not the end — neither of her literary life (in more ways than one, as we shall see here) nor of her fans' appetite for "all things Austen." Even setting aside internet fan fiction, more than a hundred published sequels and tie-ins to her work are available for the pleasure of those of us who cannot let go. There are mysteries with *Pride and Prejudice* characters solving dastardly Regency crimes; adaptations shifting the focus to minor characters; modern film and fiction updates such as *Clueless, Bridget Jones's Diary* and the Bollywood *Bride and Prejudice*; fan-focused works like *Austenland, Jane Austen Ruined My Life*, and *Mr. Darcy Broke My Heart*; dating advice guides, cookbooks, quiz books, tour books, paper dolls, and graphic adaptations, all to keep Austen's world of romance, decorum, and wry wit alive and well.[1] And then came the monsters. Is their arrival in Austenland a new form of homage — or simply an outrage?

Given Austen's almost unique status as both popular icon and canonical literary figure, Austen scholars have long debated issues about reading communities and practices that current studies of "fandom" examine. In her essay "Austen Cults and Cultures," Claudia L. Johnson traces the long history of the "faddish commodification" of Austen's works and person and of the way many Austen readers, such as novelist Henry James, feel that Austen "is loved in the wrong ways by the wrong sorts of people."[2] Who, of course, is to determine the "right" way to love Austen? Natalie Tyler adopts a whimsical yet helpful strategy for reframing internecine Austen squabbles; via a multiple choice quiz, she invites readers to determine which of the four main "schools" of Janeism they profess. Each has its own reading practices: "Janeites" treat Austen as "comfort food," "Gentle Janes" look to Austen for advice on life and love, "Ironic Janes" revel in her satire and read her "more for delight than for inspiration or instruction," while "Subversive Janes" believe that Austen's "subversive messages may be read between the lines" and hence enjoy ferreting out transgressive subtexts.[3]

In a market flooded with Austenalia, the Regency writer's fans, label them as you will, love her in many ways indeed through sequels, adaptations, and other forms of literary homage. But where does the recent onslaught of monster adaptations fit in? From the text alone, it is a little hard to say if Seth Graham-Smith's *Pride and Prejudice and Zombies* (2009), which set off the Austen monster trend, is fan fiction or just the opposite. His work keeps a percentage of Austen's text intact, while unleashing the undead upon her characters. A consideration of Amazon.com reader reviews of the book shows that responses vary widely. Some self-proclaimed Austen haters adore the book and revel in seeing the blood hit the muslin, while Austen fans range from considering the novel a fun parody, to seeing it as a clever idea imperfectly executed, to expressing howling indignation over the insult to Austen's original. In any event, the floodgates were open, and soon werewolves, sea monsters, mummies, and vampires made their appearances in new "monster mash-up" adaptations following the same template: download text, insert monsters.[4]

To date, vampires have been the only creatures versatile enough to survive past this specific "cut, paste, and adapt" formula and appear in more original renderings. In this essay I will briefly consider the first vampire adaptations to move past the template set out by Graham-Smith's book before focusing on the two texts which most invite the "homage or outrage?" question: Michael Thomas Ford's *Jane Bites Back* (2010) and Janet Mullany's *Jane and the Damned* (2010). Ultimately, however odd or inappropriate such adaptations may seem to some readers (Tyler's "Janeites" and "Gentle Janes" come to mind), a consideration of the works in question reveals how they nonetheless embody the most important dynamics of traditional, monster-free Austen fan fiction. I will also explore the relationship Ford and Mullany's novels have to the complex, ever-evolving world of vampire mythology as depicted in contemporary film and literature.

In the fall of 2009, after the April debut of *Pride and Prejudice and Zombies*, two bloodsucking spin-offs of *Pride and Prejudice* appeared — *Mr. Darcy, Vampyre*, by Amanda Grange and *Vampire Darcy's Desire*, by Regina Jeffers.[5] A sequel to *Pride and Prejudice*, Grange's text reveals that Mr. Darcy's legendary aloofness has more to do with his dark secret than with being arrogant or shy. Grange portrays Mr. Darcy as bearing his "curse" reluctantly, and in the mode of vampires tragic rather than evil; like Barnabas Collins of the classic television series *Dark Shadows*, Mr. Darcy is eager to return to his human state for the woman he loves.

Regina Jeffers, author of *Vampire Darcy's Desire*, adopts a distinctly more lurid style. Her Mr. Darcy retains his morals in the afterlife, but her Wickham is completely corrupted by the power of vampirism:

Wickham lowered his head again, drinking his fill of Lucy's blood — feasting on her existence. The act of tasting her in the most personal of ways brought the erection the woman had thought to enjoy, and Wickham sated himself with a copulation with her lifeless, rapidly cooling body. It was pure power — the lustful lapping of the woman's life fluid. It was the taking of a human life; it was the build-up of emotions — the control — *his* control — and the submission — *her* submission.[6]

Jeffers states in her novel's introduction that she is a member of the Jane Austen Society of North America (JASNA) and undertook the work reluctantly at the prompting of her publisher, hoping thus to "maintain some integrity in the story," since "the project" — a vampire adaptation of Austen's most beloved novel — "would go forward with or without me."[7] Graham-Smith acknowledges that the idea for his *Pride and Prejudice and Zombies* came from his editor, and Jeffers's admission reveals that her novel also began as a marketing concept, one calculated to accommodate the current mass-market vogue for romantic vampires fueled by the success of Stephenie Meyer's Twilight Saga, HBO's *True Blood* (based on Charlaine Harris's Sookie Stackhouse novels), and the television adaptation of L. J. Smith's series, *The Vampire Diaries*.[8]

How far are publishers (and writers) willing to pursue new ideas playing to the popularity of good-guy vampires, and of Austen as well?[9] To the ultimate outrage — a vampiric assault on the very person of Jane Austen herself. The year 2010 saw the publication of two novels with Austen as a vampire: Ford's *Jane Bites Back* and Mullany's *Jane and the Damned*. Novelized adaptations of Austen's life are nothing new to Austen fan fiction. There are more than a dozen such novels in print, from Barbara Ker Wilson's *Jane Austen in Australia* (1984; recently republished as *The Lost Years of Jane Austen*), to Jon Spence's well-researched *Becoming Jane Austen* (2003), to more fanciful works like Michael O'Rourke and Sally Smith's time-travel fantasy *The Man Who Loved Jane Austen* (2000; reprinted in 2006 under authorship of Sally Smith O'Rourke).

A common thread in virtually all fictionalized accounts of Austen is match-making — not by Austen, but for her. Even Rudyard Kipling, well before the recent flood of fan fiction, paired Austen off in his playful, touching poem, "Jane's Marriage".[10] Austen, after all, has given her readers a world in which women do not have to compromise their dignity to "win" a man, where true love triumphs, where one can believe in happily-ever-after. It just does not sit well with many of her fans that the creator of such loving couples as Emma and Mr. Knightly, and Lizzy and Darcy, should never experience any coupling herself. So authors have set about finding adventure and romance for Austen, whether spun from the sparse hints of unfulfilled romance in her life or created, whole cloth. The most popular of all such works is Stephanie Barron's ten-volume Jane Austen mystery series, and the romantic tension between Austen and Barron's fictional creation, Lord Harold Trowbridge, the "Gentleman Rogue," is one of the series' principal charms. In a plenary speech at the 2010 Annual General Meeting of JASNA, Barron wryly discussed the fallout for having killed off Trowbridge in the seventh volume of the series; this choice, although it makes narrative sense, apparently cost her many readers who had adored following Austen's chaste but intense romance.

But Austen as a *vampire*? Re-animating Austen's corpse may seem an extreme (or unacceptable) fictional choice, one completely at odds with the spirit of Austen fan fiction, created by and for the doting followers of modest, genteel, decorous Jane Austen. But as Tyler's cataloging of Austen fans highlights, not everyone's Austen is so modest, genteel, or decorous; quiz responses that land one in the "Subversive Jane" category include a fondness for singer k. d. lang, sex columnist Susie Bright, and *Gone with the Wind*'s scandalous Scarlett O'Hara.[11] Further, a close look at Ford's *Jane Bites Back* and Mullany's *Jane and the Damned* reveals that these works are largely driven by the same dynamics as most non-vampiric fictions about Austen — namely, getting Aunt Jane a little action, both in life and love.

Ford's comic novel has a modern setting, with Austen as a bookstore owner in upstate New York.[12] The opening chapters establish the main theme of the work: that much of what Austen failed to get in life, she can have in her after-life — a public career, love, *power*. In the first chapter Austen hosts a book signing for Melodie Gladstone, the author of *Waiting for Mr. Darcy*, a self-help title snapped up by chattering, Darcy-hunting women ready to vow pre-wedding abstinence to win their Mr. Right. Ford simultaneously satirizes overeager Janeites and the authors who exploit both readers and Austen herself.[13] All sweetness during the event, Gladstone becomes another person once the book buyers are gone:

> Jane smiled politely and said, "This tour must be exhausting for you."
> "It's a fucking nightmare," Melodie replied. Jane cringed. "Every night it's the same thing. 'Don't have sex until you've found the right one. Keep yourself pure. Wear this stupid locket and one day your prince will come.' What a load of crap. But they eat it up." She waved her hand in the air. "You've seen the numbers."[14]

What Janeite would not want to see such a cynical manipulator get her comeuppance? At the first opportunity, Austen whisks Gladstone off and takes a bite — non-fatal, as befits her good breeding — from the woman who had boldly declared her right to a "piece of the Austen pie."[15] Layers of irony are one of the pleasures of Ford's text, the style of which suggests that he fits nicely into Tyler's catalogue of fans as an "Ironic Jane," interested more in "delight" than in "inspiration or instruction."[16] While some would argue that Ford himself is exploiting Austen in a climate when vampire romance is riding high, it is hard not to enjoy Austen feeding on the woman who freely admits to using Austen as a meal ticket.

Vampire narratives frequently enact the fantasy of vampires taking revenge on those who have wronged them in their human state, directly or by proxy; watching the "shitkicker slaughter" scene (so labeled in the DVD chapter menu) from the 1987 classic *Near Dark*, one can imagine how many times the character played by Bill Paxton must have been beaten up in high school. While the exploitative Gladstone functions as a stand-in for authors in general who might have done Austen wrong, Ford also offers up another who actually did — fellow nineteenth-century author Charlotte Brontë. In Brontë's opinion, infamous among Austen fans, *Pride and Prejudice* is no more than an "accurate daguerreotyped portrait of a common-place face; a carefully-fenced, highly cultivated garden, with neat borders and delicate flowers — but no glance of a bright vivid physiognomy — no open country — no fresh air — no blue hill — no bonny beck."[17] Ford's Austen has a chance to reply to this postmortem assault: "What nonsense. Just because Austen's heroines aren't flinging themselves all over the moors and mooning over disfigured men ..."[18] Better still, she has the chance to revenge herself directly on Brontë, since the Victorian writer turns out to also be a vampire, one who keeps the mummified remains of her siblings Anne, Emily, and Branwell around for company and is tormented by Austen's greater fame. Setting Charlotte's house on fire (with Charlotte inside) is not something Jane *plans* ... but accidents happen.

Best of all, when virginal Austen becomes vampire Austen, she gets to have exciting, other-worldly sex — with none other than Lord Byron. Known to be fond of older women, the poet, thirteen years Austen's junior, turns her into a vampire like himself and leads her to stage her "death" in 1817 at age 41, to avoid causing her family pain. Short of Bram Stoker, no literary figure could be more appropriate for the role of Austen's seducer than the dashing

Romantic author, whose friend and doctor John William Polidori authored *The Vampyre*.[19] Although the fictitious Austen eventually flees Byron's attentions, he resurfaces in the tiny town where she has sequestered herself, complicating her life and coercing his way back into her bed:

> Byron was gone in the morning, the only proof of his having been there the pounding in Jane's head like the clanging of church bells. Her whole body ached, and she could barely stand the light. She'd forgotten what it was like when two of her kind joined together. All of their senses became heightened, but the drawback was that their frailties did as well. Jane was ravenously hungry.[20]

Numerous vampire novels, films, and television series explore the notion of vampire sex as uniquely intense and powerful, whether between vampires or in human/vampire couples. Prominent among these are J. R. Ward's steamy Black Dagger Brotherhood novels and the series by Lara Adrian and by Kresley Cole. In Charlaine Harris's Sookie Stackhouse novels, vampire blood functions as a type of aphrodisiac when ingested by humans, prolonging and intensifying sexual encounters. While aimed at a t'ween/teen audience, Stephenie Meyer's Twilight Saga trades on sexual tension through the speculation (maintained until the final novel) about what sex will be like for Bella with her vampire boyfriend, Edward. Bella's insistence on losing her virginity to him before being transformed into a vampire, in order to fully enjoy the intensity of the experience, allows for an exploration of sex with a powerful, dangerous partner — tempered, in Meyer's universe, by Edward's determination to suppress the violence in his character.

In granting Austen immortality, Ford therefore also grants her a chance for preternaturally good sex — as well as seduction by one of the most exciting literary figures ever. But however earth-shaking in bed, Lord Byron is not husband material, so the novel presents Austen with traditional romance as well. In this case vampirism is more of a hindrance than a help. As with the question of vampire sexuality, numerous works have explored the star-crossed nature of human/vampire relationships, perhaps the most famous of them, the Buffy/Angel pairing in Joss Whedon's *Buffy the Vampire Slayer*. Unlike the temperamental Byron, Austen's suitor Walter Fletcher is sweet, reliable, and can hang drywall (think *Sense and Sensibility*'s Colonel Brandon in flannel shirts, rather than a flannel waistcoat). But Austen fears that if he learns she is *undead*, she will lose him. Her first attempt at disclosure does not go well:

> Jane knew that if she was going to tell Walter the truth, it would be now. She closed her eyes. "But I'm...," she began. She could sense Walter's nervousness as he waited for her to continue. *Just say it!* The voice in her head cried. *Just tell him already!*
> "I'm celibate," she blurted out.
> She opened her eyes a little and looked at Walter's face. *Celibate?* she thought. *That's what you thought of first?*[21]

Since Ford's book has a sequel, the problem of the big revelation is left open, although the couple do finally manage to declare their feelings and make it to the bedroom.

Hot sex with Lord Byron notwithstanding, love, romance, and domesticity are of central importance in Ford's novel. Although his work has unique elements within the burgeoning world of vampire subgenres, its closest affinities are with the "vampire-next-door" variety. Rather than establishing a highly developed alternative context such as one finds in Richelle Mead's Vampire Academy novels or P. C. Cast and Kirstin Cast's House of Night series, "vampire-next-door" novels instead fold vampirism into a garden-variety contemporary setting. In works of this type, such as those by Michelle Rowen (Immortality Bites series), Lynsay Sands (Argeneau Vampires), and Molly Harper (Nice Girl series, which contains a fun Jane Austen connection), vampirism adds a colorful dimension to the basic challenges of romance and dating. When is the right time to mention that you are "sunlight challenged"? What if his mom and dad won't like him dating a ... *you know*? And isn't it great to be able to pig out and not gain weight?! Significant moral or philosophical issues connected with death, immortality, and power are, for the most part, avoided in favor of light-hearted comedy.

One intriguing feature of vampire literature is the wide field of possibility for adding to or altering vampire mythology. This provides a constant (and entertaining) source of friction among vampire aficionados, some of whom — not unlike Austen purists ready to defend their dear Jane against modernizers and adapters — insist on sticking to the "facts" about vampires. The most famous recent debate involves Stephenie Meyer's luminescent vampires, who inspired angry websites, hostile Facebook groups, and T-shirts insisting that "Real Vampires Don't Sparkle." Ford makes several modest contributions to vampire mythology, among them the idea that vampires experience their human death and vampiric rebirth as an intense dream, one that is different for each individual. By and large, however, Ford's work is more allied with Austen fan fiction than with the ever-expanding realm of vampire literature that encompasses works as diverse as Poppy Z. Brite's broody, pansexual *Lost Souls*, Christopher Moore's hilarious *Bloodsucking Fiends* and its sequels, and John Ajvide Lindqvist's stark, poignant *Let the Right One In*. While Ford lays claim to a small corner of vampire territory, his work is best calculated to delight Janeites who wish Austen could have just had a bit more *fun* in her life (and who are willing to accept her having an after-life to get it).

In *Jane and the Damned*, Janet Mullany also grants her undead Austen love, eroticism, and power — but there are significant differences both in tone and the treatment of vampire themes. Mullany's novel is an historical romance, rather than a comedy, one set in Austen's own time period. There is a distinctly more serious attempt to reproduce Austen's voice and to examine the dynamics of her relationships with her parents and her only sister, Cassandra. The novel opens as a series of conflicts converge. The date is 1796; Austen has just received her first book rejection, and, as she approaches her twenty-second birthday, spinsterhood looms:

> How many years would it be before the matrons at assemblies and balls murmured about poor Miss Jane, who almost certainly would not marry now, for she was sadly faded and had too sharp a tongue for her own good? How long before she sat behind the matrons, a spinster's cap on her faded hair, and listened to the malice and gossip, herself

an object of pity and mild derision — the gentlewoman of limited means with a small talent for music and writing.[22]

But more than age and failed novels threaten her tranquility — Napoleon and the French army also menace. With their Revolution and its radical changes under control, the French begin to turn their eyes northward to the wealthy island monarchy. And as if that were not trouble enough, Miss Austen and her family have one more concern — the Damned. Vampires, normally seen in only the most fashionable cities and resorts, have arrived in Austen's small Hampshire village to amuse themselves with some country pleasures.

Mullany's vision of vampires and their culture is more thoroughly developed than Ford's. Their existence is publically known, treated by some humans as a blasphemous affront to decency and by others as a morbidly titillating scandal. Vampires are aristocrats by blood and by nature, and their foibles are a subject of fearful, fascinated gossip for commoners. When the Damned shock the locals with their appearance at a simple country dance, Austen too is agape:

> It was the gentlemen she found most fascinating, even if there were not enough of them and so far none of them had made a move to dance, not even with the ladies who accompanied them. They stood among the Hampshire shopkeepers and local gentry like thoroughbred horses in a field of donkeys, beautiful and dangerous, stilled power in their limbs, mystery in their eyes.[23]

Mullany's vampires have many of the powers that have become standard in vampire fiction over the last twenty years; they can read minds, perform a type of "glamour" hypnotism, and they are all extremely beautiful. She makes her own contributions to the genre, however, by giving them the capacity to heal wounds with their breath and to dematerialize into darkness, thus cloaking themselves at night as they hunt ("It's like bathing in warm ink," Austen exclaims when she first masters the technique).[24] The Damned also have a special capacity to connect to inanimate objects, sense their histories, and convey these images to humans, an experience at times exotic and alluring and, at others, profoundly disturbing. When Austen's vampiric seducer draws off one of her cotton gloves, she is mentally transported to the ugly truth of the fabric's source: "Somewhere, dark-skinned people, mournful and angry, plucked white buds from bushes beneath the burning sun."[25] Along with providing an interesting twist on vampire powers, Mullany's choice implies an allegiance within Tyler's universe of Austen fans — surely only a "Subversive Jane" would shock the "Janeites" and "Gentle Janes" of the world by drawing attention to the subtext of Caribbean slavery, as did Patricia Rozema before her in the controversial 1999 adaptation of *Mansfield Park*.[26]

Powerful in distinctive ways, the Damned are the otherworldly *crème de la crème*, sharing their existence in an élite social grouping similar to that of the vampires in the Underworld film series or Melissa de la Cruz's Blue Blood novels, mingling with humans only to feed or amuse themselves. Their standards for recruitment are high, and a fledgling vampire is appointed a "Bearleader," a term Mullany borrows from the eighteenth- and nineteenth-century practice of a young monied Briton setting off for the Grand Tour of the Continent accompanied by an older gentlemen, who is charged with refining the youth's manners. Austen's Bearleader advises her on matters of dress, etiquette, and vampire hierarchy; he even points out when she should (and should not) allow her extended fangs to be seen by other vampires, a condition delicately referred to as *"en sanglant."*[27] The perennial question of vampire weaknesses also operates within the framework of Mullany's aristocratic vision. Garlic is not dangerous, but it is overpowering and distasteful to beings of refinement. Vampires cast no reflection, but this is a state one arrives at gradually, like shedding a low-born accent over time. As for sunlight, it is not fatal to vampires, Austen is told by a fellow fledgling vampire, although "it's thought to be vulgar to be seen in daylight."[28]

Considering the blue-blooded nature of Mullany's vampires, one is forced to ask: does Jane Austen, daughter of a country clergyman, actually belong in this elegant circle? The handsome, arrogant vampire who — on a whim — feeds from her at the country dance, is about to leave her to die, when the memory of their lively encounter gives him pause:

As he replaced the glove on her arm, pulling the tight cotton over her too-pale flesh, he remembered her passion, her courage in lecturing him on how he squandered immortality. Miss Jane, the respectable vicar's daughter, as one of the Damned. It was unthinkable. She could be little more than the descendant of country gentry with possibly some distant aristocratic relations' blood in her veins ... How would she fare if granted the gift herself?[29]

Austen may not have had much noble blood, but she is, he senses, *special*. And so he turns her. Mullany's adoption of an aristocratic milieu for her vampires allows her to use vampirism as the ultimate honor in her fan fiction since Austen, to her admirers, *is* an aristocrat, albeit a literary one.

Despite differences between Ford's and Mullany's novels, both are driven by a dynamic of Austen getting in death what she enjoyed little or none of in life — power, eroticism, romantic love. While Mullany attempts to create a reasonably faithful portrait of Austen's late eighteenth-century, pre-Regency world, she also invents a fictional what-if scenario that allows Austen to transcend traditional gender roles. What if the French actually *had* invaded England? The arrival of French troops and the rapid surrender of numerous towns, including Bath, where Austen and her family have traveled after the arrival of the vampires in Hampshire, throws the English into an uproar. It also allows Austen her first kill, when a French soldier corners her:

> "Eh, *ma petite*, you walk alone?" His voice rasped. "You like to welcome a Frenchman to your town, yes?"
>
> ... he laughed and lunged toward her. He was against her now, almost overwhelming her with his stink and lust and the heat of his blood, grabbing at her skirts. She raised one hand and ripped at his stock and jacket, tearing the fabric — how strong she was, how powerful — and lunged for his neck beneath the greasy pomade-scented black hair.
>
> Now she was the one who attacked.[30]

Although displeased at fighting alongside humans, the Damned take the lead in driving the French out, and Austen is caught up in the adventure — she adopts male dress, learns to swordfight, and becomes a ruthless killer, all in the interest of serving England. What has she to fear? As her Bearleader points out, "You're no shrinking spinster now."[31]

Vampirism is highly sexualized in Mullany's work, but the interesting twist on this common theme is the intrusion of dark sexuality into the morally restrained world of Jane Austen, a contrast made sharper in Mullany's book through the contemporary pre-Regency setting — Ford's modern Austen, who has seen a thing or two, has no good reason to be easily shocked. Chaste but ever curious, Mullany's Austen quizzes a maid to discover how humans could willingly submit to the bite of the Damned:

> "Ooh, miss, it's better than anything. Better than gin or plum cake or Christmas, and you won't get a baby from it. And the Bible says you can do it and it's not a sin."
>
> "It does? Whereabouts?" Try as she could, Jane could not think of any Bible passage condoning relations with vampires.
>
> "Well, miss, it doesn't say you can as much as it doesn't say you can't."[32]

Austen's transformation into a vampire is a highly erotic, nearly orgasmic experience, "the heat and glory of the moment" transporting her to "a place where the throb of her blood became a pleasure too great to bear."[33] As her powers and confidence increase she enjoys flirtations with other vampires and with her own victims, and sexual tension develops between her and her Bearleader. Although pained by the separation from her family that vampirism imposes, when it becomes clear that Luke Venning wants her as his official Consort, Austen is thrilled, poised to enjoy her new existence with the being — if not the "man" — she loves.

Mullany introduces two distinct variations on vampire legends, ones allowing vampirism to function at the level of both plot and metaphor. Vampires have many things: strength, beauty, psychic abilities, cunning. What they do not have is artistic talent. They cannot play musical instruments, and they cannot write novels. Their own lives become a thing of cold, stately beauty; they do not produce art, they *are* art. Faced with giving up not only her family but her beloved novel-writing as well, Austen balks. Fortunately, in Mullany's vampire universe, there is an option, one well-suited to entertain Austen fans. Vampirism can be cured — but only by the special healing waters of Bath. Austen's intended Consort begs her not to return to a fleeting human existence:

> "You write a few books that entertain your family and you win a little fame, perhaps even some money, while you live. And after, what then? Your books languish forgotten on dusty bookshelves and you are but a name on a binding ... You think your books offer you a chance at immortality? Oh, Jane, do not delude yourself."[34]

She has to choose between the dark gift, grudgingly bestowed but well used, and her own as-yet- untried gift for fiction. And so ... Austen makes the choice that gives birth to Lizzy and Darcy, and Marianne and Elinor, and Emma and Mr. Knightly, to all her own fledglings. After having her chance at power and danger and beauty and even love, Austen makes the choice that proves her would-be Consort wrong: she *will* have immortality, death notwithstanding.

Thus, for the vicarious pleasure of Austen lovers, the fictional Austens of Ford and Mullany receive the gift of immortality, with its powers and its problems, even if that gift is at last rejected. Both Ford and Mullany create fan fiction similar in spirit to previous free novelizations of Austen's life, albeit more exotic. Many authors have sought to provide Austen with change, excitement, and romance. Purists may reject any fictionalization about Austen, monsters or no monsters — but, ultimately, Austen's admirers are as diverse as those who enjoy vampire fiction and films. Fans of spatter-action like *John Carpenter's Vampires* and *Blade* are typically not the same people paying to see Edward Cullen from *Twilight* use his enhanced vampire speed to open the car door for his prom date, and neither group may have the patience to make their way through Bram Stoker's entire novel.

Indeed, if Austen's fans fall into the distinct schools of Janeism previously discussed —"Janeites," "Gentle Janes," "Ironic Janes," and "Subversive Janes" — then perhaps there is a parallel to be drawn with vampire aficionados. "Stephenie Meyerites," many of whom make internet confessions to endless re-readings of the Twilight Saga, can empathize with the "comfort food" Janeites, while "Stokerites," loyal to nineteenth-century vampire values, can pair off with the traditionalist "Gentle Janes." "Ironic Janes" would get on quite well with "Christopher Mooreites" and enjoy Ford's *Jane Bites Back* together. As for "Subversive Janes," the readers most likely to approve of Mullany's *Jane and the Damned*, they could find their match in sexy, edgy, darkness-loving "Poppy Z. Britists."

And so, to return to the original question. In a universe where two worlds as rich and varied as those of Austen fan fiction and of vampire literature intersect, one fan's outrage — over sparkling vampires or an undead Regency writer — is another's homage.

Notes

1   Coverage of this material would require a book in itself, but among the most original and entertaining spin-offs are the Jane Austen Mysteries by Stephanie Barron, Carrie Bebris's multi-volume Mr. and Mrs. Darcy mystery series, Paula Marantz Cohen's *Jane Austen in Boca* (New York: St. Martin's Press, 2002) and *Jane Austen in Scarsdale: Or Love, Death and the SATs* (New York: St. Martin's Press, 2006), and the series of sequels by Elizabeth Aston (the premise being that Lizzy and Darcy have five daughters). Other amusing variations include: *Lost in Austen: Create Your Own Jane Austen Adventure*, by Emma Campbell Webster (New York: Riverhead Books, 2007), *Pride and Promiscuity: The Lost Sex Scenes of Jane Austen*, by Arielle Eckstut and Dennis Ashton (New York: Simon and Schuster, 2001), and *Two Guys Read Jane Austen,* by Steve Chandler and Terrence N. Hill (Bandon, OR: Robert D. Reed Publishers, 2008). Fans who want as much Austen in their life as possible can pursue *Cooking with Jane Austen* by Kirstin Olsen (Westport, CT: Greenwood Press, 2005), *Tea with Jane Austen* by Kim Wilson and Tom Carpenter (Madison, WI: Jones Books, 2004), *In the Garden with Jane Austen* by Kim Wilson (Madison, WI: Jones Books, 2008), *A Walk with Jane Austen* by Lori Smith (Colorado Springs: Waterbrook Press, 2007), and *In Paris with Jane Austen* by Vera Quin and Veronique Yapp (Great Malvern, UK: Cappella Archive, 2005).
2   Claudia L. Johnson, "Austen Cults and Cultures," in *The Cambridge*

Companion to Jane Austen, ed. Edward Copeland and Juliet McMaster (Cambridge: Cambridge University Press, 1997), 212. *Janeites: Austen's Disciples and Devotees* (Princeton: Princeton University Press, 2000), edited by Deirdre Lynch, also addresses fandom at length.

3   Natalie Tyler, *The Friendly Jane Austen: A Well-Mannered Introduction to a Lady of Sense & Sensibility* (New York: Viking, 1999), 7–13.

4   See, for example: Jane Austen and Seth Graham-Smith, *Pride and Prejudice and Zombies* (Philadelphia: Quirk Books, 2009); Jane Austen and Ben H. Winters, *Sense and Sensibility and Sea Monsters* (Philadelphia: Quirk Books, 2009); Jane Austen and Adam Rann, *Emma and the Werewolves* (Canada: Coscom Entertainment, 2009).

5   Ann Hassell's adaptation *Pride & Prejudice's Vampires* (Charleston, SC: Netherfield House Press, 2010) follows the "cut and paste" formula and will not be considered here. Colleen Gleason's novella "Northanger Castle," a spin-off of her own Gardella Vampire Series, is an amusing vampire parody of *Northanger Abbey* (in the anthology comprised of the works of Mary Balogh, Colleen Gleason, Susan Krinard, and Janet Mullany, *Bespelling Jane Austen* (Don Mills, ON: Harlequin, 2010).

6   Regina Jeffers, *Vampire Darcy's Desire* (Berkeley: Ulysses Press, 2009), 280.

7   Jeffers, *Vampire Darcy's Desire*, v.

8   Sharkey, Alix, "Seth Grahame-Smith Interview," *The Telegraph*, 30 April 2010, http://www.telegraph.co.uk/culture/books/7656909/Seth-Grahame-Smith-interview.html.

9   Margot Adler examines the media surge in popularity of the "do-good" vampire in "For Love Of Do-Good Vampires: A Bloody Book List," *NPR.org*, accessed August 24, 2011, http://www.npr.org/templates/story/story.php?storyId=123115545.

10 One could argue that Kipling is actually Austen's first post-mortem matchmaker, since he conjures up a husband for her in the poem (published in 1926) only after she has died and gone to heaven.

11 Feminist critics have provided much-needed revisions of the image of a modest, gentle, spinsterly Aunt Jane who wrote only for amusement, cultivated first by Austen's brother Henry (against the evidence of Austen's own letters) in his Preface to the posthumous publication of *Northanger Abbey* and *Persuasion*; this safe, constricting image was later echoed in other writings by family members, editors, and various literary critics. Devoney Looser's *Jane Austen and Discourses of Feminism* (London: Palgrave Macmillan, 1995) provides a helpful analysis of the range of feminist revisionings of Austen.

12 Stacey Abbott catalogues the variety of occupations held by vampires in *Celluloid Vampires: Life after Death in the Modern World* (Austin: University

of Texas Press, 2007); bookseller can be added to the list.
13 Dating advice books on Austen vary enormously in tone from the primly earnest to the playful; among the number are *Dating Mr. Darcy*, by Sarah Arthur (Wheaton, IL: Tyndale, 2005), *Jane Austen's Guide to Dating*, by Lauren Henderson (New York: Hyperion, 2005), and *Dear Jane Austen: A Heroine's Guide to Life and Love*, by Patrice Hannon (New York: Plume, 2007).
14 Michael Thomas Ford, *Jane Bites Back* (New York: Ballantine Books, 2010), 8.
15 Ford, *Jane Bites Back*, 9.
16 Tyler, *The Friendly Jane Austen*, 12.
17 Brian Southam, ed., *Jane Austen, The Critical Heritage* (London: Routledge and Kegan Paul, 1968), 126.
18 Ford, *Jane Bites Back*, 88.
19 Stephanie Barron's most recent Jane Austen mystery, *Jane and the Madness of Lord Byron* (New York: Bantam, 2010), includes a flirtatious scene between Austen and Lord Byron.
20 Ford, *Jane Bites Back*, 128.
21 Ibid., 161–62.
22 Janet Mullany, *Jane and the Damned* (New York: Avon, 2010), 4.
23 Mullany, *Jane and the Damned*, 9.
24 Ibid., 142.
25 Ibid., 21.
26 Patricia Rozema directed and wrote the screenplay for the 1999 Miramax Studios *Mansfield Park*. Her liberal adaptation draws freely from Austen's letters and juvenilia and essentially recasts Fanny Price as Austen herself, while depicting Sir Thomas Bertram as a slave owner (and a rapist) and pointing out the family's dependence on the proceeds of slavery, based on allusions in Austen's novel to property held in Antigua. Pre-dating Rozema was Edward Said's reading of *Mansfield Park* in *Culture and Imperialism* (New York: Knopf, 1993), which also exposes the role of slavery in the "domestic comforts" of England.
27 Mullany, *Jane and the Damned*, 53.
28 Ibid., 120.
29 Ibid., 22.
30 Ibid., 68.
31 Ibid., 56.
32 Ibid., 79–80.
33 Ibid., 21.
34 Ibid., 290.

16

I Demand an Undying Devotion to the Play: *Rosencrantz and Guildenstern are Undead*

Fiona Martin

Since the first production of Shakespeare's *Hamlet* at the turn of the seventeenth century, the play has attracted performers, fascinated audiences, and stimulated scholarly discussion and debate — a form of immortality which has been further perpetuated from the twentieth century onward by film versions of the play.[1] The attitudes of literary critics and theater reviewers toward Shakespeare productions, however, remain widely divergent. Ann Thompson and Neil Taylor, for example, observe, "In the last fifty years, the play's iconic status has led to countless attempts to adapt, rethink, debunk and vandalize it."[2] The judgment implied by the word "vandalize" suggests the continuing divide between "high" and "popular" cultures, and draws attention to the issues potentially arising when a canonical text is appropriated and newly interpreted.[3]

Rosencrantz and Guildenstern Are Undead (2010), written and directed by Jordan Galland, participates in this tradition of variation and experimentation.[4] The film combines homage to Shakespeare's *Hamlet* (1602), W. S. Gilbert's short comedy *Rosencrantz and Guildenstern* (1891),[5] and Tom Stoppard's *Rosencrantz and Guildenstern are Dead* (1968),[6] with a number of otherwise disparate elements: vampires, the legend of the Holy Grail, Rosicrucianism, and film. This indie film is a locus of intertextuality, insofar as it alludes to — and assumes that the viewer has some knowledge of — pre-existing literary texts and films; it is thus "constituted through a multiplicity of textual elements."[7] It may also be considered a fan text, in the sense that it is evidently intended to appeal to various fan groups, including disciples of Shakespeare, film enthusiasts, and those devoted to vampires and/or the esoteric. However, while it ostensibly participates on the levels of both high and popular culture, it is unclear exactly which type of fan the film is intended to attract, and whether there is enough material from any one of the perspectives above to sustain audiences possessing specific and specialized interests. Indeed, one reviewer predicted that "[S]erious theater or Shakespeare fans will likely be turned off by the shallow engagement with the source material, and horror and/or vampire fans will be disappointed by the lack of suspense and gore."[8]

From my own perspective as a scholar of early modern literary texts, this observation is certainly justified, precisely because of the film script's tenuous connection to the actual text of *Hamlet*. This raises two related questions: first of all, if the film signals its indebtedness to both Shakespeare and Stoppard, to what extent does this embody a promise of a significant level of engagement with the source materials?[9] Secondly, does the suggestion that the film has distinct literary origins not imply that the integration and interplay of the appropriated matter with the new material will be meaningful in a way that maintains its connectedness to the *Hamlet*-related texts to which it alludes?[10]

These questions may be countered with further questions, of course, in regard to the issue of individual expectations. For instance, why should any form of "poaching"[11] come burdened with promises, and who is to determine what constitutes a "significant level of engagement" with the original texts? As Henry Jenkins states, "... a poached culture requires a conception of aesthetics emphasizing borrowing and recombination as much or more as original creation and artistic innovation."[12] To acknowledge this form of creativity, then, should not such "borrowings" and "recombinations" be celebrated, rather than being perceived as misguided? While I acknowledge that the responses to these issues must be largely subjective, I still maintain that the original questions are worth asking, because I also believe that the use of earlier works within another work implies a responsibility both to the original sources and to the audience. Although *Rosencrantz and Guildenstern Are Undead* might be approached from many angles — and quite lucratively from the perspectives of both movies and multimedia — my concern here is specifically for the literary texts (primarily *Hamlet*) to which the film is indebted.

Shakespeare himself borrowed freely from other writers. "Throughout Shakespeare's career as a playwright," Stephen Greenblatt observes, "he was a brilliant poacher — deftly entering into territory marked out by others, taking for himself what he wanted, and walking away with his prize under the keeper's nose."[13] Stoppard's approach in *Rosencrantz and Guildenstern are Dead* is rather different from Shakespeare's form of poaching; he has constructed a drama directly parallel to, and concurrent with, the action of *Hamlet*, and it is clear that he is thoroughly familiar with Shakespeare's text. The approach in *Rosencrantz and Guildenstern Are Undead* is different again: because it incorporates multiple genres — Galland characterizes the film as both a "surreal romantic comedy" and a "smorgasbord" — it seems to lean toward parody rather than homage.[14] The film's quirky assemblage of ingredients attempts to narrow the gap between high and popular cultures, and perhaps even attempts to subvert the high cultural elements themselves.

In addition to my predominantly literary and dramatic focus, I will also briefly discuss the written texts that are the basis respectively for the interest in vampires, and of Rosicrucianism. The film is supplemented by an official website, and I acknowledge its possible appeal to fans in a discussion of the website's "Shakespiracy" link. Before investigating further the film's appropriation of materials, however, I include here a synopsis, highlighting the elements that are most relevant to the present discussion.

The background story of the film centres around:

> a four hundred-year-old duel over the Holy Grail, between a master vampire named Horatio and his nemesis, the former vampire Prince Hamlet, who drank from the Holy Grail, curing himself of the vampire curse, and then travelled the world, erasing much of Horatio's legacy ... while still retaining his own everlasting life. Today, the vampire Horatio is known as the playwright Theo Horace, who always hires a young, controllable human to direct his plays, and turns every actress in his play into a vampire bride.[15]

In the present day, Theo (John Ventimiglia) hires Julian (Jake Hoffman) to direct his off-Broadway adaptation of *Hamlet*, entitled *Rosencrantz and Guildenstern Are Undead*, while Julian's ex-girlfriend Anna (Devon Aoki) plays Ophelia, and his friend Vince (Kris Lemche) is cast as the prince.[16] The transformations of Anna, Vince, Carlo/Rosencrantz (Carlos Velazquez) and Mickey/Guildenstern (Mike Landry) into vampires — and the discovery of the "two thousand-year-old-conspiracy" through the secret society agent, Charlotte — is followed, ultimately, by a confrontation between Theo and the "real" Hamlet, who triumphs over his adversary by driving a stake through Horatio's heart.

Now that Julian's on-again girlfriend is a vampire, he is anxious to obtain the grail himself and cure Anna of her curse. Yet the film is, after all, a romantic comedy, and when Anna points out to Julian that immortality means "we can be together forever," he quickly chooses to join her as one of the undead.[17]

This synopsis should indicate the use of the Shakespeare and Stoppard texts, primarily, as a combined point of departure for the film. The questions raised earlier, regarding the relationship between the canonical and popular elements in the film, cannot be addressed without discussing the intertextual nature of the film, and how the "poached" material has been manipulated. Fundamentally, except for a few of Shakespeare's more famous quotations, the texts are essentially subsumed within Galland's playful pastiche.[18]

In the play-within-the-film, Theo dramatizes the history of the conflict between himself and the Prince. Shakespeare's *Hamlet* was the first of four plays masterminded by Theo; the second was W. S. Gilbert's *Rosencrantz and Guildenstern*; the third, Stoppard's *Rosencrantz and Guildenstern are Dead*. Each of these plays is present, in some form, in Theo's fourth play. During the process of rehearsing, we hear fragments of Shakespeare's lines, performed by the actors in Elizabethan-style costuming, within attractively stylized sets. The following speech, spoken by Vince/Hamlet, is characteristic of the comic treatment of some of the best-known lines from *Hamlet*: "Ah, well aimed, Horatio — your arrows have outrageous fortune. You may be good with arrows and bows; myself, I'm good with ribbons and bows. Who designed your clothing? That outfit just screams, 'Something is rotten in the state of Denmark.' Is that a

Roman toga? It's got to — go!" Julian questions these lines, as they do not appear in the script; menacingly, Theo retorts, "I *like* it. We're modernizing."[19]

As a character, Theo provides the essential link between the "usually" separate worlds of Shakespeare and vampires. He appears to be intimate with the text of *Hamlet*, but he is also recognizably part of the post-Stoker evolution of the vampire. Even without stage makeup, for instance, Theo bears a resemblance to the vampire figure in *Nosferatu*, so that he is recognizably a product of the visual representations of the undead in classic films. Part of Theo's strategy for maintaining his charismatic power over humans and vampires is through the manipulation of the texts of others. The figure of Shakespeare himself is given a brief scene in Theo's play, in a dramatized flashback during which Horatio insists that "Spakesheare" writes the words "Rosencrantz and Guildenstern are Dead." The playwright is depicted merely as Theo's puppet, and is shown at the beginning of the scene struggling to find the right word: "To be, or not to be — that is the — dilemma?"[20] The most direct instance of homage toward Shakespeare — still in a comic context — occurs when Theo/Horatio says to the real Hamlet, "I turned you into a vampire; also, by having Shakespeare write that epic tragedy, I turned you into a god." Unfazed, Hamlet first retorts, "The only tragedy here is who in the hell is Rosencrantz and Guildenstern's acting coach?" — then follows up with, "is this a soliloquy or an aside I'm doing?"[21]

While Gilbert and Stoppard do not appear as characters in Theo's play, one rehearsal scene incorporates part of Gilbert's First Tableau, staged beneath the title, *Rosencrantz and Guildenstern*. Although it is not mentioned in the film, Gilbert's Claudius is responsible for writing a play entitled *A Right Reckoning Long Delayed*; it is intended as a tragedy, but fails miserably, Rosencrantz explains, as it is "a piece of / pompous folly / intended to excite no loftier / emotion than laughter and / surprise."[22] Galland's representation of the "real" Hamlet may be modeled on W. S. Gilbert's character, who is described (in Gilbert's play) as "idiotically sane / With lucid intervals of lunacy."[23]

The humour in this film, then, is closer to the spirit of Gilbert's comedy, rather than Stoppard's play, for the potentially serious is always undercut by a comic inversion of the viewer's expectations. This extends to the very mechanics of play-writing itself. In Theo's play, Rosencrantz says: "This play that Horatio wrote with Shakespeare makes us look like idiots, so I found this guy, W. S. Gilbert, who write [sic] a play where we're the heroes. It's cool, no?" When Guildenstern expresses concern that Horatio will think they're still alive, Rosencrantz suggests, "We could write a newer play and call it *Rosencrantz and Guildenstern are Dead*, or something," while Guildenstern muses, "Now, can we get Tom Stoppard to write it?"[24]

Like Stoppard's characters, Mickey/Guildenstern appears to have been gifted with slightly more intellect than Carlo/Rosencrantz; moreover, they are constantly seen together, even behind the scenes. Further influence of Stoppard's text is evident in the exchanges of dialogue between the two characters; in an echo of the confusion over which one is which, Carlo proposes a number of alternatives to their names, which Mickey and Julian immediately reject. In *Rosencrantz and Guildenstern Are Undead*, Carlo speaks almost entirely in slang, while Mickey is chiefly obsessed with the details of his appearance and gestures onstage. At one point he interrupts the rehearsal to ask, "Jules, does that work with the two fingers like that? Do I need to get my thumb involved somehow?"[25] The subtle mingling of humor and pathos in Stoppard's play is entirely absent from the film, and the emphasis, instead, is on satirizing theatre "types."

Curiously, the lines which may suggest homage to the characters' verbal tennis match in Stoppard's play are given not to Rosencrantz and Guildenstern, but to Vince. When he meets with Charlotte, she advises him to be careful if Theo asks him questions: "... repeat what he says as if you don't understand, with a question mark." "A question mark?" Vince asks, to which she replies, "That's perfect."[26]

Although *Hamlet* and the plays derived from it are the most obviously literary texts in the film, vampires are also part of an established literary tradition.[27] In an interview, Galland relates, "When I was eleven I read *Dracula* and decided that one day, I wanted to make a vampire film. I read everything about vampires I could get my hands on."[28] At 14, he played the part of Rosencrantz in a "high school version" of Stoppard's play, and was also "strongly drawn" to *Hamlet*:

One day I thought of the title *Rosencrantz and Guildenstern Are Undead* and began seeing that the supernatural evil of vampires resonated within the story and language of *Hamlet*. I was compelled to explain these connections. The Holy Grail conspiracy was something that had intrigued me throughout my childhood. It added another exciting layer to the historical elements of my script.[29]

In suggesting that he has identified the "resonance" of vampire evil "within the story and language of *Hamlet*," Galland is maintaining a fiction that extends beyond the film itself, and is further developed on the official film website.[30] The vampire content that he perceives "within" the text of *Hamlet*, and which he feels "compelled to explain," is of course Galland's own projection of vampire mythology onto the text. Each of the levels of the "Shakespiracy" on the website is accompanied by YouTube clips, presented in the same style (animations with voiceover) as the DVD in the film. These short excerpts provide "information" on the following topics: "Rosenkreutz and Goldenstone," "Shakespeare and Vampires," "Hamlet and the Holy Grail," "King James I and the Lost Passage," and "Pirates and Ancient Rome." This part of the website is designed to be interactive; provision for leaving comments encourages feedback from visitors.

In order to successfully maintain this fiction, however — to impart to it an air of authority, no matter how tongue-in-cheek — the "information" used as supporting material needs to be plausibly presented. As Galland observes of the DVD in the film, "When I was writing about it, I wanted it to feel like a real thing."[31] Although on the one hand these video clips function as a simple parody of the "infomercial," Galland has also drawn upon elements of existing scholarship in order to imply a reasonable knowledge of his various subjects. However, he can only hope to entertain a fan group that is unconcerned about the accuracy and credibility of the material used, for both the film and the website contain errors, and much of the "scholarship" touched upon by the website is surprisingly out of date. This observation pertains to Rosicrucianism, to *Hamlet*, and to Shakespeare himself.

Three major Rosicrucian texts appeared in the second decade

of the seventeenth century. Although Galland does not identify the original treatises that have evidently inspired his "Shakespiracy," the date assigned to the "Rosicrucian and Goldenstonian" manifesto in the film is 1615, the year in which the second text, the *Confessio Fraternitatis*, appeared. Likewise, the name "Goldenstone" may be derived from the third text by Johann Valentin Andreae, entitled *The Chemical Wedding of Christian Rosenkreutz* (published 1616, the year of Shakespeare's death); in it, the eponymous hero is initiated into a secret brotherhood of spiritual alchemy and earns the title of "Knight of the Golden Stone."[32] In the "Shakespiracy" link on the film website, the manifestoes are described as being filled with "references to the Kabbalah, Hermeticism and Alchemy," along with the "claim" that it was Andreae who had discovered the tomb of the vampires Rosenkreutz and Goldenstone in 1601.[33] In an interview with Janice Brown, Galland observes:

> There was a lot of material I had to cut from the screenplay that's based on historical conspiracy theory — I'd found these correlations between the text of *Hamlet*, the theory that Shakespeare may not have written some of his most famous plays, and vampire mythology ... I spent a lot of time researching and making those connections so that if you search online, it would almost appear that I hadn't made it all up![34]

While a little more material from the alchemical point of view might have provided an illuminating context for the concept of vampire immortality, it is obviously not essential. There is, however, an oversight on the film website in regard to *Hamlet*. According to Galland, a "mystery" surrounds Hamlet's age: "In act five scene one Hamlet says it was 'three and twenty seven years' since Yorick was buried. The math doesn't add up. Hamlet just finished college, so how could he have known Yorick?"[35] This is erroneous on two counts. In this scene, the gravedigger tells Hamlet that he has been a sexton for 30 years, and that he began his work "on the very day that young Hamlet was born." Hamlet is therefore 30; Yorick has been buried for "three and twenty years," so his death occurred when Hamlet was seven.[36] Secondly, Hamlet has not finished "college": near the beginning of the play, Claudius announces that Hamlet's intention to go "back to school in Wittenberg" is "most retrograde to our desire," indicating that the Prince is still a student.[37]

Despite the film's integration of vampire material with *Hamlet*, there are essentially only two phrases from the play which are used to support the vampire theme. The first fragment, "Now could I drink hot blood," is misquoted both on the website, and in the four times that Vince utters it during the film.[38] The second is paraphrased during a rehearsal scene, in which Vince/Hamlet asks Anna/Ophelia how she knew he was a vampire. She replies, "Look at you — pale as your shirt — your knees knocking each other;" whereupon Vince/Hamlet finishes with, "You don't like the shirt? It's my new design — sheep's feather."[39] In one interview, Galland relates how, in earlier drafts of the script, he had listed "quotes" that could be related to vampires; insofar that this material may have added greater interest to the film, it seems a curious decision to have deleted it.[40]

Also on the website's video clips, Galland raises the question of the authorship of Shakespeare's plays, but includes only the rather outdated theory (originating in the nineteenth century, most notably with Delia Bacon)[41] that Francis Bacon was the author of the Shakespeare canon; none of the more recent candidates are mentioned.[42] Likewise, Galland has obliquely referred to the tradition that Shakespeare incorporated his name into a translation of Psalm 46 for the King James Bible.[43] On the website, this becomes a "cryptic passage in the bible" revealing the "hidden location of the Holy Grail," which was "omitted" from the King James version.[44] Although Galland is clearly being playful with his materials, adjusting them to suit his own purposes, the overall feeling is that his approach to these Shakespearean contexts is particularly free, an impression which the misspelling of the names John Dee and Johann Valentin Andreae further reinforces.[45]

Jenkins observes of "poached" culture that it can be "a patchwork culture, an impure culture, where much that is taken in remains semidigested and ill-considered."[46] I consider this to be an apt description of *Rosencrantz and Guildenstern Are Undead*. For while the film does not promise — or require — a consideration of the appropriated texts from a rigorous, academic perspective, it does seem to promise, yet not deliver, a significant level of engagement with those texts. While the film seems to attempt a hybridization of high and popular cultural elements, it fails to engage with the kind of questions — issues of individual consciousness and will, death and immortality, the supernatural — that have repeatedly sent readers and spectators back to *Hamlet* for more than 400 years.

So what type of fan is *Rosencrantz and Guildenstern Are Undead* ultimately intended for? It may be, in the end, that I am asking the wrong question, approaching the film from the viewer's perspective, rather than that of the writer and director. In an interview with Dan Schechter, Galland was asked whether he thought that all the "promotional stuff" for the film would "help." Galland replied, "It depends on what your goal is, really, because, I mean, you can reach a handful of people and they get — they can enter your world — and that's ... an amazing personal reward, and it feels very successful and satisfying."[47] Here, the implication is that Galland is preoccupied less with possible fan groups, and more with sharing the product of his creative vision.

As an enthusiast for live Shakespeare performances, I consider the visual impact of Theo's theatrical sets and costumes to be the most successful aspect of the film. Yet I also hope that the fans of *Rosencrantz and Guildenstern Are Undead* who are new to Shakespeare will be encouraged to discover this iconic playwright for themselves, and to forge — if not an "undying devotion" to *Hamlet* — at least the beginning of an intimate and rewarding relationship with Shakespeare's text.

Notes

1 William Shakespeare, *Hamlet*, ed. Ann Thompson and Neil Taylor, The Arden Shakespeare, Third Series (London: Thomson, 2006).
2 Ann Thompson and Neil Taylor, Introduction, *Hamlet*, ed. Ann Thompson and Neil Taylor, The Arden Shakespeare, Third Series (London: Thomson, 2006), 120.
3 These designations are borrowed from Roberta Pearson, "Bachies, Bardies, Trekkies, and Sherlockians," in *Fandom: Identities and Commu-*

nities in a Mediated World, ed. Jonathan Gray, Cornel Sandvoss, and C. Lee Harrington (New York and London: New York University Press, 2007), 98–99. Pearson includes Elizabethan drama amongst the "rarefied realms" of culture, pointing out that while the "study of high culture still undeniably thrives in the academy," from the perspective of popular culture, "high culture figures only as a repressive other against which to celebrate the virtues of the popular."

4   *Rosencrantz and Guildenstern Are Undead*, DVD, director Jordan Galland, (2009, New York: C Plus Pictures, 2010).
5   W. S. Gilbert, *Rosencrantz and Guildenstern, Gilbert and Sullivan Archive*, accessed August 22, 2011, math.boisestate.edu/gas/other_gilbert/rosencrantz/script.html.
6   Tom Stoppard, *Rosencrantz and Guildenstern are Dead* (London: Faber and Faber, 1968).
7   Cornel Sandvoss, "The Death of the Reader? Literary Theory and the Study of Texts in Popular Culture," in *Fandom: Identities and Communities in a Mediated World*, ed. Jonathan Gray, Cornel Sandvoss, and C. Lee Harrington (New York and London: New York University Press, 2007), 23.
8   Joshua Bell, "Rosencrantz and Guildenstern Are Undead," *Film Critic.com*, June 3, 2010, http://www.filmcritic.com/reviews/2010/rosencrantz-and-guildenstern-are-undead/.
9   Reviewers of the film have commented on the frustration of expectations created by the title. Andrew Schenker observes that, "despite its clever title," the film fails to "explore the comic possibilities inherent in the vampire-Hamlet pairing." "*Rosencrantz and Guildenstern Are Undead*," *Slant Magazine*, May 31, 2010, http://www.slantmagazine.com/ film/review/rosencrantz-and-guildenstern-are-undead/4845; Joe Lozito describes *Undead* as "a clever title desperately in search of a movie to back it up," and concludes that the film is "never more than the sum of its one-liners," "*Rosencrantz and Guildenstern Are Undead* Review," *Big Picture Big Sound*, June 14, 2010, http://www.bigpicturebigsound.com/ Rosencrantz-and-Guildenstern-Are-Undead.shtml, while Josh Bell suggests that the "quality humor in *Undead* pretty much begins and ends with its title," *Film Critic.com*, June 3, 2010, http://www.filmcritic.com/reviews/2010/rosencrantz-and-guildenstern-are-undead/.
10 Perhaps of relevance here is John Tulloch's study of the audiences of specific Chekhov productions. He distinguishes between the "Chekhov fans" (who were familiar with the plays and were aware of "critical traditions") and "star fans" (those who "went to a particular production because they loved seeing a particular star actor.") He observes that the two groups had "rather different measures for

excellence." Star fans tended to have "much less knowledge of 'Chekhov'," and they "tended to be happy if the production was 'uncomplicated,' direct,' and 'easy to follow.'" Tulloch, "Fans of Chekhov: Re-Approaching 'High Culture'," in Gray, Sandvoss and Harrington, eds., 117, 112, 119.

11 I use the term "poaching" to refer to the practice of using material from other works in a manner that is relatively unconstrained, so that — in the present context — it serves the purposes of the film-makers rather than representing an attempt to incorporate specific elements that appear in the original works.

12 Henry Jenkins, *Textual Poachers: Television Fans and Participatory Culture* (New York and London: Routledge, 1992), 224. I acknowledge that similar questions about poaching may be usefully raised in relation to Stoker's *Dracula*, but an investigation of the horror genre in regard to this "vampire" text is beyond the scope of this essay.

13 Stephen Greenblatt, *Will in the World: How Shakespeare Became Shakespeare* (New York: W. W. Norton & Company, 2004), 152.

14 Nicole Holland, "Indie Filmmaker Finds the Holy Grail," *Independent Film Quarterly*, accessed January 29, 2011http://www.independentfilmquarterly.com/ifq/interviews/jordan-galland.htm.

15 "As I Lay Undying," *Rosencrantz and Guildenstern Are Undead*.

16 During the "Job Interview With a Vampire," Theo asks Julian, " … do you suffer from any blood vessel abnormalities, iron deficiencies, vitamin B12 deficiencies and/or intravenous drug usage?" When Julian answers in the negative, Theo breathes, "Too good to be true!" and informs his new director, "I demand an undying devotion to the play."

17 The popular appeal of this notion, embodied in Stephenie Meyer's Twilight Saga, is clearly something of which Galland is aware. Interviewer Dan Schechter teases Galland as they discuss the possibility of various trinkets to be used as promotional items for the film; he comments, "This is capitalizing on the success of Twilight?" — to which Galland laughingly replies, "Exactly." Dan Schechter, "Interviews: Director Jordan Galland," *Rosencrantz and Guildenstern Are Undead*.

18 Compare this approach with that of Stoppard, or of Jean Betts, in her play *Ophelia Thinks Harder* (Wellington, NZ: The Play Press, 2003). Betts's text bears the name "Wm. Shakespeare" alongside her own — acknowledging the "collaborative" nature of the play — and is subversively comic while still engaging intimately with the text of *Hamlet*.

19 "Grave New World," *Rosencrantz and Guildenstern Are Undead*.

20 In the First Quarto (the 'Bad' Quarto) of 1603, the line reads, "To be, or not to be — ay, there's the point" (7.115) — this, and Galland's variation, suggest the humor inherent in any deviations from a well-established

text. *Hamlet: The Texts of 1603 and 1623*, ed. Ann Thompson and Neil Taylor, The Arden Shakespeare, Third Series (London: Thomson Learning, 2006), 92.
21 "Death of a Pale Man," *Rosencrantz and Guildenstern Are Undead*.
22 From the Third Tableau in Gilbert's *Rosencrantz and Guildenstern*. Gilbert and Sullivan Archive, accessed August 25, 2011, math.boisestate.edu/gas/other_gilbert/rosencrantz/script.html.
23 From the Third Tableau in *Rosencrantz and Guildenstern*.
24 "Death of a Pale Man," *Rosencrantz and Guildenstern Are Undead*.
25 "Grave New World," ibid.
26 "Dial S for Shakespiracy," ibid. During this same scene with Charlotte, there is a visual similarity to the question-and-answer game scene in the film version of Stoppard's play ("Role-Playing," *Rosencrantz and Guildenstern are Dead*); the circular fountain in the background in Galland's film perhaps recalls the ornamental apple tree in Stoppard's. In that scene, Rosencrantz eats an apple; in Galland's film, Charlotte produces an apple and offers it to Vince, saying, "An apple a day keeps the demons away." Earlier in the film, Julian is impressed with Theo's apple-eating exercise during a workshop, ironically observing to the others, " … there's no separation between him and his character — he *is* his character!" "Grave New World," *Rosencrantz and Guildenstern Are Undead*.
27 Bram Stoker's *Dracula* (first published in 1897) was preceded by novels in the Gothic tradition, including Horace Walpole's *The Castle of Otranto* (published 1765); William Beckford's *Vathek* (published in English in 1786); Ann Radcliffe's *Mysteries of Udolpho* (1794); Matthew Lewis's *The Monk* (1796); and C. R. Maturin's *Melmoth the Wanderer* (1820). The grail legend has an even longer history, as the subject of medieval romances by such writers as Sir Thomas Malory, Chrétien de Troyes and Wolfram von Eschenbach.
28 Holland, "Indie Filmmaker."
29 Ibid.
30 *Shakespiracy.com*, accessed August 24, 2011, http://shakespiracy.blogspot.com/.
31 Afi Dallas, "Afi Dallas Video Interview: Writer/Director Jordan Galland (Rosencrantz and Guildenstern Are Undead)." *Vimeo*, May 8, 2009. gordonandthewhale.com. http://gordonandthewhale.com/afi-dallas-video-interview-rosencrantz-and-guildenstern-are-undead-writerdirector-jordan-galland/ (accessed February 17, 2011).
32 The first Rosicrucian treatise, the *Fama Fraternitatis*, appeared in 1614. For a discussion of the manifestoes, see Frances A. Yates's influential book, *The Rosicrucian Enlightenment* (London: Routledge, 1972), a copy of which may be seen in the film on the character Bobby Bianchi's dresser.

See also *A Christian Rosenkreutz Anthology*, ed. Paul M. Allen (Blauvelt, NY: Rudolf Steiner Publications, 1968), for Thomas Vaughan's 1652 translations of the *Fama* and the *Confessio*, as well as the first English translation of *The Chymical Wedding* (1690) by Ezechiel Foxcroft.

33. "Level 1: Rosenkreutz and Goldenstone," accessed January 29, 2011, http://shakespiracy.blogspot.com/.
34. Janice Brown, interviewer, "Jordan Galland and the Art of Spooky: Search Party and Rosencrantz and Guildenstern Are Undead," NYC Spotlight, *Sonic Scoop*, accessed February 17, 2011, http://www.sonicscoop.com/2010/04/23/jordan-galland-the-art-of-spooky/.
35. "Level 2: Shakespeare and Vampires," http://shakespiracy.blogspot.com.
36. *Hamlet*, Act 5, scene 1, lines 153, 139, 163–64.
37. The footnotes to the Arden edition elaborate on these issues. Thompson and Taylor acknowledge that Hamlet's age "would make him an unusually mature student by Elizabethan standards," (note 113, 174) and also that there is a variation on these dates in the First Quarto. In the earlier text, the editors point out, the gravedigger says that Yorick has "lain in the earth 'this dozen yeare', perhaps indicating that Hamlet is 18 rather than 30, an age which would seem more appropriate to his status as a student" (note 153, 420).
38. In a similar lack of fidelity to the text, Hamlet's line at 1.5.170 is altered, in the film, to "There are more things in heaven and earth / Than are dreamt of in your philosophy, Horatio."
39. "A Streetcar Named Ophelia," *Rosencrantz and Guildenstern Are Undead*. The original line (2.1.78) is part of a speech in which Ophelia describes to her father Hamlet's strange behavior toward her, leading Polonius to the conclusion that "this is the very ecstasy of love." (line 99).
40. Afi Dallas, "Afi Dallas Video Interview."
41. See S. Schoenbaum, *Shakespeare's Lives*, New Edition (Oxford: Clarendon Press, 1991), esp. 385–94.
42. "Level 2: Shakespeare and Vampires," http://shakespiracy.blogspot.com/.
    Amongst other proposed contenders for Shakespearean authorship — though perhaps no more creditable than Bacon — are Christopher Marlowe and the Earls of Derby, Rutland and Oxford.
43. In his biography of Shakespeare, Anthony Burgess observes, "whether he had anything to do with it or not, he is in it ...The forty-sixth word from the beginning is *shake*, and the forty-sixth word from the end ... is *spear*. And, in 1610, Shakespeare was forty-six years old. If this is mere chance, fancy must allow us to think that it is happy chance." Burgess, *Shakespeare* (New York: Alfred A. Knopf, 1970), 234.

44 "Hamlet and the Holy Grail," "King James I and the Lost Passage," http://shakespiracy.blogspot.com/.
45 Similarly, in the film "Rosicrucians" is spelled incorrectly on the cover of Charlotte's DVD.
46 Jenkins, *Textual Poachers*, 283.
47 Dan Schechter, "Interviews: Director Jordan Galland."

17

The Critic As Vampire:
Parasitic Relations in Media Studies and Popular Culture

Roy Parkhurst

Provocation

The following discussion attempts to look at a particular case of the study of popular culture in a transitional period of media criticism. It begins with a narrow but hopefully pointed history of the interaction between modernist critical theory and popular culture; this followed the great Marxist wave of the early to mid-twentieth century, when the tradition of formalism ceased to be a productive means for dealing with mass media texts and was subsequently displaced by postmodernist structuralism and poststructuralism after the 1960s.[1] At the end point of this historical trajectory the case of Buffy studies will be taken as an ambiguous scholarly sub-field that could be seen as the end point, the last gasp, of a particular species of media criticism. It is easy to see Buffy studies as a rather absurd mannerism of an exhausted critical paradigm that has been frequently ridiculed in the popular press. Conversely, toward the end, this discussion will also speculate on what it would mean to reverse the way we think about the purposes of media scholarship, and to take Buffy studies as the beginning of a new critical space — one that is only just opening up to a more holistic and engaged reflection on the evolving study of transmedia and its social media underpinnings, and under the emergence of new cultural paradigms no longer tethered to the "entertainment industrial complex," as they have been for over half a century. Taken instead as the transition (or phasespace) to a more interdisciplinary engagement with complexity in contemporary culture, it may turn out that Buffy studies is our new benchmark critical "artifact" of what may be seen, in retrospect, as the beginnings of a new era in cultural and media studies.

The history of academics and popular culture has been and continues to be fraught with intellectual debate. In the 1980s John Fiske[2] and associates set the agenda for the relationship between American cultural studies and popular culture, bypassing the problem of "value" by focusing on audiences and audience reception and the transformation of the meanings of popular entertainment media.[3] Emerging from the shift to reception theory and reader-response criticism, and informed by insights gleaned from the phenomena of entertainment audiences, "value" had to be recontextualized in terms of uses and social contexts rather than in relation to traditional canon-formation rooted in the inherent values of works.[4] This shift away from formalism to uses of popular culture marked the entrance of scholarship into the complex world of postmodernity.[5] During the heyday of structuralist and poststructuralist theorizing from the 1960s to the 1990s, it became increasingly easy to place popular culture into academic contexts. During this "instrumentalist" phase of critical interpretation, theory was easily applied to *any* texts, including the most inane of mass phenomena. In the formative phase of structuralist and poststructuralist epistemology, "great works" offered examples of thinking that could be turned into theory, but once this set of methodologies was established, it became part of the professionalist turn in scholarship to produce a plethora of "readings" of various texts, both canonical and popular, which filled our books and journals to the bursting point. Since the "post-theory" shift and deeper skepticism of poststructuralist and other social constructionist models of interpretation, there is a continuing strain in academic research and publishing across generations of scholars.[6] The older or more conservative scholars could triumphantly claim that sense has potentially returned to work in the humanities; the postmodern generation still forges ahead with predominantly poststructuralist readings; and a younger generation of scholars looking for alternatives and difference from their immediate generational predecessors seek desperately for new approaches to both canonical and populist works.

Allegories for a History of Criticism

A particularly good allegory of this process is staged satirically in Don DeLillo's postmodern novel *White Noise*.⁷ The main protagonist is a well-situated professor at the imaginary institution of College-on-the-Hill. As the protagonist Jack Gladney himself explains:

> I am chairman of the department of Hitler studies at the College-on-the-Hill. I invented Hitler studies in North America in March of 1968. It was a cold bright day with intermittent winds out of the east. When I suggested to the chancellor that we might build a whole department around Hitler's life and work, he was quick to see the possibilities. It was an immediate and electrifying success.⁸

The new faculty member, Murray Jay Siskind, admires Gladney, and waxes lyrical about how Gladney's department has become internationally known for being a center of Hitler studies: "You've evolved an entire system around this figure, a structure with countless substructures and interrelated fields of study, a history within history. I marvel at the effort. It was masterful, shrewd and stunningly preemptive. It's what I want to do with Elvis."⁹

It is, of course, this final statement that sets the scene for a new paradigm in the humanities in the United States of the 1980s. Perhaps the real professor we should defer to here is Ray Browne, who established the Department of Popular Culture at Bowling Green State University in 1973. Like Gladney, Browne seemingly invented the serious, academic study of popular culture. The program began as a Master of Arts degree, quickly expanded to the undergraduate majors, and now contributes to the PhD in American Culture at that institution.

However, from the very beginning, controversy has surrounded the scholarly study of popular culture among academics. The rise of cultural studies, a slightly more humanistic variation of what draws largely upon the social sciences, provided the larger theoretical framework in which material culture could be understood. This history has been well documented and frequently commented upon, but it is the relationship between a particular period and its characteristics (the postmodern) and a particular form of theoretical discourse (the poststructuralist) which has greatly shaped humanistic scholarship since the 1970s. Considerations of popular culture and mass entertainment are not that recent, and the first wave of serious critique probably emerged from the Frankfurt School and was picked up more generally among critics on the left during the 1930s. *Mass Culture: The Popular Arts In America* — a book I will return to shortly — was published in 1957 and contained a variety of critical discussions going back to the mid-nineteenth century.[10] While historically there is a wide variety of this sort of literature, it has been diverse and unfocused in the sense of a "field of study," until the rise of postmodern culture. Fredric Jameson, in one of the early, oft-cited discussions of a postmodern periodization, described one of its primary features as:

> the effacement in it of some key boundaries or separations, most notably the erosion of the older distinction between high culture and so-called mass or popular culture. This is perhaps the most distressing development of all from an academic standpoint, which has traditionally had a vested interest in preserving a realm of high or elite culture against the surrounding environment of philistinism, of schlock and kitsch, of TV series and *Reader's Digest* culture, and in transmitting difficult and complex skill of reading, listening and seeing to its initiates.[11]

The consequences of this "effacement" have many dimensions. In the cited passage Jameson goes on to talk about contemporary writers who incorporate popular culture elements directly in their work and therefore erode the distinction between a literary and a popular form. He also adds that this has been fueled by contemporary theory imported from Europe — such as that of Foucault — a rather amorphous discourse that is not exactly philosophy, sociology, history, political science, aesthetic criticism, or anything in particular. The evolution of these tendencies is most apparent in the acceptance of popular culture as a legitimate object of study from the 1970s. Jameson also makes an important point later in the essay, suggesting that modernism succeeded in at least producing a "critique" of contemporary culture which has also been displaced with the rise of postmodernism. In the wake of such changes in legitimation of the object of study, many younger academics, having grown up on a vast smorgasbord of mass entertainment that constituted the texture of everyday life, began to apply the new theoretical methods to popular culture itself, with great success. Social constructionist and the various structuralist and poststructuralist approaches found in popular culture a huge repository of possible "readings" that generated a fast and steady flow of publications, just what was needed for young, up-and-coming scholars.[12] A new canon replaced the traditional one, and with it came the freedom to apply revisionist techniques to the latter. DeLillo's young academic, Murray, a "visiting lecturer on living icons," tells Gladney that he understands "the music, I understand the movies, I even see how comic books can tell us things. But there are full professors in this place who read nothing but cereal boxes." Gladney replies with a very telling point: "It's the only avant-garde we've got."[13]

This position was first expressed by Leslie Fiedler, one of the first literary scholars of the 1950s and 1960s to suggest that popular culture would be the new vanguard in criticism. In his 1964 essay "The Death of Avant-Garde Literature" Fiedler observes:

> That we have been living through the death of avant-garde literature over the past couple of decades most of us now know. What we are still trying to find out is how to come to terms with that fact, beyond deploring or applauding it, or, in stoical despair, simply refusing to do either.[14]

In other well-known essays, such as the 1970 "Cross the Border — Close the Gap," a title that becomes the catchphrase of postmodern criticism by the 1980s, Fiedler suggests that the only avant-garde available to the critic will be a new kind of criticism, and that:

> a renewed criticism certainly will no longer be formalist or intrinsic; it will be contextual rather than textual, not primarily concerned with structure or diction or syntax, all of which assume that the work of art "really" exists on the page rather than in a reader's passionate apprehension and response. Not words-on-the-page but words-in-the-world

or rather words-in-the-head, which is to say, at the private juncture of a thousand contexts, social, psychological, historical, biographical, geographical, in the consciousness of the lonely reader (delivered for an instant, but an instant only, from all of those contexts by the *ekstasis* of reading): this will be the proper concern of the critics to come.[15]

This very prophetic essay, though at the time mostly ignored, introduced a discussion of something that he expressly called a "Post-Modernism." This is the subject of DeLillo's satire. Elvis studies will become Buffy studies in due course. If avant-garde texts cease to inspire or to even be produced, the young critic shall become the new avant-garde. Twenty years after Jameson's "distress" about postmodern culture, an older generation of once radical critics will lament the demise of a vibrant culture. This is most apparent twenty years later, in Terry Eagleton's somewhat bitter rejoinder to the over-zealous adoption of his academic best-seller *Literary Theory: An Introduction*, written in the midst of the postmodern turn.[16] In his reflective grumble, *After Theory*, the opening line states that "[t]he golden age of cultural theory is long past." While he acknowledges that "[a]nother historic gain of cultural theory has been to establish that popular culture is also worth studying,"[17] he also disparages the seriousness of such pursuits, whereby:

> Quietly-spoken middle-class students huddle diligently in libraries, at work on sensationalist subjects like vampirism and eye-gouging, cyborgs and porno movies.
> Nothing could be more understandable. To work on the literature of latex or the political implications of navel-piercing is to take literally the wise old adage that study should be fun. It is rather like writing your Master's thesis on the comparative flavour of malt whiskies, or on the phenomenology of lying in bed all day. It creates a seamless continuity between the intellect and everyday life. There are advantages in being able to write your Ph.D. thesis without stirring from in front of the TV set.[18]

These students "once wrote uncritical, reverential essays on

Flaubert, but all that has been transformed. Nowadays they write uncritical, reverential essays on *Friends*."[19] This has been the unfortunate conundrum of a criticism of popular culture that emerges from "pleasure," as Eagleton refers to it. Here we have an important link to where this postmodern turn in humanistic scholarship has gone. The academic is now also the fan.

The Vampire in the Classroom

Acknowledgement of Eagleton's annoyance with such topics as "vampirism" provides a means to explore a certain historical continuity between DeLillo's postmodern Elvis and our Buffy. Why *Buffy*? It seems quite clear that in regard to recent developments and fads in critical theory, the rise of Buffy studies represents a pivotal moment that both looks back to this great wreck of culture for which an older generation of scholars — now possibly regretting the media glare that surrounds them — was partially responsible, and signals the exciting new directions emerging in scholarship today.

Interestingly enough, one of the first major retrospective statements in the formation of Buffy studies also explicitly acknowledges in a somewhat reflexive (embarrassed) manner DeLillo's satire as well as its own fannish enthusiasm. David Lavery's "'I wrote my thesis on you!': *Buffy* Studies as an Academic Cult" reflects on the rise of Buffy studies, its champions and detractors, and the wide-ranging interest or use of *Buffy the Vampire Slayer* in diverse contexts.[20] Lavery points out that by 2005 there would be at least 13 full-length studies of *Buffy the Vampire Slayer* and a vast and various literature of conference papers, journal articles and book chapters dealing with the television phenomenon. Buffyology had definitely turned into an academic industry of sorts by the mid-2000s. Sparked by one of the earliest studies, *Fighting the Forces: What's at Stake in Buffy the Vampire Slayer*, and with numerous, dedicated conferences and the creation of *Slayage: The Online International Journal of Buffy Studies* in 2001, the field of inquiry was established.[21]

Stepping back from the surrounding critique of postmodernism, critical theory, and popular culture that has framed this reflection, it might be just as valid to say that *Buffy* belongs in a canon of sorts because of its qualities, not despite them. Rhonda Wilcox, in *Why*

Buffy Matters: The Art of Buffy the Vampire Slayer, suggests just this interpretation. Wilcox defends *Buffy* as great art and Joss Whedon as a kind of genre television *auteur*; both deserve all the study that is accorded them. This might be a plausible argument. Clearly, *Buffy* was one of the first popular culture phenomena with an adolescent target market that took its feminism seriously. With the purposeful and consistent writing of Whedon and company, there was an unusually high coherence across seven seasons of the television series and the five-season *Angel* spin-off show.[22] In this regard, *Buffy* has sustained a large body of scholarly criticism that supports Wilcox's thesis. In the current educational environment, the usefulness of a major phenomenon of popular culture for stimulating students' confrontation with critical studies cannot be overestimated. A volume like *Buffy in the Classroom* is a particularly good example of this opportunity for educators.[23] Unfortunately, one of the perennial problems of teaching popular culture in a critical theory environment, while wonderfully successful at grabbing the interest of the student, is that it is only as interesting as the material is well known. Among colleagues only fifteen years my junior, *Buffy the Vampire Slayer* was practically an unknown quantity. While several of these academics were hiding secret fan adoration for *True Blood* in particular, and also followed other popular vampire media such as Stephenie Meyer's Twilight books and films or *The Vampire Diaries* television series, many of them had never seen *Buffy the Vampire Slayer*. With enthusiastic and well-informed academic faculty already too young to be *Buffy* fans, what hope would there be that our students, another 15 years younger than that, would have any relationship to a show that went on the air about the time they were four or five years old? The only recourse would be to some kind of history of the vampire in popular media.[24] I pitched this reflection on Buffy studies to the editors of this anthology specifically because *Buffy* was excluded from what otherwise looked like a fairly comprehensive review of contemporary vampire media. Why was *Buffy* excluded? Was it no longer contemporary? No longer relevant? Was vampire scholarship already over-saturated with the Buffyverse?

My initial thoughts on this were related to the postmodern context described above: a context in which criticism itself has become part of the society of the spectacle. In this environment, criticism is frequently regarded as an academic commodity form competing for market share, and is characterized by tensions between the entrenched old scholars and the rising young stars of media studies; an ongoing rush to publication to keep the tenure mills grinding away; and a shallow depth of field in which media history can be viewed. I also speculated that, like the experience I had with my younger colleagues, *Buffy* was just a little too dated for them to have the same immersive, fan relationship that I had with the show. One of my colleagues was quite surprised, after finally watching two or three seasons of *Buffy*, by how "everything had already been done in that show" when it came to the possible teen allegories of the contemporary vampire. In any case, I posed the question of what might be gained in the ongoing and contested relationship between humanistic scholars and popular culture by pausing to reflect on Buffy studies and its legacy, and further that the generational divide is symptomatic of the increasingly ephemeral discourses of cultural and media studies in relation to popular culture and their adoption of critical "fads."[25] The contrast between the defense of Buffy studies — particularly its status within the arts, and as social science — and the sarcastic, derisory reactions of popular journalism to the scholarly field, raises interesting questions that continue to haunt cultural and media studies even after the era of the so-called "culture wars."[26]

Vampirism as Allegory

If *Buffy the Vampire Slayer* is an exemplary case of teenage allegory, it is interesting to ask questions about how Buffy studies might function as a critical allegory. The legacy of such a reading protocol can be traced back to the Yale School of Deconstruction and the influences this had on subsequent readings of postmodern culture during the 1980s.[27] This partially entails the rhetorical contrivance of looking for parallels of various kinds between otherwise only remotely related phenomena that seem to show similar structural attributes.[28] One of these potential parallels is possibly found in vampirism itself, as I will suggest in the following few paragraphs.

In pitching this consideration of Buffy studies to the editors, I had another hunch about the allegorical value of the vampire to a critical theory. It was simply the phrase that constitutes the main title of this chapter, "The Critic as Vampire," which was produced as a variation on J. Hillis Miller's well-known defense of deconstruction in "The Critic as Host" from 1979. In this famous argument, Miller defends the somewhat perverse interpretations of Derridean deconstruction for literary studies, and the book of which it was a part became a kind of manifesto for the Yale School of Deconstruction.[29] In typical deconstructive rhetoric, Miller is able to reverse the relationship between the parasite and its host by the end of the essay. The parallels seemed inescapable to me. The figure of the vampire is a particularly good case of a parasite that feeds on human life but gives little back. In Miller's essay, the question of whether or not the deconstructive critic was a kind of parasite on the literary text, gaining professional sustenance from it without giving anything significant back to the literature, was a pressing one for the rise of literary theory, which seemed very esoteric and unnecessarily dense at the time. The question of our parasitism is still of interest, particularly in an academic environment where the humanities have ceased to occupy the center of a liberal education. Why do we need philosophy, literary, film or media studies, art history, classics, and so on, in the world after postmodernism? Is the professional humanist a parasite merely in higher education or of culture at large? One possible answer to these questions would be to consider Michel Serres's alternative account of parasitism in the history of culture, and its value in encouraging the robust growth of any system faced with problems.[30]

Contemporary media studies probably does not benefit greatly from the kind of defense made by Miller in his essay. The application of "symptomatic" readings, a characteristic of the postmodern critic's approach of which deconstruction would be a typical example, has become ubiquitous in criticism. What remains intriguing about Miller's essay (as well as Serres's) is the complex ambiguities of the parasite/host relationship. Where Miller begins to explore the strange etymologies of related concepts such as guest and host in the history of the language, there may be some useful parallels in the history of the critic/text relationship that has been further complicated by the contemporary context. The elaborate constructs of contemporary media criticism, such as in the case of a pseudo-field like Buffy studies, seems to continue some parasitic relationship between critics and texts. The vampire as beast, or even the street urchin sociology of the "vamp" figure, reproduces a classic case of parasitism, a process of gaining sustenance from the host culture without giving anything back. Humanist academics have certainly been accused of something parallel, of feeding off a society that may not really need them. Perhaps the contemporary media studies critic identifies all too closely with the figure of the vampire after all. Whereas the material word served a particular function in Miller's deconstruction of parasitism, for the media studies criticism of popular culture, this parasitism must be seen in more metaphorical terms, but in terms that are still brilliantly ambiguous and that suggest possible new directions for media studies today. Among the elements that complicate this parasitical picture is the new role that the fan is playing in media studies and in the culture at large, a point to which I will return towards the end.

A good way of entering into this reflection on parasitism (or vampirism, in this case) is to look allegorically at one of the more original constructs in Whedon's world of *Buffy the Vampire Slayer*: the vampire Angelus, or Angel, as he is known in the modern, human world. Angel is a vampire with a soul. If anything, the one thing a vampire cannot have under any circumstances is a soul; this is a lack that defines the amoral character of the modern vampire, and establishes that it is "evil." In popular vampire mythology, the lack of a soul explains why the vampire cannot love or even feel in particular ways that would identify it as human. It is after all a dead body, animated by some supernatural power — "undead," in the parlance of vampires — and this also explains why the soul, the single most important human attribute, must not be present. In this more metaphysical sense, the negative "essence" of vampirism is partially determined by the absence of soul. Unlike the zombie, however, the vampire does possess consciousness, and this is what allows it to "pass" as human, if clever enough, in the human world. But in the end, the vampire is a sociopath, only interested in its own satisfactions, whether blood-lust or sexual, or — in the amusing case of Spike — material comforts. Angelus was a particularly nasty vampire for several centuries; his soul is returned to him by a potent gypsy curse. He is tortured by his conscience for the rest of eternity (since he is still immortal) because of his past, appalling deeds to humankind. He tries to repent for those deeds by joining forces against the world of demons and vampires, and also by experiencing love and loss. In a sense, Angel is possessed by a soul that disrupts the "natural" order of his vampirism. Angel's soul is thus parasitic on his vampire self, his otherwise amoral, sociopathic, evil essence. His soul sucks away the pleasures of vampirism, forcing him to resort to a life of pig's blood, of protecting humans from the true nature of vampirism, and of regret for his bloody past.

One wonders if this is not also the critic's humanist soul. The humanist in today's academy is an equally ambiguous figure. Not completely sure of his or her role in society or even in the increasingly bureaucratic, business-defined university, the humanist struggles to be relevant today.[31] With the professional humanist part "research output/source of income to the institution" and part "seeker of knowledge," can the contemporary humanist transcend its parasitic status? At what point would we be able to reverse this and make the humanist a host of the social good? In a similar manner to Miller in his time, there is some important soul-searching to be done regarding the ongoing, parasitical relationship between critic and object of study, where popular culture is concerned. This is particularly significant for media studies in general, which increasingly finds popular culture its main concern. Popular culture generally emerges from the economics of the "entertainment industrial complex," and it has only recently been challenged by new means and methods. In either case, however, it is unclear how media studies criticism contributes to that culture. Again, the appearance of the parasitic figure seems inevitable. The critic may subsist (in an academic career) on the fodder of popular culture, but what the critic contributes to that culture seems esoteric, rarefied, even irrelevant.

Sacrificed to the Fan's Pyres

At this stage let us return to and contemplate the question of fandom, fans, and fan culture in this larger media construct which the rest of this book more fully investigates as it relates to the vampire transmedia phenomenon.[32] Initially this seems something of a stretch, and admittedly, it is instrumentalist or tokenist insofar as it tries to feed off the more general concerns of this book as a whole.

However, there is something particularly interesting about the fan construct in contemporary media studies, something that has not been fully realizable before. On the one hand, we have an ongoing ambiguity, even a conflict of interests between fan and critic, especially when the critic also happens to be a fan of the popular culture it is presumably explaining. Beyond that, we now inhabit a media environment that is quite different from that of the postmodern humanist. The ecology has changed significantly with the spread of new communications technologies, the internet of Web 2.0, and social media empowerment. What was "mass culture" in the early twentieth century evolved into the more differentiated demographics of "popular culture" consumers. We have since entered into a new dynamic, in which popular culture is no longer simply manufactured for its targeted audiences in the modern, one-way-communication model well-articulated by Shannon and Weaver in the 1940s, but is now part of a complex play of power, desire, and exchange that has redefined the media ecology.[33] Both of the old models have ceased to be productive. The constructionist "sociology of art" approach — that of the disinterested critic — was a broad media criticism that, historically, tended to produce a rather vague and general account of mass culture that said very little about specific works or individuals save their ideological submission to larger cultural forces. In a more postmodernist approach, where enthusiasm for and celebration of the object of study dominated the scene (the critic as fan), the critic irrationally celebrated the consumption of the work like any popular audience and often produced little new critical knowledge about its object of study.

So why should the place of the "fan" have changed the media ecology now, when it did not before? The answer is complex and is deeply connected to the altered, more two-way media environment and the technologies which enabled it. From a very traditional perspective, the fan is now quantifiable in ways it never was before. We can look up a hot topic in current affairs and see that 22,451 respondents have voiced a negative opinion on a Facebook page within 24 hours, and so on. The consumer, the audience, and the fan can now set the agenda for cultural workers at all levels, including the intellectual labor of higher education.[34] The new media environment is itself an empirical ecology where statistics and datamining dominate the discussion. There is no vague speculation or guesswork required to get a sense of the zeitgeist in a very rapid progression of mass opinion in a given situation. Media producers now make major production decisions from week to week based on the online responses they mine in the datasphere.[35] Once the voice of the fan itself becomes part of the text — part of the world of the work, and how the work inhabits the world — then something new emerges. Both extreme critiques thus become less relevant in the new environment. Both the critic as parasite (as a force that takes sustenance from the work but gives nothing back to it) and the enthusiastic fan (who, because blinded by fandom, produces neither critical knowledge nor properly reflects on the work's true value), are transformed by the knowledge that fanaticism itself produces in relation to works, whether of high art or of popular culture.

We now live in a cultural and media environment driven by new technologies of social media and online sharing and networks of deeply complex connectedness that have transformed our understanding of cultural consumption. We have returned in some sense to the world of concrete entities that have always escaped a postmodernist proclamation of undecidability. If in the philosophy of deconstruction, the undecidable character of language prevents interpretation, or makes it impossible to say which is parasite and which is host, the return to real entities that can be quantified, qualified, and speculated upon reinvigorates the value of interpretation. We can no longer rely on a social critique of either the "fact" or "fairy" type.[36] New forms of critical engagement are emerging through critical and speculative realism, in actor-network theory, in non-linear dynamics and complexity studies, that will transform the critical ecology as much as the media ecology has been transformed.[37] What this means for media studies is still not clear, but there are clues.

Escaping the Fan Mire

Fan studies has produced its own body of literature now and this may also inform the future of media studies in the new environment. The etymology of "fan" reminds us of its strong connections to the fanatic in particular and fanatacism in general, but, as some theorists have recently suggested, fanaticism may have been instrumental in major cultural movements throughout history without getting its due appreciation. Like Serres's figure of the parasite, the interference of noise initially disrupts cultural development but eventually leads to the culture's ability to transcend its state and move on to the next level. Fanaticism similarly produces a disruption that has initiated major changes in culture.[38] Lavery, in his reflexive review of the state of Buffy studies, cites Matt Hills in defense of the positive role that fandom now plays in the field:

> academic work might be able to adopt greater cultural authority (which is after all what it imagines that it purchases through performing rationality) by surrendering some of its moral dualisms and repositioning itself. However, this is not a call for greater 'accessibility' or for the jettisoning of 'jargon.' Instead it is a call for *impassioned thought* rather than the parroting of academic discursive mantras. It is a call for an academic 'affective reflexivity' which admits its own neoreligiosities, its own fandoms...[39]

We are now in the critical world of datamining as much as textual interpretation. Something of this problem has been acknowledged in the critique of popular culture studies, particularly when treated as a form of sociology. The early Bernard Rosenberg and David Manning White anthology, *Mass Culture: The Popular Arts in America*, included a 1948 essay by Irving Howe entitled "Notes on Mass Culture," in which the author begins with a problem for popular culture studies that is very indicative of an era and a persistent manner of thought which has only recently come under scrutiny:

> When we glance at the pseudo-cultural amusements that occupy the American people's leisure time, we soon wonder: what happens to the anonymous audience while it consumes the products of mass culture? It is a question that can hardly be answered systematically or definitively, for there is no way of knowing precisely what the subterranean reactions of an audience are — and it will certainly not do merely to ask it. We can only speculate, and the answer to our question, if one is to be had at all, can be found only within ourselves.[40]

The critic-fan dualism suggested by the rest of Howe's essay continued to define problems for the scholarly study of popular culture. The rise of social constructionist philosophies and methods only encouraged a social critique during the postmodern period. But we are now in a position to understand these things differently, as we have direct access to a huge array of "data" about audiences and fans through their online presence. *Buffy the Vampire Slayer* and a number of important cultural phenomena coincide with this shift, placing *Buffy* both at the end of a postmodernist paradigm (at all levels of the term) and also at the beginning of a new paradigm not yet periodized, but which opens up popular culture and its mass products to a new space of critique that has concrete agents, realities, and affects.[41] That is why the focus on fan culture and fan studies does mark out part of a new critical appraisal that deals with new relations in the media ecology. While these new critical paradigms are only in their early formation, fan studies will play an important role in this process. As I have been trying to approach this topic from both ends of an historical process, Buffy studies should be seen as *both* the end point of a process of cultural criticism that emanated from postmodern epistemologies, *and* as the beginning of a new paradigm of cultural studies that must explore the more complex, networked, online world of the internet and the wider penetration of entertainment in an era where the audience is as important as texts and authors in the broader media landscape.[42] That "subterranean" audience is no longer an unknown quantity in the new networked society, and the new criticism that will rise to address these issues — such as the essays in the rest of this book — are in their infancy, and will evolve and adapt in accordance with the changing media environment.

Notes

1   A particularly good discussion of this tension in the history of American literary studies between the historically-oriented critic (New Left) and the formalist-oriented critic (New Criticism) can be found in Gerald Graff, *Professing Literature: An Institutional History* (Chicago: Chicago University Press, 1987). The most celebrated discussion of the rise and fall of New Left cultural thought in the United States is Alan M. Wald,

The New York Intellectuals: The Rise and Decline of Anti-Stalinist Left from the 1930s to the 1980s (Chapel Hill: University of North Carolina Press, 1987). These sorts of histories set the stage for the young theory Turks who spread Continental influences in University humanities from the 1960s on. Similar references to the formation of Film Studies, in particular, would add another dimension to how media studies evolved in subsequent decades.

2 John Fiske, *Understanding Popular Culture* (Boston: Unwin Hyman, 1989), and *Reading The Popular* (Boston: Unwin Hyman, 1989).
3 It is important to note here that the discussion of media criticism throughout is centered in an American cultural studies tradition and that there are other traditions which have treated these subjects in differing manners and with a different emphasis; in the UK, particularly, a tradition extends from such founding figures as Raymond Williams to the approach of Stuart Hall. An enlightening discussion of Fiske's impact on cultural studies and shift toward the "pleasures of consumption" in the postmodern context can be found in the concluding pages of Graeme Turner, *British Cultural Studies: An Introduction* (London: Unwin Hyman, 1990), 221–25.
4 Additionally, more specific audiences, such as those associated with "cult" media, have also had a big impact on the refocusing of media criticism on media reception; see, for example, J. P. Telotte, ed., *The Cult Film Experience: Beyond All Reason* (Austin: University of Texas Press, 1991); and Sara Gwenllian-Jones and Roberta E. Pearson, eds., *Cult Television* (Minneapolis: University of Minnesota Press, 2004).
5 While one wouldn't think the terms postmodernism, postmodernity and postmodern should be that troublesome in viewing the history and development of media studies, the terms continue to be annoyingly contested. Note that the use that appears here specifically draws upon a theory of historical periodization that roughly extends from the end of WWII to the mid-1990s, as proposed by Fredric Jameson and subsequent critics. See Jameson, *Postmodernism or, The Cultural Logic of Late Capitalism* (Durham, NC: Duke University Press, 1991).
6 This is most prominent in the publications announcing a "post-theory" paradigm shift, such as in David Bordwell and Noël Carroll, eds., *Post-Theory: Reconstructing Film Studies* (Madison: University of Wisconsin Press, 1996); Daphne Patai and Will H. Corral, eds., *Theory's Empire: An Anthology Of Dissent* (New York: Columbia University Press, 2005); or Martin McQuillan, Graeme MacDonald, Robin Purves and Stephen Thomson, eds., *Post-Theory: New Directions In Criticism* (Edinburgh: University of Edinburgh Press, 1999). Note also that this particular genealogy of media studies is biased toward a methodological foundation

established in cinema studies rather than literary criticism, where more complex evolutions have been emerging.

7   Don DeLillo, *White Noise* (New York: Viking Penguin, 1985).
8   Ibid., 4.
9   Ibid., 11–12.
10 Bernard Rosenberg and David Manning White, eds., *Mass Culture: The Popular Arts in America* (New York: The Free Press, 1957). Andrew Ross gives an interesting survey of the history of these complex relationships in *No Respect: Intellectuals and Popular Culture* (New York: Routledge, 1989), but much of the literature has been highly skeptical of the significance of the study of popular culture and its postmodern uses.
11 Fredric Jameson, "Postmodernism and Consumer Society," in *The Anti-Aesthetic: Essays on Postmodern Culture*, ed. Hal Foster (Port Townsend, WA: Bay Press, 1983), 112.
12 In fact, the academic publishing "bubble" as such may soon burst, as many recent commentators on higher education in the United States have pointed out. Mark C. Taylor, in his *Crisis on Campus: A Bold Plan for Reforming Our Colleges and Universities* (New York: Knopf, 2010), comments that "the scholarly monograph has no future," 46. A scathing critique of both over- and questionable academic publishing, and a sobering read, comes from the executive editor for humanities at Harvard University Press, Lindsay Waters, in *Enemies of Promise: Publishing, Perishing, and the Eclipse of Scholarship* (Chicago: Prickly Paradigm Press, 2004).
13 DeLillo, 10.
14 Leslie Fiedler, *The Collected Essays of Leslie Fiedler*. Volume II (New York: Stein & Day, 1971), 454.
15 Leslie Fiedler, "Cross the Border — Close the Gap," in *The Collected Essays of Leslie Fiedler*, Volume II (New York: Stein & Day, 1971), 463.
16 Terry Eagleton, *Literary Theory: An Introduction* (Minneapolis: University of Minnesota Press, 1983), and *After Theory* (New York: Basic Books, 2003).
17 Eagleton, 1, 4.
18 Ibid., 2–3.
19 Ibid., 5.
20 David Lavery, "'I Wrote My Thesis On You!' *Buffy* Studies as an Academic Cult," *Slayage* 4, nos. 13–14 (2004): http://slayageonline.com/Numbers/slayage13_14.htm.
21 Rhonda V. Wilcox and David Lavery, eds. *Fighting the Forces: What's at Stake in Buffy the Vampire Slayer* (Lanham, MD: Rowman & Littlefield, 2002).

Authors and Critics as Fans 309

22 See endnote 32 for some of Whedon's extensions of the Buffyverse through transmedia.
23 Jodie A. Kreider and Meghan K. Winchell, eds., *Buffy in the Classroom: Essays on Teaching with the Vampire Slayer* (London: McFarland, 2010).
24 Such as Tim Kane, *The Changing Vampire of Film and Television* (London: McFarland, 2006).
25 See for example Noël Carroll, *Mystifying Movies: Fads and Fallacies in Contemporary Film Theory* (New York: Columbia University Press, 1991).
26 Here, I am contrasting studies such as Rhonda Wilcox, *Why Buffy Matters: The Art of Buffy the Vampire Slayer* (London: I. B. Tauris, 2005), or Durand, Kevin K., ed., *Buffy Meets the Academy: Essays on the Episodes and Scripts As Texts* (London: McFarland, 2009), with the conservative backlash associated with Allan Bloom and the ensuing "culture wars" in American higher education in the 1990s. See Allan Bloom, *The Closing of the American Mind* (New York: Simon and Schuster, 1988).
27 The best-known figures of the Yale School were Harold Bloom, Geoffrey Hartman, Paul de Man, and J. Hillis Miller, to whom the following section is partially dedicated. For the deconstructivist reading of allegory see especially Paul de Man, *Allegories of Reading* (New Haven: Yale University Press, 1979). For the more explicit adaptation of theories of allegorical reading to postmodernism in particular, see Craig Owens, "The Allegorical Impulse: Toward a Theory of Postmodernism," in *Art After Modernism: Rethinking Representation*, ed. Brian Wallis (New York: Godine, 1984), 203–35. Owens makes a very apropos description of the allegorical impulse: "Let us say for the moment that allegory occurs whenever one text is doubled by another," 204. It is this impulse that also informs the doubling of reading throughout my text.
28 This particular use of "structural" is only vaguely related to the more historical sense of structuralism as an intellectual movement. My use of "structural" here has more affinity with Michel Serres's concept of "isomorphism" in culture, that appears throughout his work in various forms. Another alternative to the post-theory rejection of deconstruction and its ilk can be found in the "productive" side of Derridean deconstruction, identified as a "general grammatology," which Gregory L. Ulmer has built in relation to an "applied grammatology" in literary criticism, cultural studies, and media studies. See Ulmer, *Applied Grammatology: Post(e)-Pedagogy from Jacques Derrida to Joseph Beuys* (Baltimore: Johns Hopkins University Press, 1985); *Teletheory: Grammatology in the Age of Video* (New York: Routledge, 1989); and *Heuretics: The Logic of Invention* (Baltimore: Johns Hopkins University Press, 1994). In film studies applications see Robert Ray, *The Avant-Garde Finds Andy Hardy* (Cambridge, MA: Harvard University Press, 1995) and *How A Film Theory Got*

Lost and Other Mysteries in Cultural Studies (Bloomington IL: Indiana University Press, 2001); for a recent review and application of the "heuretic" method derived from applied grammatology, see Jeff Rice and Marcel O'Gorman, eds., *New Media/New Methods: The Academic Turn from Literacy to Electracy* (West Lafayette, IN: Parlor Press, 2008), which extends Florida School theory to media studies applications.

29 J. Hillis Miller, "The Critic As Host," in *Deconstruction and Criticism*, by Harold Bloom, Paul de Man, Jacques Derrida, Geoffrey Hartman, and J. Hillis Miller (New York: Continuum, 1984), 217–53.

30 Michel Serres, *The Parasite* (Baltimore: Johns Hopkins University Press, 1982). His most sustained application of an historical reading of the figure of the "parasite" can be found in *Rome: The Book of Foundations*, trans. Felicia McCarren (Stanford, CA: Stanford University Press, 1991). In some respects, I am "doubling" on this sense of the figure of the vampire which I also see as a para-site for a larger discussion, that is, "along side the site of the critical discourse."

31 See Bill Readings, *The University in Ruins* (Cambridge, MA: Harvard University Press, 1996); Sheila Slaughter and Gary Rhoades, *Academic Capitalism and the New Economy: Markets, State, and Higher Education* (Baltimore: Johns Hopkins University Press, 2004); and Frank Donoghue, *The Last Professors: The Corporate University and the Fate of the Humanities* (New York: Fordham University Press, 2008).

32 Transmedia here is derived from current media theory, in which divergent iterations of a related communication are rolled out on multiple platforms. See Henry Jenkins, *Convergence Culture: Where Old and New Media Collide* (New York: New York University Press, 2006), for a more sustained discussion of the implications of transmedia. It is worth noting that the work of Joss Whedon is itself part of a transmedia strategy. When *Buffy the Vampire Slayer* ended its television run after seven seasons, Whedon continued the story in an ongoing series of comic books which were identified as *Buffy the Vampire Slayer, Season 8* (Milwaukee, WI: Dark Horse Comics, nos. 1–40 (March 2007–January 2011). Similarly, Buffy characters Angel and Spike also had their own spin-off comics of new tales. Whedon also invented a "future" slayer called Fray, who stars in her own comic. During the Buffy reign, numerous comics, books, and merchandizing in the typical franchise context proliferated. Anthologies of music compiled from the soundtracks of the shows appeared, as have recent rumors that the Buffy franchise may be revived in a future feature film venture. Fan sites and fan fictions abound online and they have expanded the Buffy field considerably. Cross-over vampire encounters also occur in the fan fiction, such as Hideyuki Kikuchi's Vampire Hunter D encountering Buffy Summers in the futuristic wasteland.

33 I use this phrase somewhat loosely as indicative of a new way of thinking about the contemporary media environment, but it has some affinities with the use by Matthew Fuller in *Media Ecologies: Materialist Energies in Art and Technoculture* (Cambridge, MA: MIT Press, 2005). A number of contemporary media theorists now refer to themselves as "media ecologists" and this seems to have partly emerged out of some of the work on "mediology" which rethinks the media environment as ecosystem. See Régis Debray, *Media Manifestos*, trans. Eric Rauth (London: Verso, 1996), particularly the section on "Toward an Ecology of Cultures," 108–30. In film studies there is also a move toward merging a more cognitive science approach with the context of ecosystem. See Joseph D. Anderson and Barbara Fisher Anderson, eds., *Moving Image Theory: Ecological Considerations* (Carbondale: Southern Illinois University Press, 2005) in particular.

34 A particularly significant and instructive example of this phenomenon in literary studies occurred when novelist David Foster Wallace was first celebrated via online fans of his work, predating the attention of literary scholars. In fact, it was through the efforts of the fans in online social media that Wallace was brought to literary prominence in many respects. For a fascinating discussion of this process see Adam Kelly, "David Foster Wallace: The Death of an Author and the Birth of a Discipline," *IJASonline: Irish Journal of American Studies*, no. 2 (Summer 2010): http://www.ijasonline.com/Adam-Kelly.html.

35 There are a large number of examples of television series producers following the online chatter of fans and malcontents alike to drive their narrative decisions about characters, plotlines and so on. Brands are now lurking online or setting up social media websites to respond rapidly to consumer complaints and criticisms. In many respects, the contemporary consumer has gained newfound powers of persuasion as never before.

36 This phrase, from Bruno Latour, has partly inspired some of this discussion of the limitations of the two options in favor of a third, incompletely articulated option. See Latour, "Why Has Critique Run Out of Steam? From Matters of Fact to Matters of Concern," *Critical Inquiry* 30, no. 2 (Winter 2004): 225–48.

37 There are a number of emerging trends in what was cultural and media studies. While we do not need to abandon these terms, we must expand our view of methodology and critical function in the new critical ecology. There's more to do with popular culture perspectives than the auto-ethnography of a fan critic. Important trends include critical and speculative realism (Bhaskar, Harman), recent French philosophy (Meillassoux, Laruelle, Brassier), returns to ontology (Stiegler, Badiou, Rancière), social networks (Bourriaud, Latour), returns to critical phe-

nomenology (Hansen, Marks), complexity studies (Taylor, Delanda), critical epistemology (Serres, Stengers), and the emergence of media archaeology (Zielinski, Elsaesser, Kittler, Huhtamo, Parikka), and so on. While this is just a brief list of quite radically divergent but also quite new approaches to critical problems, this should indicate that there are potential new areas and methods where cultural and media studies may venture.

38 Michel Serres, *The Parasite* (Baltimore: Johns Hopkins University Press, 1982). Serres's different interpretation of the figure of the parasite (noise or interference, in certain French usages) shows that the ongoing presence of various forms of parasitism forces the larger context to respond through improvements, refinements, and innovations, superseding its previous, flawed conditions. Political philosopher Alberto Toscano has recently made a parallel, argumentative case for the status and significance of historical "fanaticism" in *Fanaticism: On the Uses of an Idea* (London: Verso, 2010). Toscano shows convincingly that the irrational and disruptive marginality that is religious fanaticism has actually been at the historical center of political life and has shaped it significantly.

39 Matt Hills, *Fan Culture*, Sussex Studies in Culture and Communication (London and New York: Routledge, 2002), 183–84.

40 Irving Howe, "Notes on Mass Culture," in *Mass Culture: The Popular Arts in America*, ed. Bernard Rosenberg and David Manning White (New York: The Free Press, 1957), 496.

41 In the Buffy studies subfield see in particular Mary Kirby-Diaz, *Buffy and Angel Conquer the Internet: Essays on Online Fandom* (London: McFarland, 2009).

42 For example, see Henry Jenkins's *Fans, Bloggers, and Gamers: Media Consumers in a Digital Age* (New York: New York University Press, 2006); *Textual Poachers: Television Fans and Participatory Culture* (New York: Routledge, 1992); Karen Hellekson and Kristina Busse, eds., *Fan Fiction and Fan Communities in the Age of the Internet* (London: McFarland, 2006); and Jonathan Gray, Cornel Sandvoss, and C. Lee Harrington, eds., *Fandom: Identities and Communities in a Mediated World* (New York: New York University Press, 2007).

Contributors

Jonathan F. Bassett earned a BA in psychology from Furman University in 1996 and a PhD in social psychology from Georgia State University in 2002. He is currently Associate Professor in the Department of Psychology at Lander University, where he teaches introductory psychology, research methods, statistics, social psychology, and the psychology of death and dying. He is the recipient of several teaching awards, including the Lander University Young Faculty Scholar Award, the Lander University Distinguished Professor Award, and the South Carolina Psychological Association's Outstanding Teacher of Psychology Award. His research interests are in the areas of Terror Management Theory, attitudes about death and dying, and the scholarship of teaching and learning. He is author or coauthor on more than two dozen papers that have appeared in journals such as *Death Studies, Mortality, Omega Journal of Death and Dying, Personality and Individual Differences, Social Psychology,* and *Current Research in Social Psychology.* He serves on the editorial board for *The Open Social Science Journal* and *The Open Psychology Journal.* Jonathan is President Elect of the South Carolina Psychological Association and is a member of several professional organizations including the Association for Psychological Science and the Society for Personality and Social Psychology.

Candace Benefiel is an Associate Professor and humanities reference librarian at Texas A&M University, and a PhD student there as well, focusing on the vampire in literature. She has a BA from Rice University, an MLIS from the University of Texas at Austin, and an MA from West Texas State University. She has published in the *Journal of Popular Culture, Wilson Library Bulletin, College and Research Libraries,* and other journals. Her poetry has appeared, among other places, in *Borderlands, The Concho River Review,* and *Classical Outlook.* Her book, *Reading Laurell K. Hamilton,* was recently published by ABC-Clio.

Brigid Cherry is a Senior Lecturer in Communication, Culture and Creative Arts at St Mary's University College, Twickenham, UK where she teaches courses on horror cinema, cult film and television, and youth culture. Her research has focused on horror and science fiction, particularly the female horror film audience and online science fiction fan cultures. She has recently published work on the feminine aesthetic of horror cinema, cultural borrowings in alternative music video, fan canons, and *Doctor Who* fans' responses to the return of the series. Her Film Guidebook on *Horror* was published by Routledge in 2009 and she is co-editor of *Twenty-First-Century Gothic*, published in 2011. She is currently editing a collection on *True Blood*, and writing a monograph on the narrative of *Lost*.

Melissa de Zwart is an Associate Professor, Adelaide Law School, University of Adelaide. She has published extensively on copyright, content regulation, the internet and new media, including social networking sites, online games and other virtual communities. She is a member of the Advisory Board, the Virtual Policy Network (UK based, not for profit think tank re virtual worlds) and the ENISA (European Network and Information Security Agency) Virtual Group of Experts on Security Issues in Virtual Worlds and Gaming (EU). In her spare time she likes reading vampire fiction, cosplay and blogging. She is a Member of the Australian Government's Classification Review Board.

Katie Hoskinson earned her BA in literature at Bowling Green State University and completed her Masters of Arts at the University of Dayton in May 2011. Her earlier writing about gender in Stephenie Meyer's *Twilight* series was recognized with the Thomas L. Wymer award. She has previously been published in *Prairie Margins* literary journal. She is presently living and working in Memphis,

Tennessee, awaiting the final installment of the *Twilight* films with bated breath.

Rick Hudson is an academic specialising in the study of literature and culture from primarily a Bakhtinian perspective. His specific fields of interest are horror, science fiction and fantasy narratives in literature film, television, and comics. As well as being an academic he is a professional writer of horror fiction, being the author of three novels and numerous short stories. He has also worked as a writer in comic strips and game design.

David Huxley is a Senior Lecturer on the Manchester Metropolitan University BA (Hons) Film and Media Studies course. His subject specialities are Cartoons and the Comic Strip, The Horror Film and Censorship, Hollywood Film, and Animation. He is the author of *Nasty Tales: Sex, Drugs and Rock n Roll in the Underground* (2001), has written widely on American and British generic comics, and has written and illustrated a range of adult and children's comics. His recent conference papers include: "For Sadists Only: The Reception of Horror Film in Britain 1958-1968," MMU, 2006; "Is the Final Girl Dead? A Morphology of the American Slasher Film," MMU, 2007; "To Deprave and Corrupt: Censorship and the Cultural Status of British Comics 1954-1988," University of Toronto, 2008. He is currently co-editing and writing a chapter for *European Nightmares; European Horror Cinema Since 1945* (Wallflower Press). He is the editor of *The Journal of Graphic Novels and Comics* (Routledge, 2010-present).

Malin Isaksson is a Senior Lecturer of French in the Department of Language Studies, Umeå University, Sweden. Her research interests span reception studies, popular culture, contemporary French literature, gender and queer theory. In a project called *Tough Girls' Love*, she analyzes femslash about strong female characters from television series and has published articles on fan fiction about the vampire slayers Buffy and Faith (*Buffy the Vampire Slayer*). She is also working on a book about vampire fan fiction, with Maria Lindgren Leavenworth, in a project funded by the Swedish Research Council.

Jennifer Jenson is Associate Professor of Pedagogy and Technology in the Faculty of Education at York University. She has published on gender and technology, education and gameplay, the design and development of digital games, and educational technology policy and policy practices. Her current work includes the design and development of a video game about dogs. She is a self-confessed lover of all things Buffy, including having played the gameboy version of the video game.

Maria Lindgren Leavenworth is an Assistant Professor at the Department of Language Studies, Umeå University, Sweden. Her doctoral thesis The Second Journey: Travelling in Literary Footsteps (2000, revised 2010) focused on contemporary travel writers who utilize earlier travelogues as both imaginative and literal maps. Within the field of travel writing and nordicity she has written articles on Selina Bunbury (in *New Contexts: Re-Framing Nineteenth Century Irish Women's Prose*, 2008), Bayard Taylor and S. H. Kent (in *Nordlit* 2010 and *Studies in Travel Writing* 2011) and Dan Simmons's novel *The Terror* (in *Arctic Discourses* 2010). She has also analyzed the essentialising function of the cold in Ursula K. Le Guin's *The Left Hand of Darkness* (in *Cold Matters* 2009). Within the field of fan studies she has published an article on J. R. Ward's Black Dagger Brotherhood and connected slash fan fiction (*Extrapolation* 2009), a chapter in the anthology *Bringing Light to Twilight* (2011) and, co-authored with Malin Isaksson, an article about queer desires in fanfic (*Tidskrift för litteraturvetenskap* 2009). Leavenworth and Isaksson's current project FAN(G)S: Fan Fiction and the Vampire Trope is financed by the Swedish Research Council.

Susana Loza is an Assistant Professor of Media Culture at Hampshire College in Amherst, Massachusetts. She received BA degrees in Political Science and Psychology from Stanford University, and her PhD in Comparative Ethnic Studies from the University of California at Berkeley. Her dissertation, Global Rhetoric, Transnational Markets: The (Post)Modern Trajectories of Electronic Dance Music, examines the racial, gender, socioeconomic, and philosophical dimensions of digital pop music. Her scholarly publications include articles on Orientalism and film noir, techno music and sonic communities, the sexual politics of digital sampling, and the resurgence of minstrelsy in popular culture. Professor Loza is currently working on a project entitled Post-Racial Performativities: Race, Sex, and Popular Culture in 21st Century America. As scholars Eric Lott (Love and Theft) and Phillip Deloria (Playing Indian) remind us, Americans have historically used racial drag as a way to simultaneously build and buttress the ever-shifting parameters of whiteness and American identity. Post-Racial Performativities contemplates the fundamental, albeit changing, role that racial masquerade plays in American popular culture.

Fiona Martin began her studies at the University of Guelph in Ontario, Canada and completed her doctorate at The University of Waikato in Hamilton, New Zealand in 2010. Her predilection for blood and violence is usually focused on death and dying speeches in early modern plays. She is a member of the Australian and New Zealand Shakespeare Association (ANZSA) and the Australian and New Zealand Association for Medieval and Early Modern Studies (ANZAMEMS). Fiona is the author of "'O die a rare example': The Condemned Body on the Jacobean Stage," *Early Modern Literary Studies*, Special Issue 19 (2009): 8.1–24, and "'Almost with ravished listening': A Most Rare Speaker in *King Henry VIII (All Is True)*," in *Rapt in Secret Studies: Emerging Shakespeares*, ed. Darryl Chalk and Laurie Johnson (Newcastle upon Tyne: Cambridge Scholars Publishing, 2010): 113–30.

Kimberley McMahon-Coleman is a former secondary school English teacher, who has written over forty workshops for students undertaking Higher School Certificate examinations. She teaches in Learning Development at the University of Wollongong. She holds a Masters in Educational Leadership from Charles Sturt University and a doctorate from the University of Wollongong. Her doctoral thesis examines shamanism and Indigenous diaspora in the work of Alootook Ipellie and Sam Watson. She is a past editor of the newsletter of the Association for Canadian Studies in Australia and New Zealand (ACSANZ). Her work has been published in a number of journals, including *Australasian-Canadian Studies* and

Kunapipi, and in R. K. Dhawan and Stewart Gill's book, *Canadian Studies Today: Responses from the Asia Pacific*. She is currently writing a book with Dr Roslyn Weaver from the University of Western Sydney, focussing on the figure of the shapeshifter in literature and popular culture, and how it is used as a metaphor for difference.

Kirstine Moffat is the Convenor of English at the University of Waikato in Hamilton, New Zealand. She is a New Zealand Literature specialist, with publications in *The Journal of New Zealand Literature, New Literatures Review, Victorian Settler Narratives, Hearing Places*, and *Moving Worlds*. As well as being an avid consumer of books and films, music is also one of Kirstine's passions. She started to learn the piano when she was five and is currently completing a Royal Society of New Zealand Marsden funded research project on the cultural history of the piano in colonial New Zealand.

Joan Ormrod is a senior lecturer in Film and Media Studies in the Department of Media at Manchester Metropolitan University. She co-edited *On the Edge: Leisure, Consumption and the Representation of Adventure Sports* with Dr Belinda Wheaton. She has published in sports and media journals and anthologies on topics such as gender and exploitation films, place and cultural identities, consumerism and surfing. She is interested in the relationships between culture, audiences and the mass media. Her current research is on the development of pop music through teenage girls' comics. She also co-edits Routledge's *The Journal of Graphic Novels and Comics* with Dr David Huxley with whom she has organised conferences on graphic novels and comics.

Roy Parkhurst is an American writer and filmmaker living and working in New Zealand. He is currently Senior Lecturer in critical studies, digital media, and postgraduate studies in the College of Creative Arts, Massey University at Wellington. His current scholarly research areas include screen studies and media archaeology within a continental philosophy context.

Anita Sarkeesian is a feminist pop culture critic who produces an ongoing web series of video commentaries from a feminist/fangirl perspective at FeministFrequency.com. She uses her web show to explore representations of race, gender, sexuality, class, and ability in popular culture. Her videos are used as educational tools in classrooms and are screened at conferences and film festivals worldwide. She speaks internationally about feminist media criticism, online video production, remix video, and fair use.

Gareth Schott is a Senior Lecturer in the School of Arts, University of Waikato, New Zealand. He has published extensively in the emerging field of game studies over the last decade, contributing research on the topics of female gaming, game fandom and participatory cultures, the application of multi-modality theory to analyzing game texts, metrics of violence and research into players, player cultures and player experience. His research has been funded by the Arts and Humanities Research Board (AHRB) and University for Industry (UfI) in the UK and Royal Society of New Zealand in NZ. He is one of the authors of *Computer Games: Text, Narrative and Play* published by Polity Press.

Amy Elizabeth Smith teaches professional writing, creative writing, and literature at the University of the Pacific in Stockton, California, in the United States. She has an undergraduate degree in Music from West Virginia University and a Masters and PhD in English from Penn State. In 2012 she will publish a literary travel memoir entitled *All Roads Lead to Austen: A Year's Journey with Jane*. The book describes a year spent traveling and holding reading groups on Jane Austen in Guatemala, Mexico, Ecuador, Chile, Paraguay, and Argentina. She also teaches a course on vampire films and fiction and has been a vampire fan since *Dark Shadows*.

Catherine Strong is a Lecturer in Sociology at Charles Sturt University in Australia. Her work focuses on how social power plays out in the context of popular culture. Work that she has done in this area includes looking at women's place in rock music and how popular culture is remembered. She has recently published a book called *Grunge: Music and Memory* with Ashgate.

Bibliography

BOOKS AND JOURNALS

Abbott, Stacey. *Celluloid Vampires: Life after Death in the Modern World*. Austin: University of Texas Press, 2007.

Abbott, Stacey, ed. *The Cult TV Book: From* Star Trek *to* Dexter, *New Approaches to TV Outside the Box*. New York: Soft Skull Press, 2010.

Allen, Paul M. "The English Translation of *The Chymical Wedding*." In *A Christian Rosenkreutz Anthology*, edited by Paul M. Allen, 61–162. Blauvelt, NY: Rudolf Steiner Publications, 1968.

Angel, Joanna, and Brenda Staudenmeier. *Burning Angel*. New York: Goliath, 2008.

Anon. "The Top 50 Greatest Screen Vampires of All Time." *SFX Special Edition: Vampires*. Bath: Future Publishing, 2009: 13–35.

Arata, Stephen D. "The Occidental Tourist: Dracula and the Anxiety of Reverse Colonization." *Victorian Studies* 33, no. 4 (1990): 621–45.

Arp, Robert. "Coming Out of the Coffin and Coming Out of the Closet." In Dunn and Housel, eds., 93–108.

Auerbach, Nina. *Our Vampires, Ourselves*. Chicago: The University of Chicago Press, 1995.

Bacon-Smith, Camille. *Enterprising Women: Television Fandom and the Creation of Popular Myth*. Philadelphia: University of Pennsylvania Press, 1992.

Backstein, Karen. "(Un)safe Sex: Romancing the Vampire." *Cineaste* 35, no. 1 (2009): 38–41.

Bakhtin, M. M. *Rabelais and his World*. Translated by Hélène Iswolsky. Bloomington, IL: Indiana University Press, 1984.

Balogh, Mary, Colleen Gleason, Susan Krinard, and Janet Mullany. *Bespelling Jane Austen*. Don Mills, ON: Harlequin, 2010.

Banks, Miranda J. "A Boy for All Planets: *Roswell, Smallville* and the Teen Male Melodrama." In Davis and Dickinson, eds., 17–28.

Barbeau, Adrienne. *Love Bites*. New York: Thomas Dunne Books, 2010.
Barker, Martin. *Comics: Ideology, Power and the Critics*. Cultural Politics. Manchester: Manchester University Press, 1989.
Barron, Stephanie. *Jane and the Madness of Lord Byron*. New York: Bantam, 2010.
Barzilai-Nahon, Karine. "Gatekeeping: A Critical Review." *Annual Review of Information Science and Technology* 34, no. 1 (2009): 1–79.
Bate, David. *Photography: The Key Concepts*. Oxford and New York: Berg, 2009.
Bebris, Carrie. *The Intrigue at Highbury (Or, Emma's Match)*. New York: Tor, 2010.
_____. *The Matters at Mansfield (Or, The Crawford Affair)*. New York: Forge, 2008.
_____. *North by Northanger (Or, The Shades of Pemberley)*. New York: Forge, 2006.
_____. *Pride and Prescience (Or, A Truth Universally Acknowledged)*. New York: Forge, 2004.
_____. *Suspense and Sensibility (Or, First Impressions Revisited)*. New York: Forge, 2005.
Becker, Ernest. *The Denial of Death*. New York: The Free Press, 1973.
_____. *Escape From Evil*. New York: The Free Press, 1975.
Belk, Russell W. *Collecting in a Consumer Society*. Collecting Cultures. Oxford and New York: Routledge, 1995.
Bellin, Joshua David. *Framing Monsters: Fantasy Film and Social Alienation*. Carbondale: Southern Illinois University Press, 2005.
Benefiel, Candace R. "Blood Relations: The Gothic Perversion of the Nuclear Family in Anne Rice's *Interview with the Vampire*." *Journal of Popular Culture* 38, no. 2 (2004): 261–73.
Bennett, Tara. "Yours Truly." *SFX Special Edition: Vampires*. Bath: Future Publishing, 2009: 86–89.
Benshoff, Harry M. *Monsters in the Closet: Homosexuality and the Horror Film*. Inside Popular Film. Manchester: Manchester University Press, 1997.
Berger, John. *Ways of Seeing*. Harmondsworth: Penguin, 1972.
Betts, Jean, and Wm. Shakespeare. *Ophelia Thinks Harder*. 1994. Wellington, New Zealand: The Play Press, 2003.
Bhabha, Homi K. *The Location of Culture*. London and New York: Routledge, 1994.
Blayde, Ariadne, and George A. Dunn. "Pets, Cattle, and Higher Life Forms on *True Blood*." In Dunn and Housel, eds., 33–48.
Bode, Lisa. "Transitional Tastes: Teen Girls and Genre in the Critical Reception of *Twilight*." *Continuum: Journal of Media and Cultural Studies* 24, no. 5 (2010): 707–19.

Bonilla-Silva, Eduardo. *Racism Without Racists: Color-Blind Racism and the Persistence of Racial Inequality in the United States*. 3rd ed. Lanham, MD: Rowman & Littlefield, 2010.

Bonilla-Silva, Eduardo, and Victor Ray. "When Whites Love a Black Leader: Race Matters in *Obamerica*." *Journal of African American Studies* 13, no. 2 (2009): 176–83.

Botting, Fred. *Gothic Romanced: Consumption, Gender and Technology in Contemporary Fictions*. Abingdon, UK: Routledge, 2008.

Bourdieu, Pierre. *Distinction: A Social Critique of the Judgment of Taste*. Translated by Richard Nice. Cambridge, MA: Harvard University Press, 1984.

Bourdieu, Pierre, and Jean-Claude Passeron. *Reproduction in Education, Society and Culture*. Translated by Richard Nice. Sage Studies in Social and Educational Change 5. London: Sage, 1977.

Bordwell, David and Noël Carroll, eds. *Post-Theory: Reconstructing Film Studies*. Madison: University of Wisconsin Press, 1996.

Brown, Mary Ellen, ed. *Television and Women's Culture: The Politics of the Popular*. Communication and Human Values 7. Sydney: Currency Press, 1990.

Bryson, Bethany. "'Anything but Heavy Metal': Symbolic Exclusion and Musical Dislikes." *American Sociological Review* 61, no. 5 (1996): 884–99.

Burgess, Anthony. *Shakespeare*. New York: Alfred A. Knopf, 1970.

Burke, Kenneth. *Language as Symbolic Action*. Berkeley and Los Angeles: University of California Press, 1966.

Bury, Rhiannon. *Cyberspaces of their Own: Female Fandoms Online*. Digital Formations 25. New York: Peter Lang, 2005.

Busse, Kristina. "Introduction." In "In Focus: Fandom and Feminism: Gender and the Politics of Fan Production." *Cinema Journal* 48, no. 4 (2009): 104–107.

Busse, Kristina, and Karen Hellekson. "Introduction: Work in Progress." In Hellekson and Busse, eds., 5–32.

Buszek, Maria Elena. *Pin-Up Grrrls: Feminism, Sexuality, Popular Culture*. Durham, NC: Duke University Press, 2006.

Calhoun, Crissy. *Love You to Death: The Unofficial Companion to* The Vampire Diaries. Toronto: ECW Press, 2010.

Carriger, Gail. *Soulless: An Alexia Tarabotti Novel*. The Parasol Protectorate. New York: Orbit, 2009.

Carroll, Noël. *Mystifying Movies: Fads and Fallacies in Contemporary Film Theory*. New York: Columbia University Press, 1991.

Carter, Margaret L. "The Vampire as Alien in Contemporary Fiction." In Gordon and Hollinger, eds., 27–44.

Case, Sue-Ellen. "Tracking the Vampire." *Differences: A Journal of Feminist Cultural Studies* 3, no. 2 (1991): 1–20.

Castronova, Edward. *Synthetic Worlds: The Business and Culture of Online Games*. Chicago: University of Chicago Press, 2005.

The Chemical Wedding of Christian Rosenkreutz. 1616. Translated by Joscelyn Godwin. Introduction and Commentary by Adam McLean. Magnum Opus Hermetic Sourceworks 18. Grand Rapids MI: Phanes Press, 1991.

Clark, Danae. "Commodity Lesbianism." *Camera Obscura* 25/26 (January/May 1991): 181-201.

Clarke, Amy M. "Introduction: Approaching Twilight." In *The Twilight Mystique: Critical Essays on the Novels and Films*, edited by Amy M. Clarke and Marijane Osborn, 3–14. Jefferson, NC: McFarland, 2010.

Clasen, Tricia. "Taking a Bite out of Love: The Myth of Romantic Love in the Twilight Series." In Click, Aubrey, and Behm-Morawitz, eds., 119–34.

Classen, Constance. *The Colour of Angels: Cosmology, Gender and the Aesthetic Imagination*. London: Routledge, 1998.

Clemens, Kirsten. "Graphic Novels and the Girl Market." *The CEA Critic* 72, no. 3 (2010): 71–85.

Click, Melissa A., Jennifer Stevens Aubrey, and Elizabeth Behm-Morawitz. "Introduction." In Click, Aubrey, and Behm-Morawitz, eds., 1–17.

Click, Melissa A., Jennifer Stevens Aubrey, and Elizabeth Behm-Morawitz, eds. *Bitten by* Twilight: *Youth Culture, Media, and the Vampire Franchise*. Mediated Youth 14. New York: Peter Lang, 2010.

Cohen, Jeffrey Jerome. "Monster Culture (Seven Thesis)." In *Gothic Horror: A Guide for Students and Readers*, edited by Clive Bloom, 198–217. Basingstoke: Palgrave Macmillan, 1998.

Coleman, Susanna. "Making Our Voices Heard: Young Adult Females Writing Participatory Fan Fiction." In *Writing and the Digital Generation: Essays on New Media Rhetoric*, edited by Heather Urbanski, 95–105. Jefferson, NC: McFarland, 2010.

Craft, Christopher. "'Kiss Me with Those Red Lips': Gender and Inversion in Bram Stoker's *Dracula*." In *Dracula: The Vampire and the Critics*, edited by Margaret L. Carter, 167–94. Studies in Speculative Fiction 19. Ann Arbor: UMI Research Press, 1988.

Creed, Barbara. *The Monstrous-Feminine: Film, Feminism, Psychoanalysis*. Popular Fictions Series. London: Routledge, 1993.

Curtis, William M. "'Honey, If We Can't Kill People, What's the Point of Being a Vampire?': Can Vampires Be Good Citizens?" In Dunn and Housel, eds., 65–78.

Dargan, Richard S. "Foreword." In *FVZA: Federal Vampire and Zombie Agency*, written by David Hine, illustrated by Roy Allan Martinez, 6–7. California: Radical Publishing 2010.

Davidson, MaryJanice. *Undead and Unwed*. New York: Berkley Sensation, 2004.

Davis, Glyn, and Kay Dickinson, eds. *Teen TV: Genre, Consumption and Identity*. London: British Film Institute, 2004.
Day, William Patrick. *Vampire Legends in Contemporary American Culture: What Becomes a Legend Most*. Lexington: University Press of Kentucky, 2002.
de Beauvoir, Simone. *The Second Sex*. New York: Vintage Books, 1989.
de Zwart, Melissa. "Angel(us) is my Avatar! An Exploration of Avatar Identity in the Guise of the Vampire." *Media & Arts Law Review* 15, no. 3 (2010): 318–39.
Deleuze, Gilles, and Félix Guattari. *A Thousand Plateaus: Capitalism and Schizophrenia*. Translated by Brian Massumi. Athlone Contemporary European Thinkers. London: Athlone Press, 1988.
DeLillo, Don. *White Noise*. New York: Viking Penguin, 1985.
Delpech-Ramey, Joshua. "Deleuze, Guattari, and the 'Politics of Sorcery'." *Substance* 39, no. 1 (2010): 8–23.
Denike, Margaret. "Homonormative Collusions and the Subject of Rights: Reading *Terrorist Assemblages*." *Feminist Legal Studies* 18, no. 1 (2010): 85–100.
Derecho, Abigail. "Archontic Literature: A Definition, a History, and Several Theories of Fan Fiction." In Hellekson and Busse, eds., 61–78.
Dery, Mark. "Flame Wars." In *Flame Wars: The Discourse of Cyberculture*, edited by Mark Dery, 1–10. Durham, NC: Duke University Press, 1994.
Dijkstra, Bram. *Evil Sisters: The Threat of Female Sexuality and the Cult of Manhood*. New York: Alfred A. Knopf, 1996.
———. *Idols of Perversity: Fantasies of Feminine Evil in Fin-de-Siècle Culture*. New York and Oxford: Oxford University Press, 1986.
Dika, Vera. "From Dracula — With Love." In *The Dread of Difference: Gender and the Horror Film*, edited by Barry Keith Grant, 388–400. Texas Film Studies Series. Austin: University of Texas, 1996.
DeLillo, Don. *White Noise*. New York: Viking Penguin, 1985.
Doane, Janice, and Devon Hodges. "Undoing Feminism: From the Preoedipal to Postfeminism in Anne Rice's Vampire Chronicles." *American Literary History* 2, no. 3 (1990): 422–42.
Donath, Judith. "Signals in Social Supernets." *Journal of Computer-Mediated Communication* 13, no. 1 (2007): 231–51.
Donath, Judith S. "Identity and Deception in the Virtual Community." In *Communities in Cyberspace*, edited by Marc A. Smith and Peter Kollock, 29–59. London: Routledge, 1999.
Donnelly, Peter, and Kevin Young. "The Construction and Confirmation of Identity in Sport Subcultures." In *Contemporary Issues in the Sociology of Sport*, edited by Andrew Yiannakis and Merrill J. Melnick, 399–412. Champaign, IL: Human Kinetics, 2001.
Duggan, Lisa. "Queering the State." *Social Text* 39 (1994): 1–14.

———. *The Twilight of Equality: Neoliberalism, Cultural Politics, and the Attack on Democracy*. Boston: Beacon, 2004.

Dunn, George A., and Rebecca Housel, eds. *True Blood and Philosophy: We Wanna Think Bad Things With You*. Blackwell Philosophy and Pop Culture Series. Hoboken, NJ: John Wiley & Sons, 2010.

Durand, Kevin K., ed. *Buffy Meets the Academy: Essays on the Episodes and Scripts as Texts*. London and Jefferson, NC: McFarland, 2009.

Dyer, Richard. "Children of the Night: Vampirism as Homosexuality, Homosexuality as Vampirism." In *Sweet Dreams: Sexuality and Gender in Popular Fiction*, edited by Susannah Radstone, 47–72. London: Lawrence and Wishart, 1988.

———. *Heavenly Bodies: Film Stars and Society*. New York: St. Martin's Press, 1986.

———. *White*. London and New York: Routledge, 1997.

Eagleton, Terry. *After Theory*. New York: Basic Books, 2003.

Early, Frances H. "Staking Her Claim: *Buffy the Vampire Slayer* as Transgressive Woman Warrior." *The Journal of Popular Culture* 35, no. 3 (2001): 11–27.

Edwards, Lynne Y., Elizabeth L. Rambo, and James B. South, eds. *Buffy Goes Dark: Essays on the Final Two Seasons of* Buffy the Vampire Slayer *on Television*. Jefferson, NC: McFarland, 2009.

Elrod, P. N. *The Vampire Files: Bloodlist*. Vampire Files. New York: Ace Books, 1990.

Eng, David L. "Freedom and the Racialization of Intimacy: *Lawrence v. Texas* and the Emergence of Queer Liberalism." In *A Companion to Lesbian, Gay, Bisexual, Transgender, and Queer Studies*, edited by George E. Haggerty and Molly McGarry, 38–59. Oxford: Wiley-Blackwell, 2007.

Eyerman, Ron, and Bryan S. Turner. "Outline of a Theory of Generations." *European Journal of Social Theory* 1, no. 1 (1998): 91–106.

Eysenbach, Gunther, and James E. Till. "Ethical Issues in Qualitative Research on Internet Communities." *British Medical Journal* 323, no. 7321 (2001): 1103–105.

Faludi, Susan. *The Terror Dream: Fear and Fantasy in Post 9/11 America*. London: Atlantic, 2008.

Feagin, Joe R. *Racist America: Roots, Current Realities, and Future Reparations*. New York: Routledge, 2000.

Fiedler, Leslie. *The Collected Essays of Leslie Fiedler*. Volume II. New York: Stein & Day, 1971.

Fielding, Helen. *Bridget Jones's Diary*. London: Picador, 1996.

Firestone, Robert W. "Individual Defenses against Death Anxiety." *Death Studies* 17 (1993): 497–515.

———. "Psychological Defenses Against Death Anxiety." In *Death Anxiety Handbook*, edited by Robert Neimeyer, 217–41. Washington: Taylor & Francis, 1994.

Fiske, John. "The Cultural Economy of Fandom." In *The Adoring Audience: Fan Culture and Popular Media*, edited by Lisa A. Lewis, 30–49. London and New York: Routledge, 1992.

———. *Understanding Popular Culture*. Boston: Unwin Hyman, 1989.

Foltyn, Jacque Lynn. "Dead Famous and Dead Sexy: Popular Culture, Forensics, and the Rise of the Corpse." *Mortality* 13, no. 2 (2008): 153–73.

Ford, Michael Thomas. *Jane Bites Back*. New York: Ballantine Books, 2010.

Foster, David William. "José González Castillo's *Los invertidos* and the Vampire Theory of Homosexuality." *Latin American Theatre Review* 22, no. 2 (1989): 19–29.

Foy, Joseph J. "Signed in Blood: Rights and the Vampire-Human Social Contract." In Dunn and Housel, eds., 51–64.

Fry, Christine L. "The Life Course as a Cultural Construct." In *Invitation to the Life Course: Toward New Understandings of Later Life*, edited by Richard A. Settersten Jr., 269–94. Society and Aging Series. Amityville, NY: Baywood, 2003.

Garner, Alex, Jeff Mariotte, Mindy Lee, and Gabriel Hernandez. *Covert Vampire Organization*. US: IDW Publishing, 2004.

Gelder, Ken. *Reading the Vampire*. Popular Fictions Series. London and New York: Routledge, 1994.

Goffman, Erving. *The Presentation of Self in Everyday Life*. London: Penguin, 1990.

Goldberg, David Theo. *The Threat of Race: Reflections on Racial Neoliberalism*. Blackwell Manifestos Series 2344. Malden, MA: Wiley-Blackwell, 2009.

Gordon, Joan, and Veronica Hollinger, eds. *Blood Read: The Vampire as Metaphor in Contemporary Culture*. Philadelphia: University of Pennsylvania Press, 1997.

Gordon, Joan, and Veronica Hollinger. "Introduction: The Shape of Vampires." In Gordon and Hollinger, eds., 1–7.

Grange, Amanda. *Mr. Darcy, Vampyre*. Naperville, IL: Sourcebooks, 2009.

Gray, Claudia. "The War Between the States." In Red and Vee, eds., with Leah Wilson, 35–49.

Gray, Jonathan. "Antifandom and the Moral Text: Television Without Pity and Textual Dislike." *American Behavioral Scientist* 48, no. 7 (2005): 840–58.

———. "New Audiences, New Textualities: Anti-Fans and Non-Fans." *International Journal of Cultural Studies* 6, no. 1 (2003): 64–81.

Gray, Jonathan, Cornel Sandvoss, and C. Lee Harrington. "Introduction: Why Study Fans?" In Gray, Sandvoss, and Harrington, eds., 1–16.

Gray, Jonathan, Cornel Sandvoss, and C. Lee Harrington, eds. *Fandom: Identities and Communities in a Mediated World*. New York and London: New York University Press, 2007.

Greenblatt, Stephen. *Will in the World: How Shakespeare Became Shakespeare.* New York: W. W. Norton & Company, 2004.

Gwenllian-Jones, Sara. "Web Wars: Resistance, Online Fandom and Studio Censorship". In *Quality Popular Television,* edited by Mark Jancovich and James Lyons, 163–77. BFI Modern Classics. London: British Film Institute, 2003.

Gwenllian-Jones, Sara, and Roberta E. Pearson, eds. *Cult Television.* Minneapolis: University of Minnesota Press, 2004.

Haggerty, George E. "Anne Rice and the Queering of Culture." *NOVEL: A Forum on Fiction* 32, no. 1 (1998): 5–18.

Halberstam, Judith. *Skin Shows: Gothic Horror and the Technology of Monsters.* Durham, NC: Duke University Press, 1995.

———. "Technologies of Monstrosity: Bram Stoker's *Dracula.*" *Victorian Studies* 36, no. 3 (1993): 333–52.

Hale, Shannon. *Austenland.* New York: Bloomsbury USA, 2007.

Hamilton, Laurell K. *Guilty Pleasures.* Anita Blake, Vampire Hunter. New York: Berkley Books, 2002.

Hammond, Mary. "Monsters and Metaphors: Buffy the Vampire Slayer and the Old World." In Gwenllian-Jones and Pearson, eds., 147–64.

Haraway, Donna J. *Modest_Witness@Second_Millennium.FemaleMan©_ Meets_ OncoMouse™: Feminism and Technoscience.* New York: Routledge, 1997.

Hardy, Jonathan. "Mapping Commercial Intertextuality: HBO's *True Blood.*" *Convergence* 17, no. 1 (2011): 7–17.

Haritaworn, Jin, Tamsila Tauqir, and Esra Erdem. "Gay Imperialism: Gender and Sexuality Discourse in the 'War on Terror'." In *Out of Place: Interrogating Silences in Queerness/Raciality,* edited by Adi Kuntsman and Esperanza Miyake. York, UK: Raw Nerve Books, 2008.

Harman, Graham. *Prince of Networks: Bruno Latour and Metaphysics.* Melbourne: re.press, 2009.

Harrington, C. Lee, and Denise D. Bielby. "A Life Course Perspective on Fandom." *International Journal of Cultural Studies* 13, no. 5 (2010): 429–50.

Harris, Charlaine. *A Touch of Dead.* Southern Vampire Mysteries Series. London: Gollancz, 2010.

———. *All Together Dead.* Southern Vampire Mysteries Series. London: Gollancz, 2007.

———. *Club Dead.* Southern Vampire Mysteries Series. London: Orion, 2003.

———. *Dead and Gone.* Southern Vampire Mysteries Series. London: Gollancz, 2009.

———. *Dead as a Doornail.* Southern Vampire Mysteries Series. London: Orion, 2005.

———. *Dead in the Family*. Southern Vampire Mysteries Series. London: Gollancz, 2010.

———. *Dead Reckoning*. Southern Vampire Mysteries Series. London: Gollancz, 2011.

———. *Dead to the World*. Southern Vampire Mysteries Series. London: Orion, 2004.

———. *Dead Until Dark*. Southern Vampire Mysteries Series. New York: Ace Books, 2001.

———. *Definitely Dead*. Southern Vampire Mysteries Series. London: Gollancz, 2006.

———. *From Dead to Worse*. Southern Vampire Mysteries Series. London: Gollancz, 2008.

———. *Living Dead in Dallas*. Southern Vampire Mysteries Series. London: Orion, 2002.

Harvey, Alyxandra. "In Which Intrepid Heroines Discuss the Merits of the Bad Boy versus the Reformed Bad Boy with the Help of a Couple of Dead Women Who Know About Such Things." In Red and Vee, eds., with Leah Wilson, 67–84.

Heard, Ruthie. "Interview with the Vampire Fandom." In Crissy Calhoun, *Love You to Death: The Unofficial Companion to The Vampire Diaries*, 189–96. Toronto: ECW Press, 2010.

Hellekson, Karen. "A Fannish Field of Value: Online Fan Gift Culture." *Cinema Journal* 48, no 4 (2009): 113–18.

Hellekson, Karen, and Kristina Busse, eds. *Fan Fiction and Fan Communities in the Age of the Internet*. Jefferson, NC: McFarland, 2006.

Hendershot, Cyndy. "Vampire and Replicant: The One-Sex Body in a Two-Sex World." *Science Fiction Studies* 22, no. 3 (1995): 373–98.

Hills, Matt. *Fan Cultures*. Sussex Studies in Culture and Communication. London and New York: Routledge, 2002.

———. "Media Academics as Media Audiences: Aesthetic Judgments in Media and Cultural Studies." In Gray, Sandvoss, and Harrington, eds., 33–47.

Hine, David (writer), and Roy Martinez (artist). *FVZA: Federal Vampire and Zombie Agency*. California: Radical Publishing, 2010.

Hollinger, Veronica. "Fantasies of Absence: The Postmodern Vampire." In Gordon and Hollinger, eds., 199–212.

Hollows, Joanne. *Feminism, Femininity and Popular Culture*. Manchester and New York: Manchester University Press, 2000.

Holmes, Janet. *Women, Men and Politeness*. Real Language Series. London and New York: Longman, 1995.

Housel, Rebecca, and J. Jeremy Wisnewski, eds. *Twilight and Philosophy: Vampires, Vegetarians, and the Pursuit of Immortality*. Blackwell Philosophy and Pop Culture Series. Hoboken, NJ: John Wiley & Sons, 2009.

Howe, Irving. "Notes on Mass Culture." In *Mass Culture: The Popular Arts in America*, edited by Bernard Rosenberg and David Manning White, 496–503. New York: The Free Press, 1957.

Hudson, Dale. "Vampires of Color and the Performance of Multicultural Whiteness." In *The Persistence of Whiteness: Race and Contemporary Hollywood Cinema*, edited by Daniel Bernardi, 127–56. London and New York: Routledge, 2008.

Hudson, Rick. "The Derelict Fairground: A Bakhtinian Analysis of the Graphic Novel Medium." *The CEA Critic* 72, no. 3 (2010): 35–49.

Huntemann, Nina B., and Matthew Thomas Payne. "Introduction." In Huntemann and Payne, eds., 1–18.

Huntemann, Nina B., and Matthew Thomas Payne, eds. *Joystick Soldiers: The Politics of Play in Military Video Games*. New York and London: Routledge, 2010.

Hunter, James Davison. *Culture Wars: The Struggle to Define America*. New York: Basic Books, 1991.

Huyssen, Andreas. *After the Great Divide: Modernism, Mass Culture, Postmodernism*. Theories of Representation and Difference. Bloomington and Indianapolis: Indiana University Press, 1986.

Jameson, Fredric. "Postmodernism and Consumer Society." In *The Anti-Aesthetic: Essays on Postmodern Culture*, edited by Hal Foster, 111–25. Port Townsend, WA: Bay Press, 1983.

Jancovich, Mark, Antonio Lázaro Reboll, Julian Stringer, and Andy Willis, eds. *Defining Cult Movies: The Cultural Politics of Oppositional Taste*. Inside Popular Film. Manchester: Manchester University Press, 2003.

Jeffers, Regina. *Vampire Darcy's Desire*. Berkeley: Ulysses Press, 2009.

Jenkins, Henry. *Convergence Culture: Where Old and New Media Collide*. New York and London: New York University Press, 2006.

———. *Fans, Bloggers, and Gamers: Exploring Participatory Culture*. New York and London: New York University Press, 2006.

———. *Textual Poachers: Television Fans and Participatory Culture*. Studies in Culture and Communication. New York and London: Routledge, 1992.

Jenkins, Henry, Tara McPherson, and Jane Shattuc, eds. *Hop On Pop: The Politics and Pleasures of Popular Culture*. Durham, NC: Duke University Press, 2003.

Jenkins, Tricia. "'Potential Lesbians at Two O'Clock': The Heterosexualization of Lesbianism in the Recent Teen Film." *The Journal of Popular Culture* 38, no. 3 (2005): 491–504.

Jenson, Joli. "Fandom as Pathology: The Consequences of Characterization." In *The Adoring Audience: Fan Culture and Popular Media*, edited by Lisa A. Lewis, 9–30. London and New York: Routledge, 1992.

Johnson, Derek. "Inviting Audiences In: The Spatial Reorganization of

Production and Consumption in 'TVIII'." *New Review of Film and Television Studies* 5, no.1 (2007): 61–80.

Kane, Kathryn. "A Very Queer Refusal: The Chilling Effect of the Cullens' Heteronormative Embrace." In Click, Aubrey, and Behm-Morawitz, eds., 103–18.

Kane, Tim. *The Changing Vampire of Film and Television: A Critical Study of the Growth of a Genre*. Jefferson, NC: McFarland, 2006.

Kaplan, Deborah. "Construction of Fan Fiction Character Through Narrative." In Hellekson and Busse, eds., 134–52.

Kaplan, H. Roy. *The Myth of Post-Racial America: Searching for Equality in the Age of Materialism*. Lanham, MD: Rowman & Littlefield, 2010.

Kastenbaum, Robert. "A World Without Death? First and Second Thoughts." *Mortality* 1 (1996): 111–21.

Kemp, Cornelia, and Susanne Witzgall, eds. *Das zweite Gesicht: Metamorphosen des fotografischen Porträts/The Other Face: Metamorphoses of the Photographic Portrait*. Munich: Prestel, 2002.

Kilpatrick, Nancy. "Archetypes and Fearful Allure: Writing Erotic Horror." In *On Writing Horror*, edited by Mort Castle, 171–75. Revised ed. Cincinnati: Horror Writers Association, 2007.

King, C. Richard, and David J. Leonard. "Wargames as a New Frontier: Securing American Empire in Virtual Space." In Huntemann and Payne, eds., 91–105.

King, Stephen. *Danse Macabre*. New York: Everest House, 1981.

Kirby-Diaz, Mary, ed. *Buffy and Angel Conquer the Internet: Essays on Online Fandom*. London: McFarland, 2009.

Klause, Annette Curtis. *The Silver Kiss*. New York: Dell, 1990.

Klein, Naomi. *No Logo: Taking Aim at the Brand Bullies*. Toronto: Knopf Canada, 2000.

Kokkola, Lydia. "Virtuous Vampires and Voluptuous Vamps: Romance Conventions Reconsidered in Stephenie Meyer's "Twilight" Series." *Children's Literature in Education* 42, no. 2 (2011): 165–79.

Kreider, Jodie A. and Meghan K. Winchell, eds. *Buffy in the Classroom: Essays on Teaching with the Vampire Slayer*. London: McFarland, 2010.

Kustritz, Anne. "Slashing the Romance Narrative." *Journal of American Culture* 26 (2003): 371–86.

Lakoff, Robin Tolmach. *Language and Woman's Place*. New York: Harper and Row, 1975.

Lancaster, Kurt. *Interacting With Babylon 5: Fan Performances in a Media Universe*. Austin: University of Texas Press, 2001.

Latham, Rob. *Consuming Youth: Vampires, Cyborgs, and the Culture of Consumption*. Chicago: University of Chicago Press, 2002.

Latour, Bruno. *Reassembling the Social: An Introduction to Actor-Network-Theory*. New York: Oxford University Press, 2005.

———. "Why Has Critique Run Out of Steam? From Matters of Fact to Matters of Concern." *Critical Inquiry* 30, no. 2 (2004): 225–48.

Leatherdale, Clive. *Dracula: The Novel and the Legend: A Study of Bram Stoker's Gothic Masterpiece*. Wellingborough, UK: Aquarian Press, 1985.

Lefebvre, Henri. *The Production of Space*. Translated by Donald Nicholson-Smith. Oxford: Blackwell, 1991.

Leogrande, Cathy. "My Mother, Myself: Mother-Daughter Bonding via the Twilight Saga." In Click, Aubrey, and Behm-Morawitz, eds., 155–71.

Levine, Donald N. *The Flight from Ambiguity: Essays in Social and Cultural Theory*. Chicago: University of Chicago Press, 1985.

Levine, Elana, and Lisa Parks, eds. *Undead TV: Essays on* Buffy the Vampire Slayer. Durham, NC and London: Duke University Press, 2007.

Lewis, Lisa A., ed. *The Adoring Audience: Fan Culture and Popular Media*. London and New York: Routledge, 1992.

Lifton, Robert Jay. *The Life of the Self: Toward a New Psychology*. New York: Simon & Schuster, 1976.

Light, Alison. "'Returning to Manderley': Romance Fiction, Female Sexuality, and Class." In *Feminism and Cultural Studies*, ed. Morag Shiach, 371–94. Oxford Readings in Feminism. Oxford: Oxford University Press, 1999.

Lindgren Leavenworth, Maria. "Variations, Subversions, and Endless Love: Fan Fiction and the *Twilight* Saga." In *Bringing Light to Twilight: Perspectives on a Pop Culture Phenomenon*, edited by Giselle Liza Anatol, 69–81. Houndmills: Palgrave MacMillan, 2011.

Lindsay, David, Melissa de Zwart, and Francesca Collins. "My Self, My Avatar, My Rights: Rights of Avatar Identity and Integrity in Virtual Worlds." In *Humanity in Cybernetic Environments*, edited by Daniel Riha, 147–57. Oxford: Inter-Disciplinary Press, 2010.

Lipsitz, George. *The Possessive Investment in Whiteness: How White People Profit from Identity Politics*. Rev. and expanded ed. Philadelphia: Temple University Press, 2006.

Longhurst, Brian, Gaynor Bagnall, and Mike Savage. "Place, Elective Belonging, and the Diffused Audience." In Gray, Sandvoss, and Harrington, eds., 125–38.

Lott, Eric. "Whiteness: A Glossary." *Village Voice* 38, no. 20 (1993): 38–39.

Lovell, Terry. *Consuming Fiction*. Questions for Feminism. London: Verso, 1987.

Lynch, Deidre, ed. *Janeites: Austen's Disciples and Devotees*. Princeton: Princeton University Press, 2000.

Mann, Bonnie. "Vampire Love: The Second Sex Negotiates the Twenty-First Century." In Housel and Wisnewski, eds., 133–46.

Marchetti, Gina. "From Fu Manchu to *M. Butterfly* and *Irma Vep*: Cinematic Incarnations of Chinese Villainy." In *Bad: Infamy, Darkness, Evil, and*

Slime on Screen, edited by Murray Pomerance, 187–99. Cultural Studies in Cinema/Video. Albany: SUNY Press, 2004.
McClelland, Bruce A. *Slayers and Their Vampires: A Cultural History of Killing the Dead*. Michigan: University of Michigan Press, 2006.
_____. "Un-*True Blood*: The Politics of Artificiality." In Dunn and Housel, eds., 79–90.
McCloud, Scott. *Understanding Comics*. Northampton, MA.: Kitchen Sink Press, 1993.
McCrea, Barry. "Heterosexual Horror: Dracula, the Closet, and the Marriage-Plot." *NOVEL: A Forum on Fiction* 43, no. 2 (2010): 251–70.
McGeough, Danielle Dick. "*Twilight* and Transformations of Flesh: Reading the Body in Contemporary Youth Culture." In Click, Aubrey, and Behm-Morawitz, eds., 87–102.
McQuillan, Martin, Graeme MacDonald, Robin Purves and Stephen Thomson, eds. *Post-Theory: New Directions In Criticism*. Edinburgh: University of Edinburgh Press, 1999.
McRobbie, Angela. "Notes on 'What Not to Wear' and Post-Feminist Symbolic Violence." In *Feminism after Bourdieu*, edited by Lisa Adkins and Beverly Skeggs, 99–109. Oxford: Blackwell, 2004.
Mellins, Maria. "Dressing up as Vampires: Virtual Vamps — Negotiating Female Identity in Cyberspace." *Networking Knowledge: Journal of the MeCCSA Postgraduate Network* 1, no. 2 (2007): 1–13.
Melton, J. Gordon. *The Vampire Book: The Encyclopedia of the Undead*. Second Edition. Canton, MI: Visible Ink Press, 1999.
Meyer, Stephenie. *Breaking Dawn*. London: Little, Brown and Company 2008.
_____. *Eclipse*. London: Little, Brown and Company, 2007.
_____. *New Moon*. London: Little, Brown and Company, 2006.
_____. *Twilight*. London: Little, Brown and Company, 2005.
Miller, Genevieve. *Vampire Knits: Projects to Keep You Knitting From Twilight to Dawn*. New York: Potter Craft, 2010.
Miller, J. Hillis. "The Critic As Host." In *Deconstruction and Criticism*, by Harold Bloom, Paul de Man, Jacques Derrida, Geoffrey Hartman, and J. Hillis Miller. New York: Continuum, 1984.
Mills, Charles W. *The Racial Contract*. Ithaca: Cornell University Press, 1997.
Minahan, Stella, and Julie Wolfram Cox. "Stitch'n Bitch: Cyberfeminism, a Third Place and the New Materiality." *Journal of Material Culture* 12, no. 1 (2007): 5–21.
Modleski, Tania. "Femininity as Mas(s)querade: A Feminist Approach to Mass Culture." In *High Theory/Low Culture: Analysing Popular Television and Film*, ed. Colin MacCabe, 37–52. Manchester: Manchester University Press, 1986.

_____. *Loving With a Vengeance: Mass-Produced Fantasies for Women*. New York and London: Methuen, 1982.

Moore, Christopher. *You Suck: A Love Story*. New York: Harper, 2007.

Moretti, Franco. "The Dialectic of Fear." *New Left Review* 136 (November–December 1982): 67–85.

Mullany, Janet. *Jane and the Damned*. New York: Avon, 2010.

Murray, Simone. "'Celebrating the Story the Way it is': Cultural Studies, Corporate Media, and the Contested Utility of Fandom." *Continuum: The Journal of Media and Cultural Studies* 18, no. 1 (2004): 7–25.

Nakamura, Lisa. *Cybertypes: Race, Ethnicity, and Identity on the Internet*. New York and London: Routledge, 2002.

Nelson, Robin. "HBO Premium: Channelling Distinction through TVIII." *New Review of Film and Television Studies* 5, no. 1 (2007): 25–40.

Nixon, Nicola. "When Hollywood Sucks, or, Hungry Girls, Lost Boys, and Vampirism in the Age of Reagan." In *Blood Read: The Vampire as Metaphor in Contemporary* Culture, edited by Joan Gordon and Veronica Hollinger, 115–28. Philadelphia: University of Pennsylvania Press, 1997.

Odell, Colin, and Michelle Le Blanc. *Vampire Films*. Harpendon, UK: Pocket Essentials, 2000.

Patai, Daphne and Will H. Corral, eds. *Theory's Empire: An Anthology Of Dissent*. New York: Columbia University Press, 2005.

Pattillo, Beth. *Jane Austen Ruined My Life*. New York: Guideposts Books, 2009.

_____. *Mr. Darcy Broke My Heart*. New York: Guideposts Books, 2010.

Pearson, Roberta. "Bachies, Bardies, Trekkies, and Sherlockians." In Gray, Sandvoss, and Harrington, eds., 98–109.

Platt, Carrie Anne. "Cullen Family Values: Gender and Sexual Politics in the Twilight Series." In Click, Aubrey, and Behm-Morawitz, eds., 71–86.

Polidori, John William. *The Vampyre and Ernestus Berchtold; or, The Modern Œdipus*. Edited by D. L. Macdonald and Kathleen Scherf. Peterborough, ON: Broadview Press, 2007.

Pollner, Melvin. *Mundane Reason: Reality in Everyday and Sociological Discourse*. Cambridge, UK: Cambridge University Press, 1987.

Powell, Anna. "Duration and the Vampire: A Deleuzian Gothic." *Gothic Studies* 11, no. 1 (2009): 86–98.

Priester, Paul. "The Metaphorical Use of Vampire Films in Counseling." *Journal of Creativity in Mental Health* 3 (2008): 68–77.

Puar, Jasbir K. *Terrorist Assemblages: Homonationalism in Queer Times*. Next Wave: New Directions in Women's Studies. Durham, NC: Duke University Press, 2007.

Puar, Jasbir K., and Amit S. Rai. "Monster, Terrorist, Fag: The War on Terrorism and the Production of Docile Patriots." *Social Text* 20, no. 3 (2002): 117–48.

Pugh, Sheenagh. *The Democratic Genre: Fan Fiction in a Literary Context.* Bridgend, UK: Seren, 2005.
Punter, David, and Glennis Byron. *The Gothic.* Blackwell Guides to Literature. Oxford: Blackwell, 2004.
Radway, Janice A. *Reading the Romance: Women, Patriarchy, and Popular Literature.* Chapel Hill: University of North Carolina Press, 1991.
Red, and Vee, eds., with Leah Wilson. *A Visitor's Guide to Mystic Falls: Your Favorite Authors on The Vampire Diaries.* Dallas: SmartPop Books, 2010.
Redman, Peter. "Invasion of the Monstrous Others: Heterosexual Masculinities, the 'AIDS Carrier' and the Horror Genre." In *Border Patrols: Policing the Boundaries of Heterosexuality,* edited by Deborah Lynn Steinberg, Debbie Epstein and Richard Johnson, 98–118. London: Cassell, 1997.
Reinsborough, Patrick, and Doyle Canning. *Re:Imagining Change: How to Use Story-Based Strategy to Win Campaigns, Build Movements, and Change the World.* Oakland, CA: PM Press, 2010.
Rheingold, Howard. "A Slice of Life in My Virtual Community." In *Global Networks: Computers and International Communication,* edited by Linda M. Harasim, 57–80. Cambridge, MA: MIT Press, 1993.
Rice, Anne. *Interview with the Vampire.* New York: Knopf, 1976.
Richardson, Diane. "Desiring Sameness? The Rise of a Neoliberal Politics of Normalisation." *Antipode* 37, no. 3 (2005): 515–35.
Roberts, Betty B. *Anne Rice.* New York: Twayne, 1994.
Rosenberg, Bernard, and David Manning White, eds. *Mass Culture: The Popular Arts in America.* New York: The Free Press, 1957.
Ross, Andrew. *No Respect: Intellectuals and Popular Culture.* New York: Routledge, 1989.
Rubin, Gayle S. "Thinking Sex: Notes for a Radical Theory of the Politics of Sexuality." In *The Lesbian and Gay Studies Reader,* edited by Henry Abelove, Michèle Aina Barale and David M. Halperin, 3–44. New York: Routledge, 1993.
Ryan, Marie-Laure. *Avatars of Story.* Electronic Mediations. Minneapolis: University of Minnesota Press, 2006.
Sanders, Joe, and Rich Brown. "Glossary of Fanspeak." In *Science Fiction Fandom,* edited by Joe Sanders, 265–69. Contributions to the Study of Science Fiction and Fantasy 62. London: Greenwood Press, 1994.
Sandvoss, Cornel. "The Death of the Reader? Literary Theory and the Study of Texts in Popular Culture." In Gray, Sandvoss, and Harrington, eds., 19–32.
―――. *Fans: The Mirror of Consumption.* Cambridge, UK and Malden, MA: Polity Press, 2005.
Schneider, Kirk J. *Horror and the Holy: Wisdom-Teachings of the Monster Tale.* Peru, IL: Open Court, 1993.

Schneider, Steven Jay. "Mixed Blood Couples: Monsters and Miscegenation in U.S. Horror Cinema." In *The Gothic Other: Racial and Social Constructions in the Literary Imagination*, edited by Ruth Bienstock Anolik and Douglas L. Howard, 72–89. Jefferson, NC: McFarland, 2004.

Schoenbaum, S. *Shakespeare's Lives*. New Edition. Oxford: Clarendon Press, 1991.

Schopp, Andrew. "Cruising the Alternatives: Homoeroticism and the Contemporary Vampire." *Journal of Popular Culture* 30, no. 4 (1997): 231–43.

Scodari, Christine. "Yoko in Cyberspace with Beatles Fans: Gender and the Re-Creation of Popular Mythology." In Gray, Sandvoss, and Harrington, eds., 48–59.

Sender, Katherine. "Sex Sells: Sex, Taste, and Class in Commercial Gay and Lesbian Media." *GLQ: A Journal of Lesbian and Gay Studies* 9, no. 3 (2003): 331–65.

Senf, Carol A. "'Dracula': Stoker's Response to the New Woman." *Victorian Studies* 26, no. 1 (1982): 33–49.

Serres, Michel. *The Parasite*. Baltimore: Johns Hopkins University Press, 1982.

———. *Rome: The Book of Foundations*. Translated by Felicia McCarren. Stanford, CA: Stanford University Press, 1991.

Shakespeare, William. *Hamlet*. Edited by Ann Thompson and Neil Taylor. The Arden Shakespeare. Third Series. London: Thomson Learning, 2006.

———. *Hamlet: The Texts of 1603 and 1623*. Edited by Ann Thompson and Neil Taylor. The Arden Shakespeare. Third Series. London: Thomson Learning, 2006.

Shea, Brendan. "To Bite or Not to Bite: *Twilight*, Immortality and the Meaning of Life." In Housel and Wisnewski, eds., 79–92.

Sheffield, Jessica, and Elyse Merlo. "Biting Back: Twilight Anti-Fandom and the Rhetoric of Superiority." In Click, Aubrey, and Behm-Morawitz, eds., 207–22.

Slotkin, Richard. *The Fatal Environment: The Myth of the Frontier in the Age of Industrialization, 1800-1890*. Middletown, CT: Wesleyan University Press, 1986.

Smith, Catherine. "Queer as Black Folk?" *Wisconsin Law Review* (2007): 379–407.

Smith, L. J. *The Awakening*. The Vampire Diaries 1. New York: HarperTeen, 1991.

———. *The Fury* and *Dark Reunion*. The Vampire Diaries 3 and 4. New York: Harper Teen, 1991.

———. *Midnight*. The Vampire Diaries: The Return 3. New York: HarperTeen, 2011.

———. *Nightfall*. The Vampire Diaries: The Return 1. New York: HarperTeen, 2009.

———. *Shadow Souls*. The Vampire Diaries: The Return 2. New York: HarperTeen, 2010.

———. *The Struggle*. The Vampire Diaries 2. New York: HarperTeen, 1991.

Smith, L. J., and Alloy Entertainment. *Bloodlust*. The Vampire Diaries: Stefan's Diaries 2. New York: HarperTeen, 2011.

———. *The Craving*. The Vampire Diaries: Stefan's Diaries 3. New York: HarperTeen, 2009.

———. *Origins*. The Vampire Diaries: Stefan's Diaries 1. New York: HarperTeen, 2010.

Smith, Marc A., and Peter Kollock, eds. *Communities in Cyberspace*. London: Routledge, 1999.

Soja, Edward W. *Thirdspace: Journeys to Los Angeles and Other Real-and-Imagined Places*. Malden, MA and Oxford: Blackwell, 1996.

Solomon, Sheldon, Jeff Greenberg, and Tom Pyszczynski. "Terror Management Theory of Self-Esteem." In *Handbook of Social and Clinical Psychology: The Health Perspective,* edited by C. R. Snyder and Donelson R. Forsyth, 21–40. Pergamon General Psychology Series 162. New York: Pergamon Press, 1991.

Solomon, Sheldon, Jeff Greenberg, Tom Pyszczynski, Florette Cohen, and Daniel M. Ogilvie. "Teach These Souls to Fly: Supernatural as Human Adaptation." In *Evolution, Culture, and the Human Mind,* edited by Mark Schaller, Ara Norenzayan, Steven J. Heine, Toshio Yamagishi, and Tatsuya Kameda, 99–110. New York: Psychology Press, 2010.

South, James B., ed. *Buffy the Vampire Slayer and Philosophy: Fear and Trembling in Sunnydale*. Popular Culture and Philosophy 4. Chicago: Open Court, 2003.

Southam, B. C. *Jane Austen: The Critical Heritage*. Vol. 1. The Critical Heritage Series. London: Routledge and Kegan Paul, 1968.

Stam, Robert. *Subversive Pleasures: Bakhtin, Cultural Criticism, and Film*. Parallax Re-visions of Culture and Society. Baltimore: John Hopkins University Press, 1989.

Stevenson, John Allen. "A Vampire in the Mirror: The Sexuality of Dracula." *Publications of the Modern Language Association of America* 103, no. 2 (1988): 139–49.

Stoker, Bram. *Dracula*. Edited by Maud Ellmann. Oxford: Oxford University Press, 1996.

Stoller, Debbie. *Stitch 'n Bitch: The Knitter's Handbook*. New York: Workman Publishing, 2003.

Stoppard, Tom. *Rosencrantz and Guildenstern are Dead*. London: Faber and Faber, 1968.

Strinati, Dominic. *An Introduction to Theories of Popular Culture*. 2nd ed. London and New York: Routledge, 2004.
Suicide, Missy, ed. *SuicideGirls*. Los Angeles: Feral House, 2004.
Summers, Sarah. "'*Twilight* Is So Anti-Feminist That I Want to Cry': *Twilight* Fans Finding and Defining Feminism on the World Wide Web." *Computers and Composition* 27, no. 4 (2010): 315–23.
Telotte, J. P., ed. *The Cult Film Experience: Beyond All Reason*. Austin: University of Texas Press, 1991.
Tepper, Michelle. "Usenet Communities and the Cultural Politics of Information." In *Internet* Culture, edited by David Porter, 39–54. New York and London: Routledge, 1997.
Thompson, Ann, and Neil Taylor. "Introduction." *Hamlet*. Ed. Ann Thompson and Neil Taylor, 1–137. The Arden Shakespeare. Third Series. London: Thomson, 2006.
Thornton, Sarah. *Club Cultures: Music, Media and Subcultural Capital*. Hanover: University Press of New England, 1996.
Toscano, Alberto. *Fanaticism: On the Uses of an Idea*. London: Verso, 2010.
Tulloch, John. "Fans of Chekhov: Re-Approaching 'High Culture'." In Gray, Sandvoss, and Harrington, eds., 110–22.
Turkle, Sherry. *Life on the Screen: Identity in the Age of the Internet*. New York: Touchstone, 1995.
Tushnet, Rebecca. "Economies of Desire: Fair Use and Marketplace Assumptions." *William and Mary Law Review* 51, no. 2 (2009): 513–46.
———. "User-Generated Discontent: Transformation in Practice." *Columbia Journal of Law & the Arts* 31, no. 4 (2008): 101–20.
Twitchell, James B. *The Living Dead: A Study of the Vampire in Romantic Literature*. Durham, NC: Duke University Press, 1981.
Tyler, Natalie. *The Friendly Jane Austen*. New York: Viking, 1999.
Tyree, J. M. "Warm-Blooded: *True Blood* and *Let the Right One In*." *Film Quarterly* 63, no. 2 (2009): 32.
Ulmer, Gregory L. *Applied Grammatology: Post(e)-Pedagogy from Jacques Derrida to Joseph Beuys*. Baltimore: Johns Hopkins University Press, 1985.
———. *Heuretics: The Logic of Invention*. Baltimore: Johns Hopkins University Press, 1994.
———. *Teletheory: Grammatology in the Age of Video*. New York: Routledge, 1989.
Ward, J. R. *Dark Lover*. The Black Dagger Brotherhood. New York: New American Library, 2005.
Wilcox, Rhonda. *Why Buffy Matters: The Art of Buffy the Vampire Slayer*. London: I. B. Tauris, 2005.
Wilcox, Rhonda V. "'Set on This Earth Like A Bubble': Word as Flesh in the Dark Seasons." In *Buffy Goes Dark: Essays on the Final Two Seasons*

of Buffy the Vampire Slayer *on Television*, edited by Lynne Y. Edwards, Elizabeth L. Rambo, and James B. South, 95–113. Jefferson, NC: McFarland, 2009.

Wilcox, Rhonda V., and David Laverty, eds. *Fighting the Forces: What's at Stake in* Buffy the Vampire Slayer. Lanham, MD: Rowman & Littlefield, 2002.

Wiles, David. *Greek Theatre Performance: An Introduction*. Cambridge, UK: Cambridge University Press, 2000.

Williamson, Milly. *The Lure of the Vampire: Gender, Fiction and Fandom from Bram Stoker to Buffy*. London: Wallflower Press, 2005.

———. "Spike, Sex and Subtext: Intertextual Portrayals of the Sympathetic Vampire on Cult Television." *European Journal of Cultural Studies* 8, no. 3 (2005): 289–311.

Winnubst, Shannon. "Vampires, Anxieties, and Dreams: Race and Sex in the Contemporary United States." *Hypatia* 18, no. 3 (2003): 1–20.

Wise, Tim. *Colorblind: The Rise of Post-Racial Politics and the Retreat from Racial Equity*. City Lights Open Media. San Francisco: City Lights Books, 2010.

Wisker, Gina. "Love Bites: Contemporary Women's Vampire Fictions." In *A Companion to the Gothic*, edited by David Punter, 167–79. Blackwell Companions to Literature and Culture. Oxford: Blackwell, 2001.

Wlodarz, Joe. "Beyond the Black Macho: Queer Blaxploitation." *The Velvet Light Trap* 53 (2004): 10–25.

Wood, Robin. *Hollywood from Vietnam to Reagan*. New York: Columbia University Press, 1986.

Wright, Bradford W. *Comic Book Nation: The Transformation of Youth Culture in America*. Baltimore, MD: John Hopkins University, 2003.

Yaksich, Michael J. "Consuming Queer: The Commodification of Culture and its Effects on Social Acceptance." *Elements* (Spring 2005): 24–35.

Yarbro, Chelsea Quinn. *Hôtel Transylvania: A Novel of Forbidden Love*. Chronicles of Saint Germain. New York: St. Martin's Press, 1978.

Yates, Frances A. *The Rosicrucian Enlightenment*. London: Routledge, 1972.

Zanger, Jules. "Metaphor into Metonymy: The Vampire Next Door." In Gordon and Hollinger, eds., 17–26.

WEBSITES/INTERNET

Adler, Margot. "For the Love of Do-Good Vampires." *National Public Radio*. February 18, 2010. http://www.npr.org/templates/story/story.php?storyId=123115545.

American Vampire League. 2011. http://americanvampireleague.com/.

BloodCopy.com. 2008. http://www.youtube.com/watch?v=ZEhG5DKmkHQ.

Anderson, John Frederick. *The Gaze in Portraiture*. Accessed August 24, 2011.

http://www.dshed.net/digitised/reveal/resources/the_gaze_adv_part1.html.

Anderson, Steve. "*True Blood* Title Sequence." *Critical Commons*. 2010. http://criticalcommons.org.

Anne Rice.com. Accessed August 24, 2011. http://www.annerice.com.

Ausiello, Michael. "Vampire Diaries Ratings: They Don't Suck!" *Inside TV*. September 11, 2009. http://www.insidetv.ew.com/2009/09/11/vampire-diaries-ratings-they-dont-suck.

Bailey, Courtney. "Feminist Art and (Post)Modern Anxieties." *Genders* 32 (2000). http://www.genders.org/g32/g32_bailey.html.

Bell, Josh. "Rosencrantz and Guildenstern Are Undead." *Film Critic.com*. Reviewed June 3, 2010. http://www.filmcritic.com/reviews/2010/ rosencrantz-and-guildenstern-are-undead/.

Bendix, Trish. "Kristin Bauer Could Play the Next Lesbian Vampire on *True Blood*." *After Ellen*. November 3, 2009. http://www.afterellen.com/blog/trishbendix/kristin-bauer-could-be-the-next-lesbian-vampire-on-true-blood.

———. "*True Blood* Mini-Cap 3.2 'Beautifully Broken'." *After Ellen*. 2010. http://www.afterellen.com/blog/trishbendix/true-blood-mini-cap-3-2-beautifully-broken.

Benz, Frau Sally. "Tuesday *True Blood* Roundtable: Night on the Sun." *Feministe*. 2010. http://www.feministe.us/blog/archives/2010/08/10/tuesday-true-blood-roundtable-night-on-the-sun/.

Bierly, Mandi. "*True Blood* Comic Book Series Coming in July. Hold on to your Fangs. Or Fang." May 13, 2010. *Blood Copy.com*. http://popwatch.ew.com/2010/05/13/true-blood-comic-book-series/.

Blood Copy.com. Accessed August 24, 2011. http://www.archive.bloodcopy.com.

"Breaking Dawn." *Publishers Weekly*. August 4, 2008. http://www.publishersweekly.com/ 978-0-316-06792-8.

Brown, Janice. "Jordan Galland and the Art of Spooky: Search Party and Rosencrantz and Guildenstern Are Undead." *Sonic Scoop*. April 23, 2010. http://www.sonicscoop.com/2010/04/23/jordan-galland-the-art-of-spooky/.

Busse, Kristina. "Fandom-is-a-Way-of-Life versus Watercooler Discussion; or, The Geek Hierarchy as Fannish Identity Politics." *Flow TV* 5 no. 13 (2006). http://flowtv.org/2006/ 11/taste-and-fandom/.

Callander, Michelle. "Bram Stoker's Buffy: Traditional Gothic and Contemporary Culture." *Slayage: The Journal of The Whedon Studies Association* 1, no. 3 (June 2001). http://www.slayageonline.com/essays/slayage3/callander.html.

CBR News Team. "IDW, HBO Announce *True Blood* Comic." Friday, April 2, 2010. http://www.comicbookresources.com/?page=article&id=25537.

Charlaine Harris.com. Accessed August 24, 2011. http://www.charlaineharris.com.

Coppa, Francesca. "Women, *Star Trek*, and the Early Development of Fannish Vidding." *Transformative Works and Cultures* 1 (2008). http://journal.transformativeworks.org/ index.php/twc/article/view/44.

Cordova, Heather. "L. J. Smith and Vampire Diaries Rumors — Author Confirms They're True." *Vampire-diaries.net*. February 9, 2011. http://www.vampire-diaries.net/books/l-j-smith-vampire-diaries-rumors-author-confirms-theyre-true.

Cousins, Johannah. "Sex in *Twilight*: An Argument for Bella," *Psych Central*. March 15, 2010, http://blogs.psychcentral.com/pop-psychology/2010/03/sex-in-twilight-an-argument-for-bella.

Dallas, Afi. "Afi Dallas Video Interview: Writer/Director Jordan Galland (*Rosencrantz and Guildenstern Are Undead*)." *Vimeo*. May 8, 2009. http://gordonandthewhale.com/afi-dallas-video-interview-rosencrantz-and-guildenstern-are-undead-writerdirector-jordan-galland/.

Dargan, Richard S. "Incident Reports." *FVZA: The Federal Vampire and Zombie Agency*. Accessed September 20, 2010. http://www.fvza.org/incidents.html.

Day, Heather. "*True Blood* Comics are a Mega Hit." *Truebloodnet.com*. December 10, 2010. http://truebloodnet.com/true-blood-comic-books-mega-hit/.

Dean, Michelle. "'The Bridge of You and Me Ain't Never Gonna Happen': Against *True Blood*." *Bitch*. September 14, 2010. http://bitchmagazine.org/post/tube-tied-the-bridge-of-you-and-me-aint-never-gonna-happen-against-true-blood.

De Leon, Kris. "'The Vampire Diaries': Updates on Team Damon, Werewolves, and a Shocking Death." *Buddy TV*. Accessed August 24, 2011. http://www.buddytv.com/articles/the-vampire-diaries/the-vampire-diaries-updates-on-35832.aspx.

Emma. "Interview: Alan Ball from *True Blood*." *Fan Bolt*. June 26, 2009. http://www.fanbolt.com/headline/7203/Interview:_Alan_Ball_from_True_Blood.

Fellowship of the Sun. 2011. http://www.fellowshipofthesun.org/.

Fisher, D., and C. Schubert. "Timber Towns in Trouble." *Progressive* 56, no. 4 (1992): 28.

http://web.ebscohost.com.

Flanagan, Nan. "About: The American Vampire League." *American Vampire League*. 2008. http://americanvampireleague.com/about/index.html.

Frank, Steven. "*True Blood* Episode 308 Recap: 'Yes, Daddy!'" *After Elton*. 2010. http://www.afterelton.com/tv/recaps/trueblood/308.

Moonlightaholics.com. Accessed August 22, 2011. http://moonlightaholics.com/viewforum.php?f=704.

Gabe. "Can the *True Blood* Metaphor Get Any More Fucked Up?" *Videogum*. 2008. http://videogum.com/23001/how_much_worse_can_the_true_bl/everyones-a-critic/.

Gilbert, W. S. *Rosencrantz and Guildenstern: A Tragic Episode, in Three Tabloids, Founded on an Old Danish Legend*. 1891. *Gilbert and Sullivan Archive*. Accessed August 24, 2011. Gilbert and Sullivan Archive.math.boisestate.edu/gas/ other_gilbert/rosencrantz/script.html.

Gitlin, Lauren. "Sexy Vampire Alert: Alan Ball Dishes on *True Blood*." *Television Without Pity*. 2008. http://www.televisionwithoutpity.com/telefile/2008/09/suck-on-this-alan-ball-dishes.php.

Gay & Lesbian Alliance Against Defamation. "Where We Are on TV: 2010–2011 Season." *GLAAD.org*. 2010. http://www.glaad.org/publications/tvreport10/overview.

Goldberg, Michelle. "Vampire Conservatives." *The Daily Beast*. 2009. http://www.thedailybeast.com/blogs-and-stories/2009-07-18/vampire-conservatives/.

Gray, Chris. "It's *Twilight* Time in the Pacific North West." *USA Today*. November 6, 2009, sec. Life. http://web.ebscohost.com.

Gross, Michael Joseph. "Gay Is the New Black?" *The Advocate*. July 23, 2009. http://www.advocate.com/News/Daily_News/2008/11/16/Gay_is_the_New_Black_/.

Halterman, Jim. "Interview: *True Blood* Creator Alan Ball." *The Futon Critic*. September 5, 2008. http://www.thefutoncritic.com/interview/2008/09/05/interview-true-blood-creator-alan-ball.

Harding, Kate. "Touched by a Vampire." *Salon.com*. July 30, 2008. http://www.salon.com/books/review/2008/07/30/Twilight.

Henheffer, Tom. "*Twilight* Central's Sobbing Pilgrims." *Maclean's* 122, no. 45 (2009): 74.

http://web.ebscohost.com.

Hill-Meyer, Tobi. "About This Contributor: Tobi Hill-Meyer." *Bilerico Project*. September, 2008. http://www.bilerico.com/contributors/tobi_hill-meyer/.

———. "*True Blood* a Metaphor for Trans Folks?" *Bilerico Project*. September 22, 2010. http://www.bilerico.com/2010/09/true_blood_a_metaphor_for_trans_folks.php.

Holland, Nicole. "Jordan Galland: Indie Filmmaker Finds the Holy Grail." *Independent Film Quarterly*. Accessed August 24, 2011. http://www.independentfilmquarterly. com/ifq/interviews/jordan-galland.htm.

Holmes, Trevor. "Becoming-Other: (Dis)Embodiments of Race in Anne Rice's *Tale of the Body Thief*." *Romanticism on the Net* 44 (2006). http://www.erudit.org/revue/ron/2006/ v/n44/014004ar.html.

Humphreys, Sal M. "The Challenges of Intellectual Property for Users of

Social Networking Sites: A Case Study of Ravelry." In *Proceedings Mind Trek*, 2008. http://eprints.qut.edu.au/14858/.
Humphreys, Sal M. "The Challenges of Intellectual Property for Users of Social Networking Sites: A Case Study of Ravelry." In *Proceedings Mind Trek*, 2008. http://eprints.qut.edu.au/ 14858/.
Jace. "From Dusk Til Dawn: Talking with Alan Ball About *True Blood* Season Two." *Televisionary*. 2009. http://www.televisionaryblog.com/2009/06/from-dusk-til-dawn-talking-with-alan.html.
Jacobs, W. W. *The Lady of the Barge and Others, Entire Collection. Project Gutenberg*. The Project Gutenberg EBook#12133, 2006. http://www.gutenberg.org/fiels/12133/12133_h/12133h.htm#c2.
Jenkins, Henry. "Fandom, Participatory Culture and Web 2.0." *Confessions of an Aca/Fan: The Official Weblog of Henry Jenkins*. Accessed August 24, 2011. http://henryjenkins.org/2010/01/fandom_participatory_culture_a.html.
———. "On Mad Med, Aca-Fandom and the Goals of Cultural Criticism." *Confessions of an Aca-Fan: The Official Weblog of Henry Jenkins*. Accessed January 25, 2011. http://henryjenkins.org.
Juergens, Brian. "*True Blood* Review and Interview with Creator Alan Ball." *After Elton*. 2008. http://www.afterelton.com/TV/2008/9/alan-ball_trueblood?page=0%2C0.
Kelly, Maura. "Knitting as a Feminist Project? Untangling the Contradictions of the 'New Knitting' Movement." *Proceedings of the American Sociological Association Annual Meeting*, July 31, 2008. http://www.allacademic.com/meta/p241231_index.html.
Kiros, Magda. "Jordan Galland: Triple Threat Assessment." *Playback*. Accessed February 17, 2011. http://www.ascap.com/playback/2009/08/RADAR/Jordan_Galland. aspx.
Kungl, Carla T., ed. *Vampires: Myths and Metaphors of Enduring Evil*. Oxford: Learning Solutions On-line Publication, 2004. http://www.inter-disciplinary.net/ publishing/id-press/ebooks/vampires-myths-and-metaphors-of-enduring-evil/.
"Lafayette Reynolds Quotes." *TV Fanatic*. 2010. http://www.tvfanatic.com/quotes/characters/lafayette-reynolds/.
Lauren. "Tuesday *True Blood* Roundtable, 'Everything Is Broken'." *Feministe*. August 17, 2010. http://www.feministe.us/blog/archives/2010/08/17/tuesday-true-blood-roundtable-everything-is-broken/.
Laverty, David. "'I Wrote My Thesis On You!': *Buffy* Studies as an Academic Cult." *Slayage* 4, nos. 13–14 (2004): http://slayageonline.com/Numbers/slayage13_14.htm.
Le Fanu, Sheridan. *Carmilla. Project Gutenberg*. Accessed August 3, 2011. http://www.gutenberg.org/files/10007/10007-h/10007-h.htm.

Lim, Thea, Joseph Lamour, Tami Winfrey Harris, Latoya Peterson, and Andrea Plaid. "The Snot Factor, Death and Sex, & Improper Firearm Use: *True Blood* S03 E08." *Racialicious*. 2010. http://www.racialicious.com/2010/08/11/the-snot-factor-death-and-sex-improper-firearm-use-true-blood-s03e08/.

Lim, Thea, Tami Winfrey Harris, Andrea Plaid, and Latoya Peterson. "Racialicious Presents the *True Blood* Roundtable." *Racialicious*. June 22, 2010. http://www.racialicious.com/2010/06/22/racialicious-presents-the-true-blood-roundtable/.

Lo, Malinda. "Notes & Queeries: The Allure of the Lesbian Vampire." *After Ellen*. June 24, 2009. http://www.afterellen.com/column/2009/6/notes-queeries.

Lucianovic, Stephanie V. W. "Why doesn't *Twilight* have a Team Bella?" *MSNBC.com*. June 27, 2010. http://today.msnbc.msn.com/id/37545960/ns/today-entertainment.

Manning, Shaun. "McMillan & Andreyko Spill '*True Blood*'." *CBR.com*. March 1, 2011. http://www.comicbookresources.com/?page=article&id=31073.

Martin, Denise. "TCA: Alan Ball: '*True Blood*' Is Not a Metaphor for Gay People." *Los Angeles Times*. July 10, 2008. http://latimesblogs.latimes.com/showtracker/2008/07/tca-alan-ball-t.html.

Martin, Renee. "*True Blood*: Bad Blood." *Womanist Musings*. June 14, 2010. http://www.womanist-musings.com/2010/06/true-blood-bad-blood.html.

———. "*True Blood*: Everything Is Broken " *Womanist Musings*. August 16, 2010. http://www.womanist-musings.com/2010/08/true-blood-everything-is-broken.html.

———. "When Is Gay Love Not Problematic on Television?" *Womanist Musings*. March 1, 2010. http://www.womanist-musings.com/2010/03/when-is-gay-love-not-problematic-on.html.

McEwan, Melissa. "On *True Blood*." *Shakesville*. June 15, 2010. http://shakespearessister.blogspot.com/2010/06/on-true-blood.html.

Meyer, Stephenie. "The Story Behind the Writing of *New Moon*." *The Official Website of Stephenie Meyer*. Accessed April 10, 2011. http://www.stepheniemeyer.com/nm_thestory.html.

Miller, Laura. "Touched by a Vampire." *Salon.com*. July 30, 2008. http://www.salon.com/books/review/2008/07/30/Twilight.

Monroe, Irene. "Gay Is Not the New Black." *The Huffington Post*. 2008. http://www.huffingtonpost.com/irene-monroe/gay-is-emnotem-the-new-bl_b_151573.html.

Newitz, Annalee. "Let's Face It: *True Blood* Hates Gay People." *io9.com*. November 1, 2008. http://io9.com/#!5071755/lets-face-it-true-blood-hates-gay-people.

Nicholson, Brad. "Dead Space's Horror Influence Comes from Life, Not Space Monsters." *Gamezone*. Accessed April 4, 2011. http://www.destructoid.com/dead-space-s-horror-influence-comes-from-life-not-space-monsters-103619.phtml.

Pentney, Beth Ann. "Feminism, Activism, and Knitting: Are the Fibre Arts a Viable Mode for Feminist Political Action?" *Thirdspace, A Journal of Feminist Theory and Culture* 8, no. 1 (2008). http://www.thirdspace.ca/journal/article/viewArticle/pentney/210.

Peterson, Matthew. "Interview with L. J. Smith." *The Author Hour*. November 19, 2009. http://theauthorhour.com/l-j-smith/.

Peterson, Michael, Laurie Beth Clark, and Lisa Nakamura. "Vampire Politics." *FlowTV*. November 3, 2009. http://flowtv.org/2009/12/vampire-politicslisa-nakamura-laurie-beth-clark-michael-peterson/.

Polidori, John William. *The Vampyre: A Tale*. Project Gutenberg. Accessed August 2, 2011. http://www.gutenberg.org/files/6087/6087-h.htm.

Press, Joy. "Vampires That Don't Suck." *Salon.com*. September 3, 2008. http://www.salon.com/entertainment/tv/int/2008/09/03/ball/index.html.

Puar, Jasbir. "In the Wake of It Gets Better." *The Guardian*. November 16, 2010. http://www.guardian.co.uk/commentisfree/cifamerica/2010/nov/16/wake-it-gets-better-campaign.

PuppetMaster. "Kristen Stewart Interview, TWILIGHT." *MoviesOnline*. Accessed January 30, 2011. http://www.moviewsonline.ca/movienews_16118.html.

"Quotes for Lafayette Reynolds (Character) from '*True Blood*'." *IMDb*. Accessed August 24, 2011. http://www.imdb.com/character/ch0060862/quotes.

Radish, Christina. "Interview: Alan Ball on Making *True Blood*." *Media Blvd*. Accessed August 24, 2011. http://www.mediablvd.com/magazine/the_news/ celebrity/ alan_ball_on_making_true_blood_200811021391.html.

Red, and Vee. *Vampire-Diaries.net*. Accessed October 17, 2010. www.vampire-diaries.net.

Reese, Jennifer. "*Breaking Dawn*." *Entertainment Weekly*, August 8, 2008. http://www.ew.com/ew/article/0,,20217628,00.html.

Rhodes, Joe. "After All the Funerals, a Prime-Time Auteur Digs up the Undead." *The New York Times*. August 3, 2008. http://www.nytimes.com/2008/08/03/arts/television/03rhod.html.

Rodriguez, Lee. "*True Blood #1*." *Panels on Pages.com*. July 20, 2010. http://panelsonpages.com/?p=25980.

"Rosencrantz and Guildenstern Are Undead." *Vampires.com*. February 2, 2010. http://www.vampires.com/rosencrantz-and-guildenstern-are-undead/.

Sarah. "*True Blood*'s Nest." *True Blood News.com*. May 13, 2010. http://www.trueblood-news.com/true-blood-comic-book-4-covers.

Sarkeesian, Anita. "Beyond *True Blood*'s Sensationalism [Transcript of Youtube Video]." *Feminist Frequency*. November 21, 2009. http://www.feministfrequency.com/2009/11/beyond-true-blood-sensationalism.

Scarlett, Stefanie. "Professor Critical of 'Twilight' Gender Roles." *The Journal Gazette*. July 8, 1010. http://www.journalgazette.net/article/20100708/FEAT/307089990/-1/FEAT11.

Schenker, Andrew. "Rosencrantz and Guildenstern Are Undead." *Slant Magazine*. May 31, 2010. http://www.slantmagazine.com/film/review/rosencrantz-and-guildenstern-are-undead/4845.

Schuker, Lauren A. E. "Harry Potter and the Rival Teen Franchise." *Wall Street Journal Online*. July 9, 2009. http://online.wsj.com/article/SB10001424052970204261704574276261288253316.html.

Scott, Suzanne. "All Bark and No Bite: Siring the Neutered Vampire on Buffy the Vampire Slayer." In *Vampires: Myths and Metaphors of Enduring Evil*, edited by Carla T. Kungl. Oxford: Learning Solutions On-line Publication, 2004. http://www.inter-disciplinary.net/publishing/id-press/ebooks/vampires-myths-and-metaphors-of-enduring-evil/.

_____. "Repackaging Fan Culture: The Regifting Economy of Ancillary Content Models." *Transformative Works and Cultures* 3 (2009): http://dx.doi.org/10.3983/twc2009.0150.

Scott, Tobias. "Alan Ball on *True Blood* and Its Relationship to the Source Material." *The A.V. Club*. September 7, 2008. http://www.avclub.com/content/interview/alan_ball.

Seidman, Robert. "'*True Blood*' Renewed by HBO for a Fourth Season." *Zap 2 It*. June 21, 2010. http://tvbythenumbers.zap2it.com/2010/06/21/true-blood-renewed-by-hbo-for-a-fourth-season/54804.

Sharkey, Alix. "Seth Grahame-Smith Interview." *The Telegraph*. 30 April 2010, par. 17. http://www.telegraph.co.uk. http://www.telegraph.co.uk/culture/books/7656909/Seth-Grahame-Smith-interview.html.

Smith, L. J. "About these Just for Fun Polls," *Official Site of L. J. Smith*. November 20, 2010. http://www.ljanesmith.net/www/blog/2010/277-about-these-just-for-fun-polls.

Smith, L. J. "Thank you but don't boycott." *Official Site of L. J. Smith*. Accessed February 22, 2011. http://www.ljanesmith.net/www/blog/297-thank-you-but-dont-boycott.

Smith, S. E. "Finally, I Have Watched *True Blood* Season Two." *This Ain't Livin'*. June 12, 2010. http://meloukhia.net/2010/06/finally_i_have_watched_true_blood_season_two.html.

Snicks. "13 Gay Badasses We Love." *After Elton*. July 29, 2010. http://www.afterelton.com/people/2010/07/thirteen-gay-badasses.

_____. "'*True Blood*' Episode 310 Recap: 'I Smell a Rat!'" *After Elton*. August

23, 2010. http://www.afterelton.com/tv/recaps/trueblood/310.
Sobel, Gianna. "An Interview with Michael McMillian." *Inside True Blood. com*. February 18, 2011. http://www.inside-true-blood-blog.com/.
Stewart, Dodai. "The *True Blood* Finale Is All Questions & No Answers." *Jezebel*. September 13, 2010. http://jezebel.com/#!5636669/the-true-blood-finale-is-all-questions--no-answers.
Sullivan, Jane. "Dracula and the Human Factor." *The Age*. June 7, 2006. http://www.theage.com.au/news/books/dracula-and-the-human-factor/2006/06/02/1148956490961.html?page=fullpage.
Sundstrom, Laura. "*True Blood* Is Right Wing's Worst Nightmare." *Young Feminist Adventures*. July 21, 2009. http://youngfeministadventures.blogspot.com/2009/07/true-blood-is-right-wings-worst.html.
Tanklefsky, David. "Vampire Diaries Sets Debut Record for CW." *Broadcast and Cable*. September 11, 2009. http://www.broadcastingcable.com/article/ 346165_Primetime_Ratings_Vampire_Diaries_Sets_Debut_Record_ForCW.php.
Trendacosta, Katharine. "You're Doing it Wrong: *Twilight*." *Glibberal*. Accessed August 24, 2011. http://glibberal.com/3100/.
"*True Blood* General Gabbery >>3-3: "It Hurts Me Too [Forum]." *Television Without Pity.com*. June 29, 2010. http://forums.televisionwithoutpity.com/lofiversion/index.php/t3196618-250.html.
"*True Blood* General Gabbery >> 3-9: "Everything Is Broken [Forum]." *Television Without Pity.com*. August 15, 2010. http://forums.televisionwithoutpity.com/index.php?showtopic =3197707&st =195.
"Vampire Attack in Wellington." *Dominion Post*. May 6, 2010. http://www.stuff.co.nz/national/crime/3662417/Vampire-attack-in-Wellington.
"Vampires Come to Life in *True Blood*." *Canwest News Service*. September 4, 2008. http://www.canada.com/topics/entertainment/story.html?id=47530f3e-7aa4-49d7-9152-2b5b2f697d30.
Wesley, Vanessa. "Top 10 Lafayette Reynolds Quotes from *True Blood*." *Wet Paint*. February 8, 2011. http://www.wetpaint.com/true-blood/articles/top-10-lafayette-reynolds-quotes-from-true-blood.
Williamson, Milly. "Vampire Transformations: From Gothic Demon to Domestication?" In *Vampires: Myths and Metaphors of Enduring Evil*, edited by Carla T. Kungl. Oxford: Learning Solutions On-line Publication, 2004. http://www.inter-disciplinary.net/ publishing/id-press/ebooks/vampires-myths-and-metaphors-of-enduring-evil/.
Winfrey Harris, Tami. "*True Blood* Epiphany: If Bill Compton Were a Black Man, He'd Be Clarence Thomas." *What Tami Said.com*. September 1, 2009. http://whattamisaid.blogspot.com/2009/09/true-blood-epiphany-if-bill-compton.html.
_____. "*True Blood*, Tired Stereotypes." *Racialicious*. September 24, 2008. http://www.racialicious.com/2008/09/24/true-blood-tired-stereotypes/.

Woerner, Meredith. "Best *True Blood* Ending Ever. Ever. Ever. Ever." *io9.com.* 16 August, 2010. http://io9.com/5613435/best-true-blood-ending-ever-ever-ever-ever.

_____. "First Six Pages of the *True Blood* Comic are Just as Dirty as the Show." *io9.com.* May 13, 2010. http://io9.com/5538531/first-six-pages-of-the-true-blood-comic.

Wood, Evan Rachel, interview by Katy Hall. "Evan Rachel Wood Talks Nudity, Lesbian Vampire Sex." *The Huffington Post.* August 27, 2009. http://www.huffingtonpost.com/2009/08/27/evan-rachel-wood-talks-nu_n_270421.html.

Woodward, Beth. "Whedon Week: Buffy vs. Bella: The Battle of the Vampire Love Sagas," *CC2K: The Nexus of Pop-Culture Fandom*.us. August 9, 2009. http://www.cc2konline.com/movies/script-reviews/1378-whedon-week-buffy-vs-bella-the-battle-of-the-vampire-love-sagas.

Wortham, Jenna. "HBO Brews a Viral Campaign With Tru Blood." *Wired.com.* July 9, 2008. http://www.wired.com/underwire/2008/07/hbo-brews-a-vir/.

Yabroff, Jennie. "A Bit Long in the Tooth." *Newsweek.* December 6, 2008. http://www.newsweek.com/2008/12/05/a-bit-long-in-the-tooth.html.

Zinoman, Jason. "A Shirt Shortage Strikes Bon Temps: *True Blood*'s Very Sexy, Very Gay Season 3 Debut." *Slate.com.* June 14, 2010. http://www.slate.com/id/2256939/.

Films

Bride and Prejudice. Director Gurinder Chada. New York: Miramax, 2005.

Clueless. Director Amy Heckerling. Los Angeles, CA: Paramount Pictures, 1995.

Cursed. Director Wes Craven. New York: Dimension Films, 2005.

Daybreakers. Directors Michael Spierig and Peter Spierig. Santa Monica: Lionsgate, 2010.

I Know What You Did Last Summer. Director Jim Gillespie. Los Angeles: Columbia Pictures, 1997.

Interview with the Vampire: The Vampire Chronicles. Director Neil Jordan. Burbank, CA: Warner Brothers, 1994.

The Lost Boys. Director Joel Shumacher. Burbank, CA: Warner Brothers, 1987.

Return of the Living Dead. Director Dan O'Bannon. Century City, Los Angeles: MGM, 1985.

Rosencrantz and Guildenstern are Dead. Director Tom Stoppard. New York: Cinecom Pictures, 1991.

Rosencrantz and Guildenstern Are Undead. Director Jordan Galland. West Hollywood, CA: Indican Pictures, 2010.

Scream. Director Wes Craven. New York: Dimension Films, 1996.
Scream 2. Director Wes Craven. New York: Dimension Films, 1997.
Scream 3. Director Wes Craven. Dimension Films, 2000.
Scream 4. Director Wes Craven. Dimension Films, 2011.
Twilight. Director Catherine Hardwicke. London: Summit Entertainment, 2008.
Underworld. Director Len Wiseman. Culver City, CA: Screen Gems Pictures, 2003.

Television
Beverly Hills 90210. Created by Darren Star, Aaron Spelling and E. Duke Vincent. Los Angeles: Fox Entertainment, broadcast 1990–2000.
Buffy the Vampire Slayer. Created by Joss Whedon. Burbank, CA: Warner Brothers, broadcast 1997–2001.
Dark Shadows. DVD. Created by Dan Curtis. Los Angeles: MGM, 2009.
Dawson's Creek. Created by Kevin Williamson. Burbank, CA: Warner Brothers, 1998–2003.
Moonlight: The Complete Series. Created by Ron Koslow and Trevor Munson. DVD. Burbank, CA: Warner Home Video, 2009.
Party of Five. Created by Christopher Keyser and Amy Lippman. Los Angeles: Fox Entertainment, 1994–2000.
Sanctuary. DVD. Created by Damian Kindler. UK: Contender Home Entertainment, 2007.
True Blood: The Complete First Season. DVD. Created by Alan Ball. New York: HBO Home Entertainment, 2009.
True Blood: The Complete Second Season. DVD. Created by Alan Ball. New York: HBO Home Entertainment, 2010.
Twilight in Forks: The Saga of a Real. DVD. Director Jason Brown. Universal City, CA: Summit Entertainment, 2010.
The Vampire Diaries. The Complete First Season. Created by Kevin Williamson. Burbank, CA: Warner Brothers, 2009.
The Vampire Diaries. The Complete Second Season. Created by Kevin Williamson. Burbank: CA: Warner Brothers, 2010.

Discography
Bauhaus. "Bella Lugosi's Dead." On *Crackle*. Beggars Banquet 7243 8465 5822, 1998, compact disc. Originally released in 1979.
Cramps, The. *Big Bad from Badsville*. Epitaph 6516–1, 1997, 33⅓ rpm.
_____. *Smell of Female*. Big Beat Records NED6, 1983, 33⅓ rpm.
_____. *Songs the Lord Taught Us*. IRS Records SP007, 1980, 33⅓ rpm.
_____. *Stay Sick*. Enigma Records ENVLPD 1001, 1989, 33⅓ rpm.
Damned, The. *Damned, Damned, Damned*. Stiff SEEZ1, 1977, 33⅓ rpm.

_____. *Grave Disorder*. Nitro 15844-2, 2001, compact disc.
_____. *Machine Gun Etiquette*. Chiswick CWK 3011, 1979, 33⅓ rpm.
My Chemical Romance, "Vampires Will Never Hurt You." On *I Brought You My Bullets, You Brought Me Your Love*. Eyeball Records 9866233, 2004, compact disc.
Nox Arcana: *Transylvania*. Monolith 18267, 2005, compact disc.
Sex Pistols. *Never Mind the Bollocks, Here's the Sex Pistols*. Virgin V2086, 1977, 33⅓ rpm.
Siouxsie & the Banshees. *The Scream*. Polydor POLD 5009, 1978, 33⅓ rpm.

Video Games

Conflict: Desert Storm II: Back to Baghdad. Video game. Developer Pivotal Games. US: SCi, Gotham Games, 2003.
Resident Evil. Playstation video game. Directed by Shinji Makami. Japan: Capcom, 1996.

Index

30 Days of Night, 41, 43–44

Austen, Jane, 7, 257–271

Ball, Alan, 92, 96, 100, 106–107, 120, 122, 129, 170, 206, 209, 215–216, 239
Barbeau, Adrienne, 21, 25–26
Barron, Stephanie, 260
Becker, Ernest, 21, 23, 24–25
Being Human, 4, 139
Benshoff, Harry, 98, 106
Bible, 18–19
Blade, 56, 270
Blood; AIDS, 37, 91; Animal, 75, 174, 223–225, 302; Fairy, 27, 208; Human, 65, 177–178, 206–207, 209, 218, 223–224, 226–227, 229–231, 233–234, 242, 245–246, 263, 269, 300–301; Synthetic, 8, 92, 205–208, 218–219, 243–244; TruBlood, 8, 128, 144, 145, 207–209
Bloodsucking Fiends, 265, 271
Brite, Poppy Z., 265, 271
Brontë, Charlotte, 4, 262
Buffy the Vampire Slayer, 4, 8, 11, 37, 55–68, 121–123, 132, 139, 145, 150, 157, 216, 239, 241, 247–249, 264, 291–292, 296–301, 305–306;

Angel, 4, 37, 57, 61–63, 139, 145, 241, 247–250, 264, 298, 301–302; Buffy Summers, 11, 55–68, 247–249, 264
Byron, Lord, 6, 37, 263–64

Charmed Circle of Sex, 101–102

Dark Shadows, 37, 126, 139, 259
Dracula, 3, 4, 6, 37, 40, 41, 43, 51, 56, 91, 123, 150, 175, 223, 249, 280, 286

Existential anxiety, 17–28

Fang banger, 98, 129, 225
Fear of death, 15–16
Federal Zombie and Vampire Agency, 4, 33–48
Firestone, Robert W., 21–22, 25
Fiske, John, 36, 292
Ford, Michael Thomas, 258–259, 261–263, 265, 270

Gay and Lesbian Alliance Against Defamation (GLAAD), 92, 94, 96, 108
Gay Window Advertising, 93, 102
Genre; Dark Romance, 9, 37, 42, 75, 81, 92, 123, 140, 172, 224, 235,

262; Gothic, 5, 56, 68, 137, 141, 158–159, 173, 176, 182; Horror, 9, 15–16, 37–38, 42–43, 75–76, 81, 107, 139, 150, 158–160, 163, 171, 173–175, 182, 276; Melodrama, 37, 42, 47, 55; Paranormal Romance, 119, 139–140; Romance, 37, 42, 47, 73–76, 81, 92, 123, 157, 174, 176, 182, 197, 209, 224, 235, 239, 257, 260, 265, 270; Supernatural, 3–4, 9–11, 16–17, 37–38, 60, 65, 67, 92–93, 96, 105, 120, 170–173, 176, 241, 244, 281, 284, 301
Gilbert, W. S., 275, 278–280
Gray, Jonathan, 7, 78, 188–189

Hamlet, 275–284
Harrington, C. Lee, 7, 9, 188–189
Harris, Charlaine, 4, 8, 20, 92, 119–120, 170, 206–207, 213–217, 225, 260, 263
Harry Potter, 9, 138–139, 140, 150, 169
Heteronormative, 103–105
Heterosexual, 103–105
Hills, Matt, 144, 151, 179, 194, 305
Home Box Office (HBO), 10, 16, 92–93, 104, 119, 123–124, 206–210, 213, 216–217, 225, 239, 260
Homonationalist, 93, 94, 96, 98
Homonormative, 91–108

Immortality, 17–28
Interview with the Vampire, 37, 42, 56, 139

Jacobs, W. W., 18–19
Jane Bites Back (Michael Thomas Ford), 258–265, 270–71
Jane and the Damned, 258–261, 265–271

Jane Austen Society of North America (JASNA), 259
Jeffers, Regina, 259–60
Jenkins, Henry, 36, 45, 47, 141, 147, 228, 276, 283
Johnson, Claudia, 257

King, Stephen, 56, 123
Kipling, Rudyard, 260
Klause, Annette Curtis, 20, 24

Lesbian/Gay/Bisexual/ Transgender/Intersexual/ Questioning, 93, 94, 108
Lindqvist, John Ajvide, 265
Lost Boys, The, 170, 178
Love Bites, 21, 25

"Mary Sue", 46, 57, 59, 229, 234
Masculinity, 35, 47–48, 101
Mead, Richelle, 4, 264
Meyer, Stephenie, 4, 12, 58–59, 62, 65, 67, 75, 78, 80, 85, 169, 187, 189–193, 195, 223, 239, 245–246, 260, 263, 265, 270, 271, 298
Moonlight, 139, 223–235
Moore, Christopher, 19, 22, 265, 281
Mullany, Janet, 258–261, 265–271
Myth, 4, 6, 9, 12, 34–35, 41–42, 45, 75, 91, 95, 120, 123, 132, 178, 191, 194–196, 199, 259, 265, 281–282, 301

Neoliberalism, 93–4, 102, 108
Nosferatu, 98, 279

Participatory Culture, 36, 47, 142–143
Polidori, John William, 3, 56, 223, 263

Rice, Anne, 42, 56, 157, 160, 205, 214, 224, 242
Rosencrantz and Guildenstern Are Undead, 7, 275–284
Rozema, Patricia, 267

Sanctuary, 38, 139
Sandvoss, Cornel, 7, 140, 188–189
Shakespeare, William, 275–284
Shapeshifter, 10, 75, 101, 171, 224
Silver Kiss, The, 20, 24
Six Feet Under, 120, 123, 208–209
Smith, L. J., 169, 170, 173, 175–178, 180–182, 260
Sopranos, The, 10, 123, 208
Southern Vampire Mystery Series, 4, 8, 92, 120, 129, 206–207, 218, 225, 260, 263
Stoker, Bram, 3, 43, 51, 56, 91, 123, 150, 165, 175, 223, 249, 262, 270, 279, 286, 287
Stoppard, Tom, 275–280

True Blood, 4, 7–11, 16–17, 19, 22, 24–28, 37, 56, 58, 91–108, 119–133, 139, 145–146, 148–152, 157, 169, 205–219, 225, 239–243, 260, 298; American Vampire League, 8, 96, 97, 99, 105–106; Bill Compton, 3, 17, 22, 26–27, 37, 92, 97, 101, 105, 120–121, 128–129, 131, 145, 150, 205–206, 207–208, 218, 225, 232, 241–245, 247; Bon Temps, 10, 17, 19, 24, 92, 100, 205, 207, 216; Eric Northman, 4, 16, 26, 102–104, 120–122, 128–129, 131, 144–147, 150, 205, 208, 218, 232; Fangtasia, 16, 99; Fellowship of the Sun, 8, 24, 26; Godric, 16, 26, 145; Hadley Hale, 99, 102–103; Hoyt Fortenberry, 19; Jason Stackhouse, 24, 120, 128–129; Jessica Hamby, 19, 120, 145, 210; Jesus Velasquez, 99; Lorena Krasiki, 26, 243; Lafayette Reynolds, 99–101, 120–121, 128, 145; Maryann Forrester, 17, 24; Merlotte's Bar and Grill, 121, 205, 243; Pamela de Beaufort, 99, 102–103, 131; Nan Flanagan, 96, 99, 102–103; Russell Edgington, 20, 99, 104–107, 128; Sam Merlotte, 24, 101, 128, 150; Sookie Stackhouse, 16, 22, 26, 27, 92, 97, 103, 120–1, 128–131, 205–208, 213–214, 218–225, 234, 241, 243–244, 260, 263; Sophie-Anne LeClerq, 17, 99, 102–103; Talbot, 99, 103–4; Vampire Rights Amendment, 92; Yvetta, 99
Twilight Saga, 4, 8–11, 37, 42–43, 55–59, 61–64, 67, 73–86, 91, 103, 123, 130, 139–140, 143–152, 169–170, 187–199, 223, 239–241, 245–246, 249, 260, 263, 270, 298, 314; Alice Cullen, 67, 76, 144, 150, 192, 196; Bella Swan, 10, 55–68, 75, 130, 191–193; *Breaking Dawn*, 75, 67, 140; Carlisle Cullen, 75, 140, 250; *Eclipse*, 155, 245; Edward Cullen, 3–5, 10, 37, 58–68, 75–79, 81, 130, 140, 143–146, 150, 152, 218, 245, 246–247, 249–251, 263, 270; Forks, 59, 76, 149, 187–199; *New Moon*, 251
Tyler, Natalie, 258, 261–262, 267

Underworld, 4, 150, 157, 267

Vampire; Contemporary, 3, 5, 7, 9, 16, 27, 35, 47, 55, 56, 92, 160–161, 169, 239, 241, 249,

298–299; Domestic, 3, 5–6, 8, 36, 91, 264; Immortality, 3, 9, 11, 16–19, 21–28, 41, 64, 67, 91, 106, 141, 224, 231, 244, 263–264, 268, 270, 275, 278, 282, 284, 301; Mainstreaming, 7–8, 74, 92, 105, 205–206, 208–209, 243–244; Supernatural, 3, 4, 9–11, 16–17, 37–38, 60, 65, 67, 92–93, 96, 105, 120, 170–173, 176, 241, 244, 281, 284, 30; Sympathetic, 6–7, 16, 20, 36–37, 42, 44, 46–47, 206, 224, 232, 239, 245, 247

Vegetarian, 75, 91, 223, 240, 245–246, 250

Vampire Academy, 4, 264

Vampire Chronicles, The, 139, 205, 242

Vampire Diaries, 4, 8, 42, 91, 169–182, 260; Salvatore, Damon, 171–182; Salvatore, Stefan, 4, 171–182

Werewolf, 10, 75, 175

Whedon, Joss, 122, 216, 239, 264, 298, 301

Williamson, Kevin, 170, 173–177, 181

Williamson, Milly, 3, 6, 140, 218

Xena: Warrior Princess, 58, 130

Yabroff, Jennie, 91

You Suck: A Love Story, 19, 22–23

Zombies, 17, 33–35, 38, 40, 163–164, 258–259, 301

www.ingramcontent.com/pod-product-compliance
Lightning Source LLC
Chambersburg PA
CBHW032101230426
43662CB00034B/131